KV-576-730

Graeme Aitken was born in Central Otago, New Zealand but has lived for the past ten years in Sydney, Australia. His first novel, *Fifty Ways of Saying Fabulous*, was published successfully in both Australia and the UK, and is currently being adapted for screen.

Also by Graeme Aitken

fifty ways of saying fabulous

vanity fierce

GRAEME AITKEN

review

Copyright © 1998 Graeme Aitken

The right of Graeme Aitken to be identified as the Author of
the Work has been asserted by him in accordance with the
Copyright, Designs and Patents Act 1988.

First published in 1998
by Random House Australia, Pty Ltd

First published in Great Britain in 1998
by REVIEW

An imprint of Headline Book Publishing

First published in paperback in 1998

10 9 8 7 6 5 4 3 2 1

All rights reserved. No part of this publication may be
reproduced, stored in a retrieval system, or transmitted,
in any form or by any means without the prior written
permission of the publisher, nor be otherwise circulated
in any form of binding or cover other than that in which
it is published and without a similar condition being
imposed on the subsequent purchaser.

All characters in this publication are fictitious
and any resemblance to real persons, living or dead,
is purely coincidental.

ISBN 0 7472 5299 8

Printed and bound in Great Britain by
Clays Ltd, St Ives plc

Headline Book Publishing
A division of Hodder Headline PLC
338 Euston Road
London NW1 3BH

To Dean Baxter

First and foremost, thank you to Julia Stiles, my editor, for her advice and enthusiasm. I am also grateful to Graeme Head, Alan Brotherton and Steven Thurlow for their close reading of the manuscript at various stages.

I am especially indebted to Geraldine Cooke and Paul Bailey for all their early championing of my work.

part one

PROLOGUE

'If you can't be good, be clever.'

Those were my mother's words to me as she toasted me on my eighteenth birthday. She informed me that this piece of wisdom had become something of a family motto over the years, passed down from generation to generation, from mother to daughter.

My mother's explanation of this tradition filled me with alarm. I am her son not her daughter. My immediate reaction was to interpret her toast as a slur upon my masculinity, that she had somehow perceived a deficiency in me, when I had believed myself to be presenting to her and to the world a demeanour that was inscrutably, exemplarily macho.

Why were Nana's words of caution being repeated to me? Was my mother trying subtly to prod a confession out of me? Was that why she had ordered French champagne? Not because I was of an age to appreciate a sophisticated bubbly, but in order to loosen my restraint and my tongue? Or was I merely being paranoid? I was, after all, my parents' only child. My mother had no-one else to continue this tradition with.

I checked my wild impulse to blurt out an ill-timed confession and took a mouthful of champagne instead. I looked her in the eye and nodded sagely, as if I was giving appreciation to her counsel as well as to the champagne.

In fact, having recovered from the initial affront, I realised what an extraordinary thing it was for my mother to have said. She had brought me up to be good: well behaved, polite, to 'say something nice or say nothing at all'. Now she appeared to be repudiating all that. She was giving me permission to flout whatever rules and conventions I liked as long as I was clever about it. Misbehave but don't get caught.

3

Of course I had misunderstood her, but I didn't realise that until many years later. My mother was referring to sex. To be specific, contraception. Had I been her daughter, perhaps she might have explained herself more explicitly. But because I was her son, the son she had some private qualms about, she had no wish to initiate an intimate conversation. Such a conversation might reveal that her advice had come too late: her son was already active. Or, heaven forbid, that he was *passive*. So she let her words stand alone, not realising how cryptic they were.

I was eighteen. I was on the brink of a new life. I would finish school, decide what to do with myself and move out of the parental home. My mother's motto came at exactly the right time. I had spent the last eighteen years being obedient and well behaved. I was flushed and thrilled by the realisation that now I was an adult, it was apparently quite permissible to behave badly. I took her advice to heart. With a drunken, foolish grin I held up my glass for a refill.

CHAPTER ONE

I was always the golden boy. That was the name so many people gave me – my relatives, my teachers, my parents' friends – but I particularly relished hearing it from my peers. I adored when they said it as a taunt, unaware of how twisted with jealousy their voices sounded. *The golden boy*. Blond, blue eyed and seemingly blessed with countless advantages and talents.

Blessed. That was how Mr Preston described me on my last day at school. His voice so choked that his words were almost inaudible. Mr Preston was head of the English department and my teacher five years in a row. He was also in charge of the school's dramatic society. A fitting appointment. Mr Preston could be very dramatic. Especially when it came to praising me.

He was my favourite teacher. I told him that all the time although it wasn't particularly true. In fact, the inverse was true. I was *his* favourite. Teachers weren't supposed to have favourites, but as it was so patently clear that Mr Preston wanted the two of us to have a special bond, I obliged him by confiding what he liked to hear. But it's what he said to me on my last day of school that's significant. Not him. I never forgot Mr Preston's compliment. Surprisingly, as I'm often flattered. But what he said enchanted me. I liked its connotation: that my success wasn't merely due to luck or privilege, but to something more profound. Providence. I had been singled out. Chosen. Blessed.

I thanked Mr Preston. I had been groomed by my mother in how to receive a compliment. 'If you don't acknowledge praise graciously and enthusiastically, no-one will bother to take the trouble with you again.'

Elisabeth adored compliments. She sought them with the

calculation of a game hunter, although to the casual observer she appeared to receive them with nonchalance. But I knew better. She kept count and an evening when she didn't achieve double figures was considered disastrous. 'Fifteen compliments on this new dress,' she might boast in the car on the way home from a party. 'What do you think of that?' And my father and I would be obliged to offer up number sixteen and number seventeen. If the praise failed to materialise upon expectation, Elisabeth was likely to sulk. Or drink.

My mother reminded me many times that giving birth to me had demanded a sacrifice of her, had robbed her of some of her beauty. 'Not that I regret its loss,' she assured me. 'Because *you will* do me proud.'

I understood what she meant. She wasn't implying that I was unwanted; she spoke to fire ambition in me, to make me understand that there had been an investment made and she expected to see returns. I was to be a credit to her at all times and win her *fresh* compliments by being the perfect son.

It was a vain, selfish remark for a mother to make, but that was Elisabeth's way. She always spoke plainly to those of us she had no need to fool or impress. And she was vain. Terribly vain. The mirror was to her what a bottle of liquor is to an alcoholic. She had mirrors in every room of the house, even the toilet.

But my mother does have some justification for her grand behaviour. She was once something of a star. A famous beauty in her youth, she went on to have a career as an actress, largely in television. When she acts the prima donna, I indulge her. I'm grateful to have inherited her looks. I have her eyes, her height, her smile and her hair. Thankfully. My father is not at all desirable in any of these respects. He wears glasses, is short and balding and his teeth are not his own.

I'm always being told that I'm my mother's son. I'm never sure whether it's a compliment or not, a remark on our physical similarities or some more insidious observation. I am acutely aware that I take after her too much in some respects. Our hair colour for example. We're the exact same shade of blond. Arctic Blonde it says on the bottle. I started using her hair colourant when I was sixteen. I hated that my hair was darkening, becoming so dull and mousy. The golden boy *had* to be blond. I'm sure Elisabeth suspects but she's never said a word. I think it adds credence to her claims that she's a natural blonde if she can point to her son with the exact same hair colour.

I have my mother's stature too. I shot up early, when I was eleven, so much so that I was embarrassed by my height. When I hit six foot (taller than my father by two inches) I panicked. I fretted that I wasn't going to stop. I was teased relentlessly at school. I used to stoop to try to appear smaller but Elisabeth would not tolerate that. 'Posture,' she would reprimand me, flicking me beneath the chin with her index finger, the way you might flick away an insect, but so forcefully it hurt.

She insisted that it was an advantage to be head and shoulders above everyone else. I wasn't persuaded. Instead, I took another of her sayings and put it into practice. She was forever telling me that a goal was achievable if you only believed in yourself. 'Convince yourself and you're practically over the finishing line.'

So I set about convincing myself to stop growing. I had a little mantra which I repeated faithfully every morning and night. 'I'm six foot tall and that's quite sufficient thank you. I'm going to stop growing now.'

By some stroke of coincidence, my growth did seem to dwindle to a halt. My prayers were answered, as they often seemed to be. Slowly, my schoolmates began to catch up with me. I had just been an early developer. However, there was an unforeseen downside to what I had managed to accomplish. Development halted in another all-important area. Down below. Between my legs. I kept measuring myself hopefully as I progressed through my teens, but the only thing to develop was my own sense of despair at what I had inadvertently managed to inhibit.

It wasn't until I was seventeen that I learnt I hadn't drawn the short straw through the power of my own thought. I had merely inherited my father's penis. 'It's very average,' I overheard my mother complain one evening to her closest confidant, Vic, my self-styled uncle. 'He claims anxiety over prostate cancer in his family has made it shrink over the years, but I don't recall any significant difference from when we were first married.'

So it seemed that not only was what I already possessed to be the extent of it, but prostate cancer loomed as my fate in old age as well.

I consoled myself that it could have been worse. I'm exactly six inches. Which is average. It's claimed by a lot of people and in a lot of places that six inches is average. Unfortunately Uncle Vic destroyed that small comfort by what he said in reply to my mother. 'The people who claim six inches is average are all men. The word small doesn't feature in a man's vocabulary when it comes to cock size. It starts at average and soars from there.'

Elisabeth and Uncle Vic tittered together. I knew that Uncle Vic was something of an authority on male genitalia. My dislike of him grew more pronounced from that day.

The size of my penis was my one deficiency, although it wasn't really a deficiency. It was merely average. Despite what Uncle Vic said, it was average. But the thing was, nothing else about me was average. I was generally regarded as exceptional. I wanted to be exceptionally endowed too. I consoled myself that at least this problem (really quite minor) wasn't on constant display. It wasn't like the indignity of pimples, there on your face for everyone to see and sneer at. It was something that could be kept secret. Perhaps forever.

But enough about that: it's my face that's my fortune and my eyes are my very best asset. Wide, forthright and vividly blue. So blue, I'm often asked if I wear tinted contact lenses. 'No,' I reply indignantly. Unjustly, it's the one time people don't seem to believe me. But that's of little consequence. Most of the time my eyes endow everything I do or say with an air of innocence and veracity. I can tell the most outrageous lies and generally be believed. That's another thing I get from my father; he's a liar, by profession. At least, according to Elisabeth. She always pronounces 'lawyer' with such a grand British accent that it ends up sounding more like liar. My father detests this, which she well knows. But she's so often the victim of one of his dry, laconic barbs, this joke is her one effective retaliation. It always irritates him.

I've inherited my father's wit and his way with words. The two of us may be deficient in the size stakes, but we could probably persuade anyone to believe otherwise if we chose to.

It's quite a combination, beauty and wit, though Elisabeth considers them wasted on a man. 'What use can you put them to?' she demanded of me once.

My father answered for me. 'Reading law at university.'

Elisabeth sighed her dissatisfaction, to make it plain that such a course would be to squander my gifts. 'Beauty isn't merely a foot in the door,' she proclaimed. 'It's a quality that demands the door be opened for you and opened wide.'

I had no doubts that at least was true. My only dilemma was which door should I allow myself to be ushered through next.

From a very young age, if I showed the slightest inclination for a particular pursuit, Elisabeth would enrol me in lessons for it. Throughout my childhood and adolescence I was always studying and endlessly practising something. Singing lessons. Acting lessons. Piano lessons. Drawing lessons. But my accomplishments weren't confined to the arts. I was to be a sportsman as well, though Elisabeth wouldn't permit me to play any team sports. 'Too dangerous,' she insisted. She'd had a suitor, a boy she claimed was the love of her life, who was knocked senseless during a ruck on the rugby field. 'He never knew his own name again, let alone mine.'

When I expressed an admiration for perky, pigtailed Tracy Austin bounding about centre court at Wimbledon, Elisabeth enrolled me for tennis lessons. I was only five years old at the time. My racquet was almost as big as I was, but I soon became accustomed to wielding it. Elisabeth had a volley board built against the back of the garage and I practised my strokes there every day. She took me around the tournament circuit. By the time I was ten, my coach declared the school competition grade beneath me and had me join a club that played in the adult grade. By age twelve, I was number one on the club ladder.

My reputation as something of a boy wonder was enhanced even further during my first year of high school. I won a place in the school's top tennis team, an unheard-of feat for a junior. I auditioned for the drama club and was noticed by Mr Preston, who immediately cast me as the lead in *Oliver* that year. Even though it was only a school production, it received a lot of attention because of me. Elisabeth alerted the media. Her son was making his debut. I also joined the debating club and impressed Mr Frost who ran it. 'Remarkable eloquence in one so young,' he told me time and time again. He made me reserve for the school team, which was another great honour.

I was never intimidated by being placed with those who were much older than me. If they scoffed at my youth and dismissed me, I was delighted. It made it so much easier to whip them when I faced them in competition. Surprise was a great advantage.

The end of year prize-giving, my first year in high school, was a triumph. I won so many prizes, the applause when I got up from my chair *again* began to grow listless. I could actually discern the enthusiasm of Elisabeth's clapping amongst the applause, that's how subdued it became. I won the junior tennis cup, the junior debating prize, the junior drama club prize, the Year Seven English prize and the modern languages prize. It felt like the Academy Awards.

After that sweep of success, I resolved to do even better the following year. I studied the list of prizes published in the school magazine and worked out which ones I could feasibly win. The following year I took up badminton, squash, hockey and Latin. I also made myself eligible for obscure prizes that most pupils were unaware of, such as the prize for an essay on the life of a distinguished old boy. I was rewarded for my research and subsequent application by doubling my record. I won ten prizes. It was unheard of. I was photographed and interviewed, not only by the local newspaper, but also by the *Daily Telegraph*. My parents bought me a cabinet with glass doors to display all my prizes in.

I continued to dominate the prize-giving in the years that followed, but I became more selective. My success had made me a target for mockery: some of it light-hearted, some of it pointed and malicious. I did not want to become the victim of my own achievements. I didn't necessarily have to win the most prizes, but I did have to win the most prestigious. I had a new aim in mind and it required that, in addition to being a success, I was popular too. I could not afford to be widely resented if I was to be made head prefect in my final year at school.

I knew it would not be easy. Head prefect was a popularity award that almost always went to a top sportsman. Scholastic achievement was supposed to be considered, but seldom was, even by the teachers. There could be no disputing that I had distinguished myself, but my achievements were of a more dubious kind. They had been wrought on the tennis court, not the rugby field; in the French class, not the physics class. These were not the conventional accomplishments of a head prefect. They did not carry the same prestige. Another mark against me was that I had no family tradition at the school. My father wasn't an old boy, let alone my grandfather, who I suspected had never even attended high school, although he claimed otherwise.

The other obstacle was the popularity factor. Prefects were voted for by the senior school. I was well known, if not for my own achievements, then as the son of my famous mother. However, success didn't necessarily translate into popularity, but all too often into jealousy and resentment instead. The drama club in particular was a hotbed of indignant envy. I realised it would be easier to make the younger boys like me than to win over some of my grudging peers. Therefore, at the beginning of my Year Eleven, I began my private campaign. I encouraged my reputation as a good sort. I did not lord my seniority over those boys who were junior to me as so many did, teasing or persecuting them for kicks. I made a particular effort towards those hapless souls who had been written off on account of their spectacles, obesity, acne, race or religious upbringing. I learnt their real names, and used them instead of their appallingly apt nicknames.

My efforts paid off. The following year I was voted in as one of the twelve prefects. From there, it was up to the teachers to select a head and a deputy. My chances were very promising. I was very popular with the teachers. I had always been a model student and consistently topped my year in English, French and history. I had worked out how to win top marks and the teachers' sympathy at the same time. The secret was to regurgitate everything those teachers ever said, word for word, back at them. But I went a little further than that. I would quote their opinions back at them and acknowledge the source. They were so impressed that I had memorised their words and treated them as if they were authoritative scholarly sources, I always got top marks. I had been well taught by my mother. Flattery can get you almost anything.

Mr Fletcher, the principal, was terse when Marcus Lloyd and I were summoned to his office on the day the head prefect announcement was to be made. I couldn't stop myself grinning at him. Fletcher was a big rugby supporter. His displeasure could only mean that his staff had insisted I be made head prefect over Marcus, the captain of the first fifteen. My presumption was correct. Fletcher announced the decision and shook our hands. Marcus was then dismissed as Fletcher felt compelled to tell me privately that I wasn't his personal choice.

'I've been persuaded of your merits by certain members of my staff,' he began drily. 'To my mind, there are some glaring deficiencies in your record of achievement. Over the years we have become accustomed to a head prefect who excels at either cricket or rugby, preferably both. You play neither.'

'I've represented the school in tennis since I began here, sir,' I pointed out.

Mr Fletcher raised his eyebrows. 'Yes. I've been made to understand that tennis is your thing.'

There was a silence. 'Head prefect isn't school sportsman of the year, is it?' I said, trying to bring some light to the conversation.

'That's one prize you'll never win,' flashed Mr Fletcher.

'No,' I agreed. 'I would prefer to be the dux.'

Mr Fletcher snorted. 'I recognise that you have ambition, Spear.'

I smiled confidently.

'But you must take care,' he continued, 'that your ambition is not mistaken for impertinence.'

I lowered my eyes and murmured a 'yes, sir'.

When I was dismissed, I found Mr Preston hanging around in the foyer outside Fletcher's office. 'I wanted to be the first to congratulate you,' he beamed, clasping my hand with both of his as he shook it.

'I believe I owe some of my success to you,' I replied brightly. 'Mr Fletcher indicated I had some champions on the staff and I'm certain he meant you, *Derek*.'

It was the first time I had ever used Mr Preston's first name and I did so quite deliberately. It was a liberty to take with a teacher, but I knew it was exactly what Mr Preston longed to hear. It would be another of those small intimacies between us which I doled out to him occasionally, and which I knew he treasured, probably even fantasised over at bedtime. I knew because occasionally he would startle me by mentioning remarks I'd made to him and completely forgotten about.

Mr Preston's smile became more bashful. 'It wasn't only me. Mr Frost was very persuasive on your behalf as well. But between us we did sway the vote in your favour. Convinced them all that with your speech-making abilities, you'd be a credit to the school on public occasions. Lloyd was Mr Fletcher's choice. As if he could utter a sentence without the use of a profanity. Finally I managed to convince Mr Fletcher what an embarrassment he would be when he was called upon to make a speech.'

Scholastically Marcus Lloyd was something of a disaster, but he was captain of the first fifteen and a fast bowler for the first eleven. He neglected his studies in favour of his sporting achievement and his teachers tended to make allowances for him. Elisabeth would've considered him uncouth. He smoked. He drank. It was rumoured he smoked dope. He went out with Philippa James, who was unanimously considered to be the ultimate babe of our sister school. Marcus was butch, bad and totally irresistible to me.

He and I were thrown together increasingly after our new status was conferred. It wasn't long before he boasted to me that he was cheating on Philippa. He had a woman twice his age, a university tutor whom he met for liaisons at her Newtown flat. 'She's taught me a thing or two,' he boasted one afternoon in the prefects' lounge.

'What about Philippa?' I couldn't help protesting.

She and I always played opposite one another in our school co-productions and I was fond of her – she was to be Mary Magdalene to my Jesus Christ Superstar that year. 'Unlike Mary Magdalene, Philippa doesn't fuck. *Yet*,' he added ominously.

Marcus's virility and treachery aroused me desperately, but sadly he had little time for me. My mother was 'hot for an old girl' but I was a wimp. I didn't play rugby and that alone was enough to condemn me.

I flirted with Philippa throughout the rehearsals for *Superstar*. Her connection with Marcus made her suddenly attractive to me, but there was another reason. I needed to quickly salvage my reputation which had been sullied by Mr Preston and an indiscreet remark he'd made during one of the early rehearsals. He had started rattling on to me, in front of the entire cast, about how I must apply to drama school for the following year. 'With your looks and diction you are destined to tread the boards professionally,' he declared in his usual theatrical manner.

Several of the cast misheard him or didn't know what diction meant or perhaps chose not to. They sniggered that Mr Preston had ambitions for me as a gigolo. 'With your looks and dick . . .'

I was horrified. Mr Preston had a definite reputation round the school. I rescued the situation by finding him alone one day and threatening to quit the show. 'There have been remarks made,' I told him with a tear in my voice, 'that you favour me above others. Some boys have made obscene insinuations.'

Mr Preston stared at me with such intensity, I feared he was going to seize and kiss me. I quickly continued. 'Derek, you must be more strict with me. Tell me off in front of the others. Fail me for an English essay or something, though please don't count the mark towards my assessment.'

'And you must stop calling me Derek. Even in private moments like this. It's best if you don't,' Mr Preston said gravely.

I blushed and nodded.

My intervention restored the damage. Mr Preston stopped fawning over me in public and he shocked my English class by calling an essay I'd done 'sloppy' when he handed it back to me. I allowed the essay to sit on my desk for several minutes so that those sitting next to me could see the mark – 5 out of 20 – in red pen up the top of the page. The real mark – 19 out of 20 – was written in pencil on the final page of the essay along with his adoring comments.

The gigolo joke died when the show finished and it never really spread beyond the *Superstar* cast. Mr Preston managed to restrain himself for most of the rehearsal period, though he did get carried away with his camera at the first dress rehearsal, taking photographs of me strung up on the crucifix in my loincloth. Luckily the rest of the cast believed his frantic snapping was for publicity purposes and thought nothing of it as he edged closer and closer, until he stood directly beneath me, his lens pointed up between my legs, the shutter clicking furiously. I was strapped to the crucifix. Exposed. I could not defend my modesty or hide my mounting erection.

The following night, I waited until Mr Preston entered the dressing room before I began to undress. I pretended not to have noticed him and swiftly began to slip out of my clothes. But he lingered for only a moment before apologising and withdrawing. I turned, as if disturbed, my underwear held aloft in one hand, as he backed out the door.

Although the entire school was convinced of Mr Preston's leanings – he was known as Dirty Derek or Ditsy Derek – I began to have my doubts. I felt certain that a real homosexual would have found me impossible to resist at that moment. I had been so provocative yet he had failed to act. Although the look on his face did seem to contradict his inertia. There had been such yearning in his eyes as he fled from the dressing room, so strong it seemed to pain him.

I found I enjoyed provoking that look onto Mr Preston's face. A liaison between us was utterly forbidden and that was the crux of his appeal. I didn't find him attractive. I couldn't get over the fact that his moustache was a different colour to his hair and looked as though he'd borrowed it from the dramatic society's make-up box. But he was my teacher, my master, and I relished having him in thrall to me. I had the power to expose him if I chose. It would be a scandal which might tarnish me briefly but would undoubtedly ruin Mr Preston.

Every night after that, I tormented him. I would hum a line or two of Mary Magdalene's famous song 'I don't know how to love him' when I passed by him. I had to have my body darkened with greasepaint for the crucifixion scene and I always made a point of asking for a volunteer from the cast to apply it in front of Mr Preston. He wanted to do it more than anyone else. I could see it in his eyes, begging me to ask this favour of him, but to ask it in private. It was impossible for Mr Preston, with his reputation, to volunteer in front of an audience.

I looked spectacular up there on the crucifix. Everyone said so. I was lifted up high. Bathed in a golden light. Before the crowd, beneath those lights, I could feel myself glowing. The golden boy was ascendant. Mr Preston stood off in the wings, mouthing silently at me, 'You are a superstar, *my superstar.*'

Beneath me on her knees, Philippa James looked up with more than admiration in her eyes, and so at the end of performance party I let it slip to her about Marcus and the university tutor. She seemed crushed and fell silent for several minutes, but after some champagne (I had poured it into Sprite cans) she began to smile again and then to laugh and even to flirt with me. After several cans of 'Sprite', I watched Mr Preston's eyes widen as she flicked a few drops of champagne onto my painted chest then slowly wiped away the paint around my nipple with a dainty finger.

On Monday it was the talk of the school that Philippa had dumped Marcus and was going out with me. A few days later she asked me over to watch a video of the *Superstar* show. I presumed it was an invitation that extended to the entire cast, but when I arrived I discovered that it was an invitation to me alone. We were on a date.

I wasn't nervous about the situation. Marcus had complained about Philippa's frigidity so often. 'She should be playing the Virgin Mary not Mary Magdalene in that play. That would've been type casting.' Philippa wanted nothing more than to kiss and cuddle and I was greatly relieved that she always slapped my hand away if it should stray too far up her thigh.

'It's such a nice change to be with someone who can understand that I have limits,' confided Philippa, speaking of herself as if she was a parking place. 'Marcus was an animal. He had no respect.'

'Tell me,' I encouraged her and she did.

For once I managed to get an erection, which I pressed against her thigh hastily.

I began to spend whole weekends with Philippa. I'd stay over at her house on Saturday night, though of course we didn't share a bedroom. We kissed good night after both brushing our teeth. She went to her room and I went to her brother Simon's room. He was three years younger than Philippa. He didn't take much convincing to allow me into his bed. 'How'd you like to save your sister from losing her virginity?' I said to him that first night I slept in his room.

His cute little face puckered up with concern and puzzlement. 'What?'

'I need some relief, man.' I threw back my bedclothes to show him my cock, hard through my cotton pyjama shorts. 'You get my meaning?'

Simon would do anything I asked, though he liked to make it clear before each particular act that he was only doing it to relieve his sister of the responsibility. 'I'll do it for Philippa's sake,' he would tell me solemnly, nobly, before he went down on me.

Going out with Philippa lent a certain prestige and normality to my reputation. Everyone – my parents, Mr Fletcher, my friends – seemed to think it was a marvellous development. There was an undercurrent of relief in their satisfaction. I had been acutely aware of how peculiar it seemed that I should be so highly eligible yet had never had a steady girlfriend.

So I embellished the background to my romance with Philippa. I confided that I had in fact been infatuated with her for years, ever since I had played Rolf to her Liesl in *The Sound of Music*. I claimed to have suffered in silence throughout all those years she had dallied with the unsuitable Marcus Lloyd, unable to contemplate another. It made perfect sense to everyone. My reputation was redeemed.

My story was so splendidly convincing, I actually began to believe in it myself and felt hurt and betrayed when I first realised that Philippa still had feelings for Marcus. There were small actions that gave her away. She mentioned his name, not often, but enough to make me realise that she still felt compelled to know what he was doing. When the tennis season began and she came to watch my matches, I noticed her eyes kept wandering over to the cricket pitch where Marcus was playing. And when we went to parties, she always scanned the crowd as soon as we arrived, to check whether he was there. If he was, her manner changed. She became very vivacious, laughing and talking with great animation. She also became more physically demonstrative with me, clinging to my arm or perhaps resting a hand on my thigh. She was performing. Of course, we both were. My ego was hurt until it occurred to me that our situation was utterly perfect. I was using her to the same extent as she was using me. It was advantageous to both of us to pretend to be in love.

It was in the kitchen at one of those parties that Marcus approached me and broached the subject of Philippa for the first time. 'Betcha not fucking her,' he jeered.

'If I was, I wouldn't tell you or anyone at all for that matter. I consider sex to be a private matter.'

'You didn't consider my sex life *a private matter* when you told Phil about it a few months back.'

Which was a very good answer and about the cleverest thing I'd ever heard come out of Marcus Lloyd's mouth.

Dating Philippa seemed the ideal subterfuge. It proceeded perfectly until the day, three months into our 'going out', when she announced that she wanted me to take her virginity. Luckily, I'm a fast thinker. That's why I'm so formidable on the school debating team. 'Philippa, I'd love to do it,' I said, all earnest conviction. 'More than anything. But you do have to be certain about this. Absolutely certain.'

'I'm certain.'

'Even though you're still in love with Marcus,' I said gently. Philippa blushed.

'Philippa, you shouldn't give up your virginity to me in an attempt to make Marcus jealous. We can achieve that without actually doing the deed.'

'We can? How?'

And I explained.

She telephoned her friend Julie immediately. She gave her such a good account of our lovemaking that even I got hard listening to her narrate how we'd done it. Afterwards, when she'd hung up and we were rolling round on the couch in each other's arms, screaming and laughing, I began to worry that she was going to give herself to me out of gratitude for such a masterful plan she was grinding herself against my crotch with such ardency.

The plan worked perfectly. Marcus seized me and threw me up against the lockers the next day at school, his forearm jammed against my throat, his face leering into mine. 'You fucked my girlfriend.'

'Not true,' I gasped.

'What?'

Marcus released me.

'She's not your girlfriend any more . . .'

Marcus lunged towards me again.

'. . . but she'd like to be,' I added quickly. 'Marcus, we didn't go all the way. Philippa couldn't because . . . because she still loves you.'

Marcus got a little lost in thought at that moment. His big brown eyes softened and a small frown creased his brow. I sighed. I could well understand Philippa's irrepressible attraction to him.

Philippa was genuinely regretful when she told me that the plan had worked *too* well. 'I didn't just make him jealous. He wants me back and, though it's irrational, I want him back too.'

I let her rattle on, making her apologies, bemoaning her weakness, praising my decency – I love compliments! 'You're such a nice guy. In lots of ways, I wish it was going to be you, the first time.'

'Oh well,' I said. 'We can always have a threesome.'

Philippa giggled. 'That's what I love about you. We always had such a laugh together.'

I laughed too, though I had been perfectly serious.

Everyone was very sorry that my relationship with Philippa had ended. I let it be known that I was heartbroken, damaged, quite unable to contemplate another . . .

I threw myself into my school work. It was to be my final prize-giving and I wanted the ultimate accolade.

When I was made dux, it was like that moment in *Superstar*, on the crucifix, only better. Mr Fletcher gave such a stirring speech about my achievement. 'Our first dux from the arts stream ever in the school's history,' he proclaimed.

I shook Mr Fletcher's hand and accepted the trophy. Behind us, the staff of the school, led by my five class teachers, swept to their feet and applauded. The entire school followed suit. It was unprecedented. A standing ovation.

But afterwards Mr Preston took the edge off my victory. He told me, when he bounded up to congratulate me, that strictly speaking I shouldn't have been the dux. 'This is in the strictest confidence, you must never repeat it to anyone,' he warned me and I nodded, intrigued.

Mr Preston couldn't help himself. He wanted me to appreciate what he'd done for me. His final act of benevolence. 'Raymond Cheok had higher marks than you overall,' he admitted. 'But then it's easier to get a perfect score in science subjects, whereas it's virtually unheard of in arts subjects. We took that factor into account and made an adjustment. There's no doubt that you're the most outstanding English student we've had pass through the school in years and years. We all felt that fact should be recognised.'

Over Mr Preston's shoulder I could see Raymond Cheok being consoled by his parents. He had his back to me but it looked as though he was weeping.

'I mustn't monopolise you,' Mr Preston continued. 'Everyone wants to congratulate you. But you will come and see me tomorrow and say goodbye, won't you?'

'Of course,' I said automatically.

I had hoped to avoid him. I knew he was going to try to make some arrangement for us to see each other over the summer. Now that I was no longer his student, he had nothing to fear. But equally I had nothing to gain. I knew why he had made me aware that I was indebted to him, but I felt no obligation. Only anger that he had insinuated himself, and his role in my victory, into my day of glory and tarnished it. I resolved to slip away from school the following day without allowing him the chance for a private chat.

I avoided his classroom the next day, but as the afternoon drew on, he came in search of me and found me leaving Mr Fletcher's office, having said my goodbyes there.

'Stephen!'

Mr Preston strode towards me from across the vestibule. 'I thought I'd missed you.'

I stopped and smiled weakly. 'I was just on my way to see you. I thought I'd say goodbye to you last.'

The smile my remark prompted was cloying.

'I would have been sorry not to say goodbye to you,' said Mr Preston. 'Though I'm sure we'll hear how you get on. We usually do hear with the top boys. Especially if they disgrace themselves, though I know you won't do that, Stephen.'

His voice lingered on my name and he stared at me just a moment too long. I looked away and Mr Preston became awkward himself and started rummaging in his bag. 'I have something for you. A book I thought you might like to read now that you have some leisure time for reading.'

He held it out towards me. It was a paperback. Thomas Mann's *Death in Venice*. 'You don't need to return it. It's a gift. But I did write my name and telephone number in the front of it. I thought you might like to discuss it when you finish reading it.'

It was the way he said the title, in an undertone, and the frankness with which his eyes sought mine that made me feel hemmed in. For once I had no ready reply or excuse. I could feel myself blushing. Suddenly there was the clatter of feet on the stairs above our heads and Marcus Lloyd and two of his friends, Cross and Cometti, rounded the corner of the stairway. They stopped when they saw us. The surprise on their faces made me feel guilty, as if I'd been caught at something illicit. I edged away from Mr Preston as discreetly as I could. Then I realised. It was they who were in the wrong. All three of them had cigarettes dangling from their fingers.

Marcus exchanged glances with his friends and then strode confidently on, down the stairs. 'It's the last day of school, sir,' Marcus shrugged with an abashed grin.

That smile of his was totally adorable. I would have forgiven him any vice. I felt like suggesting that we go off, just the two of us, and get drunk to celebrate the end of school. Perhaps if he was drunk enough, and Philippa was still withholding herself, there might be some possibility . . .

'Yes, Lloyd,' said Mr Preston in a voice which was much quieter than the usual authoritative tone he used with Marcus.

'See you, sir,' said Marcus, sauntering on and out through the door, his friends trailing after him.

'Goodbye, Lloyd.'

'I bet you'll miss us, sir,' Cross called back over his shoulder.

'I doubt that very much, Cross,' Mr Preston retorted.

'But he'll miss *Stephen.*'

Marcus said it in an undertone, but his words carried back, no doubt as he'd intended, a sardonic twist in his voice as he spoke my name. Cross and Cometti barked their laughter. My eyes met Mr Preston's briefly. He looked as startled and guilty as I felt. I jerked my gaze away. Marcus's taunt had stabbed me, punctured the erotic visions stirring in my mind, but even though he mocked me, I still wanted him. Badly.

Mr Preston began to speak, but I knew I didn't want to hear it, didn't want to hear him admit to what Marcus had suggested. I turned away but he caught me by the arm and I was surprised by the strength of his grip. 'I know you'll do well, Stephen,' he began, and then his voice choked up with emotion. 'You're blessed with many advantages. Blessed.'

I muttered a thank you, pulled away from him and darted out the door. Marcus and his friends were larking up ahead of me. I was tempted to run after them, to suggest getting some beers, offering to pay, but as I watched them, their cocky walks, their boisterous laughter, I knew it was useless. My hopes were groundless. The main gate was in front of me and I hurried through it, nervous of Mr Preston coming after me.

I turned down the street without looking back.

The book arrived in the post a week later. Mr Preston had been holding it out to me when Marcus and his friends had interrupted us, and I had forgotten all about it. There was no accompanying note. I ripped out the incriminating inscribed page and threw it away. I shelved it in my bookcase. I had no intention of reading it. I had an idea of what it was about. But the book seemed to lurk on the shelf, making insinuations. Its spine caught my eye constantly. It was like a taunt. Finally I wrapped it up and gave it to Uncle Vic for Christmas. He thanked me, praising my choice. 'A classic tale of unrequited love,' he declared.

'Of course it ends tragically,' he muttered when he insisted on giving me a thank you kiss on the cheek.

I submitted to the kiss and ignored his remark. I was the golden boy and confident that for me, love would never be tragic.

CHAPTER TWO

I missed school. I'd enjoyed such success there, I mourned its passing. I do believe I suffered from a slight depression over that summer. It was such a drastic change for me: to go from my daily due of praise, compliments and top marks to being mercilessly nagged by my parents as to what I was going to do with myself next.

I had found that the best way to deal with 'the career question' was to say nothing, and generally the person interrogating me would answer it themselves. I would nod and agree to whatever they had in mind for me, dismissing their suggestions automatically.

My tennis coach had been nagging me for years to forget ideas of university and turn professional. Mr Preston was forever telling me to follow in my mother's footsteps and apply to drama school while Mr Frost tried to convince me that I should have a career in politics. Even Mr Fletcher had ideas for me. A masters in English literature, then a teaching position back at the old school and a quick rise through the ranks. 'Who knows, you could be head of the department by the time you're thirty. Look at Mr Preston.'

Emulating Mr Preston was the last thing I wanted to do, but I pretended to be deeply impressed by the plan. It was a compliment that Mr Fletcher, who had been so cool at the outset of my year as head prefect, wanted me to return to the school.

My father told everyone that I was going to law school 'like his old man'. Elisabeth would pretend to support my father's intentions for me, but she held her own firm views as to what the pinnacle of career achievement was. She had no ambition for me to be an actor. 'One show-off in any family is quite enough,' was what she said when anyone made that suggestion.

Privately she stressed to me that the life of an actor could be very bleak, with long spells of going without work. 'It's no life for a man,' she informed me, dismissing all her own male actor friends in that sentence, but then deep down she didn't consider them to be real men anyway. 'What you need is the security of a good solid profession. A doctor.'

The subject of my career brought Elisabeth's conservative housewife persona to the fore. All the notions that her own mother had nagged her with throughout her adolescence in the fifties suddenly began to sound sensible to her. Nana had wanted Elisabeth to marry a doctor – a doctor's wife had cachet. When instead she married my father, a lawyer, Nana considered him a second-rate choice.

Throughout my last year at school, Elisabeth was always pointing out to me the advantages of being a doctor. The fact that I gave up all science and mathematical subjects once the syllabus permitted it didn't worry her. 'You always watched "The Young Doctors" on TV every night, year after year. You always said you wanted to be a doctor,' she insisted.

It was true I had loved that programme, but I couldn't remember ever declaring that I wanted to be a doctor. If anything, I wanted to be the patient. I had crushes on several of the cast and had fantasies about being examined by them.

So when Elisabeth thrust an application form for medical school at me, I dutifully filled it in. It was ridiculous. I would never be considered without a science background, but Elisabeth refused to accept that, so I sent it off, along with all the other application forms for courses that people kept insisting I must apply for. Over the summer I was expected to stop procrastinating and make my decision.

But I couldn't. I couldn't focus. I was too preoccupied. My hormones were humming and I was in a state of almost perpetual arousal. I was cracking erections constantly and inappropriately; though one advantage of being modestly endowed down there, they weren't so readily discernible. All previous restraints had fallen away from me. I no longer had to be a model of discretion and good behaviour. Elisabeth had said as much herself at my birthday dinner. I was eighteen. I could legally go to bars and I was itching to. I longed to explore the world that I knew lay out there, strung out along Oxford Street, which Uncle Vic's tales had unwittingly tempted me with. But I didn't dare venture there. Not until I had told Elisabeth my news. If I didn't tell her, someone else surely would. She had a coterie of homosexual friends, the way most women would have a circle of girlfriends. If Vic or one of her other friends saw me in one of those places, she would learn of it.

But I couldn't bring myself to tell her. I was so unsure of how she would receive the news. Although she professed to adore her 'fag fan club' and their outrageous conversation, I wasn't convinced. It seemed to me that she had her private reservations. She had occasionally made dismissive remarks about her friends, implying that it was not a lifestyle to be emulated by her only son. 'It's very sad,' she told me after one of her afternoons around the gin bottle with them. 'Ultimately they *always* end up alone.'

She had probably drunk quite a lot to say such a thing, but it was when she was drunk that you often caught a glimpse of the real Elisabeth. Sober, you could never be quite sure what mask she had assumed or when she had stopped playing a part.

Elisabeth was a man's woman, not a woman's woman. She had only a few women friends whom she saw infrequently for lunch, and they were like her: loud, showy and prone to not listening to what anyone else had to say. Elisabeth was at her best when she was being fawned over by her gay friends or engaging in flirtatious banter with someone else's husband. It was behaviour that did not endear her to other women. She was too much the vamp. At parties she was always to be found amongst the men, chatting and laughing, while the other wives clung together and gossiped, often about Elisabeth. She liked to be admired and cosseted, and of course other women never indulged her with the sincerity she expected. She would feel slighted and couldn't help herself giving those women 'a little fashion advice' in turn. It was never received with good grace. She was dismissed as a shameless coquette. I overheard such remarks occasionally. They were uttered so that I would hear. I burned with shame and anger but I could not defend her. There was too much truth in what had been said for that.

But I was proud of my mother and how splendid she always looked. Throughout my school years I was the envy of all my classmates. Boys sought me out as a friend merely because I was her son and she was famous. She'd gone straight from acting school in London to a small television role in the BBC production of 'The Forsyte Saga'. Her role was tiny but when the series screened on Australian television in 1968, the local media made a huge fuss of her. The *Australian Women's Weekly* adored her. London symbolised international success. The BBC epitomised quality and crinolines. Elisabeth returned to Australia in triumph. Anyone who hadn't seen the series would've imagined Elisabeth must've been the lead, she received so much attention.

She traded on this new fame for several years without working a great deal. Then her agent convinced her into a number of short dramatic stints in some key, cult television series. These roles kept her fixed in the general public's mind as a star: a barmaid in 'Number Ninety-Six', a stint incarcerated in 'Prisoner', a haughty socialite in 'Return to Eden'. She was a 'name', one of those actors who is popular with Sydney Theatre Company subscribers. They liked to see her onstage at the Opera House at least once a year; someone in the programme they knew and felt confident criticising at the interval. She was good for box office; the artistic director recognised that fact and regularly cast her in supporting roles in the latest David Williamson. She was never offered Shakespeare or Chekhov.

On the basis of her celebrity, I cultivated friendships with some of the most popular boys in the school. Even when I was a junior, the older boys who generally disdained juniors sought me out. They angled for invitations to my home, even to sleep over on the weekends. They dreamed of somehow catching my mother *déshabillée*, which of course never happened. It was I who watched them strip naked before they put on their pyjamas. Later, when the light had been switched off, I would sneak across to their bed. Almost always, the blankets would be thrown back to welcome me.

In that respect Elisabeth was an asset as a mother. But when it came to telling her what I had to tell her, there were two massive drawbacks. First was what I believed to be her underlying antipathy to homosexuals, despite her public delight in their company. And second was the fact that she simply knew too much about the gay scene. Thanks to the candidness with which Uncle Vic and her other friends outlined their exploits, my mother was well aware of the extremes of the gay underworld. Of course she had never been to any of these venues, but thanks to Uncle Vic she knew the names of all the popular bars, nightclubs and saunas, and even the location of several nocturnal beats. She knew exactly what went on in these places, what men did to one another there. Every time I thought about telling her, I could imagine that knowledge reflected in her face. My nerve always failed me.

Uncle Vic was my mother's closest friend, the female confidante she lacked. They had become friendly when they were both in their mid-twenties. Vic was a buyer for David Jones back then, and Elisabeth was doing some modelling for the store. Apparently Vic was very handsome in his day and Elisabeth was attracted to him. But he dashed her hopes when, instead of asking her out, he asked to borrow her fur muff and matching hat to wear to a masquerade ball. She agreed, but only on the condition that he take her along for the night. That marked the beginning of their friendship and also set something of a pattern: Elisabeth attending parties where she was one of the few real women present; Vic trading on the glamour she lent him, whether it was a muff or merely her presence as she grew more famous.

Throughout the seventies and eighties Uncle Vic was perpetually single. He assured my mother that he liked it that way. 'Fancy free's the way to be,' he would trill whenever she enquired if he was seeing anyone.

I wished Elisabeth wouldn't ask. Vic needed no encouragement to talk about his sex life and it always embarrassed me. I was surprised my mother didn't try to hush him when, in front of me, he started talking about the things he did in bed. Finally I asked her why she permitted it. 'You're old enough to hear it,' she said breezily. 'Besides, I know it's more likely to revolt you than titillate you.'

But Elisabeth had miscalculated there. Uncle Vic's stories made me aware of a whole new world. Places whose sole purpose was for men to meet like-minded men, who were often nothing like the effeminate homosexuals I was aware of from films and television and as evidenced by Uncle Vic himself. Vic displayed photographs of some of his friends and lovers, and both Elisabeth and I were impressed by their looks and apparent innocuousness. 'He doesn't look gay to me,' she said disbelievingly of one particularly macho, moustached specimen, voicing my own thoughts.

Uncle Vic assured us proudly that he was. 'I still ache from the things he did to me three nights ago.'

My mother and Uncle Vic shrieked with laughter.

I couldn't understand how Uncle Vic could attract such a masculine-looking man. To my mind Uncle Vic's appearance was tragic. He had clung gamely on to the clone look for years after it was popular and then, when he finally did give himself a much needed make-over, instead of opting for something tasteful for a man of his years (fifty-two), he started getting himself up in the dance party look that was popular at that time. He dressed in bike shorts and Smiley T-shirts that highlighted the swell of his belly rather than his biceps or chest. Perhaps he might have got away with it at night, in a club where it was dark and everyone was on drugs, but Uncle Vic considered his new look day wear as well.

'Mutton dressed as lamb,' my mother would say of him, even to his face occasionally.

'Some people prefer mutton,' Vic would reply archly. 'It may not be as tender as lamb but there is more of it, and size, my dear Liddy, is everything in the gay world.'

That was the one thing Uncle Vic did have going for him. The swell in his bike shorts was of gargantuan proportions. I didn't know how he could walk around like that in broad daylight without being arrested. It was obscene.

'Couldn't you suggest to him that if he possessed a bike to go with the bike shorts he wouldn't look so ridiculous?' I asked Elisabeth.

But Elisabeth just shrugged and then made a joke of my remark by repeating it to Vic in front of me. 'That's the whole point of it,' Vic chortled. 'I'm in search of something or rather someone to ride.'

Elisabeth joined in his laughter.

I was baffled by her behaviour. She could revel in Vic's vulgarity, yet at other times, when he wasn't around, she could be prudish and disapproving of him. It was impossible to gauge her true feelings. Her opinion seemed to vary depending on whom she was discussing homosexuality with.

Her response to the existence of AIDS seemed to give some clue to her true feelings. She saw a report about it on the television news and phoned Uncle Vic up in hysterics, insisting he come over immediately. When he walked in the door she threw herself upon him weeping. 'Tell me you haven't got it. Tell me you're not going to die.'

'Well actually I'm not,' said Uncle Vic cheerfully.

He elaborated. Apparently he'd had a problem down below which had persisted for more than eighteen months and prevented him from indulging in the highest risk activity for contracting HIV. By the time he'd got himself 'back in working order', AIDS had been news in the gay press for some time and safe sex guidelines had been issued. Uncle Vic had taken an HIV test and his result had been negative.

After Vic left, my mother was subdued. 'I'm so relieved,' she said.

But her voice didn't sound relieved. She sounded suspicious and a little disappointed.

Elisabeth had had her role snatched from her. She had put on such a performance when Vic arrived – the tears, the hysteria, the way she had seized him – she had decided in her own mind that he had *it* and that she would play the merciful nurse to her debauched dying friend. Not that she wanted Vic to die. But part of her couldn't help believing that someone who was as promiscuous as Vic must eventually suffer for it. Her own mother had convinced her so effectively that there was always a price to pay for promiscuity. 'Poor Vic must have suffered dreadful anxiety over this,' she finally concluded.

But she didn't sound sympathetic. She sounded vindicated.

The television news had a lot of reports about AIDS at that time and I watched Elisabeth closely whenever such a story came on. When conservative groups argued that AIDS was God's punishment for homosexuals, Elisabeth protested vigorously to my father and me how misguided such an assertion was. But then she deflated her own argument by remarking that the conservatives did have a point. 'The plague does seem to be singling out homosexuals. It does make you wonder.'

It was obvious to me that Elisabeth's initial comments were a lecture she'd had from Vic and which she felt obliged to reiterate. Her personal opinion was more equivocal.

Her ambiguous behaviour began to convince me that although she could be enthusiastic about the most extreme excesses of Uncle Vic's sexuality, when it came to me confessing something as innocent as a chaste attraction to another boy, she would hose me down with a torrent of invective. So I said nothing and probably would have gone on saying nothing if she hadn't confronted me. She found an incriminating magazine in my room. Not a porno. It was a girls' magazine. Quite innocent to the casual eye. But of course Elisabeth didn't have a casual eye. She had a prying, spying, suspicious eye. She took note of the special photo spread of Christopher Atkins from *Blue Lagoon* in his loincloth, which had been the very reason I'd stolen it from my elder cousin Janine when I was eight years old.

'I found this under your bed,' she said to me in an accusing tone.

Even though it was about ten years old, it was still popular material for me to jerk off to. I'd made use of it the previous night and evidently forgotten about it in the morning. Elisabeth insisted on access to my bedroom, despite all my protestations. Her excuse was that she had to vacuum and make my bed. I told her I would do that myself but she always retorted that I wouldn't do it to her satisfaction. 'I can't abide squalor or a job only half done. What would visitors think?'

'What would visitors be doing in my bedroom?'

'Visitors pry about,' said my mother vaguely. 'It's their way.'

It was Elisabeth's way. I knew that she searched my room, looking for 'signs'. One of her friends had a sixteen-year-old heroin addict for a son. So as Elisabeth vacuumed and tidied, she kept an eagle eye out for syringes, razor blades, compact mirrors, cigarette papers and other such evidence. She also liked to keep tabs on what I was up to: what books I was reading, what magazines I was buying, who was writing letters to me, what I was writing in my diary. The things on my desk and on my bedside table were always disturbed when I came home from school.

I tried making my bed myself so she wouldn't have an excuse to enter, but her response to that was to whisk the sheets off the bed and wash them. When I confronted her over this, she breezily replied that the sheets had been *dirty*. She gave the word special emphasis and then looked at me intently. I gave up after that and was very careful not to leave anything incriminating around. But obviously I had been careless.

'Oh,' I said, as the magazine dangled in front of my eyes. 'I liked that movie.'

'Yes,' said Elisabeth, pursing her lips. 'I remember being obliged to escort you to see it because you were too young to go on your own. I thought you had a crush on Brooke Shields.

You had her poster on your bedroom wall.'

That was true. I had also written in my diary that I was obsessed with her, to put Elisabeth off the scent of my true infatuation. Obviously she had read that entry.

Elisabeth thrust the photo spread at me. 'Brooke doesn't appear in any of these pictures,' she said ominously.

I probably could've invented some convincing lie if I'd wanted to, and Elisabeth would have enthusiastically believed it. But instead I said nothing and let my failure to deny anything speak for me.

'I knew it, I knew it,' Elisabeth finally said wearily, sinking into a chair. 'I used to watch you ironing your tennis shorts and worry. I'd think to myself, that's a little extreme, though I never said a word. But those shorts were crimplene. All they needed was a bit of a shake. But no, that wasn't good enough. You insisted on ironing them yourself and I was too upset to offer to do it for you. I knew what it signified but I didn't want to believe it. But only a queen in the making would go to such lengths.'

'I was a fool to allow it,' she mused after a few moments of silence, as if banning me from using the iron would somehow have prevented the inevitable.

Suddenly she glanced up at me, her eyes wide, her expression dramatic. 'Whatever you do, don't tell your father. He'll blame me. Raising you was always my responsibility and now I'll be blamed for ruining his only son.'

'I'm not ruined.'

Though Elisabeth said nothing in reply, the way she arched her eyebrows implied she disagreed. Strongly.

She sat there in the armchair studying me and I began to blush. Suddenly she jumped out of her chair and darted across the room to me. Her hand seized my wrist, her fingers pressed viciously into my flesh.

'You are careful, aren't you?'

I nodded, but still she clutched my hand, staring at me sternly. She didn't need to say any more. It was that moment I'd been dreading. Her eyes boring into me, imagining that I had indulged in all the activities that Vic and her other friends related to her with such candour.

I squirmed to get out of her grip. 'I'm nothing like Uncle Vic,' I protested.

'I should hope not,' said my mother. 'Your Uncle Vic is a terror.'

Maybe the mention of Uncle Vic made Elisabeth realise she was being overly dramatic. If I ran off to Uncle Vic for the sympathetic ear I failed to find in her, she would be humiliated. She released my hand and her tone of voice lightened. 'You're lucky you have a modern mother,' she informed me. 'I have an open mind on this particular issue. We can discuss it any time you choose.'

Having delivered that little speech, Elisabeth made a hasty exit lest I take her up on her offer of a heart-to-heart.

In the days and weeks that followed there were small signs that this news had affected her. She smiled at me too much. I recognised that smile. It was the same tense, tight smile she offered those women whose husbands she flirted with. She also developed a sudden respect for my privacy. Her cleaning missions came to an abrupt halt. 'You're old enough to deal with all that yourself,' she said quickly when, two weeks after 'our talk', I finally queried whether she intended to change my linen.

It was what I'd wanted for years – privacy – but my mother's retreat didn't feel like the triumph it should have been. It felt like a rejection. She'd been only too eager to wash away the evidence of my fantasies when she presumed them to be heterosexual. Now that she knew better, my sheets, and by inference my sexuality, were too sordid a matter for her to deal with.

As for my father, I felt slightly relieved that Elisabeth had insisted I not tell him. I had no idea how he would take it. He was a husband and father who managed to absent himself even when he was present. But who could blame him? After twenty years of playing attentive audience to Elisabeth, it was only natural that he would focus his attention elsewhere (upon the newspaper, the television, the carpet) instead of upon her latest performance. The only time he ever showed any genuine relish for our family conversation was when the subject of my career came up; then he would argue the benefits of taking up law as if he were in an actual courtroom. I had a feeling that when the time came to tell him, I could mollify him by agreeing to be a lawyer if he would accept that his son was gay.

However, as it happened, I told him inadvertently. I'd arrived home after being out all night and ran into my father in the kitchen. He was having an early breakfast. 'Well, well,' he said. 'You must've had a good night. Care to tell me about her?'

My father got it wrong on two counts. I'd had a bloody awful night and it hadn't been a her. For the first time I'd allowed myself to be picked up in a bar. But it had been a disaster and I'd ended up spending three hours in McDonald's waiting for the trains to start up so I could get myself home. I was deeply tired, hung-over and in a vicious mood. 'Actually it was a him,' I snapped, regretting the remark as soon as I'd uttered it.

I walked off without glancing back to see what his reaction was.

The guy had approached me when they turned on the lights at the Albury to make everyone go home. 'I'm Reece,' he introduced himself. 'I've been watching you all night. I'd love to take you home.'

I was startled. I hadn't noticed him looking at me. I'd been mesmerised by an Italian guy who'd been returning my gazes with an encouraging smile all night, but who had nevertheless walked out the door with his arm slung round the shoulders of someone else. I looked Reece over, trying not to be too obvious about it. He certainly had a sensational body. I was drunk. I was also feeling quite worked up. I had thought tonight would be the night. Reece pressed his crotch against my leg and I realised that it still could be. 'I live nearby,' Reece added hopefully.

I shrugged. 'Okay.'

We got a taxi to his place in Elizabeth Bay. He started kissing me and undoing my fly in the lift. From there he pulled me by the buckle of my undone belt through his front door, into the bedroom and sat me on the bed. Standing over me, he dropped his pants. His cock sprang out and I took it in my mouth. Then, to my amazement, Reece picked up the telephone beside the bed and began to make a phone call. I stopped what I was doing and stared up at him, incredulous.

'Hey, don't stop,' Reece protested as he dialled. 'Open wide!'

He pushed his hips forward so that his cock brushed against my lips. Reluctantly I opened my mouth and he guided it back in. I couldn't understand what or who could be so important that he had to make the call at that very moment, but when he began to speak, it slowly dawned on me.

'Hi, it's me . . . Yeah I did . . . Oh yeah, real cute young thing . . . He's a blond, blue eyes, just out of school . . . Doesn't seem like he learnt how to suck cock there . . . Yeah, he's got my cock in his mouth . . . He's just kinda lolling it around in there . . . Feels nice . . .'

I stopped, got to my feet and grabbed the phone off him with the intention of hanging it up. 'Hey, he wants to talk to you,' Reece announced excitedly, clinging to the phone before relinquishing it to me.

Reece stood in front of me, grinning. He kept nodding at me, encouraging me. 'Talk, talk,' he whispered as he began to unbutton my shirt.

Reece began to lick one of my nipples. When he wrapped his hand over my own and guided the phone up to my ear, I let him. The guy on the other end did all the talking anyway. He identified himself as Mike. 'You've been sucking on Reece's cock? Been liking it too, I hear . . . I'm lying here imagining that . . . I've got a big cock you'd like to suck too, I bet . . . Reece likes sucking it and being fucked by it . . . He *loves* being fucked . . . When you start to fuck him, I want you to tell me how you like it. How you like fucking my boyfriend.'

I was so surprised I dropped the phone. *His boyfriend?* At that exact same moment Reece finally slithered my underwear down. I noticed that my cock didn't spring out in the same abundant eager way that Reece's had. I was also aware that he was making the same comparison. He looked up at me, his face like that of a child at Christmas time, his dismay unmistakable.

Reece got to his feet. 'Maybe I'll fuck you instead,' he suggested.

I would've liked to have said no to that, but as it was clear that he was disappointed in my cock, I felt pressured to do something to please him. I hesitated. 'Okay,' I finally agreed. 'But be gentle. It's the first time.'

Reece had been absorbed putting on a condom. 'Yeah?' he said, his face suddenly transformed by excitement. 'Tell Mike that. Talk down the phone to Mike. Tell him it's your first time. He'll love that. Where's the phone?'

Reece scrabbled under the bed and found the receiver. 'You still there?' he queried into it.

I hoped Mike might have hung up, but of course he hadn't. Reece began to chat away to him, advising him that he was going to do the fucking and that I was a virgin and itching for it. I couldn't bear it any longer. I grabbed the phone and put my hand over the mouthpiece so Mike couldn't hear. 'I'd prefer it, Reece, if it was just the two of us, without the phone,' I told him firmly.

'Without Mike?' said Reece incredulously. 'Oh no. He wouldn't like that. Mike and I have an agreement, you see. If we fool around, the other one has to be in on it too. Then we both know exactly what's going on. Talk to Mike. He's very easy to talk to. You'll make him very excited if you just say a few things down the phone to him. A few filthy things.'

Suddenly I knew exactly what to say. 'Your boyfriend is an absolute slut,' I informed Mike.

But instead of getting angry, Reece was delighted. 'That's it exactly,' he congratulated me.

Mike was blabbering away in my ear, agreeing with me and

giving me plenty of examples of Reece's whorish behaviour. The more I heard, the more uncomfortable I felt about him fucking me. How safe had he been in the past? But then Reece wrapped his arms around me, pulled me against himself and I began to waver again. I was curious to try it. I also knew it would not be easy at this late stage to extract myself from what was imminent. Mike was talking in my ear, telling me what Reece was going to do to me, how much I was going to like it, and I began to feel soothed and reassured, as well as aroused, by his erotic patter. I found myself agreeing with what Mike was telling me.

Reece thrust it in. I couldn't believe the pain. It seemed to sear right through my gut. My eyes watered. I felt ripped in half. I screamed down the phone at Mike. On the other end, he was chanting in a frenzied fashion, 'Yes, yes, yes.' Reece had me by the hips. I could feel him pulling back to thrust into me again and I wrenched myself away from him. I fell off the bed, getting free of him, and lay there on the floorboards, curled up, feeling wounded, convinced that something inside me had surely been ruptured, that I couldn't even have got to my feet if I'd wanted to. Reece knelt on the bed, staring down at me, his hand working his penis, his head cock-angled, the phone wedged between his ear and his shoulder. Gradually the pain began to ease and I finally felt able to speak. I lashed out at him. 'I told you to be gentle. I told you it was the first time.'

He mumbled his apologies. 'I thought you were just trying to turn me on. You know. Role-playing. Acting all innocent.'

Slowly, I got to my feet and began putting my clothes back on. 'Hey, where are you going? Mike, he's getting dressed. I've got a big one here for you.'

'Too big for me.'

He continued trying to persuade me back into bed, repeating the entreaties Mike was making as well. I ignored them. When I began to leave, he followed me to the door, grappling at the buttons on my fly which I had just done up. Finally I got the door open and escaped through it. I couldn't see any stairs, so I was obliged to wait for the lift while Reece stood in the doorway of his flat, masturbating furiously. I jabbed the button impatiently. Eventually the lift arrived and the doors opened. I glanced back at Reece. His head was thrown back. He was about to come. I rapped on his neighbour's door before ducking into the lift. That spectacle deserved an audience.

Much later that same day, back at home in my own bedroom, I awoke to find my father sitting on my bed, looking down at me gravely. I felt like turning over, insisting on further sleep, when he began to speak.

'Son, I'm glad you told me. To be honest, it wasn't news I wanted to hear but it's best you've told me. I know what it's like having a secret hoarded away. I have one too.'

My father hesitated and for one horrible moment I thought he was going to tell me that he was gay too and that it was hereditary like the baldness.

'I have a mistress.'

Once he'd got it out, his words began to spill out quickly. 'We've seen one another for almost ten years now. Your mother knows but prefers not to know and I'm only telling you . . . I suppose I'm telling you so you realise that I can understand. I mean, not your preference, I don't really understand that, but I can relate to the secrecy. How you've had to keep something fundamental a secret from the world. Do you understand what I'm saying?'

I nodded groggily and my father left the room. I fell back to sleep and when I woke up again, late in the afternoon, I wasn't entirely sure if my father had indeed come to my room and made his confession or whether I'd dreamt it. But the way he met my eyes when I joined him and Elisabeth downstairs, and his swift secret smile, made me understand it was no dream.

My father's confession gave me insight into Elisabeth's muted reaction to my news. No discussion between the two of us had ever come about and I sensed that she wouldn't welcome me raising the subject. I'd felt disappointed and slighted, but now I could understand her behaviour. She would simply have preferred to go on believing that I was an innocent, even if it was a ludicrous self-deception. I felt the same way about my father's secret. Details of his sex life was the absolute last thing I wanted to know about. I would've infinitely preferred to go on believing that he was faithful to my mother. His confession had been a nasty, unwelcome intrusion. I knew, I rather wished I didn't, and I prayed the subject would never flare up into a nasty scene or further embarrassing confessions.

That night I overheard my parents having a fight in their bedroom. I pressed my ear to the wall and discovered they were fighting about me.

'What do you expect?' my father was saying. 'You taught him to knit! I came home from work one day and there you were the two of you, sitting in front of the television, knitting. And he was so pleased with himself, holding it up for me to see and telling me so proudly that he was knitting a holder for the spare toilet-paper roll. Then when this object was finally finished, every time I went to the loo in my own house, I was confronted by it, sitting there on top of the toilet, reminding me that my son, my only son, was a knitter.'

The next morning when I went to the bathroom, the knitted cover wasn't sitting on top of the toilet. I looked around for it and eventually discovered it, inside the bowl. I left it there. From my father's tone the previous night, I wouldn't have been surprised if he'd done a shit on top of it before trying to flush it out of sight for good.

I hadn't wanted my mother to tell Uncle Vic my news. I couldn't adequately explain to her why. 'He's not going to try and seduce you, if that's what you're worried about,' my mother said scornfully.

I blushed. That thought had crossed my mind, but it wasn't the real reason. What made me cringe about Uncle Vic knowing was that I worried it might encourage him to draw closer to me. That he would think we had something in common and should become mates. I could imagine him nudging me and raising his eyebrows, all innuendo. 'We're one of a kind, eh, boy?' There had always been a distance between us. I was polite rather than friendly towards him. If we found ourselves alone in each other's company, this reserve became more marked, our conversation faltering into uneasy silences.

As far as I was concerned, nothing had changed. I still felt worlds away from Uncle Vic. I had always considered him faintly ridiculous: his effeminate behaviour, his loud and lewd remarks, his vain attempts to cling to his youth. It had always embarrassed me when I'd been compelled to go out in public with him and my mother. Uncle Vic could never be discreet and my mother was his perfect foil. She adored being the centre of attention. Once I started going out to the bars on Oxford Street I began to worry that I would run into Vic, who would then attach himself to me and insist on having a night of it together.

Despite me expressly forbidding her to mention it, Elisabeth must've phoned Vic immediately and then arranged for him to come over to have a little chat with me. Her manner was so high-spirited, when he turned up and she excused herself to make some tea, I knew she was up to something. I had never known her to get so excited about making a pot of tea before. Sure enough, as soon as she'd left the room, Vic turned to me, his expression sober. 'Your mother's told me your news . . .'

I began to protest but Vic talked over me. 'She mentioned you didn't want her telling me, but she has. Out of concern, Stephen. She's worried that you don't know enough about safe sex and she wants me to make sure you do. I guess she thinks that I must know what I'm doing, what with all the sex I've had over the years and I've still managed to end up negative.'

Vic smiled tentatively but I stared back at him coldly. I was furious that my mother had disobeyed me. Vic dropped his gaze and fumbled in his pocket. He pulled out some coloured leaflets which he laid upon the couch. 'I've brought you some brochures on safe sex. It explains everything and you can look at them at your leisure . . . without having to endure listening to me.'

He looked up at that point and our eyes met. I felt a brief flush of shame. His expression was so contrite. But I preferred him that way. I couldn't bring myself to smile, to make him feel more at ease. To do so, I was sure, would be to invite back his loud and flashy side.

'Good luck,' said Vic quietly.

'I'll be all right,' I mumbled back.

'Yes, I think you probably will be,' said Vic. 'I'm sure you won't be lonely for long.'

I was quite certain I wouldn't be either.

'It's been different for me,' Vic began and inwardly I groaned. I could guess what was coming. 'You're young, masculine, intelligent. When I was your age . . .'

But Vic stopped mid-sentence. I glanced over at him. He looked embarrassed. 'Excuse me,' he said, rising suddenly. 'Of course you don't want to hear about me.'

Vic hurried from the room. I was startled. Had my disinterest been so transparent? I could hear the murmur of his and my mother's voices in the kitchen. I wandered over to the couch where Vic had been sitting and picked up the brochures that he'd left there. I was glancing through them when Elisabeth appeared. She stood, poised in the doorway, hands on her hips, lips pursed. I knew I was in for a blasting.

'How could you behave so contemptuously towards my dearest friend?' my mother demanded.

I affected a look of innocence. I was beginning to feel certain that I must've sighed or yawned or something when Vic started to speak.

'Because I won't put up with it in my house. You can get out and find your own place to be rude and ungracious in.'

'What am I supposed to have done?'

'You've upset Vic.'

'I didn't say anything.'

'Well you obviously did something. Treated him with your usual contempt, I expect. I'm telling you, Stephen, you can mend your manner, or you can find somewhere else to live.'

'Go on,' I jeered. 'Find some excuse. Kick me out because I've told you I'm gay.'

'Are you? I wonder how you can be when you behave with such a total lack of empathy towards Vic . . .'

'We're nothing alike.'

'You're both attracted to men, aren't you? Aren't you?'

I shrugged. My mother strode across the room and looked me in the face.

'Your Uncle Vic has had it tough. Do you think it was easy for him coming out back in the early sixties? It was practically unheard of then. But he had the courage to do it. He was like a pioneer and he had to put up with a hell of a lot of shit, and I mean literally. Human turds on his doorstep. I only know that because I happened to visit him one day and found him cleaning it all up.'

'I didn't know,' I mumbled.

'There's a lot you don't know about Vic. He's suffered a lot of very cruel abuse over the years – physical as well as verbal. But he's loud. He's camp. He's flamboyant. He laughs it off. It's his way of coping. He wasn't laughing when he came into the kitchen before. He looked close to tears to me.'

'I'm sorry,' I mumbled.

'Don't tell me,' Elisabeth snapped. 'Tell your Uncle Vic, and drop the snotty attitude when you do it.'

My mother turned and marched out of the room. But it was too late to offer an apology, even if I'd wanted to. Uncle Vic had gone home.

It was some weeks before I happened to see him again. I spotted him at the Albury, in the piano bar, seated at a table with a gaggle of mostly middle-aged men. I couldn't see because he was seated, but I had a feeling he'd be wearing those psychedelic bike shorts of his. Then he noticed me. We stared at one another for a moment and then he looked away. I was taken aback. He hadn't smiled. He hadn't waved me over to join him and his friends, not that I would've wanted to, but still I expected him to offer. Suddenly I felt very conspicuous. No doubt Vic would tell my mother that he had seen me out, alone, at the Albury, looking predatory.

I didn't feel predatory. I felt shy and awkward and embarrassed. I wondered about approaching Vic, saying hello and offering to buy him a drink. But I hesitated. I was loath to do it in front of all his friends. I could imagine how they would react to my appearance, cooing at one another behind their glasses, making lewd insinuations about Vic and me. Just then the pianist began to play and the performer began an affected, sibilant rendition of some Broadway show tune. The crowd roared its approval, clapping and whistling.

It was too much for me. I fled next door to the other bar, intending to come back and seek Vic out when the show had finished. But where the cabaret bar was too old-fashioned, the cruise bar was too intimidating. The sleek, confident barmen. The coiffed and muscled clientele. Everyone seemed to know everyone else. They stood together laughing and chatting. The place was packed. I stood against the wall, sipping my drink, waiting hopefully for someone to come up and talk to me or even look at me with interest. When the glass was drained and I had failed to attract even a fleeting glance, I gave up and went back next door.

The show was still in full swing. Vic and his friends were joining in on the chorus. He didn't notice me. There were too many people to have to push past to get to where he sat and I wasn't particularly confident of a warm welcome when I reached him. I walked out onto the street. There seemed no point in hanging around uselessly. If I hurried I could still catch the last train back home to Wahroonga.

CHAPTER THREE

I took great pleasure in announcing to my mother soon after her threat to throw me out that I was moving out of my own accord to live in Kings Cross. On William Street.

Elisabeth was horrified. 'People don't live on William Street, surely?'

I assured her that they did.

'Well, I can't imagine how anyone could ever get any sleep. All that traffic noise. Cars driving up and down there all night, ogling the prostitutes.'

I pointed out that my flat didn't overlook William Street, it overlooked the lane behind it. 'Actually, there's a view of a church from my lounge room.'

'You can't afford to pay rent,' Elisabeth scoffed. 'You're going to be a student.'

But that was the reason I could afford to move out. I'd had a private conversation with my father and struck a gentlemen's agreement, that Elisabeth was not to be privy to. He would pay my rent in full on the condition that I study Legal Institutions in my first year at uni. I was set to start a combination law degree, with English, History and Psychology. I knew the Legal I would be a drag but I figured I could fudge my way through it.

The flat I found was cheap, which was lucky; Elisabeth would have become suspicious had I moved into anywhere too grand. It didn't bother me that it was in the heart of William Street's sex for sale precinct. The girls literally operated from the doorstep of the building, sometimes even using the foyer as a place to freshen up their make-up or adjust their clothing. But to my mind the location was perfect: only a ten minute walk down the hill from the gay bars of Oxford Street. The building was one down from the corner of William Street and Forbes Street, above a car showroom. I was relieved to overlook the back lane. Those residents that faced onto William Street couldn't even open their windows, the traffic noise and fumes were so severe. Instead they left their front doors open onto the landing to let some air through. The apartments overlooking St Peters Lane were infinitely preferable. As well as being much quieter, they had French doors off the living room which opened out onto tiny Juliet balconies. The lane was named after St Peter's church which was situated on the corner intersecting Bourke Street, but there was another name for the lane. It had been scrawled on the wall beneath the official street sign in aerosol paint. I noticed it the first time I stood there at the balcony looking out at the view. Shame Lane.

There was a shameful side to Kings Cross and it was exemplified by the fact that in some instances the suburb did not even dare speak its own name. There was an amusing ambiguity over where I was actually living. I had presumed myself to be in Kings Cross but the mail I received was addressed otherwise and was completely contradictory. According to Telstra, I was living in East Sydney, while Sydney Electricity considered I was in Woolloomooloo. My bank said I was in Darlinghurst.

When I mentioned this to my new neighbour, Strauss, he roared with laughter. 'Darling, you're living in Betty Bay, didn't you know? Well, that's where my estate agent claims I'm living. When I came to look this place over, it was advertised as being "a penthouse apartment in Elizabeth Bay". *Elizabeth Bay?* The thing is, Kings Cross is considered so down-market in terms of real estate that it doesn't exist as an address. It's always Darlinghurst or Woolloomooloo or East Sydney, and in the fanciful imagination of some real estate agents it's Elizabeth Bay. I just adore telling people that I live on William Street, Elizabeth Bay.'

I invited Elisabeth to inspect the flat as soon as I'd moved in. I knew that otherwise she would turn up unannounced and that inevitably it would be at a bad moment. I arranged for her to visit during the day when there would be no prostitutes hanging about. She arrived with Uncle Vic. I could hear her complaining to him as she mounted the stairs that she hadn't seen any prostitutes. The first thing she asked me when I opened the door was, 'Where are they all?'

'They come out at night,' I explained.

'Well, that seems like a gap in the market. Why doesn't one of them do a day shift?'

'I think the idea is that they look their best by night.'

'Oh,' said Elisabeth. 'Yes, I see.'

Uncle Vic had wandered over to the French doors and was looking out at the view. 'It's quite pleasant by day,' he remarked.

His eyes told me he knew exactly what went on down below by night. I was grateful for his discretion. Elisabeth joined him at the doors. She glanced at the view. 'South facing,' she observed. 'It will be cold even at the height of summer.'

Then she strode into the kitchen and looked around it with distaste. I had invited her for lunch. 'Perhaps we'll go out for lunch,' she decided.

'I'm all organised to cook,' I said.

'We'll eat out,' she said in a voice that wouldn't tolerate any dissent.

The bathroom was off the bedroom and as she walked through to inspect it she made a point of averting her eyes from the unmade bed. 'If you'd make your bed, this place might not appear so much like the awful dosshouse that it is.'

Uncle Vic and I remained in the living room while my mother snorted her disapproval of the bathroom. Uncle Vic smiled sympathetically at me. 'She's putting on a bit of a show. Of course she'd like to keep you at home forever.'

Elisabeth emerged from the bathroom. 'Well, I can't imagine why anyone would want to live here, let alone pay to live here; however, I daresay you have your reasons. They're just not fit for a mother to hear.'

She fixed her eyes upon me, waiting to see if I'd respond.

When I didn't, she declared herself ready for a Bloody Mary at the Bayswater Brasserie, her favourite restaurant. 'Because it's a proper restaurant,' she was always telling me. By which she meant lots of dark wood surfaces, attentive young men attired in black and white and dazzling white linen everywhere you looked. But in fact it was the attention she loved not the decor or the service. The staff all knew her and fawned over her whenever she turned up.

Elisabeth had hit the nail on the head with that remark. I *had* moved out of home so that I could have a sex life. It was basically impossible to manage when I was living with my parents at Wahroonga. I had been going out on the weekends to Oxford Street for some time, but it was hopeless. The bars only began to get lively around the same time that I had to leave if I wanted to catch the last train back to Wahroonga. If I stayed out in the hope of meeting someone, I was forced to be out for the entire night. The trains didn't start up again until five-thirty in the morning. A taxi was out of the question on my budget. But it was also embarrassing to have to admit to anyone I did get talking to that I still lived at home with my parents. Their interest in me always seemed to curdle soon after that point in the conversation.

For the first two weeks after moving into the William Street apartment I went out to Oxford Street almost every night. The girls working the street were always performing at full throttle by the time I made my way home and they soon got to know me and would enquire how my night had been. 'Not so good if you're coming home alone again,' the tallest and most attractive of them cackled.

However, when I did finally bring a boy back, the tall one, who called herself Sass, pounced on us and encouraged all her colleagues to join in her inspection. 'Stephen's finally got a fuck,' she announced loudly.

They crowded round us, tweaking the boy's face, asking his name, speculating loudly as to what would happen once we got inside and assuring him that I had been 'an absolute monk' for as long as they'd known me. When we did finally escape them, the boy was trembling so badly I had to help him climb the stairs. 'I'm sorry but I'll have to stay the night. There's no way I can face going back out there again. They're not still there in the morning, are they?'

I reassured him that they wouldn't be.

I quickly became friendly with the regular girls and got to know them by name. I call them girls – everyone called them girls – but of course they weren't. I was always curious as to how many of the louts who leered at them out of their car windows as they kerb-crawled down William Street actually realised. They fooled a lot of people, my father included. He called in on me after he'd finished work one night and encountered Sass as he entered the building. She was the leader of the William Street girls by virtue of her success. She was the most authentic-looking, the most glamorous, the most outrageous and undoubtedly the most financially successful. My father made little comment on the apartment. All he could talk about was Sass. 'I had no idea the prostitutes were so glamorous. She was like some sort of movie star.'

I couldn't be bothered explaining. Why ruin the illusion Sass put so much work into creating? But my father was right. Sass and the other girls were like movie stars. Everything about them was so big and glossy and provocative. The actual women prostitutes who operated further along the street towards the city seemed very drab, even grim, by comparison. Certainly they rarely smiled. Whereas outside my front door a party atmosphere prevailed. Sass was the wildest. She strutted, flounced and flirted. The pavement was her stage and her audience in their cars whooped, hollered and even applauded their appreciation. The highlight of her act incorporated the use of the council rubbish bin. She would daintily balance one stiletto-clad foot on top of the rubbish bin, the other on the brink of the gutter, and then thrust her pelvis in and out, tossing her long blonde hair about behind her as the cars slowly streamed down the hill towards her. She stopped traffic.

Literally. Sass's performances were short-lived, however. She always got snapped up quickly by a punter.

I was puzzled that someone with Sass's looks and personality worked the street, and I said as much to her one night when we struck up our first real conversation. It was late, the early hours of Sunday morning. I was getting home from a night at the Shift. Sass, sitting out in the square, noticed me as I stumbled down the Chard Steps. 'No luck, honey?' she called out to me. 'It's been a slow night here too.'

She waved me over and insisted I sit down beside her. I drunkenly told her she could do better for herself. 'Honey, I hear that line so many times. All my johns tell me the same thing. But do they offer to look after me and keep me in the style that I'm accustomed to? No. The fact is that deep down most people regard me as some sort of freak and eventually that sentiment rises to the surface. You say I could do better for myself, and I used to feel the same way, but in fact I can't. I know because I've tried. There ain't many opportunities in the work line for a chick with a dick. I've tried to get conventional work – restaurants, reception – but once they realise I piss standing up, that's the end, I'm out. Even the gay places don't want girls like me. I project the wrong image. All those queens are trying desperately to be as butch as possible, while I'm doing the exact opposite. The only sort of job I can get is one that exploits what I am. Makes me out to be some sort of freak. On the stage at Les Girls, pulling my wig off at the end of the night. No, thank you. I won't do a job where I get laughed at by small-minded people. It's too humiliating. I want to be respected and, believe it or not, I can get more respect as a hooker.'

She paused for a moment. 'Sure I'd like not to have to work the street. It's a bitch in winter. But setting yourself up to work privately from home isn't easy either. It can be almost impossible getting an apartment. What do you write down as your occupation on the estate agent's form? You've got to prove you can pay the rent, but if you write down "escort", they'd never give you the place. So you lie on the form and if you're lucky you get the apartment. But even once you're signed up, there's no security. The neighbours always cause problems. You notice them sneaking looks at you in the lift, then they start to talk amongst themselves and watching who comes to visit you. Eventually you're accused of operating a brothel and get evicted. I was kicked out of one apartment, which was my home. I never worked from there. But my uncle came to visit me, the only member of my family who will have anything to do with me, and of course he was mistaken for a john. You just get so frustrated and discouraged after a while. Ultimately, this is the simplest way. Working the street. And I have to work to keep this up. It ain't cheap looking good.'

I was intrigued by Sass's accent. She had a pseudo-American way of speaking. She laughed when I asked. 'I grew up in Gympie, Queensland. But an American accent is sexier. The guys just love a Californian blonde. I've watched a helluva lot of porn videos trying to get the accent right. Actually, I do a lot of business in dirty talk. Some of those boys are just too damn nervous to be up to much else. Penises are fragile things. I'll be glad to get shot of mine once and for all. But I'll never do that if I sit here chitchatting instead of working up a bit of business.'

With that, Sass sprang to her feet and prowled across the pavement to a car that had slowed down opposite us. 'Hey, butch,' I heard her say as I got to my feet and began to walk away.

There was a definite hierarchy amongst the girls who worked that particular segment of William Street, and Sass was at the pinnacle. She was very tall. Six foot two without heels. Yet she insisted on always wearing two-inch stilettos. Her hair could add a couple of inches as well, depending on which wig she wore and how she had it styled. Her height seemed to imbue her with an unassailable confidence. She towered over the majority of her clients and claimed most of them loved it that way. 'They all want me to dominate them. Seems like they never get it that way at home. Luckily it's something that just comes natural to me.'

Her rival, Jo-Jo, said Sass looked like Centrepoint in drag, she was so tall and skinny. Naturally enough, they hated one another. Once Jo-Jo had strutted her stuff on William Street and had been the most popular girl on the strip. But that was ten years ago. Now her 'surgical enhancements' were showing their age and as she wasn't pulling in the kind of money she once had, she couldn't afford to go for some 'reconditioning'.

'She's had every tooth in her mouth pulled out so that she can give better head, that's how desperate she is to attract clients,' jeered Sass, laughing as she unfolded Jo-Jo's tragedy, failing to consider she might conceivably share the same destiny one day. But Sass was young. 'I'm only twenty-four and much prettier than Jo-Jo ever was,' she gurgled.

These days Jo-Jo was forced to lurk down Shame Lane, where the light was less cruel and the clients not as discerning. She wouldn't even venture down to the little square below the Chard Steps to sit with some of her old mates and talk on a slow night. That was Sass's territory now and Jo-Jo steered clear of it. 'They're all louts from out west anyway, or country boys with no idea what they're cruising. They don't even know the back lane exists, where the real action is.'

But if Sass dared to venture up the stairs to the intersection of Forbes Street and Shame Lane, Jo-Jo would detonate, screaming at her, chasing her away, threatening to beat her up. Their fights were as regular as clockwork. 'I respect your patch, now you respect mine and fuck off back to where you came from,' Jo-Jo would screech.

'Just checking,' Sass would reply smoothly.

'Checking what?'

'Checking the merchandise and the prices of the rival business, like any competitive businesswoman would do.'

'You're no woman.'

'And you ain't got no business,' Sass would cackle, retreating back down the stairs, a string of expletives firing from Jo-Jo like a round of ammunition.

Sass delighted in stirring Jo-Jo. She'd venture up the Chard

Steps most nights, and would always act disappointed if Jo-Jo was with a john and not there to tell her to fuck off. They woke me and the rest of my neighbours up most nights, going off at one another. Finally, we had a residents' meeting about the problem. One evening when I got home from uni, I found a note in my mailbox. *Your attendance is requested at a residents' meeting 'chez Strauss' (Flat 9) to discuss the raucous behaviour of the trannies in the back lane after midnight. The main culprits will be in attendance.*

Sass actually apologised to me personally before the meeting. She rushed over when she saw me coming home one night. 'Oh, you poor darlings,' she gushed. 'Being woken up by that witch. She's got a voice like fingernails on a blackboard. Oh, I can imagine the agony she must've been causing you all. Strauss is organising a meeting, but in the meantime, you let me know if you have any more problems and I'll fix her good and proper. Stuff her wig down her filthy loud mouth.'

Sass winked and promenaded back to her spot, the car horns tooting as she walked.

It was at that meeting that I came to know Strauss and the other residents of the apartment block. I had seen Strauss on the stairs several times and we always exchanged greetings. I said hello. Strauss said, 'Ciao bello.' That was Strauss's style. I soon learnt that he always had to appear more exotic than everyone else: in his manner, his conversation and, above all, in his appearance. Every time I saw him he looked completely different. One day his hair was a cropped jet-black stubble, the next day an Andy Warhol white thatch. He was either dressed very stylishly and formally in something black and severe, or he would be wearing a completely ridiculous outfit such as a safari suit he had dyed canary yellow.

One evening he stopped me as I passed him on the stairs, placed a white-gloved hand upon my arm and looked at me through his cat's-eye sunglasses. 'We meet again upon the stairs. Are you a resident or merely the regular trade of one of my *lucky, lucky* neighbours?'

I didn't understand what he meant by trade. 'I live here.'

'Which apartment?'

'Number seven.'

'Lovely. I know it well. I'm in the penthouse apartment, on the roof. I have that enchanting view of everyone's laundry on weekends. Thankfully, I'm generally asleep during the sunshine hours.'

With that, Strauss flounced down the stairs. I watched him descend, startled but impressed. It was the first time I'd encountered him close up. I was astonished to discover that he wore make-up.

The residents' meeting was more of a cocktail party than a meeting. Strauss opened the door wearing an ankle-length striped kaftan. Before I even had a chance to say hello he handed me a glass. 'I'm serving Orgasms,' he confided. 'I thought it was appropriate given our guests of honour tonight.'

No introductions were made. I said hello to Sass who was seated on the couch talking to a smartly dressed girl I hadn't seen before. Jo-Jo stood by the French doors, smoking a cigarette.

'Are there more people to come?' I asked.

'Oh, I scare the people who live in number four,' exclaimed Strauss. 'The Asian couple. Recent arrivals to our country, I believe. Every time I encounter the wife, she screams. I thought an invitation would only alarm her further.'

'Is Ant coming?' asked the girl.

'The delectable Antonio,' Strauss sighed. 'Yes. After he's been to the gym. He can't possibly miss a day's training. He will be arriving all flushed and sweaty at any moment, I imagine.'

I took the chair opposite the couch and the girl turned her attention to me. 'I'm Blair,' she said.

I introduced myself.

'How are you settling in?' she enquired.

'It's my first time out of home,' I admitted. 'So it's all quite new and strange.'

'It doesn't get much stranger than round here,' cackled Sass.

'Jo-Jo, for Chrissake get away from that balcony and stop brooding over the business you're missing out on.'

There was a knock at the door.

'Entrez,' Strauss called out.

The door swung open and there he was. Ant. He had indeed come straight from the gym. He was wearing a pair of cut-down sweat pants and a black Bonds singlet. Strauss bounded over to welcome him and kissed him on both cheeks. Ant didn't exactly recoil, but his stance was stiff and awkward as he submitted to the greeting, drawing back as soon as it could safely be declared over. I felt a pang of disappointment. I liked the look of him, but his reaction made me suspect that he was straight. Strauss had him clutched by the wrist and was gushingly unfolding some anecdote, his eyebrows arching, his smile twisting with flirtatious insinuations. Ant appeared to be listening intently, but his expression was inscrutable; there was no clue to whether he was interested or indifferent to what he was being told. While he was absorbed, I studied his profile.

The more I stared, the more his looks appealed to me. His face was quietly handsome. Not turn-your-head striking, but very masculine and steady looking. His hair was dark brown and cropped close to his head. His body was well displayed by what he wore. He was deeply tanned, so tanned he almost glowed, and he was very muscular. There was a great jut to his chest and his biceps looked rock-hard and ripe, like apples in his arms. And he was unshaven! Not his face, but his chest and legs. Dark hair sprouted from the scoop of his singlet. *This* was very exotic. Body hair was practically extinct on Oxford Street. All the muscle men I'd noticed and admired around the bars were perfectly hairless. I wasn't so impressed by what he was wearing. It was a bit sloppy: his pants unhemmed and dangling threads, his singlet faded and thin. I would never be seen in such a state. But on him, I rather liked it. It was rough and careless, the way I imagined he might treat me in bed.

Strauss was laughing, in snorting ripples – his story had reached its climax. Ant gave a quick terse smile. His profile was so severe. But I liked that! Gruff not gushy. Then he turned to face the rest of us in the room and the conversation ground to a sudden halt. Someone gasped. Ant's right eye was a slit, the eyelid swollen and livid. He had a black eye.

Strauss was cooing over it but was being steadfastly ignored. Ant smiled and nodded at Blair and Sass, then his good eye settled on me. It was no cursory glance. This was a look that raked me over intensely and I knew at once that I had been mistaken about where his sexual interests lay. I felt borne up by his speculative gaze, light, giddy, as if I might float away out the French doors. Then, just as suddenly, that sensation crumpled and I was plummeted back to earth, shot down by a shocking spasm of nerves. Shocking because it was such an utterly alien feeling to me.

I'm *never* shy. My self-confidence and eloquence are my greatest gifts. It was inconvenient and highly frustrating that they should suddenly desert me at such a crucial moment. But they had. I was bereft. I cast about for an opening remark, something original and witty with a teasing undertone that would initiate our conversation with a stylish flourish, but found I could think of . . . *nothing?* Meanwhile Ant's gaze pressed upon me relentlessly. There was such an intensity to that one eye, perhaps because it was temporarily doing the work of two. I felt more and more unnerved and tongue-tied with every second that passed.

I tried to focus upon his other eye, the black eye, but found it too disturbing. I caught a glimpse of the iris, a sudden flash of movement and colour between the lids. Strangely, that made me feel more exposed than I had under the scrutiny of his good eye. I looked away, which immediately made me feel foolish and defensive, unequal to the challenge of his attention. I reached for my glass and drained it automatically, then wished I hadn't. The Cointreau burnt my throat and I gagged. I could feel myself blushing.

I was too embarrassed to look up again. I stared at the carpet instead. It was an offensive sight, being in dire need not only of a vacuum but also an intensive steam clean. Dark stains (red wine? rouge? blood?) adorned it in a pattern not unlike that of the Great Lakes across the continent of America. Upon these 'lakes' lay a litter of cockroach corpses, withered olives, cigarette butts, and a solitary false eyelash, jumbo size. When a Converse clad foot crushed one of the olives into the carpet, then halted there before me, I knew I had to look up. My eyes ran up his legs and instinctively paused at his crotch. It was unavoidable, being barely half a metre from my face, exactly at eye level, and looking remarkably prominent and promising, flattered by the cling of his cotton sweat pants. I jerked my eyes up to his face. Ant gazed down at me and offered his hand. 'You live here?' he asked, slightly puzzled.

I took his hand and nodded.

'I'm Anthony.'

Up close there was a slightly bewitched air to his stare. He gave a quick abashed flicker of a smile. 'You look a little like someone I know,' he said, as if in apology for staring. 'You could be his brother.'

He paused, expecting a reply, but I could think of nothing to say to that. I had no idea to whom I was being compared. If it was even a compliment. He cleared his throat. 'What . . . what's your name?'

I realised I had forgotten to introduce myself, yet I was still clutching his hand like a halfwit. I released it abruptly, apologising and blushing.

'Stephen. Stephen Spear.'

I could think of nothing, *nothing* more to say.

'You must be in number seven,' Ant finally remarked. 'Above me. I heard you moving in.'

'I hope I didn't disturb you,' I replied without thinking and then cursed the inanity of such a remark.

It was exactly what I did want to do – disturb him. Deeply. Captivate him. Seduce him. In the past I'd had no problem charming whomever I wanted. Usually the flirtatious banter rippled off my tongue as if it had been scripted. But Anthony –

Ant – he was an entirely different proposition. Desire had never really been a motivation before. Now it was and its urgency danced through my veins. But instead of inspiring me into an imitation of Elisabeth at her finest, it rendered me useless, huddled in my chair, blushing and bumbling.

Ant reassured me that I hadn't been an intrusion. 'You get used to noise in these apartments,' he said with a sharp look at Jo-Jo.

He slid down and knelt on the carpet beside me. Our faces were at the same level. He rested his elbow on the arm of my chair. Neither of us spoke but the atmosphere between us was charged with expectation. Suddenly Strauss swooped down in a whirl of psychedelic kaftan and insinuated his body between us. '*Voilà*, Antonio,' he cried, presenting Ant's drink with a flourish, his other hand stealing up his arm to caress his bicep.

I wasn't sure whether I was more relieved or irritated by this invasion. Certainly Strauss commandeering the conversation filled the daunting silence between Ant and me and provided an opportunity for me to gather my wits, but that charge of intimacy between us had been lost. I'd had a sense that something profound and revealing might have occurred at any moment. Instead, we were obliged to listen to Strauss prattle on as he pried into the origins of Ant's injury.

'Now, darling, what have you been doing with yourself? How did you get that black eye? You brushed by me without a word of explanation but that won't do. I demand to know. And don't bother to think of a lie because I shall see straight through it. I have an instinct for distinguishing fact from fantasy.'

Ant said nothing. There was a frosty edge to his silence.

'Now don't get peevish,' Strauss continued. 'You know how overactive my imagination is. I will believe the worst of you if you don't tell me the truth. That you're dreadfully allergic to mascara or something ghastly like that.'

But even that couldn't coax a smile from Ant.

'I had a fight with someone,' he finally said stiffly.

'Hmm,' mused Strauss, arching his eyebrows. 'I believe I know with whom.'

'Yes, you do and let's leave it there.'

'Very well,' sighed Strauss. 'Perhaps you'll confide in me later when you're drunk. Or maybe Stephen can cajole the details out of you. I'll leave you two to get acquainted. Ant is about to flee to the Land of the Long White Cloud. Did he tell you?'

'What?' I was horrified that he was about to disappear before I'd had a chance to impress him. 'Where?'

'Neeeew Ziiiiland,' said Strauss in an exaggerated mockery of the accent. 'I like to refer to it by the English translation of the Maori name. It speaks so eloquently of the weather there.'

Strauss flitted back to the kitchen to mix some more drinks. Ant's face was flushed. He looked a little annoyed, or rather he looked as if he was trying to hide the fact that he was very annoyed.

'You're going away?' I asked, trying to keep the agitation I was feeling out of my voice.

'Just for a holiday to visit my family.'

I nodded, relieved. 'For long?' I asked.

'Five days. It's enough.'

I was so pleased that it wasn't for weeks that I forgot to continue the conversation. I became preoccupied planning how our romance might unfold upon his return. It took Strauss's announcement that he was putting a Nana Mouskouri record on the stereo to jerk me back to reality.

'He's a character,' I remarked for something to say.

'Yes,' said Ant with a twist to his voice. 'But the thing is you never know what character he's going to be. One day he looks like Sid Vicious, the next day he's got up like Liberace.'

'What does he do?'

'For work?' Ant frowned. 'He doesn't as far as I know. He runs a nightclub one night a week, just down the road at Club 77. We should go along some time.'

I was so thrilled and surprised by his invitation that I found myself lost for words again. By the time I'd recovered myself, Ant had carried on the conversation, with me failing to indicate any interest in his proposition.

'I guess he's on the dole, although I don't know how he could possibly support his lifestyle on the dole. He goes out so much and he must spend a fortune on clothes. Maybe he disguises himself and claims the dole under a dozen different names.'

'I *would* like to go to his club,' I said abruptly. 'With you, I mean.'

The thread of that conversation had been lost and Ant seemed faintly startled by my belated eagerness. 'Okay,' he said, but there was no enthusiasm to his voice, something I hoped was due to his irritation with Strauss, not to the prospect of my company.

Abruptly, Nana's voice, which had been in mid-chorus of 'Four and Twenty Hours', began to deepen and slow down, gradually winding down into silence. Jo-Jo had kicked the stereo's power point out of the wall. She stood by the French doors looking pleased with herself. 'Can we get cracking?' she demanded.

'That was a nasty thing to do to Nana,' Strauss protested.

Jo-Jo looked unrepentant.

'Very well,' said Strauss. 'I merely thought if everyone was made mellow by some strong drinks and some lovely music, we might be able to resolve this problem in a friendly, casual fashion. However, Jo-Jo, if you prefer everyone to be sober and serious, businesslike and brutal, so be it. I call this meeting to order.'

He paused and stared with mock solemnity first at Jo-Jo and then at Sass. 'Now, it has been brought to my attention that you two ladies are indulging in Bette Davis theatricals every night after midnight and disturbing the residents of this building from their slumber.'

'If madame would stick to her patch, then there wouldn't be a problem,' said Jo-Jo moodily.

'You're always spying on me from the top of the stairs. I'm just doing the same,' Sass retaliated.

Jo-Jo's voice rose. 'Those stairs are off-limits to you . . .'

'Thank you, but no thank you, ladies,' Strauss interrupted Jo-Jo firmly. 'We don't need a demonstration of your animated conversation. But now I know what everyone's been complaining about. I'm never in at night so I've never heard you. That's why I've taken it upon myself to mediate some sort of agreement, as I'm not affected personally. Now, I believe the first step would be to agree upon some limits.'

'Hear, hear,' said Blair.

'I don't think it would be unreasonable for Sassparilla to restrict herself to making her nightly excursions up the stairs to Shame Lane before eleven o'clock on week nights, and before midnight on weekends. Does that sound fair?'

'Why arrange visiting hours for her when she's not welcome in the first place?' grumbled Jo-Jo.

'I don't come to visit *you*. I like the view from the top of the stairs.'

'Then why don't you gaze at the fucking harbour instead of down the alley to see who I'm busy with.'

'Ladies, ladies,' protested Strauss. 'It seems to me, Jo-Jo, that from your vantage point at the top of the stairs you can look down upon Sass whenever you please. It's probably only fair that Sass should be allowed to climb the stairs to look in on you occasionally.'

'That's true,' declared Sass jubilantly, and eventually Jo-Jo, after a good deal of moaning and mumbling, was forced to agree.

'Good. But, Sass, restricted hours of calling. Okay? Can I also point out that it does nothing to fuel your clients' delusions when they hear you two bellowing at one another like warring football fans. If you want to foster an atmosphere of allurement and enticement down there in the alley, I'd keep it strictly silent.'

Jo-Jo scowled, though she did look a little thoughtful, once the irritation had faded from her face.

'Now, I believe Jo-Jo has a complaint of her own to air. Jo-Jo?'

Sass leant forward with interest.

Jo-Jo turned a baleful eye upon each of us in turn. 'Someone from these apartments threw an egg at me,' she said slowly.

Sass shrieked her approval.

'Did they hit you?' enquired Strauss.

'No,' said Jo-Jo with a toothless smirk. 'They missed.'

'Well, I doubt very much it was anyone in this room. We all have a very good aim. Is anyone going to own up?'

No-one spoke.

'Any witnesses?'

'It may have been the guy next to me, in number two,' suggested Ant. 'He owns his place. He's always complaining about the prostitutes cheapening his investment.'

'Very likely,' said Strauss. 'He has also failed to turn up tonight, which seems to be a sure sign of guilt. I'll speak to him. Jo-Jo, you're not to go exacting revenge.'

I was relieved that a likely culprit had been identified. Jo-Jo had been making a frightful noise on one of my first nights in my new apartment. Finally, in exasperation, I had thrown one of the eggs I had intended to cook Elisabeth for lunch at her. I was surprised to learn I had missed. From the pandemonium that followed, I had assumed it was a direct hit.

Jo-Jo lurched across the room on her high heels. At the door she turned, hands on her hips, and glared at us all. 'Anyone throws anything at me, eggs, anything, I'll be after them for compensation. Disruption to business. Loss of income.'

'You'll get your lawyers on to them, won't you, Jo-Jo?' taunted Sass.

'Naw,' drawled Jo-Jo. 'I'll get Slash and Eddie on to them. They're more effective than any lawyers.'

Jo-Jo hauled herself out the door, chuckling.

Surprisingly, Sass came to Jo-Jo's defence once she'd gone. 'Don't throw eggs at the poor old tart. She has enough insults hurled her way without eggs to cap it off. Besides, her mates are bad news. You don't want to know about them.'

'Be warned,' Strauss added. 'I declare a cease-fire and that it's time for another round of drinks.'

I was surprised when Ant got to his feet and excused himself. 'You're going?'

'I have to eat,' he replied. 'And then I have to pack for going away. Nice to meet you.'

Strauss rushed over with more drinks. 'Ant, you can't leave!' he cried indignantly.

'Sorry,' he said without a trace of sincerity.

He strode across the room saying goodbye to Blair and Sass as he went. At the door he paused and glanced back across the room, but it was his right profile, his black eye, that was now turned towards me. It was impossible to discern anything – longing, curiosity, indifference – from that swollen slit. I couldn't even be sure if his attention was directed at me or at our host who stood next to me and was bemoaning Ant's premature exit in my ear.

CHAPTER FOUR

When I awoke the next morning, my first thought (once I'd dulled the throb in my head with some Panadeine) was what pretext I could use to see Ant again. I'd hardly begun to give the question any attention when a knock came at my door. There had been no buzz from the security door off the street. It had to be one of my neighbours in the same state as me, begging Panadeine or something stronger. I opened the door, expecting Blair, not caring how dishevelled I must appear.

Ant was there on my doorstep.

I felt like closing the door in his face, frantically freshening up and then receiving him, but of course that was impossible.

'I heard you stirring, from downstairs, so I knew you were up,' he said by way of explanation.

I nodded. I felt very self-conscious. I was wearing an ugly emerald green velveteen robe and a pair of ugh boots. Out of necessity. Elisabeth had been right. My apartment was always cold. At that moment I wished Ant's vision was impaired in both eyes.

'I know we've only just met,' he continued, 'but I wondered if you'd mind watering my plants and collecting my mail while I'm away.'

'Sure,' I said.

'I could ask Strauss or Blair, but even though I barely know you, I can tell you'd be more reliable than either of them.'

'I'm very conscientious,' I assured him.

Ant suggested I come down to his apartment then and there so that he could give me instructions. 'Okay,' I agreed. 'Just let me put on some jeans.'

I left the bedroom door open so that he could watch me

change. I was disappointed when I glanced back to find he'd walked out of the line of vision.

I was surprised when we got downstairs to his apartment. It was so austere. The walls were pristine white and bare. There were no framed prints or paintings. The only furniture was a couch, a matching armchair positioned opposite, a stereo and a kitchen table with two chairs. My surprise must have shown on my face, as Ant began to justify his decor.

'I had a flatmate for a while and he owned a lot of stuff. I haven't got round to replacing it yet.'

A flatmate? In a one-bedroom apartment?

'I've just bought the necessities to make it liveable. You see, I'm saving to buy my own apartment.'

'No television?' I noticed.

'I wasn't allowed to watch it as a child and . . .'

'*No television?*'

'My father believed it bred sloppy minds. He had firm opinions on many things and television was one of them.'

'He sounds strict.'

'He was formidable. A schoolteacher and a very old-fashioned one. He was the rector of the school I went to from when I was thirteen. Sometimes I found myself calling him sir rather than Dad.'

Ant paused for a moment, then he became a little self-conscious and grinned at me. 'Of course, back then, I didn't agree with him about television. It seemed like the worst deprivation in the world. But when . . . my flatmate . . . took it away with him, after a month or two, I realised I didn't miss it at all.'

Still, there was a wistfulness to Ant's voice. He might not miss the television, but I suspected he missed its owner.

I sat down at the kitchen table and began to ask Ant questions about his upbringing.

He had lived all his life in Dunedin, only escaping it two years ago after he'd graduated with a degree in accounting from the University of Otago. Dunedin, it seemed, had been settled by Scots and was known as the Edinburgh of New Zealand.

The town square was overlooked by a statue of Robbie Burns; the street names were copied from the streets of Edinburgh, and the school that Ant's father ruled over even looked a little like Edinburgh Castle, with its grim grey stone facade, perched up on a hill.

'Our home, the rectory, was on the school grounds,' said Ant, 'so the school was always there in the background, towering over us. I don't particularly enjoy going back to that house, even for a visit. Bad memories.'

When he was appointed rector of this historic school in the late seventies, Angus Tallantire had introduced some academic and recreational pursuits that were dear to the heart of a Scot. He invaded the history and geography classrooms of the third form boys in their first weeks at the school and gave them an impromptu lesson in 'their heritage'. The fact that some of his pupils were of Irish or English descent, and a small number even of Maori parentage, did not give him a moment's pause. He suggested to the music teacher that the school orchestra would benefit from the inclusion of some bagpipers. When the teacher reported back that no member of the orchestra could be found to take up the instrument, Ant was volunteered by his father. He only got out of it by feigning that it aggravated his asthma.

The rector instilled fear, not through the use of corporal punishment but by regularly threatening the boys during assembly with a change to the school uniform. Shorts and long grey pants would be replaced by the compulsory wearing of the kilt. 'The kilt is the garment of warriors and gentlemen,' the rector liked to declare.

But he convinced no-one. It was a skirt. The exact same thing that their sisters were obliged to wear to school!

Ant brought out his photo album. 'That's my father,' he said, pointing to a photo of some boys posed with their teacher on a frozen pond. 'He coached the curling team himself.'

'What's that?' I asked, imagining some sort of hairdressing competition.

'It's an ancient Scottish sport, kind of like bowls on ice but with big heavy stones and broomsticks. Another of my father's innovations.'

Angus Tallantire stood on a frozen dam, legs apart, arms folded, bracing himself from the cold. His pupils were clustered around him. Snow coated the hills behind them. The ice had been cut from the blades of skates, leaving trails of white shavings on that great black expanse. It looked very cold. Everyone was wrapped up in mittens, hats, woollen bush shirts and tartan scarves, except the rector who looked snug enough behind his heavy beard. He didn't smile for the camera, but the angle of his head and the expression in his eyes contributed to the sense that his mouth was drawn in a line of grim satisfaction rather than rage. That was perhaps the only resemblance I could see between father and son: a seriousness of countenance.

'I'm in the photo too,' said Ant, pointing himself out.

It would have been impossible to recognise him. He was at one extreme of the photograph, with as much distance between himself and his father as was possible. Ant was tall and skinny. He looked cold. Hunched over. Like his father, he didn't smile but his expression was utterly morose. That photograph said it all. How unbearable his life had been as the son of the school rector.

'Wouldn't it have been easier if you'd gone to a different school?'

'Oh no,' said Ant, looking shocked. 'It was the best school for boys in Dunedin. I had to go there.'

'Did everyone know you were his son? You don't look anything like him. You missed out on the red hair.'

Ant explained that everyone was so in awe of the rector that they were very careful how they treated his son. Ant wasn't bullied or teased, but the boys had a sneering way of pronouncing his surname which transformed it into an insult. 'Though I had no real enemies, or none that cared to identify themselves too blatantly, I had no real friends either,' Ant said a little mournfully. 'No-one wanted to be invited back to my house after school or on the weekend. No-one wanted to be sat down to dinner at the rector's table and have his attention drawn to them.'

Ant slapped the photo album shut. The unnecessary force of this action made it clear that he intended to talk no more of his upbringing. He ushered me over to the plants he kept on his balcony. They were such pitiful, scraggly specimens, I felt certain they had merely been a pretext to lure me down to his apartment and out of my clothes. I didn't bother listening to his detailed instructions. Instead, I wandered off towards his bedroom to facilitate the inevitable. 'Are there more in here?' I asked ingenuously.

'No, no,' said Ant, catching my arm. 'You don't need to go in there. It's just these and the fern on top of the fridge. Now, I'd offer you a cup of tea or something but I actually have to get myself organised and start packing. My flight leaves early evening.'

Packing had been his excuse the previous night and I was about to point that out but, before I knew what was happening, I found myself manoeuvred out into the stairwell in a profusion of thanks and further watering instructions. 'Here are my spare keys,' said Ant, holding them up for me.

I took them, wished him a happy holiday and wondered if he might at least kiss me farewell, but he only smiled and closed the door upon my expectations.

I had, however, achieved something. I had the keys to his apartment clutched in my hand. Instead of returning upstairs, I walked up the street to the locksmiths on Darlinghurst Road and had the keys copied. I would have my own set when I was obliged to return the originals. They were bound to come in handy.

I let myself into his apartment later that evening when I knew he would be halfway across the Tasman Sea. I had taken note of where he had stowed his photograph album earlier that day and I went straight to the bookcase to retrieve it. I hadn't even had a chance to open it when the phone rang. It gave me a jolt, made me feel caught out for a moment, but then the machine picked up the call. A boy's voice, a voice that sounded both coy and a little uncertain, began to leave a message. After he'd identified himself, a flirtatious edge began to creep into his voice and as he continued speaking it became abundantly clear that this was some fling Ant'd had, ringing up in the hopes of further action. I was so furious to discover I had a rival that I picked up the phone with the intention of telling him to fuck off. However, once I had the phone in my hand and the boy's voice going 'Hello, hello' in my ear, it didn't seem like such a smart thing to do.

'Hello,' I said down the phone instead.

'Hello. You are there then?'

'I was busy,' I mumbled.

'It's James here. Do you remember me?'

Then it occurred to me. How easy it would be to impersonate Ant and hopefully learn a little more about him in the process, some intimate details. I adopted my best New Zealand accent. 'Hmm. James? I'm bad with names. You'll have to give me a few clues.'

'Well, we had sex together last Saturday night. I expect you'd remember that at least,' said James a little tersely.

'How was it?' I asked, forgetting for a moment that I was supposed to be impersonating Ant and would surely know. 'Did I fuck you?'

I wondered if Ant was active, passive or versatile.

James's tone changed. It became softer and more wheedling. 'Are you trying to turn me on?'

'Nope, just trying to remember.'

James gave a sort of whelp and hung up.

I replaced the receiver, satisfied. I hadn't gleaned any real knowledge about Ant's sexual habits, but I had nipped a potential encore in the bud. Knocked James out of the competition quite effortlessly.

I returned my attention to the photo album and opened it towards the back. I wasn't interested in his family photographs.

I was looking for evidence of a boyfriend and I found it immediately. The last twenty pages of the album were devoted to a blond boy who I had to admit was extremely photogenic. Big eyes. Snub nose. Perfect skin which looked as if a blade had never been obliged to whisk a solitary hair from it. He had a particular pose which he obviously knew *worked*. He stared intently at the camera, his head tilted slightly forward, his lips parted a little, a vacancy to his expression which accentuated his youth and innocence. Was this 'the flatmate' who had recently moved out?

He wore blue in almost every photograph, which brought out the colour of his eyes, and his T-shirts were so tight and skimpy I was certain they must've been bought in children's wear. There was an endless sequence of him in his Speedos on some deserted beach (and a few of him *without* the Speedos, cavorting in the waves). He was tanned. Smooth. Long limbed. He looked very young, very lithe and utterly provocative. There were a couple of head shots which were perhaps even more revealing than any of the ones in which he was naked. That expression of vacant innocence had been supplanted by a knowing smirk. It was a look meant only for the photographer but which made it perfectly clear to me that this boy was wise beyond his apparent youth.

There were only a few photographs of Ant, none of him in his Speedos unfortunately, but a number of the two of them posed together. I turned those pages swiftly, pinched by the sharp fingers of jealousy. In one particular photo there was a look of such naked adoration in Ant's eyes as he gazed at this boy that I felt a pang of guilt at the deceit of my intrusion.

I closed the album and put it back. I began to puzzle over the phone call from James. It seemed to indicate that either it was over with the young blond, or that Ant dallied in extramarital affairs. I wanted to find evidence of the former. I decided to search the apartment. I started in the bedroom, sliding back the mirrored doors of the built-ins and glancing through the shelves. There were no tiny blue T-shirts stowed there. I tried the bathroom next but found no extra tooth-brushes, no blond-enhancing shampoo, no blond hairs caked to the soap in the shower recess. As I walked out of the bathroom, I glanced over at the bed and that's when I noticed it. There was a framed photograph of Ant and the boy positioned on the bedside cabinet. It was a photograph that hadn't been in the album, a close-up of their faces. The boy stared at the camera. He looked about fifteen years old, his big eyes blank and uncomprehending, as if he'd never been photographed before. Or kissed. For Ant had one hand curled around the back of his neck and his lips pressed against the boy's cheek. Ant's eyes were closed, his head tilted upward in an expression close to rapture.

The presence of that photograph in such a prime position suggested that even if the relationship was over, feelings obviously still lingered. Deeply.

I placed the photograph face down on the cabinet and went upstairs to Strauss's apartment. He would know who this boy was and what state their relationship was in. My pretext was to thank Strauss for the drinks the previous evening. He promptly suggested we have another. Just the two of us. 'A martini,' he decided.

While Strauss set about mixing the drinks, I brought up the subject of Ant's black eye. 'He was elusive, wasn't he?' said Strauss in a rush of words. 'He tried to avoid discussing it, which meant of course that he sustained the injury doing something that he shouldn't have been.'

Strauss promenaded over, a glass in each hand, and sat down next to me on the chaise longue.

'Cheers,' he said, clinking glasses. 'My theory is that he snuck back to see that trashy ex-boyfriend of his and they had a fight.'

'Is this the blond boy?'

'Kip,' sighed Strauss. 'A terrible tramp. He could never be trusted. Poor darling Ant. Kip was his first love. An appalling choice. Ant was fresh from New Zealand with all these innocent old-fashioned expectations which I'm afraid Kip crushed terribly. They had totally different concepts of their relationship. Ant, the naive old thing, presumed it was to be monogamous and imagined it would last forever. Kip had . . . a less constraining view of it. It wasn't until Kip moved in with him downstairs, after about a year of seeing one another, that Ant began to have a few suspicions. Everyone else in the building knew of course and tried to let Ant know, as you do, but you can't tell someone something they don't want to hear. But Kip was outrageous! He seduced the census collector! And then someone else distributing pamphlets for the local Liberal MP. Innocent visitors to our building were his favourite prey for a time. They had a fuck with Kip, then afterwards, when they returned to their duties, a drink with me upstairs. Of course all the details were quickly spilled out over a gin and tonic.

'Finally Ant caught crabs off his boyfriend and couldn't deny any longer what he hadn't wanted to believe. Poor Ant. He'd never had an STD in his life. He was so pure. I do believe Kip took a conscious delight in sullying him. Anyway, I'd begun to have my suspicions about *an infestation* before Ant confided in me. Their sheets were on the clothes line so often. Practically every day for an entire week. A particularly vicious case. They had a terrible fight over that incident. Actually made more noise than those shrill prostitutes ever do. Kip departed and the relationship was declared officially over. However, unofficially, I saw Kip leaving Ant's one morning a few weeks ago, so it would seem that they've started seeing one another again but have kept it quiet. Ant wouldn't confide in me now. I warned him to keep away from Kip. Told him he couldn't keep his pants on. But of course the heart never heeds sensible advice and first love is particularly irrepressible. As for the black eye, my guess is that Ant has caught Kip out a second time, that things got physical and they threw a few punches.'

Strauss rolled his eyes, then leant closer to me to confide in a whisper, 'But what I want to know is whether they fucked after they'd punched one another.'

I found myself irritated that Strauss could possibly imagine their relationship was ongoing. 'It must be well and truly over now,' I said stiffly.

'I wouldn't put money on it. Nevertheless, it can only be a good thing that Ant is going away this week. Hopefully he'll come back having put things in perspective and come to the correct conclusion about the incorrigible Kip.'

Strauss tossed back the remains of his glass and jumped to his feet, offering to mix another round. But I made my escape – I'd learnt what I needed to know – claiming that I had to do some reading for Legal I.

That night I slept in Ant's bed.

I was lying, sleepless, in my own bed, thinking of him, when suddenly it occurred to me that there was a way I could get a little closer to him even though he was all those thousands of miles away. I padded down the stairs in my bare feet and let myself into his apartment. I didn't turn any lights on. The layout was identical to my own apartment and I made my way instinctively to the bedroom, shedding my T-shirt and boxer shorts as I went. I slipped between his sheets and buried my face in his pillow, hoping to catch some scent of him trapped there. I sniffed deeply and then again. There was a slightly stale smell to the pillow, which satisfied me. I rolled over onto my back. I was erect and I began to masturbate. I wasn't cautious when I came. In fact, I felt pleased when some of it got on the sheets. I liked the idea of leaving my mark. I fell asleep, reassuring myself that this was not an act of trespass and sacrilege, but one of devotion, perhaps even of enchantment, a ritual that would lure Ant to me on his return.

I slept in Ant's bed every night after that. I took my showers there, dried myself on his towels, then slipped into a fresh pair of his underwear. It pleased me immensely that I was walking around all day wearing his underwear beneath my clothes.

However, on the Friday night, the last night before he was due back, I went too far. I don't know what got into me. Certainly I was drunk. I'd been to a party and then to a few bars, but I would've thought that even drunk I would've had some restraining sense of caution. I ended up at the Albury, where I watched the show. When it was over, I was approached by a man who asked me my name. For some reason I said Ant. It was him I was thinking of as I stood there amidst all that commotion. It was Ant's underwear, a fancy pair of Calvin Kleins, that I was wearing. Somehow his name popped out in answer to the question.

'W-e-ll A-n-t?' said the guy, drawing out the words.

It was the way he said it. The seductive, teasing edge to the way he drawled out the name, which made me pay attention. I looked him over closely and realised that although he was balding and probably almost as old as Uncle Vic, there was something intrinsically sexy about him. The insinuations that glinted in his eyes, the T-shirt that accentuated his bulky body, the way he had his cock arranged in his jeans so that it protruded an invitation.

'I am not from here, Ant,' he said. 'Where is the best place to go?'

I looked him in the eye. 'My place.'

The guy guffawed. 'I am sure that it is so.'

We left the bar together.

I had not been able to place his accent, a strange mix of formal English and occasional Americanisms. It transpired that he was Dutch, his name was Bern and he was on his first visit to Australia. He was one of those people who, having learnt your name, use it constantly, as if in fear of forgetting it. By the time we'd walked down the hill to William Street, he had almost convinced me that I was Ant, through sheer repetition. As I was impersonating Ant, it seemed natural to use his apartment. It was also one less flight of stairs to climb and at that point, time seemed of the essence. Bern had mounted the stairs on my heels, one hand pressed against my abdomen, the other on the banister, his erection loaded against me from behind every step of the way.

Once we'd entered the apartment, Bern took over. He

guided me into the bedroom, adjusted the lighting to his satisfaction and closed the mirrored doors of the built-ins so that the bed was reflected there in its entirety. He took his time undressing me, exclaiming over me in Dutch with the occasional line of Californian porn dialogue thrown in. His own clothes were discarded in a flash. He sat himself down on the edge of the bed, then pulled me back between his legs so that we both faced the mirror. He rested his chin upon my shoulder. He placed one hand on my left pectoral, the other spread upon my inner thigh, but his fingers didn't stray or fondle. The only pressure was from his eyes, unsmiling and appraising as they studied me in the mirror, and his cock, rigid against my lower back. I felt as jittery as if it were a gun he pressed back there, the memory of that first brutal, premature attempt suddenly paramount in my mind.

Bern's intense contemplation of me went on for far too long. We must have sat there for at least five minutes and my initial surge of lust began to wane. My erection faltered. At first I had felt paranoid that Bern was disappointed with the size of my cock, that he was sitting there, staring, hoping it was going to engorge further. I began to feel impatient, then irritated and finally a little nervous. What sort of person – a dead loss or some sort of pervert? – had I brought home with me, or rather brought back to Ant's place?

Ant.

I must've sobered up some. The thought of Ant suddenly made me aware of exactly where I was and what was poised to happen there, in Ant's bedroom, in Ant's bed. Suddenly it didn't seem such a lark. Rather it was clearly an ill-conceived, exceptionally foolish act. Having sex in his bed was not going to transform this Dutchman into Ant, even if I insisted the lights be turned off.

I cleared my throat as a prelude to excusing myself from what was imminent, but Bern must have sensed a change in my mood, because suddenly he was spurred into action. He seized a handful of my hair, jerked my head back and lunged at my mouth, the appetite of a Hollywood vampire in his eyes. I was so startled I edged away from him and fell off the bed. But rather than pulling me back up, he came after me, tumbling on top of me. His hands, which had been so restrained, were now frenzied. Fondling. Stroking. Pinching. Probing. I was pinned beneath him. I found I *loved* it!

When he slid off me, I was limp and a little delirious from all that he had done to me. He picked me up off the carpet and half threw me across the bed. I was impressed by his strength. I lay there prone, my face pressed into the duvet, my arms flung out over my head. I faced away from the mirror. I could not see what Bern was doing. I could only hear him, panting above me. My knees still rested on the carpet and I was surprised when I felt his feet nestle in between them, and then firmly begin to press, edging my legs apart. 'I will fuck you now,' he informed me.

I rolled over onto my back, kicking out at him for good measure as I did. 'No you won't,' I replied jauntily.

I had decided *that* was for Ant.

I slid up onto the bed and sat there. Resolutely. He begged me in English, in Dutch, and I continued to say no. I was surprised he didn't get angry that I was denying him. But if anything his smile became broader as he continued to wheedle and plead. Finally I realised that being made to beg excited him tremendously. I relaxed. I winked at him, to signal that I'd twigged to his game, and sank back upon the bed, pursing my lips as if I was giving his suggestions some serious contemplation. Bern came after me in an eager galumph of limbs. He crouched over me on all fours, his mouth lowered down by my ear, hoarsely pleading the urgency of his need and the cruelty of my denial. Encouraged, I feigned being torn and tempted. I was beginning to enjoy myself. It was easy for me to rattle off some demure dirty talk: admiring how big and dominant he was, admitting it was practically my first time and that I had never brought anyone back to this bedroom before. I didn't even need to lie.

Bern's eyes (and penis) bulged with excitement. His fingers began to work me over expertly, pressing upon me as insistently as his whispered suggestions. When I began to feel the flush of orgasm, I reached forward to grab his cock. It seemed only to require a few quick tugs. We came within seconds of one another, Bern extravagantly careless of Ant's white duvet cover.

I lay there on my back, my head turned to the side, entranced by the sight of Bern's ejaculation threatening to slither down a fold in the duvet. I felt too spent to force myself up to look for a tissue, but that gleaming glob of semen was blatant evidence of my digression. I reached out and rubbed it into the cotton, hoping when it was dry it would blend in with other, older stains. Bern had collapsed alongside me. His exhalations smacked of satisfaction and satiation. He was ready for sleep. I nudged him awake. He opened one eye. 'You are a wonder!' he declared. 'You want more already?'

I assured him that I did not, that I wanted to sleep. Alone.

But Bern would not be banished that easily. He wanted to lie next to me all night long, then eat *brodjes* with me for breakfast the next morning. He wanted to wake up in the middle of the night and have me all over again. He wanted to have sex with me in my Speedos. He wanted to sling me over the Juliet balcony and fuck me and have me call him mate while he did it. Bern had an endless number of scenarios he wanted to entice me into. Finally I agreed we would try them all if he would only leave me to sleep now. Having wrung that promise from me, he began to put on his socks. He left the address of his hotel and room number by the telephone and I promised to visit him there the following day.

Of course I didn't. I was frantic the next day. I slept late. Once I was up, I had to rush to the laundromat with Ant's sheets, duvet cover, towels and underwear; then I had to vacuum and generally restore the apartment to the state it had been in prior to his departure. The one sign of disturbance I couldn't bring myself to remedy was the photograph by the bed. I left it there. Face down. I hoped Ant might interpret it as a sign.

Ant tapped on my door later that evening and retrieved his keys. But he wouldn't be cajoled inside and I was aware of a coolness in his manner that hadn't been there before he left. He pleaded fatigue, but a three-hour flight from New Zealand could hardly be considered arduous. I fretted for days that I had overlooked some crucial shred of evidence and betrayed my behaviour. However, it was Strauss who enlightened me. 'You forgot to water some plant in the kitchen.'

The fucking fern on the fridge.

I bought a replacement, a much more vibrant looking plant than the original, and knocked on Ant's door to present it. 'I'm sorry. I realised I forgot the fern.'

I didn't wait for an invitation. I marched in and replaced the shrivelled original, which still sat there on the fridge in testimony to my neglect. 'There. Am I forgiven?'

Ant looked sheepish. 'Did Strauss tell you . . . ?'

I interrupted the question. 'I hope everything else was in order?'

'Oh yes. Everything's fine. Look, you shouldn't have bought that.'

'Yes, I should have.'

Ant sighed, then grinned. 'Actually, there is something else. I've been having these strange phone calls ever since I got back.'

'Oh. Obscene?'

'Well yes, actually. This guy with an accent keeps calling. He knows my name. Claims he's in love with me and that we spent a glorious night together. He seems to know my address. Described the apartment block with the prostitutes outside.'

'You must've been drunk not to remember,' I teased him convincingly enough, though inside I was fuming.

I had not given Bern my number, let alone Ant's. Obviously he'd scrawled it down himself, copied it off the telephone on his way out.

'The strange thing is that I did meet someone just before I went away, and I was kind of hoping he might call. He was very insistent that he would. But his name was James. This person is called Ben. You didn't happen to turn my machine off while I was away?'

I had erased the beginning of James's greeting.

'No, I didn't touch a thing. Except the watering can of course, and even that doesn't seem to have been often enough.'

'This guy is so persistent. He's called three times and he insists on seeing me. He's got me so curious, I've said that I'll meet him.'

'What?'

'He sounds kind of sexy over the phone.'

'Are you mad? He's obviously just some pervert who's out for his thrills.'

'He knew my name and the apartment block.'

'You're in the phone book, aren't you? It doesn't take much imagination to guess that a William Street address will have prostitutes hanging around.'

Finally I managed to persuade him not to keep the assignation. However, I found out the meeting spot and went there at the appointed time. Bern was thrilled to see me, fawning all over me, but I was very firm with him.

'You must stop phoning,' I told him sternly. 'That's my boyfriend you keep talking to.'

'B-B-Boyfriend?' stuttered Bern, his face falling. 'But he answers to your name.'

'Ian. His name is Ian. Mine is Ant, short for Anthony. It can be confusing. Your accent makes Ant sound like Ian. He is getting very suspicious about what I got up to while he was away on business.'

'Of course you have a lover,' said Bern sadly, his hand straying under the table to settle on my thigh. 'You are very handsome, very desirable. Perhaps next time I visit Australia you will be single.'

He gave me his business card and I promised to look him up if I was ever in Amsterdam.

I thought I'd dealt with Bern but then I saw him again, a week later, when I was out with Ant at the Flinders. We noticed one another at the same time and of course he made his way through the crowd to say hello. He stopped in front of us, looked Ant over with evident approval and then said to me softly so that Ant couldn't hear that he wanted to sleep with both of us that night. 'I want to watch your boyfriend fuck you.'

'He's very old-fashioned,' I whispered back. 'He would be shocked by such a suggestion.'

'Ah, he would be more shocked if he knew you had been with another,' Bern retorted.

I frowned. It seemed Bern was a bit sharper than I'd given him credit for.

'I leave tomorrow,' said Bern wistfully. 'My last night in Sydney should be a special night, don't you think?'

'There's a very popular sauna across the street,' I suggested.

He stared at me disconsolately for some moments, then finally turned and walked away.

'Who was that?' asked Ant.

'Oh, some friend of my Uncle Vic's. Let's go home.'

But Ant didn't want to leave. The Flinders was where he'd met James and he was hoping to run into him again, which made *two* very good reasons to leave.

James never appeared but Bern returned, several drinks later. This time he wasn't so discreet. 'I want to sleep with you,' he declared loudly. 'The both of you. At the same time.'

Ant stared at Bern thoughtfully. Did he recognise the voice? The accent was heavier now that Bern was drunker.

'You are very lucky to have this boy,' he continued to Ant. 'Very, very lucky.'

Ant laughed. 'I think there's been a misunderstanding. We're not . . .'

'Interested,' I interrupted firmly and turned away, seizing Ant by the arm as I did.

I could hear Bern protesting loudly as I steered Ant out of the bar. 'Uncle Vic warned me that he's got a drinking problem,' I said by way of explanation.

'He thought we were a couple,' said Ant in a wondering voice.

'Yes,' I said, struggling to keep my voice neutral.

We walked home in silence. I wondered if Ant was brooding over the failure of James to appear, or whether Bern's remark had introduced the idea that was foremost in my mind into his. When we got to the front door I made sure I walked ahead of him up the stairs, taking them slowly, hoping the sight of me in my ripped-up 501s was helping to nudge along the possibility that had lingered between us ever since Bern's remark. When I reached his door, I turned to him and smiled at his feet. I was too nervous to look him full in the face.

'Thanks for the company,' Ant said.

'Any time,' I replied, loading the words with as much significance as I could.

Ant pulled his keys out of his pocket and when I heard the key slide into the lock, I looked up, desperate now for the night to continue. Ant stood there grinning at me. He leant forward and pecked me on the lips. 'Thanks for all those drinks,' he grinned. 'I think I'm ripped.'

I'd bought round after round, with the aim of getting him drunk enough to seduce. 'That's okay,' I muttered.

'I'll sleep tonight. That's for sure,' said Ant pushing his door open.

I said nothing. I certainly wasn't going to endorse that proposal.

'G'night,' said Ant.

'Good night,' I said reluctantly, and then he slipped through his door and let it close behind him.

I was so disappointed, I didn't have the heart to climb the stairs. I sank down onto the bottom step and watched the light under the crack of the door. I craned forward to decipher the noises I heard. Music softly playing. The flush of a toilet. Footsteps on the kitchen lino. Water running from a tap and then a softer, barely distinguishable gurgle of water. Was he watering his new fern at this hour?

I must've dozed off there. I was drunk too. Very drunk. I don't know how long I slept there. Minutes? Hours? But I awoke suddenly, my senses alert. Gradually I realised where I was. Then I heard it. The clatter of the front door down below and then the sound of someone making their way up the stairs. Strauss probably. I didn't want to be discovered by him, keeping vigil soulfully outside Ant's door. I jumped to my feet and scampered up the stairs, noting before I turned away that the light beneath the door had been extinguished.

Ant was undoubtedly asleep, untroubled, blithely unaware of so much that had transpired that evening; and also, it seemed, quite oblivious to me.

CHAPTER FIVE

Ant and I drew close in the months that followed. Close, but never so close that we were mouth to mouth, toe to toe and naked, which was the kind of intimacy I was aiming for. Ant seemed to have no heart for such things. In the immediate aftermath of his break-up with Kip, he had made a few hasty liaisons, but ever since I had known him, he had been celibate. To me that seemed significant. The timing seemed to imply that, yes, he had noticed me and, yes, once he had recovered from the emotional devastation that Kip had wrought upon him, he would indeed turn to me. In the meantime he would impress me with his virtue, give me to understand that he had been driven into a few one-night stands out of sheer unhappiness. When we did eventually come together, he would be renewed emotionally and physically.

Patience, however, is not my strongest suit. I like immediate gratification. As autumn turned to winter, it took all my resolve not to attempt to hasten this outcome with one of my little schemes. But I had resolved to treat Ant with the greatest delicacy. No sneaky manoeuvres that might misfire. No fibs that might be discovered. Ant was emotionally fragile and I was aware that an ill-timed move on my part might lead to a definitive rebuff.

As I won Ant's trust, he began to confide in me more and more. In the beginning I relished hearing all the dreadful details about Kip. There was a gossipy thrill to learning the worst of this person I had never met. He had lied to Ant about practically everything, from his age ('I came across his passport and found out he was older than me. He said he was nineteen') to his job ('He didn't even have a job. He spent his days smoking joints and having sex at beats'). But after a month of hearing the same story over and over again, I realised my mistake. I had been cast in the role of the supportive confidant and it had become impossible for me to say the blunt home truths that I itched to. I had been fondly praised so many times for 'my insight and understanding' that to suddenly become blunt and brutal and declare Kip to be the manipulative tramp that he was would've been too shocking a change of attitude. I was obliged to check my sharp tongue. Some days it seemed like I was curbing all my natural urges, not only my speech, but also the clamorous longings of my heart (and penis).

I took consolation in the fact that Ant and I were becoming more and more like a married couple with every day that passed. We saw so much of one another. We had dinner together every night, often spent the weekend together, and when we were obliged to be apart during the working week we spoke on the telephone several times a day. My studies suffered. I was studying cookbooks instead of legal theory; skipping tutorials so that I could prepare something extra special for Ant's dinner. It was a poor attitude, I knew, but then university had not been what I'd expected.

My fellow students were all terribly competitive and flatly refused to lend me their notes when I missed lectures, which I often did. None of my lecturers and tutors took a shine to me the way my teachers at school always had. I did well, not brilliantly in my arts subjects but Legal I was so tedious. I had no interest in it and my tutor recognised that and enjoyed humiliating me with difficult questions in front of my tute group. I only managed to scrape by as I had someone writing my essays for me – a recent graduate who worked in my father's firm. In return, I fed him a steady supply of dope and the occasional ecstasy, which I obtained from Strauss. But I suspected that his joint smoking had jaded his memory and application, because I only ever got very average marks for his essays and was even failed for a couple of them.

Even if I did take myself off to the law library, I could never concentrate there. All I could think of was Ant. How he would come upstairs to my apartment after he'd been to the gym and sit on the couch, his pecs and biceps pumped up and prominent in his snugly fitting singlet. Some evenings I felt so much like a housewife out of an American sitcom – Carol Brady, Samantha Stephens – enquiring how my man's day had been.

Though Ant was never that interested in me and my day. Once we'd eaten dinner and he'd pushed his plate away, he would begin. Every night he was compelled to talk about Kip.

'I'm no good on my own any more,' Ant said to me one night. 'I used to like living alone, but after Kip moved in I got used to coming home to someone, having someone to talk to in the evening. I don't know what I'd do without you, Stephen.'

I was thrilled when he said that. I thought it was a prelude to my much deserved reward (for housewifely devotion) between his sheets. So I refrained from pointing out that these evening conversations with Kip that he had such fond memories of had involved him listening to a pack of lies. It was clear to me that Kip was a pathological liar and some sort of sex addict. But I never said that. I pretended to agree with the excuses that Ant found for Kip's appalling behaviour and even found myself providing inventive explanations for his lies and infidelities.

My reward that night for my patient ear was, as it had been so many other nights, only our usual good-night embrace and kiss. That brief moment when I was held in Ant's arms and his mouth, chaste but astonishingly tender, descended upon my own. Initially those good-night kisses had been enough. They smacked so tantalisingly of what was to come. But as week after week passed and Ant's stories began to sound increasingly monotonous, I began to feel more and more frustrated that those kisses always failed to draw out. That night, when I had felt certain that something was going to happen and I was proved wrong once again, I could bear it no longer. His capacity to mourn and moan over Kip was beginning to seem endless. I had reached a point where I had almost begun to admire Kip as intensely as I resented him: that he still managed to exert such a hold over Ant.

Before Ant walked out my door, I placed a restraining hand upon his arm and gently suggested that he needed a distraction from Kip. 'A *physical* distraction.'

'I couldn't face the bars,' Ant muttered. 'What if I saw him there? I'd be bound to run into him. He was always going there when we were together. Of course he'll be there every night now he's single.'

'*If* he's single,' I snapped and Ant's face crumpled.

But I was fed up. I had sat with him for so many evenings, waiting for the obvious to occur to him. There was no need for him to go to the bars. No need for him to even leave the apartment block. All he had to do was allow one of those goodnight kisses to draw out for a fraction longer.

I began hiring videos on my way home from work to avoid being forced into conversations I could no longer endure. The videos were an excellent strategy. Ant complied and watched them with me. The big advantage of this new tactic was that my television was in the bedroom and so the two of us were obliged to sprawl out together on my bed to watch them. Although we might as well have been in a suburban cinema surrounded by hundreds of potential queer bashers for all Ant recognised the romantic potential of our situation. When the video finished, he invariably tried to bring up the subject of Kip. I would feign extreme fatigue. I'd yawn, stretch out and lie supine only inches from him, willing him either to take me or to shut up and leave. He always left. But some progress had been made. His goodnight kisses were now bestowed lying on my bed, instead of at my door.

At that point I couldn't help giving him a little nudge forward. I devised a simple little plan. I selected the most romantic video I could think of. Rupert Everett in *Another Country*. After a big dinner, with a particularly heavy pudding (one of Nana's famous steamed jam sinkers, which I insisted Ant have seconds of), I was confident that once Ant had settled down on my bed, Nana's sinker would cast him there for the night. I ushered him through to the bedroom, dimmed the lights, spilt my cup of tea over my side of the bed so that I was obliged to squeeze up next to him then, halfway through the action, I offered him a joint. I'd been assured by Strauss that it packed a punch. We shared it, but I, of course, did not inhale.

When the video drew to its emotional conclusion, the mood in my bedroom had become so charged with intimacy that even Ant could not fail to recognise the fact. It was then, as the credits rolled and the music swelled, that he turned and confided something to me. They weren't the words I had been expecting. Instead of a declaration of love, he mumbled how wary he was of making any more mistakes. At first I thought we were once again back on the subject of Kip, but eventually, as he stumbled over his words, it became clear that he was referring to 'another mistake'. There had been a friend – he wouldn't name him – whom he had slept with when he was at his lowest ebb over Kip. He had deeply regretted the act from the moment it was over with. 'Make friends of your lovers, not lovers of your friends,' he quoted at me and I felt obliged to move my foot which had nestled up against his own some minutes earlier.

He gave me his usual peck on the lips, a concerned brotherly smile, and departed.

The next evening, over the remnants of Nana's steamed pudding, Ant confided that he had finally taken my advice. 'What advice was that?' I asked.

'I went out and got myself laid.'

I gasped; when Ant looked up at me, I had to pretend that the custard had been too hot and I'd burnt my mouth. I went to the sink for a glass of water so that I wouldn't have to meet his eyes as he elaborated on his night, in between mouthfuls. Instead of going downstairs to bed the night before, he had gone out to Oxford Street and met someone he'd spent all night having sex with. He'd been obliged to call in sick to work, he'd had so little sleep. 'I was really in the mood, you know, for the first time in months.'

I nodded. I knew the mood exactly.

That was the beginning of Ant's spring fever, a whirl of

indiscriminate promiscuity. I couldn't decide which was worse. Having to endure those endless stories about Kip or having to hear the details of Ant's multiple conquests. I tried to make myself believe it was a mark of respect that he never turned to me at that time. I told myself that he rated me higher than all those boys he was having sex with so casually. I hadn't believed his story about sleeping with a friend in a weak moment. It was too convenient an excuse. I was certain it was merely a means of rebuffing me more kindly.

For the first time I was in the position of being the pursuer and I was finding it thoroughly exasperating. In the past I'd always been so preoccupied with fending off or succumbing to those who pursued me, I'd never had to actively pursue anyone myself. I was accustomed to admiration and compliments, even bold propositions, and I was still the recipient of those attentions at that time. But they made so little impression. They only served to make me wonder how a person I barely knew could desire me so intensely, while Ant, whom I had become so close to, could remain so indifferent to me. What was lacking in me? Was there something about my appearance or my manner that repelled him? I studied myself endlessly in the mirror, worrying. I couldn't fault my face or physique. I was physically very similar to Kip. If he was indicative of Ant's type, then I seemed to fit the bill perfectly. The only thing I could think of was that there must be something about my manner that was repugnant to Ant. I quizzed my friends. Had I become camp?

'Darling,' spluttered Strauss, 'you're asking me if you've become too camp? Are you worried that it's catching? That there's such an excess of effeminacy upstairs in number nine, that it's seeping out beneath my door at night, slithering down the sides of our building, then stealing in through the windows of your boudoir and infiltrating your manly demeanour as you slumber?'

But Strauss couldn't joke me out of my certainty that therein lay my problem. I remembered that Ant was often awkward around Strauss. It seemed obvious enough that he found his effeminacy distasteful. I began to make an effort to appear more manly around Ant, though it did not come naturally throwing 'mate' into every second sentence. I became more guarded and monosyllabic in my speech, stiff and self-conscious. Eventually I gave up. The change in my manner seemed to be puzzling rather than enticing Ant. 'Have you been on Prozac all this time and suddenly stopped taking it?' he had asked me one night.

The irony was that as I strived to be more butch, I noticed Ant becoming more and more girlish and giddy. His promiscuity had snapped him out of his brooding melancholy. He adopted a gushing, jocular manner when he described his conquests to me. Listening to him carry on was torture, but what really killed me was when he'd nonchalantly remark, 'He was great sex. I might try and see him *again*.'

I had to physically bite my tongue between my teeth to stop myself letting out a long wail of protest.

When Ant mentioned his birthday was coming up, I saw it as a last-ditch opportunity to go all out to impress him – then seduce him. He was uncertain what to do, dubious if he even wanted to celebrate. 'It was different when I was with Kip,' he said mournfully.

I insisted on taking charge. 'We'll go out for dinner, just the two of us. Somewhere smart.'

Ant winced at the potential cost and I reassured him that I would pay. It would be intimate, romantic and I would be wearing a minute blue T-shirt to emphasise my physical similarity to Kip. It *had* to work. By the time I'd finished with him, he would be replete, drunk and violable. His principles about doing it with friends would add that extra edge to the moment – the allure of the forbidden.

I made the reservation. A table for two. I told Elisabeth I needed two hundred dollars for some legal texts and she provided it without question. But then a few days later Ant confessed that several friends had demanded to know what he was doing for his birthday and had invited themselves along. He was so contrite when he asked if the reservation could be changed. It ruined my concept of the evening but it was his birthday. I could hardly refuse. Still, I clung to the fact that the two of us would at least be returning to our apartment block together after dinner and there was an opportunity in that.

By the date of Ant's birthday, the number of his party had swollen to ten and we had been obliged to change restaurants as my initial choice would not bother themselves with such a large group. We were all gay boys at the table that night – Blair had been invited but as usual was too broke to attend – and as the empty bottles mounted up on the table the conversation of course turned to sex.

It was Philippe, a loud carping queen, who introduced the topic of who had slept with Ant, and started quizzing everyone at the table. After the first few affirmative responses, I had a horrible premonition that Strauss and I would be the only people present to answer in the negative. We were the final two Philippe interrogated. The others had all answered yes and expectation on our responses was high. Even the diners at the neighbouring table had paused in their meal. It was a tasteless exercise. I would have demurred from replying at all, except I thought a couple of negative responses might help salvage Ant's reputation a little. I gave my answer quietly and avoided Ant's eyes. I wasn't particularly paying attention to Strauss. His answer was a foregone conclusion.

'I'm never one to kiss and tell myself,' Strauss began. 'Though it's a quality I adore in others. However, I don't want to be a spoilsport and ruin the fun, so I'll confess. I have indeed had the pleasure of a night with Antonio, and a cherished memory it is too.'

In the pandemonium that Strauss's answer provoked, I somehow managed to keep my head bowed so that my expression could not be observed. I sat, gripping the tablecloth until I felt I could compose myself. Strauss was seated next to me and finally I turned to him and tapped him on the leg. '*You* and *Ant*?' I whispered fiercely.

'You sound so startled, dear,' said Strauss. 'It's not such an implausible coupling, surely?'

I managed to mutter, 'No, of course not,' but the tumult of my emotions must still have been apparent in my face for Strauss felt obliged to explain the circumstances.

'Poor Ant was at a low point with Kip. I offered my usual forms of comfort. But Ant made it clear he required more than a martini and a receptive ear, so I provided the other as well. It was lovely of course, though I don't believe Ant recalls it quite so fondly. I don't know why. Maybe he awoke with my make-up rubbed off all over him. I've had complaints about that in the past. Foundation in their pubic hair. I'd have thought that it demonstrated a certain avidity.'

This was the liaison with a friend that Ant so deeply regretted and which had in effect consigned me to the off-limits category.

'Ant's harem' became the joke of the evening. Everyone was laughing and teasing Ant about it while Ant kept protesting and laughing. 'It's not that bad. I haven't slept with *everyone* here. I've never slept with Stephen.'

'Look out,' screeched the awful Philippe; I was horrified that Ant had stooped to fucking *him*. 'He's got you in mind for tonight.'

If only it were true.

I felt close to tears as Ant struggled to change the topic of conversation, but everyone was drunk and so delighted by the revelation, they refused to let it go. At one point Ant's eyes met mine and his expression was the same as when he asked me to change the dinner reservation. Humble. Contrite. Almost pleading. I don't know why but that look moved me to tears and I had to excuse myself from the table on the pretext of going to the bathroom. I stood at the urinal, failing to piss, and wept into the stainless steel drain. I couldn't understand what Ant saw in those eight others at the table that he failed to see in me. The fact that Ant had slept with both Philippe and Strauss destroyed my theory about Ant's abhorrence of effeminacy. If anything, it made me suspect he had a fetish for it. I glanced in the mirror as I washed my face. I was better looking than all of them. I was better looking than Kip for that matter. Or at least not as cheap looking.

When I returned to my seat at the table that conversation had been usurped by the arrival of the desserts. I had no appetite for the brûlée Strauss and I had ordered to share. I took the occasional mouthful but I was preoccupied by the inadequacies of the others at the table. None of them loved Ant as I did. Several of them hadn't even bothered to bring him a birthday present. I had sent flowers to his work and was paying for his dinner. I didn't know how he could even have invited some of these people tonight. Describing them as 'friends' was rather overstating the extent of the relationship. If I had been Ant, I would've been embarrassed to see several of them again.

Philippe threw himself at Ant as we were leaving the restaurant. 'I have a large gift for you to unwrap back at my place, Ant,' he cooed, his hand pressing Ant's against his own crotch, which I noted was substantial.

But Ant made his excuses. For a moment it gave me hope that perhaps we did both have the same plan in mind to finish off the night. But then, as Philippe stalked off down the street, disgruntled, Ant whispered to me how relieved he was to shake him off. 'I want to slip off to the sauna and do some celebrating there tonight.'

I ended up walking home alone. Strauss had belatedly decided that Philippe was 'thoroughly evil and delicious' and set off in pursuit of him in a taxi. It was a shock as I trudged up the stairs to my flat to come across someone slumped on the stairs outside Ant's apartment in the exact same place I had sat all those months earlier. The boy jumped to his feet and I recognised him at once, though we had never met. I had studied his photograph. I had listened to endless tirades over his misconduct. It was Kip.

He seemed to know who I was and he said hello warily, then demanded to know where Ant was.

'He's gone out.'

'Where?'

I shrugged. 'The usual places.'

Kip said nothing and I was about to turn away and continue up the stairs when he spoke again, a plaintive edge to his voice. 'He's changed the lock on his apartment. Because of me, I suppose.'

'You wouldn't return his key.'

'He told you that.'

'I've heard a lot about you. None of it complimentary.'

Kip's face was masked in shadow, so it was impossible to observe his reaction, but when he did finally speak his voice was cool and measured. 'How much has he told you then?'

'He was just unburdening himself . . .'

'How much has he told you?' There was an edge to Kip's voice. 'Did he tell you he's taken a restraining order out to stop me coming near him?'

The surprise must have shown on my face, as Kip answered for me. 'So he didn't tell you that. Or the reason why.'

That pricked my curiosity. I found it hard to believe that Ant had left anything unsaid. I had endured hearing so much. I was wondering how best to continue the conversation when Kip abruptly switched topics. 'Can I wait for a while at your place? It's not very comfortable out here in the stairwell.'

I hesitated.

'Please, Stephen. I know who you are. Ant's talked about you.'

I couldn't decide. I didn't particularly want Kip in my apartment; however, if he were to tell me things Ant had neglected to . . . I was more than a little intrigued to hear Kip's version of events. I was also surprised that Ant had spoken to Kip about me. I had been led to believe they hadn't seen one another since they broke up, before I came to know Ant.

'But if he has a restraining order out against you . . .' I began, still uncertain.

'*Who* told him to do that?' demanded Kip, his voice rising.

'That's what I want to know. He would never have done it on his own initiative.'

The door of the apartment next to Ant's opened and his Asian neighbour poked his head out quizzically. 'Sorry,' I muttered. I tugged at Kip by the arm. 'Come upstairs then, for a minute or two. We can't talk here.'

I hurried up the stairs with Kip following. Before the stairs turned at the landing, I looked back to see if Ant's neighbour was still watching. He had been joined by his wife. Their two heads poked out from the door, their eyes wide and serious.

'They never liked me, those two,' said Kip in a low voice. 'One night I was coming home with some dinner for Ant and me and we met on the stairs. The woman looked at what I was carrying and told me off. "Takeaway! All you ever eat is takeaway." '

I opened my door, turned on the light and ushered Kip in. He was still grinning at the memory, his face transformed by an expression of impish delight. It was an insight I could have done without, a glimpse of just how cute and appealing Kip could be. That was the boy Ant had fallen in love with and was finding so difficult to relinquish.

I began studying him as soon as he entered the harsher light of my apartment, taking note of his flaws. The hair that was in need of a cut. The sunburnt nose. The tarnished earrings. The face that appeared thinner than in his photographs. I even checked the inside of his arms. Somehow I felt certain he used drugs. He had that dissolute air about him I associated with drug users. Maybe it was merely that he didn't care, about Ant or about anything, for I found no evidence of track marks. Though there was an ugly scar on one wrist which the bracelet he wore tried but failed to conceal.

I continued to glance back at him as I went to open the French doors and let in some air. Kip seemed oblivious to my stares. He prowled the room, appraising my possessions. There was something edgy to the way he moved about my apartment, as if there was a surplus of energy coursing through his body which he was only barely managing to contain. Even when he stopped still, some part of his body remained in motion. Fingers tapping against his jawbone. Head swivelling from side to side as if there was some music playing within his head. Was it nerves, I wondered, or was he wired? On some drug? I wasn't experienced enough to recognise the signs if he was. Then he turned suddenly and caught me staring at him and a slow, triumphant smile twisted across his face. Those eyes of his were like the headlights of a car. It was as if they had a high-beam switch that could be turned on at will. I was trapped in the sweep of Kip's stare, and his smile began to seem both mocking and lewd. Then, unable to remain motionless for long, he swivelled those skinny hips of his and an image of him naked flashed into my head. I couldn't help myself. It was the last thing I wanted to imagine, but there was something about Kip that was so innately provocative, you found yourself imagining his long lithe limbs writhing about naked. It was plain he would be a dynamo in bed.

I offered him coffee to break the spell of the moment.

He screwed up his nose. 'Do you have a joint?'

'No.'

'Pity,' he said and that same impish look stole over his face.

He pranced over to the balcony and stood there motionless for a moment, surveying the lane below. When he turned to face me, his expression was very cold and composed. 'I've seen Ant up here in your flat a lot,' he said, a note of accusation in his voice. 'I watch him, you know, and you, from that cafe down there, the drop-in place, underneath the theatre. I call in most evenings. I've made some friends there now. I take the table by the window and keep an eye on him. I've seen him up here a lot, though I've noticed he never stays the night. I see him later in his own flat, the lights come on in our bedroom and then they go out again.'

Kip stared at me hard as if he expected me to refute the facts. When I said nothing, he raised an eyebrow and then produced a packet of cigarettes from his pocket. But instead of pulling one out and lighting it, he suddenly switched his attention from the cigarette packet to me. The intensity of his gaze was intimidating.

'You'll probably tell him I've been spying on him, won't you? Even though it's harmless. I only do it because I'm not allowed to see him. Because he's forbidden himself from me.'

'I'm sure he has his reasons.'

Kip's blue eyes flashed angrily. 'Yeah, he does. But it's a denial. You see, we're bound together, forever, and he knows it. He can never forget me.'

Kip wandered over to my bookcase and glanced at the photograph I kept there of Elisabeth and my father. 'I wonder,' he said airily, 'does Ant still have my photo on the table beside his bed?'

I was shocked by his question because it made me aware that Ant *did* still keep that photograph there. I had seen it there only the week before as I passed through his bedroom to use the bathroom. But I'd thought nothing of it. It was only now Kip had drawn my attention to it that I realised what a contradiction it was. Ant was supposed to be trying to forget Kip, yet he still kept this very vivid reminder of him in that most personal of places. I looked Kip full in the face and lied.

'Last time I saw that photograph, it was lying in the corner of the bedroom, the glass smashed, the photo torn in two.'

'Really?'

I wasn't certain if he believed my story. His tone of voice was questioning but also amused, as if he knew that I had lied and found it childishly comical. Those blue eyes of his were so piercing, you could almost imagine them reading your mind. I was unnerved by his gaze. I feigned a yawn. 'I have to go to bed.'

'I'll keep you company in there if you like.'

I was so shocked by this blunt offer that I couldn't reply. Luckily, before I had a chance to make a fool of myself by revealing that I had taken him seriously, his mouth curled up into a mischievous grin. 'Joke. Though you could probably do with some sex. I've seen quite a few strange men in Ant's apartment late at night. Pick-ups. But I never see any in yours.'

I shrugged. 'Why do you watch? Why make yourself jealous?'

'Jealous? I don't suffer from jealousy. But I can tell that you do.'

He paused momentarily, watching my reaction carefully, perhaps hoping my face would betray the truth of his words. But I held his gaze and said nothing, and after a moment he smiled faintly and continued.

'I'm curious about jealousy. I've often wished I was capable of it. Perhaps it might have made me a little more faithful to Ant.'

I feigned another yawn.

'It's all right,' said Kip. 'I'll go. But only if you give Ant a message from me, a birthday message.'

I nodded and Kip walked over to stand very close to me. I was intimidated but determined not to show it. I thought perhaps he was going to whisper something in my ear, something he couldn't bring himself to say aloud. His hand slid around the back of my neck and I leant towards him a little, intrigued by what the message could be. It was so quick I didn't have time to resist. His fingers gripped into my neck and he pulled my face towards his and kissed me. I was so taken by surprise that just as I was beginning to appreciate that Kip had one of those mouths you seemed to sink into – wet and soft and enveloping – it was over. The message had been delivered.

Kip stood in front of me, that smile playing upon his lips, and I wondered if this was another of his jokes. 'You will pass on that message, won't you?' said Kip before sauntering out the door.

'I don't know if I can do it as well,' I replied, flirting from instinct.

But Kip had gone.

I caught the door before it thudded shut and listened to his footsteps pounding down the stairs. He was running down them as if he was being pursued. I stood at my door and listened, wanting to be certain that he actually left the building and didn't hang about waiting for Ant. I heard the front door open and close, and then silence. I rushed to the balcony and stood, like a thief, hidden from view, waiting, watching the laneway. I stood there for ten minutes and then finally conceded that he must have gone home. I realised my heart had been thudding.

I wondered how old Kip actually was. Ant said he had lied about his age, that he was older than he appeared. I could believe that now, having met him. There was a knowingness in his face, a confidence in his manner and conversation that only age could have taught him.

I decided to write Ant a note, insisting that he come up to my flat when he got home, no matter how late that was. I pushed the note under his door and left my own door wedged open so that he could slip inside.

I went to bed and fell asleep. When I woke up, there he was, Ant, sitting on the edge of my bed, whispering my name. I had been dreaming of him.

'What's wrong?' he asked.

'What time is it?'

'It's late. Are you all right?'

'Kip's been here.'

Ant moved to turn the bed lamp on but I clutched his arm. 'No, it's too bright.'

Instead, I jumped out of bed and pulled the window blind up so that the light from the street spilt into the room. I was naked, deliberately naked, and I paused momentarily at the window, allowing Ant to see me silhouetted in that light, before scrambling back beneath the sheet.

Then I began to speak. I told Ant only what he needed to know. That I had found Kip lying in wait for him. That he had admitted to spying on Ant from the cafe across the road for months. I didn't mention that he had been in my apartment or the lie I had told about the photograph. I had decided to make that lie a reality. I would accidentally knock it off the bedside table the next time I happened to be in Ant's apartment.

'He came here, on my birthday,' said Ant in a voice choked with awe.

'Yes, but it was just as well you didn't see him. He was clearly out of his mind on drugs and he looked a fright.'

'What do you mean? Did he look ill?'

'Oh, skinny, run-down, edgy.'

Ant sprang to his feet and crossed to my bedroom window. He peered down across the road.

'That cafe's closed,' he said a little mournfully. 'There's no-one there now.'

'He said you'd taken out a restraining order against him.'

Ant slumped down onto the edge of my bed, his head bowed. He didn't say anything for several minutes, just sat there. Finally I reached out my hand, found his and clasped it. Ant returned the pressure of my grip. Then he sighed and flopped back onto the bed so that he was lying beside me, still holding my hand. 'Did he tell you why I took out the restraining order?'

I remembered the black eye Ant had been sporting the first time I met him. 'I can guess.'

'You know, you probably can't. You can't begin to imagine.' Ant gripped my hand tighter.

'He's unbalanced,' I suggested.

'I think he probably is.'

Ant kicked off his shoes and sighed again. 'Oh, Stephen.'

I thought it was a prelude to his pulling me to him, but instead he lay staring up at the ceiling and began to talk about his night.

'It's strange that Kip was here because I was thinking of him earlier. I had sex with a boy at the sauna who looked like him. Though the lighting there's so dim I guess any young blond would look like Kip. I thought he was perfect, exactly what I wanted. But he wouldn't let me kiss him. He just wanted to be sucked off. I obliged him, of course, but as soon as he'd come, he wrapped his towel round himself and walked out without a word. I lay in the cubicle for ages. I felt very depressed somehow, and then I must've dozed off. I was drunker than I realised. Then when I woke up, there was some old guy sucking my cock. I pushed him off me and ran for the showers, but he followed me. He was very persistent. He took the shower next to mine and started pleading in whispers to let him give me a massage. He kept saying how awful it was being old and being ignored by boys like me. I was beginning to feel sorry for him, almost contemplating the idea. You know, it was my birthday and I was thinking about growing old. But then he ran his hand up my thigh and just the feel of his hand on me, I couldn't bear it. There was such . . . reverence in his touch, it revolted me. I fled upstairs and left.'

We lay beside one another, still holding hands, in silence.

'You can get in under that sheet if you like. If you'd like a bit of a cuddle,' I said tentatively.

Ant rolled on his side and faced me. He ran a finger down my face. 'I'd like to but, to be truthful, I'd be worried that I was going to give you crabs. I always seem to get them when I go to places like that.'

'I don't care.'

'But I do. I wouldn't want to do that to you. I can still hug you from here.'

He pulled me to him, the sheet and his clothes offering a chaste protection. He fell asleep like that. One hand on my hip, the other in my hair, his breath in my face. It was only when I realised he had fallen asleep that I remembered Kip's message. I had quite honestly forgotten to deliver it.

CHAPTER SIX

My New Year's resolution was simple: seduce Ant.

Practically a year had passed since we had first met, an entire year in which he had remained blind to my charms. It baffled me. It infuriated me. But each little rebuff also made me love him all the more. The night of his birthday when he had fallen asleep next to me had been the closest to success, and to him, I'd managed to get. However, I had a plan for New Year's Eve which I considered to be infallible. I had decided to try a little chemical persuasion.

Ant always made a big fuss about being drug free. He said it was one of the first subjects he brought up with any guy he was interested in. 'What about Kip?' I asked slyly.

'That was another lie he told me,' said Ant a little mournfully.

Ever since the Sleaze Ball back in October he'd complained to me endless times about how mindless everyone had been and how impossible it was to meet anyone. 'I said hello to this boy I thought was cute, but he'd taken so many drugs, he couldn't talk. He could barely manage to smile. Do you call that having a good time?'

I did but refrained from saying so. Ant continued his tirade about the hazards of taking illegal substances. For a non-user, Ant had gone to some lengths to educate himself on the possible side effects of recreational drugs. I feigned complete ignorance. If snaring Ant meant saying no to drugs, I was prepared to pretend. However, I couldn't help feeling that his knowledge was too expert, his protestations too protracted – it seemed to indicate a fascination rather than an abhorrence.

I pointed out to Ant that if he'd taken some speed at the Sleaze Ball he wouldn't have run out of energy by four o'clock and ended up sitting down for two hours watching everyone else have a fantastic time. 'You went home at six which is when the party starts to get really good. They always play the best music in the last couple of hours and it gets so cruisy then too.'

'Does it really?' said Ant, suddenly intrigued.

I didn't consult him but when I rang my contact Eva, I ordered an extra ecstasy. I casually mentioned it to him a couple of days before the party. 'I've got a spare I bought for a friend who changed his mind about going. I thought I'd sell it to someone . . . unless of course you want to try it.'

His immediate response was predictable 'Oh no, I couldn't.' But five minutes later he was asking how much it would cost and when I told him it was his Christmas present, I knew it was a foregone conclusion. I retrieved the tablet from the bedroom and gave it to him. He studied it from every angle. 'Is it from a reputable source?' he asked.

I repeated Eva's assurances as to the quality of the drug, her anecdote that a friend had taken one from this same batch and had been flying on it for six hours at a nightclub mid-week. Ant nodded gravely, believing it all.

'I'll be with you, Ant. I'll look after you. If it's too strong for you we'll just sit down for half an hour.'

I hoped he would find it too strong. I could imagine helping an overwhelmed Ant off the dance floor to sit down, huddling up next to him, the sensation of his bare skin upon mine. All inhibitions would have been shed. Rules about intimacies with friends utterly forgotten. Surely Ant, in those circumstances, in that atmosphere, on 'the love drug' for the first time, would finally appreciate what he had remained so resolutely indifferent to for so long? Me.

I took a lot of trouble with my appearance for that party and spent all of the money Elisabeth and my father had given me for Christmas. I bought a new pair of black PVC shorts which were a criminal price, considering the minimal amount of fabric involved; however, they had an ingenious crotch enhancer sewn into them which was extremely flattering. 'Those shorts are like a Wonderbra for genitalia,' the sales assistant informed me. 'They lift and protrude to massive effect.' I was sold.

I already owned a vest which matched the shorts. I borrowed some jewellery from Strauss who had an array of funky trinkets. Knowing Ant's penchant for blonds, I spent two and a half hours at the hairdresser's having some fresh highlights put through my hair. As they were having a special I also had my eyelashes dyed at the same time. I booked sessions at the solarium every day after Christmas, leading up to the party. I had my excess body hair waxed off my chest and shoulders and even enquired about 'the intimate special', but the receptionist's explanation of the process combined with the price seemed guaranteed to dissuade even the most enthusiastic potential client. On the morning of the party I attempted it myself. Standing bent over on the bathroom sink, safety razor in hand, looking through my legs into the mirror, I made some cautious inroads into the problem area.

Strauss was hosting New Year's Eve drinks prior to the dance party and Ant called in on me on his way upstairs. 'You look great,' I enthused when he arrived at my door around nine.

Though to be truthful, I wasn't even sure if he had dressed for the party. He was wearing what he usually wore on the weekends, an old pair of Levi cut-offs and a black Bonds singlet. It was simple, classic perhaps, but uninspired. And it wasn't merely his outfit that lacked a party spirit, he did as well. When I opened the door with a lively 'Happy New Year!' he barely raised a smile. The expression on his face was morose. He muttered a hello and his eyes swept over me. I had been anticipating compliments on my appearance, maybe him even running his hands over my newly smooth and tanned body, but though he seemed transfixed momentarily by the front of my shorts, he said nothing. Instead, he turned away from me and walked over to the balcony. He stood listening to the clamour from Strauss's party up above. 'What a racket,' he said. 'I really can't be bothered going up there.'

'We can have a drink here instead if you like. I'll open some champagne.'

'No, no. I don't want to drink. It's bad enough that I'm going to be taking this . . . this pill. I'm a bit anxious about tonight, Stephen.'

I walked over to him and patted his bicep reassuringly. 'You'll be fine. I'll look after you . . .'

'It's not just the drug-taking. It's Kip. I'm worried about running into Kip.'

I tried to reassure him, told him how many thousands of tickets had been sold, how the party was big enough for him to avoid Kip easily, but I could tell he wasn't listening. 'It's exactly three years since we met. This is our anniversary. We met at this party three years ago.'

'Oh.'

'I know he'll be there tonight and if he sees me, I know he'll say something cutting. Maybe I'd be better off staying straight tonight – no drugs – so that I can handle it if we run into him. Or maybe I shouldn't go to the party at all.'

I spent over an hour making Ant cups of coffee and persuading him back into going to the party and into taking his ecstasy. Meanwhile, overhead, the champagne corks kept popping and there were shrieks of delight and applause when the music swelled even louder and Strauss presumably began doing one of his impromptu drag shows.

Even in the taxi en route to the party Ant was still dithering. 'Maybe I should get out at Oxford Street and go to the Midnight Shift instead.'

'Shall I stop?' asked the driver.

'*No!*' I shrieked at him.

It was only once we'd walked past the party security that I relaxed. I had got him there. I could hear the countdown to midnight begin as we walked into the hall. I grabbed Ant's hand and began to run, pushing through the people in front of me, pulling Ant after me. We plunged onto the dance floor at the exact moment a storm of tinsel confetti was scattered over the crowd. I flung my arms around Ant and kissed him long and lingeringly. There was tinsel in our hair, through our clothes, even caught in Ant's chest hair. All around us people were clapping and cheering. 'It's as if we got married,' I whispered in his ear.

'What's that? Oh yeah, I am glad I came now. Thanks for persuading me,' he said.

I turned away from him to watch the stage. There was a show about to start, but I noticed out of the corner of my eye a boy in Hom underwear standing next to us, simpering at Ant. Gradually he edged closer and closer until he had pressed his crotch against Ant's hip and offered up his mouth. I watched them kiss. It went on for much longer than my own kiss. The boy had one hand slapped firmly on Ant's right buttock.

'Hey, the show's starting,' I said, tugging Ant away from him.

They drew back from one another and I grabbed Ant's hand, hoping the boy would presume we were lovers. Once the show was over, and before either of them had time to think of some inane conversation opener, I whispered in Ant's ear that now was the time we should be taking our drugs. All Ant's apprehensions immediately resurfaced and he turned away from Hom Underwear, whom I glared at emphatically, making it clear that I wasn't going to tolerate any further intercourse between the two of them.

'I've been thinking,' said Ant tentatively into my ear. 'Maybe I should just take a half at a time.'

I scotched that timid suggestion. 'You'll probably just lose the other half when you're out of it.'

As a final convincing flourish, I unwrapped my own tablet from the scrap of tinfoil, snatched Hom Underwear's bottle of water, took a mouthful and swallowed the pill.

Ant was still looking doubtful but I handed him the water bottle and eventually he fumbled in his shorts and produced the pill. 'Shouldn't I go somewhere discreet and take it?'

'Ant, this is the safest place. There's not going to be any

undercover cops on the middle of the dance floor.'

Laboriously, he unwrapped it from the foil and contemplated it. 'I don't know if this is a good way to be starting the New Year. Taking drugs.'

But with that he finally put the tablet in his mouth and took a gulp of water. I snatched the bottle of water from him and passed it back to Hom Underwear who was still hanging around hopefully. 'Thanks, love,' I said. 'He wanted to rinse his mouth out after kissing you.'

Hom Underwear's cute little face fell. He stared at me, uncomprehending, as if he couldn't believe what I'd just said. I leered at him and he turned and fled into the throng of bodies behind him.

We hadn't even begun to dance and already we were sweating. Ant peeled off his singlet and I followed suit. It was so packed on the dance floor, movement was restricted to swaying about in the same spot. We were surrounded by men, practically pressed up against one another. Everyone was bare chested. Ant was the only guy in the vicinity with hair on his chest, though there was one dark guy with a five o'clock shadow spread across his chest, which after a while began to look like burnt toast. The atmosphere was charged with sex. It was so crowded, I was in the delicious position of being pressed up against Ant, but I was also desperately thirsty. Reluctant as I was to relinquish being so close to him, I had to get a drink of water. I suggested we go together but Ant indicated that he wanted to stay and dance. I hesitated. I knew from experience how easy it was to lose someone at these parties. 'Don't move until I get back,' I commanded.

I took careful note of my bearings – beneath the second mirror ball, beside the couple in matching dog collars – so I could find him again and began to push my way through the crowd. Several hands admired my new enhanced crotch as I went.

I went to the coat check and checked in my vest, then lined up at the bar, which was packed. By the time I'd been served, I must've been gone from the dance floor for at least fifteen minutes. I squeezed my way back to the exact spot where I'd left Ant, only to find that he wasn't there. I stood, dumbfounded, unable to believe that it was only half an hour after midnight and I'd already lost him. I scanned all around, in every direction, but Ant was nowhere in sight, though I did notice someone on his knees giving a blow job. The couple in dog collars noticed me looking around and one of them remarked that a collar and leash was essential at these parties.

I nodded, too distracted to pay attention.

'Boyfriends have a habit of getting lost,' the man added with a smirk at his own lover.

I was extremely irritated. But there was nothing I could do but stay put, dance and hope that he would reappear.

When I felt the first signs of the drug kicking in, I cursed it. *Stop!* This was supposed to be happening with Ant, to the two of us together. Where was he? Was the same thing happening to him? I thrust through the dancing bodies, my eyes darting in all directions, the need to find him becoming more frantic and desperate as the drug's potency began to rise up in me. I thrashed through the crowd; wherever I saw a gap, I plunged through it. When, to my surprise, I found myself right across on the other side of the hall, at the edge of the dance floor, I turned to make my way back again. But a girl I had just pushed past blocked my way, standing in front of me with her hands on her hips and a snarl on her face. 'Make up your mind,' she snapped.

Suddenly it seemed too difficult and too hopeless a task to make my way back through all those people again. I went and sat down in the seats, near the toilets, figuring that Ant would have to take a piss sooner or later. But it was difficult to keep an eye on the toilet entrance when the dance floor was so mesmerising. It was a fiesta of the senses. The thousands of people heaving in pagan unison; the lights constantly flashing and dazzling into new unpredictable colours and motions; the thump of the music so loud that it vibrated the seats, causing my water bottles to dance together on the empty seat beside me. I had to fight not to become spellbound by the spectacle. I was aware that sitting there, watching who was coming and going from the toilets, peaking on ecstasy, was no way to be spending my New Year's Eve. It was a pathetic act of desperation.

And, as it transpired, a complete waste of time. Ant never appeared. The only person I noticed was Uncle Vic, who scuttled sheepishly back into the hall, a good hour after I'd seen him head down to the toilets. The time he'd taken, and his slightly self-conscious expression, told me that he must have been 'urinating' in that section where the lights always 'failed'. Uncle Vic had a new outfit for the occasion. A pair of psychedelic bike shorts which, I was horrified to notice when I caught a view of him from behind, had had the arse cut out of them. It was clear that Uncle Vic had *not* had 'the intimate special'. Worse was to come though. I noticed him returning to the toilets an hour or so later and the bike shorts had disappeared altogether. He was wearing only a g-string, the pouch in the same psychedelic fabric as the shorts. I felt like doing him a favour, running after him and telling him to cover up, but he looked so pleased with himself I didn't have the heart to. To my amazement, and Uncle Vic's evident delight, he actually got lucky dressed that way. I saw him leaving the party around five a.m. with a not unattractive boy.

When I noticed that it had grown light, I wandered outside and sat down on a low wall near the entrance to the hall. It was a good position to watch the passing parade of people and keep an eye out for Ant. I was very surprised when I saw a boy I knew from the gym (Warwick? Warren?) peering over the rim of a rubbish skip positioned up against the opposite hall. He clambered out, brushed himself off and marched swiftly past me, pretending he hadn't seen me. Five minutes later another figure emerged from the rubbish skip, wearing only a leather vest and underwear. I couldn't help staring and wondering if he'd come dressed like that or lost his pants. The man must've noticed me staring because as he walked past he seemed to feel obliged to stop and explain. 'I met this most gorgeous guy; perhaps you noticed him, if you've been sitting there a while. Gorgeous, wasn't he? Well, he was very willing but he wouldn't leave the party and come home with me, no matter how much I begged him. He always stays until the very end of these things. Finally he agreed to have sex with me here, if we could find somewhere private. That skip was the best we could do. It was dark when we got in there and it seemed like a good idea at the time, but then I lost my shorts in there and someone threw a hot dog in on top of us.'

I expected him to head for the exit and go home, but to my surprise he went back into the hall. I noticed as he walked away from me that he had a dollop of tomato sauce across his back. There was a boy in silver lamé shorts sprawled just a few feet away from me and we exchanged smiles as the guy walked off.

That conversation made me worry anew about Ant. What if he'd been preyed upon in his vulnerable first-time-on-ecstasy state? He might have already been whisked off by some predatory type, which would explain why I hadn't seen him all night. I scanned the crowd around me with a renewed sense of urgency, searching for Ant or even someone we both knew who might have seen him. Every time my eyes fell in the direction of Silver Shorts, he smiled broadly at me. I gave him a limp grin, then ignored him, hoping he wasn't going to try to strike up a conversation. I couldn't be bothered. He cleared his throat which seemed like a prelude to an introduction, so I slid off the wall, leant back against it and pretended to go to sleep. Then I felt someone's fingers delicately, hesitantly brush my arm and I glanced round to find that Silver Shorts had slithered over to sit right next to me. 'Hello,' he said.

I was about to say something crushing in reply when I saw him, over the boy's shoulder, and the words froze on my tongue. Ant had strolled out of the hall. I watched him walk by me, only a few metres away, but I didn't call out and he didn't notice me. Ant wouldn't have noticed anybody, he was too preoccupied, grinning at the boy whose hand he was holding.

For a moment I thought it was Kip. The features were similar. Tall. Blond. Leggy. But then he turned his face towards me and I could see that this was someone else. That was my first view of Carson.

I was compelled to watch him. Somehow amongst that mass of boys who had all gone to so much trouble and expense over their outfits and bodies, it was Carson who stood out. I studied him as he walked by, trying to work out what it was about him, and saw as I did that I wasn't the only one watching him. Several heads turned to follow his progress. I wondered if he was from somewhere overseas. Then I realised – all that made Carson stand out was his utter failure to emulate the look that was so common amongst Sydney gay boys.

For a start, he had no suntan. It was almost shocking amongst all that tanned muscle, suddenly to encounter pale flesh. Everyone had a tan, whether it was from the beach, the solarium or out of a bottle. For a dance party, it was as mandatory as the drugs.

A bearded leather queen lying on the other side of me noticed me staring and murmured, 'I'd like to run my hands over that.' Although I refused to agree with him, I could see what he meant. Given the opportunity, you would feel compelled to touch him, if only to ascertain whether his skin truly was as soft and smooth as it promised to be. Not that Carson was showing off a lot of flesh. His unbuttoned shirt revealed just a glimpse of his chest and abdomen, and that was the second astonishing thing about him. He had no muscles either. He had the chest of a child. Undeveloped, smooth, pale and hairless. One lavender nipple exposed by the billowing of his flimsy white shirt.

He was dressed entirely in white. White jeans. White shirt. White trainers. For a dance party, that was very overdressed. He should have been soaked in sweat – it had been so hot and steamy on the dance floor – but he didn't appear to be. He looked cool. Suave. Alert. You couldn't help but notice him as he moved through the party-goers who lounged about on the forecourt either in extravagant, gaudy, carnival-like costumes or wearing next to nothing. Carson was dressed so austerely, almost formally by comparison, yet he didn't seem to feel out of place. He appeared perfectly oblivious to the people he manoeuvred around and the eyes that settled upon him and lingered with some admiration. Carson was leading Ant, and there was a jaunty rhythm to his step, as if he was still moving in time to the dance music. Ant, by comparison, staggered once or twice, tripped on someone's outstretched leg and gazed around himself in a dazed fashion. His hair was wet, his face slick with sweat, the expression on his face beatific. Alongside him, Carson looked so amazingly *fresh*. That was the word to describe him and what made you look twice at him. Dressed all in white, that vibrancy in his stride, he looked young, coltish and fresh.

They flopped down on the asphalt together. Ant stretched out and rested his head on Carson's thigh; Carson sat up and looked about, for the first time paying some attention to the people around him. I turned my back on them. I could think of nothing more unbearable than to be noticed by Ant and beckoned over to join them, forced to make polite conversation to some Kip clone who had usurped my night. It would be unendurable. It was then that I remembered the boy who had said hello, and I turned back to him. But he had gone. Got up and walked away and I hadn't even noticed. Now that it was clear that Ant had met someone, I began to wish that I had bothered to talk to the boy. At least then I wouldn't feel so vulnerably alone.

I glanced back over at Carson and Ant. Carson was looking in my direction and I hastily put my sunglasses on. From behind them, I could study him unobtrusively and note his flaws. I was gratified to notice that his ears stuck out, a fact that his hair tried to disguise. That summer everyone had their hair cut short with a Roman fringe. Everyone, that is, except Carson. His hair was longish with a floppy fringe that dangled in his eyes. Ant must've said something because Carson looked down at him and laughed; when he lifted his face, he was still smiling. I had to look away. At that moment Carson's face, transformed by the smile, looked so dazzlingly handsome and happy it was more than I could bear. I got to my feet and began to walk as inconspicuously as possible towards the exit.

This walk, post drugs, was quite a feat. Having to weave through all the bodies sprawled out, while also trying to keep my back to Ant so that he wouldn't notice me. I needn't have worried on this latter count. He was absorbed. I glanced back in his direction and Ant was staring up at Carson with a rapt expression. I turned away, walked forward blindly and very nearly stood on someone's leg. When I looked down to mutter an apology, who should it be but Hom Underwear, his arms round a tattooed boy in black flares. 'Well, well,' he smirked, jerking his head in Ant's direction. 'Looks like you've been discarded along with last year.'

I just stood there. I didn't know what to say. My knack for the sharp retort had deserted me. Hom Underwear sneered, his fingers straying over the tattooed boy's chest. I felt horribly alone. I turned away, making damn sure that I did tread on his leg before striding briskly on towards the exit.

I was out on the street when I remembered my vest. I'd checked it into the cloakroom, but to go back would oblige me to walk within a few paces of where Ant was sitting. I didn't know if it would be worse to be noticed by Ant and obliged to make polite conversation to this blond to whom I only wanted to be extremely objectionable, or for Ant to fail to notice me because he was so entranced. I hesitated. The vest was practically new. Then a taxi rounded the corner and zoomed up Drivers Road. I hurried towards it, not caring about the vest. Ant hadn't noticed it. He hadn't told me it looked gorgeous. I raised my hand, signalling the taxi driver, sweeping past a couple of drag queens struggling to get to their feet from the edge of the gutter where they were perched. They feebly protested their claim upon the taxi, but I was already reaching for the door handle and swiftly installing myself inside.

There was something undeniably depressing about being dropped on the corner of Shame Lane at seven o'clock in the morning, having kicked off the New Year with a night that had only been memorable for all that it had failed to achieve. One of Jo-Jo's girls still lurked across the street in the shadow of my building and she lurched towards me hopefully as I stumbled from the taxi. I didn't think I had the energy to run, but the sight of Suzy Sixty-Nine in daylight, smacked senseless, gave me some and I darted across the street and down the stairs. When I got upstairs to my apartment and opened the French doors, I noticed the taxi hadn't driven off. Instead, the driver had parked in the laneway. From my balcony I had a perfect view of Suzy going down on him.

I turned away and surveyed my flat. It wasn't a great improvement on the sordid sight in the lane. It couldn't be denied – it *was* the dosshouse that Elisabeth had declared it to be. I felt like putting my sunglasses back on.

The cockroaches were rampant. They had commandeered the entire flat. Once they had been content to confine themselves to the kitchen, but lately I had found them frolicking in my bed, nestled inside my underwear when I went to put it on one day, and even floating in my morning cup of tea. They resisted all attempts at chemical extermination and merely bubbled up with grotesque mutations which made squashing them twice as disgusting. The walls were stained with their corpses – my tennis prowess made me a devastating aim with a leather slipper.

But it wasn't only the cockroaches. The entire apartment looked ugly and neglected. The furniture was shabby. The armchair had a broken leg and was propped up by a couple of Badboy erotic titles. The fabric of the couch was worn and faded and had ripped in several places. The only new piece of furniture in the apartment was the bookcase from IKEA I had constructed myself and which was so precarious I had been forced to remove all books from its shelves. The carpet was hideous and made any attempts at beautifying the rooms redundant. At least its colour and pattern – hectic swirls of mustard, fawn and chocolate – didn't show the stains readily.

The only positive aspect I could identify was the fragrant smell of mango through the room. I'd bought a whole load of fruit – oranges, mangoes, bananas and peaches – with the idea of luring Ant back to my apartment for breakfast after the party. I stared at the fruit piled up in the bowl on the table. The thought of eating it was appealing but I couldn't be bothered peeling it, let alone cutting it up. Even the effort required to peel a banana was too great. I went to the bathroom cabinet instead, shook a couple of double strength Normisons out of the bottle and swallowed those. All I wanted to do was knock myself out for the day so that I didn't have to think about how Ant was spending his. I slipped out of my damp clothes, pulled the blinds and crawled in under the sheet. I went to sleep dreaming about persuading Ant to share an apartment with me. We could both move out and find something spacious and sunny in Elizabeth Bay with a view of the water. I was quite prepared to share a bedroom if he wanted to economise, as he always seemed to.

I woke up to the phone ringing. The machine picked up the call and I could hear my voice, so confident and happy (such a contrast to my present mood), wishing the caller a happy New Year. The machine beeped and then Ant began to speak. I jumped out of bed and ran for the phone, scrambling to turn off the machine as I picked up the handset.

'Hello, hello.'

'Well hello. I was about to hang up. Thought you must've still been out or gotten lucky.'

I wondered if he would've felt the slightest spark of jealousy if I had met someone.

'I was asleep,' I said, sinking back onto the sofa.

'But it's five o'clock.'

'Is it really?'

'Yep, and I still haven't made it home yet,' said Ant with a chuckle.

There was such self-satisfaction in that chuckle, I couldn't trust myself to speak. I'd have liked to have wrapped the phone cord round his faithless cock and squeezed and squeezed until it bulged, turned purple and fell off.

'I didn't feel like coming home to my empty flat, so I thought I'd ring and check if you were home and wanted some company?'

A slight edge of melancholy had crept into his voice. He had undoubtedly spent the day with the guy I saw him with at the party, but he was ringing, wanting to come home to me. Did he finally feel something in his post-ecstasy haze?

'That'd be nice,' I said softly.

'Great,' said Ant, his voice suddenly jubilant again. 'I've got so much to tell you. I had the most amazing night. And day. See you soon.'

He hung up and I sat, transfixed, the phone still clutched to my ear. My heart sank. He only wanted to brag about his conquest and tell me things that it would be better for me not to hear. But as painful as I knew it would be listening to him, I was curious. I felt compelled to know the worst.

Then I noticed the shorts I had worn to the party, lying in the middle of the living room where I'd stripped them off. The sight of them reminded me that I had to take a shower. I'd gone straight to bed all smelly and sweaty. I had to spruce myself up for Ant. I strode into the bathroom. Showered. Shaved. Slapped on some deodorant but hesitated over which aftershave, before settling on Obsession. Naturally! I tried on a few different clothes combinations just to confirm that my first choice (the Kip look!) was the best: a pair of faded cut-off Levis and a tight blue Calvin Klein T-shirt which brought out the blue in my eyes.

I hurried into the kitchen to check the fridge for champagne. I couldn't remember if I'd drunk all the bottles I'd bought to see me through the festive season. There was only one left, which wouldn't go far when it came to helping me cope with what I was about to hear. I glanced at my watch. Was there time to duck out and buy another bottle before Ant arrived? I didn't want to miss him or, even worse, run into him on the way back from buying it. The champagne had to seem like a spontaneous idea. 'Oh, look what I found in the fridge. Let's have a drink for the new year.' Ant could be such a puritan at times. I could imagine him protesting that he couldn't possibly drink after taking *drugs* less than twenty-four hours beforehand. To be caught in the act of buying *more* champagne – he had been with me when I bought the dozen – would only confirm his opinion that I was a terrible lush. Ant never kept alcohol in his fridge for that moment when he might happen to feel like a drink. He bought it only when the occasion demanded it, and he was no connoisseur. He would never spend more than eight dollars on a bottle of wine or champagne and thought casks were sensational value.

Then I remembered Blair. I had given her a bottle of French champagne for Christmas. I phoned her and asked if she would mind lending it back to me for the night. She didn't as long as I came and collected it and let myself in with the spare key I minded for her. 'I'm in bed and I'm not going to get out for anything or anybody,' she proclaimed.

I unearthed the key and hurried across the landing to her apartment. As soon as I'd let myself in, Blair immediately materialised in her bedroom doorway, out of the bed she had sworn she could not move from, and insisted on telling me the full, uncondensed version of her New Year's Eve and the man she'd brought home with her. The eventual punch line of the story was that when she woke up, around three in the afternoon, not only had the man disappeared, but so had the dress she had worn to the dance party. 'What's worse,' said Blair, 'I'd borrowed it from the shop and now I'm going to have to pay for it and, Stephen, you know I already have serious, serious debts.'

It was not a story I could excuse myself from readily. It had such ramifications for poor Blair. She could be fired. She managed one of the boutiques up in Paddington. Borrowing dresses was strictly forbidden. Only the owner was allowed to do it, though she seldom did as it was rare for anything in the shop to fit her. To pay for the dress was not an option for Blair. Her debts were legendary: three credit card companies, three ex-boyfriends, David Jones, Telstra, her boss, her mother and her best friend, with whom she was now feuding. To attempt to add to that was unthinkable. But Blair wasn't so concerned about the money, but the fact, the shocking realisation, that she had slept with some sort of freak.

'It's possible he wanted the dress as a trophy,' said Blair, trying to convince herself. 'To show off to his mates.'

'It's probably tied to his car aerial as we speak.'

'But surely my underwear would make a better trophy?'

'Not if it had skid marks,' I pointed out.

'Don't make fun of me,' frowned Blair. 'I've suffered enough. It's obvious I've slept with some weird sort of cross-dresser who only wanted me for my wardrobe. I just can't believe a transvestite would have such fabulous taste. That dress has a three hundred dollar price tag.'

'But would he get into it?'

'He was skinny. I remember that much about him. Oh, Stephen,' she wailed, 'he only came home with me because we were the same dress size.'

It took ten minutes to calm Blair down. When I left she was vowing that she'd never go to another gay party. 'Now that they've become so mainstream, they're obviously just attracting perverts.'

I thought of Hom Underwear and Ant's blond and agreed heartily. 'The crowd was vile.'

I hurried back to my own apartment and marched straight into the bathroom to check my appearance. I fussed with my hair, freshened my aftershave, and then the knock on the door came. I practised a devastating smile, snapped off the light and went to answer the door.

'Hi there,' I smiled, offering up my mouth for a kiss.

Ant provided a quick peck and squeezed my bicep. I couldn't help feeling paranoid that this wasn't a meaningless affectionate gesture, but a subtle test to see whether I'd been keeping up my gym routine over the festive season, which of course I hadn't.

'Hey, Blair popped in before with a late Christmas present,' I said, holding up the bottle of champagne. 'Shall we drink a toast to the new year? It's French. I can't think when I'll have a better occasion to drink it.'

It was the usual 'Oh no, I couldn't' and 'Oh go on, be a devil' for a couple of minutes before Ant finally conceded that he would perhaps have just one glass to keep me company. I hurried into the kitchen for glasses before he could have a change of heart. I gave them a quick wipe (the cockroaches) and whisked back into the living room with them. I considered spilling some champagne over his jeans so that he would be forced to take them off, but it was French champagne, the one thing I adored perhaps even more than Ant. I popped the cork, poured two glasses and we toasted to the new year.

'So what happened to you?' Ant teased. 'Get lucky?'

'It was you that disappeared,' I said hotly. 'I came back to the exact spot and you'd vanished.'

'I realised after you'd gone that I had to take a piss, but I went back to where we were.'

We argued and eventually Ant admitted that maybe he'd got confused but he'd been sure it was the same spot because 'the friendly boy in the underwear' was dancing there. He'd danced with him for a while and then the ecstasy had kicked in.

'I was like – whoa! – flying. It was incredible. I couldn't believe I could feel so great. I kept looking round for you. I was dying of thirst and really needed that water you were getting. There was no way I could've found my way to the bar myself. Then this beautiful man started dancing next to me. He was dressed all in white and he looked incandescent.'

The rest of the story was predictable. Ant noticed the guy had a bottle of water and asked for a drink, but he was so thirsty he gulped the entire bottle down. Embarrassed, he offered to buy a fresh one, and the guy agreed. The bar was in the foyer and the fresh air sweeping in helped calm Ant down a little. He could actually manage a conversation. 'I don't know who started it. Maybe it just occurred to both of us at the same time, but suddenly we were kissing.'

I reached for the champagne bottle and refilled my glass.

'What did you say his name was?'

'Carson.'

'That's a peculiar name. What's it short for? Carcinogenic?'

Ant frowned. 'Actually, it's his last name. He doesn't like his Christian name, so he uses his last name.'

'What's his real name?'

'Robert. Robbie. He inverted it. Now he's Carson Robbie.'

'Where does he live?'

'Newtown.'

I shuddered. Ant started to defend the suburb. 'Newtown is —'

'Hideous. It's miles from anywhere. The beach. Oxford Street. Decent shops. Decent restaurants. It's vile.'

'Well, Carson isn't like you. He's no eastern suburbs scene queen. He's more arty and he likes Newtown. It suits him.'

'I wouldn't go to Newtown for a fuck no matter how gorgeous he was.'

'So who did *you* meet last night?' Ant retaliated.

'No-one. I spent hours looking for you because I was worried you'd freaked out on the ecstasy. I didn't give a thought to trying to pick someone up. Of course, it transpires that I needn't have bothered worrying about you, but I did and wasted my night feeling guilty about giving you drugs.'

'You should've known I'd be all right.'

'How would I know? You'd never taken ecky before and you vanished on me.'

Ant looked a little contrite and I drained my glass, waiting for an apology. I presumed Ant was musing on the ruination of my night and feeling guilty, but after a few moments he started talking about Carson again and how fabulous his body was. I couldn't believe Ant hadn't even apologised. I was furious, but he didn't notice. He kept rattling on about how Carson didn't go to the gym, but did yoga classes instead. 'He's so flexible,' Ant boasted.

I didn't want to dwell on that. 'What does he do for work?'

'He doesn't. He's a student. And a writer. Stephen, can you believe that he's writing a book? A memoir.'

'That'll be short,' I observed archly, and Ant looked nonplussed. 'How can he write his memoirs if he's only in his twenties? That's ridiculous! Unless he's another Kip. Now Kip could write his memoirs. In a few brief years he's managed to make himself thoroughly notorious and degenerate.'

'He is nothing like Kip,' said Ant tersely.

'So he's not blond, blue eyed and winsome?'

Ant blushed. 'Okay, I have a type. What's wrong with that?'

What was wrong with that was that I fitted the requirements to perfection and it crushed me whenever he remarked on some new blond who'd caught his eye. Every time I wanted to wail, 'What about me?', and every time I had to bite back that protest. I could see that I was making Ant defensive and irritated, so I changed my strategy. My remarks had been getting too sharp. I would do better by trying to win his sympathy. I took a deep breath. 'I'm so pleased for you,' I lied. 'You're lucky to have met someone. It was so depressing for me coming home by myself to an empty apartment. No-one to talk to. No-one to cuddle up to. And of course there's the post-ecstasy depression which is so hideous when you're by yourself.'

That was Ant's cue to reach out and pull me to him, offer me some comfort, reassure me that he'd be there to give me a cuddle now and again when I needed one. But Ant wasn't looking at me with sympathy and tenderness. Rather, he was looking at me with bulging, angry eyes.

'What do you mean, post-ecstasy depression? You didn't warn me about that.'

'I thought you knew. I thought you knew all the drawbacks to every drug that is any fun, which is why you never took them.'

'I didn't know,' he grumbled petulantly. 'You should have warned me.'

'It only lasts a couple of days. Like the romances that start in an ecstasy haze.'

I regretted that remark as soon as I'd uttered it. Usually with Ant I'm on my best behaviour and manage to refrain from making any barbed retorts. But that evening I was so frustrated and annoyed and tired, it just slipped out.

'I don't know about depressed, Stephen, but I think that drug has left you feeling rather vicious.'

I gave myself a few moments before replying. 'Oh, Ant, I am sorry. I don't know what came over me. You're absolutely right. It must have been the drug.' I gazed at him contritely, then lowered my eyes as if I couldn't bear to look at him. 'I hate to admit it, Ant, but I think it was jealousy speaking. You've started the new year in this wonderful way, met this interesting up-and-coming writer, while I've spent a lonely day in my lonely bed, *masturbating*.'

Ant looked a little startled at my frank description of my day. 'If it makes you feel any better,' he mumbled, 'Carson and I didn't have sex.'

It did make me feel better. Instantly better. If Ant hadn't had sex, then perhaps there was still hope for the two of us. Tonight. After a good deal of prodding and prompting, the entire story unfolded. When Carson had invited Ant back to his place for breakfast, Ant had naturally assumed he was being invited back for sex. However, on arrival at Carson's Newtown terrace, Ant was ushered straight through to the kitchen, past the staircase that led to the bedroom, and asked how he liked his eggs. He was served breakfast outside in the garden. Afterwards, a nap was suggested. Naturally Ant assumed that this meant sex. But when, after an endless amount of kissing and cuddling, Ant could bear it no longer and slid his fingers beneath the band of Carson's underwear, Carson removed his hand. 'I think I'd prefer to wait until you're more yourself,' he told Ant firmly.

'He's anti-drugs,' I hissed.

'He's not anti-drugs. He's like me. He doesn't believe in taking them. I explained how I was bullied into it.'

'Wow, sounds like fun,' I exclaimed. 'Anti-drugs. Anti-sex. Call me old-fashioned, call me a clichéd promiscuous homosexual, but when I go home with someone, especially all the way to Newtown, I expect them to at least offer me the hospitality of sucking my cock. What's his problem?'

'He just likes to take things slowly,' said Ant hotly. 'He implied that he's had some bad experiences with sex in the past.'

'What happened? Did he sleep with my Uncle Vic?'

Ant was beginning to look uncomfortable. 'I should've known you wouldn't understand,' he mumbled.

'You're right,' I said brightly, pressing home my advantage. 'I can't understand how anybody who was lying next to you in bed could keep their hands off you.'

I had probably revealed too much of my own feelings with that remark, but I had drunk most of one bottle of champagne and was beginning to lose my sense of restraint. I sprang to my feet to open the second bottle but Ant followed me into the kitchen and planted himself in front of the fridge. 'I've made a New Year's resolution to cut back on alcohol,' he informed me. 'Maybe you should follow my example. You always have a glass in your hand. You haven't started drinking alone, have you?'

'As I don't have a boyfriend to enjoy an occasional glass with, sometimes I'm forced to,' I replied, sliding my hand behind him to open the fridge, enjoying the feel of his buttock against my hand as I groped for the handle.

Ant leapt away from the fridge as if I'd stung him. He backed away from me and sat down on the couch again. I retrieved the bottle of Yellowglen and wandered back out of the kitchen. Ant regarded me, his eyes solemn and concerned.

'Stephen, you drink too much.'

I couldn't believe it. All I wanted from him was some affection, and instead I was getting a lecture on depriving myself of one of life's few solaces. I was tempted to pop the cork in the direction of his crotch. It made such a good target, him sitting there, legs apart, his faithless gonads prominent. But I aimed the bottle away from him, opened it and replenished my glass. Behind me Ant sighed. I ignored him.

'Let's have a toast, to the new year,' I insisted, sweeping over to him and filling his glass, despite his protestations. 'It may not have got off to the start you were hoping for but I'm sure it will improve.'

'I hope so. Carson and I are having dinner together on Tuesday.'

My heart sank. 'You've arranged to see him again?'

Ant nodded.

'How nice,' I managed to say. 'A date.'

'Yes.' Ant's face erupted into a huge smile. 'It's like a proper date too. Nothing happened today, so there'll be all that romantic anticipation.'

My mind was scrambling for a means of sabotage.

'Where should we go?' asked Ant. 'I want to take him somewhere special.'

That remark truly perturbed me. 'You're not paying for him, are you?'

Ant would have to be very keen on this guy to actually buy him dinner. In the year that I'd known him, I couldn't recall him doing so much as buying me a drink at the Albury.

'It was my invitation. I should pay, I suppose.'

I recognised the reluctance in Ant's voice. That same tone edged into his voice whenever we were settling the bill in a restaurant and the issue of the tip came up. Ant refused point-blank to contribute. No matter how impeccable the service or how cute the waiter. It was a terrible situation because if I tipped my share, the amount would seem too small and demeaning for the two of us. But I wasn't prepared to pay Ant's share of the tip as well. Meanwhile, Ant would be urging me to leave nothing at all – 'This isn't America. It isn't expected' – and increasingly that seemed the best solution. Except now I was too embarrassed to return to any of those restaurants lest I encounter the same waiter. Ant had no such scruples.

'Well, if he offers to pay, maybe I'll let him,' Ant decided.

'You have just met him, after all.'

'I guess so.'

Suddenly, I had an inspiration.

'Ant,' I said gently, 'if I were you, I think I'd give it a couple of weeks before I saw him again.'

'I can't wait that long.'

'Well, I think you should.'

'Why?'

I made a show of hesitating, then lowered my voice dramatically. 'It sounds to me like he's got something. You know, a little infection. Gonorrhoea. Crabs. I'd give him a couple of weeks to get over it.'

Ant was indignant. 'Stephen!'

'Look, it's obvious. Why else would he pull the Pollyanna act on you? All the classic indicators are there, but if you choose to ignore them, that's up to you. Just don't come whingeing to me if you're afflicted with crabs *again* and can't get rid of them.'

I knew Ant had developed a pathological abhorrence of *Phthirius pubis*. I made no further attempt to converse but left him to stew. My theory was so brilliant and credible, I had begun to believe it myself. I proffered the champagne bottle and Ant, so disappointed by the sense he recognised in my scenario, forgot his New Year's resolution and held up his glass obediently. I poured for him, replenished my own glass and silently toasted my own ingenuity.

CHAPTER SEVEN

Ant did postpone his date with Carson and was vague about naming another night. He might never have bothered to contact him again if he hadn't bumped into him at Boy Charlton pool the following Sunday. Carson didn't mention Ant's failure to phone, but he did reproach him for not wearing any sunscreen. Ant tried to laugh it off but Carson was in earnest and insisted on applying some of his own lotion then and there. After that, it was only natural for Carson to end up spreading his towel alongside Ant's and the two of them to chat the afternoon away. When the sun began to dim, they decided to go for a coffee in Stanley Street, but once they'd walked up to William Street, Ant suggested he make the coffee instead, seeing they were so close to his flat. It was these circumstances that allowed me to meet Carson and get myself invited along on their first date.

I happened to be arriving back from the beach at the same time as Carson was leaving after his visit. I heard voices overhead as I walked in off the street. Curious, I mounted the stairs silently. When I recognised Ant's voice, I stopped short of the landing so that I could remain unseen and overhear the conversation. When Carson began to invite Ant to his house for dinner, I decided it was time to introduce myself.

'Hi, Ant,' I called out cheerfully, turning the corner of the stairs. 'I thought I heard your voice.'

The two of them were standing very close together outside Ant's door. Ant was barefoot and bare chested, wearing a pair of Levi cut-offs; while Carson looked like some African explorer in a pair of baggy cream shorts, flowing shirt and a wide-brimmed hat which he clutched in one hand.

'Oh hi, Stephen,' said Ant.

I bounded up the stairs and introduced myself to Carson. 'Hi. I'm Ant's neighbour, Stephen.'

I held out my hand and we shook. I held his gaze and his hand for as long as he would allow it. 'I'm Carson,' he said, tilting his head to the side and giving me a quizzical smile.

'Actually, I remember seeing you at the New Year's Eve party. You were dressed a little like you are now. All in white.'

Carson blushed with pleasure. 'That's right. How strange. I can't remember seeing you.'

'Oh well, I noticed *you*. You were like a vision. So fresh and pristine looking.'

Ant was looking puzzled. 'You never mentioned seeing Carson,' he said.

'Well I didn't know it was him, did I? We've only just met now.'

The conversation faltered at this point, which was my cue to excuse myself and continue on up the stairs, but I had no intention of doing that. I could feel Carson's eyes studying me while Ant was staring at me with mounting irritation and suspicion. I smiled at both of them, all innocence. Finally Carson began to take his leave again. 'So? Dinner on Friday?'

'Okay,' said Ant.

Carson turned to me. 'Nice meeting you, Stephen.'

'Yes, it was. I'm sure we'll run into each other again.'

'That might be a little unlikely,' said Ant, a twist to his voice. 'Carson lives in Newtown. A suburb you despise, Stephen.'

'Really?' said Carson.

I stuttered for an explanation but Carson was smiling at me kindly and didn't seem offended. 'Look, why don't you join us on Friday if you're free? I'll try and salvage your poor opinion of Newtown over dinner.'

'I'd love to,' I said.

'Good. Ant knows all the details.'

Carson beamed at me with the enthusiasm of a child. He turned back to Ant, kissed him lightly on the lips and murmured goodbye. 'Bye, Stephen,' he said, smiling at me and disappeared down the stairs.

I strolled into Ant's flat and sat down on the couch. After some moments, Ant followed me in. 'He seemed nice,' I said.

'Of course you're not coming to dinner.'

'I was invited.'

'Stephen, this is a date,' Ant pleaded.

'Is it? Why did he invite me along then?'

'To be polite.'

'Maybe he's interested in me,' I mused. 'From what you said he didn't sound that keen on you. He didn't want to have sex with you, did he?'

Ant stared at me angrily.

'Oh Ant, I'm only teasing. How about a drink?'

'A cup of tea?'

I would've preferred a gin and tonic but I said that would be lovely. While Ant was in the kitchen, I jotted down Carson's number which was written on the pad by the phone.

I phoned him the next day to demonstrate my enthusiasm for his invitation. I took down his address details and offered to make dessert and bring the wine. 'Looking forward to Friday,' I cooed down the phone before I hung up.

I was curious as to whether Carson would mention my call to Ant, but I had no way of knowing as Ant avoided me for the rest of the week. That was very uncharacteristic behaviour. We had a routine. I cooked him dinner. We watched videos together. We talked on the phone during the day. But that week he shunned me. When I phoned him at work on Monday, he claimed to be too busy to take the call and failed to call me back. I retaliated by ignoring him. I took satisfaction in the fact that he would be suffering more than I was. I was an accomplished cook and without me he'd be forced to resort to Lean Cuisine. I invited Blair and Strauss for a noisy dinner party one night to press home that point to him.

I have to admit that I felt very nervous when I knocked on Ant's door on Friday evening. I had a feeling he would tell me to fuck off when he saw that I was dressed for dinner and expecting to join him. I had dressed carefully for the occasion. I remembered how stylish Carson had looked on both occasions that I'd seen him. I wore my Gaultier Junior pants with a navy pirate shirt from Morrissey Edmiston and Blundstone boots. I knew Ant would turn up in jeans and a T-shirt and that the contrast would be noted. I'd bought a bottle of champagne, a bottle of chardonnay, a box of rum babas from a patisserie in Paddington and a bunch of lilies.

After knocking three times on Ant's door and getting no reply, I finally had to concede that he had slyly left without me. I checked my watch. It was only just after seven o'clock but I knew that Ant would never pay eight dollars to take a taxi to Newtown. He would've walked into the city to catch the bus. I gathered up the flowers and the shopping bags and hurried down the stairs. I would take a taxi and arrive first.

When Carson opened his door, he looked flustered. He began to apologise but I interrupted. 'I'm early. You go back to dinner. Just give me a vase and a couple of champagne glasses and I'll deal with these.'

Gratefully, Carson returned to his chicken curry. I arranged the flowers, opened the champagne, poured Carson a glass and took myself off on a tour of the house. 'I'll just have a wander round your beautiful home,' I called out to him. 'Do you rent?'

I was shocked but impressed when Carson admitted that he owned it. The house was a renovated terrace done in the usual way. White walls, polished floorboards, lots of wood surfaces. I headed straight for the stairs. There was little to be learnt from the dining room and living room, other than the occasional photograph which I studied carefully. Upstairs was the master bedroom which opened out onto a balcony; a second bedroom, the bathroom and a study. There was a large photograph in the bedroom of an older, distinguished looking man I'd noticed in several of the photographs downstairs. Clearly this man was not Carson's father. I glanced through his clothes rack. It was all very tasteful and expensive. There were several labels I knew had to have been bought overseas. He also had more pairs of shoes than I did, neatly arranged on a chrome rack. The bathroom cabinet was stocked with vitamins and aftershaves but curiously none of the essentials like Valium or sleeping pills. I had a quick hunt through the study for the masterpiece Carson was allegedly writing but could see no evidence of it anywhere.

I went downstairs to replenish my glass, planning to quiz Carson on exactly how he'd come by the house, when the doorbell rang. 'Let me get it,' I called out to him.

I took great pleasure opening the door and seeing the look of dismay spread across Ant's face. 'What . . . what are you doing here?' he finally demanded.

'I was invited. Remember?'

'B-B-But how did you know the address?'

I'd been expecting that question. 'I came down to your apartment at seven, all dressed, and found you'd left without me. I couldn't believe you hadn't knocked on my door before going. So I looked Carson up in the phone book.'

'How did you know his last name?' snapped Ant.

'You told me. You told me he'd changed it, inverted it, so I remembered it.'

Ant looked extremely irritated but at that moment Carson appeared behind me and Ant had to adopt an enthusiastic smile. I smiled back at him. Widely.

Carson greeted Ant, they kissed and then he ushered both of us back through to the living area. Ant proffered a couple of bottles of beer to Carson who retrieved a glass and bottle opener from the kitchen for him. We toasted – 'To Newtown' – and I could see Ant taking in our champagne flutes raised up against his beer glass. Ant began to admire the house and complimented Carson on the lilies which I'd placed on the central coffee table.

'Stephen brought the flowers,' said Carson, smiling at me.

Judging from the expression on his face, Ant's opinion of the flowers seemed to change rapidly.

'Tell me, Carson,' I said, 'how did you come by this house? Did your parents help you buy it?'

He didn't answer for a moment. 'No, it wasn't my parents,' he said eventually, avoiding looking at me. 'My father died years ago and I'm estranged from my mother.'

It wasn't an answer, but when it became clear that he didn't intend to elaborate, I decided to broach the subject when he'd had a little more to drink.

I tried again when we sat down to eat dinner. 'Have you always lived alone, Carson? It's such a large house for one. I'm sure you must've had boyfriends. Did you ever make the fatal mistake of living with any of them?'

'I suppose it was a fatal mistake,' Carson replied, his face deadpan. 'He did die.'

Carson began to laugh from the look of shock on my face and Ant joined in the laughter, delighted by my faux pas. But he laughed a little too enthusiastically and I could tell Carson resented it.

'Your boyfriend died?' I asked, all concern. 'Recently?'

'Over a year ago. It wasn't unexpected. We both knew it was likely for some years before.'

'What did he die of?' asked Ant abruptly.

Carson turned to him and I noted the colour in his face. He was irritated by the question. 'Cancer.'

It wasn't the answer we'd been expecting but I was relieved it wasn't 'the other'.

'I'm sorry,' I said. 'It must have been a great strain on you. Very distressing.'

Carson smiled wanly and changed the tack of the conversation. 'You were curious how I came by the house, Stephen. You've probably guessed now. It was Stewart's house. We lived here together, and when he died, I inherited it.'

'It's a lovely home,' put in Ant.

'Even if it is in Newtown,' said Carson with a quick grin at me. 'Actually, I'm thinking of selling and moving over your way. It was so much Stewart's house, it seems strange to be living here without him. And I think a fresh start somewhere new might be a smart move for me.'

'That must be Stewart in the photograph there,' I said. 'He was very handsome.'

Ant hadn't noticed the photograph and he sprang up from the table to study it. 'He must've been a lot older than you,' he said.

'Yes,' said Carson a little tersely.

Ant seemed to take note of the tone of Carson's voice and contritely put the photograph down and returned to the table. 'What did he do workwise?' I asked.

Carson grudgingly outlined a few details. Stewart had an import business. They had met more than ten years ago. Stewart had encouraged Carson to go to TAFE to complete his Higher School Certificate. 'I had to leave school prematurely . . . because of family problems,' he admitted.

After TAFE he'd spent a year overseas with Stewart. When they returned, Carson started a Bachelor of Arts at Sydney University. No mention was made of ever holding any jobs, which I surmised meant that Stewart had supported him for all those years, including the year they'd spent in Europe. When Stewart's health had begun to falter, Carson had gone part-time at university and looked after Stewart. I did some quick calculations. It seemed that Carson must have become involved with Stewart at a very young age, when he was sixteen or even younger.

'I'm writing my thesis this year,' Carson continued. 'I had to put it off for the last two years because of Stewart. I rather regret my choice of topic now. I've had so much reading to do.'

'What's your topic?'

' "The Sapphic in the Saga: Lesbianism in British Period Sagas." Anthony Trollope. John Galsworthy—'

'*No*,' I exclaimed. 'Not *The Forsyte Saga*! Not Fleur and Irene!'

'You've read it?'

'Of course,' I lied.

In fact, I probably knew it better than anyone who had read it. I had watched the television version, and my mother's fleeting appearance in it, countless times. I noted with satisfaction that Ant looked thoroughly bewildered, which encouraged me to pursue the subject. I pressed Carson to outline some of his theories, while I threw in occasional remarks to demonstrate my familiarity with the characters and plot. Finally, after about ten minutes of this, Ant could bear it no longer and bluntly interrupted us by enquiring how work was progressing on Carson's book. Carson blushed and looked a little embarrassed and tried to change the subject. Ant was persistent. 'How many chapters have you written this week?' he asked.

'It's a very slow process,' said Carson quickly, dismissively.

But Ant was determined to have a conversation to rival our discussion of *The Forsyte Saga*. 'I'd like to read it,' he persisted. 'It sounds a lot more interesting than a bunch of stuffy aristocrats and their love lives.'

It had been meant as a compliment to Carson's writing, but it sounded like an insult, a slur on his choice of topic, which was obviously of great, even passionate, interest to him.

'It's not at the stage to be read by anyone,' said Carson firmly.

There was an uncomfortable silence, which I broke by enquiring if Carson had a job. He smiled at me warmly, grateful to have had the topic changed. 'I'm lucky. I'm not obliged to work. I can get by quite comfortably on what I have, if I'm careful. I haven't felt like doing frivolous things with my money, travelling or going out, for some time. The New Year's Eve party was the first time I'd been to a gay party for years and I only went because I felt I should make an effort. Get out instead of starting the new year by staying at home. It was a good decision.'

But I noted that his smile was directed at me and not at Ant.

Carson asked me how old I was and I could see he was surprised when I said I was almost twenty.

'Stephen is very precocious,' said Ant in a voice that made it sound like a curse rather than a compliment.

I stretched my leg out beneath the table and encountered Carson's. I did not draw back but let my ankle rest there, against his, wondering if he would move his. He did not.

When it was time to leave, I rang for a taxi. 'Do you want to share it with me, Ant, or are you staying the night?' I asked, aware that I was being extremely tactless.

Both Ant and Carson blushed. In the silence that followed, Ant kept darting glances at Carson, hoping for some direction. When no invitation to linger was forthcoming, he muttered that he'd join me in the taxi.

Ant didn't speak at all during the ride back to the Cross. I made a few neutral comments about the dinner and the house but he didn't even reply. However, once we'd got out of the taxi, he exploded. We'd become caught up in the car crawl up William Street and the fare ended up costing fourteen dollars, which irritated Ant even more.

'What the fuck are you up to?' he demanded. 'Do you have designs on Carson?'

'No,' I said innocently.

'What happened before I arrived?'

'Nothing happened. Look, we've got some common interests, we can talk readily . . .'

'Oh, you can talk readily all right,' snapped Ant. 'You're a very smooth operator.'

And with that, Ant stalked across William Street, through the stalled traffic, ignored Sass's greeting and slammed the door as he entered our apartment building. I waited for the lights, then crossed.

'Lovers' quarrel?' asked Sass.

'You know we're not lovers,' I replied.

'But you'd like to be,' she said quickly, then laughed when I blushed. 'Darling, I was there in Strauss's apartment when you met. You were spellbound. I saw that look on your face.'

I began to stutter the need for discretion. 'It's all right, darling, I'd never say a word to him,' Sass assured me as she sashayed across to a car waiting at the kerb. 'But maybe you should tell him yourself.'

I was thoughtful as I climbed the stairs to my apartment. If my infatuation was so transparent to Sass, who else had recognised it and why hadn't Ant himself recognised it? I hesitated outside his door. I had behaved badly. I had flirted brazenly with Carson for the sheer perversity of annoying Ant; but, in a way, I couldn't help myself. It was as if I had fed off his chagrin – the more irritated he became, the more compelled I felt to outclass him in Carson's eyes. I thought of knocking on his door and acting contrite, but when I imagined him suffering behind that closed door, I found I relished that image too much to try to soothe it away. It was exactly what he deserved for all those countless times he'd wounded me with the tales of his latest conquest, not to mention the pain and indignity of being overlooked by him time and time again. I continued up the stairs with more of a skip to my step. He deserved to suffer some heartache too. It was only a fraction of the anguish he had caused me.

I phoned Carson the next morning to thank him for the dinner, and to my surprise he invited me to a play at the Opera House on Tuesday. I accepted the invitation automatically, though once I'd put the phone down I wondered if it might've been wiser to decline. I didn't want to embitter Ant permanently. He would be furious if he found out that Carson and I were going out on what sounded very much like a date. My intention had only been to dampen any prospects between the two of them, not to divert Carson away from Ant to myself. Yet that was exactly what was happening, so effortlessly too, and I couldn't help savouring being in the position of having what Ant wanted. Was it possible that he might begin to see me through Carson's eyes and finally awaken to my eligibility and charms? Or would he only see it as a rejection of himself? Might his sense of injury and jealousy harden into a bitter hatred of me?

I was so unsure of what to do that I decided it would be

best to wait for Ant to do or say something and judge the situation from that. But what Ant did was ignore me. He didn't come upstairs and visit me. He didn't phone me. When I finally ran into him on the stairs on Monday evening, he didn't respond to my smile and greeting, but excused himself curtly, with the pretext that he was late for something. He ran down the stairs, taking them two at a time, as if he couldn't get away from me fast enough.

His manner, so frosty and dismissive, alarmed me. I couldn't stop fretting over how distant he had been with me. I resolved to tell him that I would stop encouraging Carson, but I wanted him to appreciate that I would do so only out of consideration to him. I went down to his flat several times that night and knocked on his door, but he hadn't returned home. I tried to deliver my message for the last time at midnight, but he still wasn't home. I was beset with anxieties. Where was he? Who was he with? The fact that he was out so late on a Monday night reeked of some sort of sexual escapade. I knew it was a popular night at the sauna. Was he there? Even when I went to bed I couldn't sleep, I was so edgy. After lying awake for over an hour, torturing myself with scenarios of what he must be doing, I finally took two sleeping pills and passed out twenty minutes later.

I overslept the next morning. When I woke up it was already nine and I knew Ant would have left for work. I would have to speak to him that night. I decided during the course of the day that I would stand Carson up at the theatre, but I wanted Ant to appreciate that I was making this sacrifice for his sake. I waited until seven-thirty, when I knew he would be home from the gym, and crept quietly down the stairs to his apartment. I listened at the door. I could hear the stereo. He was home. I knocked on the door and waited. I heard the stereo's volume subside but there was no sound of footsteps approaching the door. I knocked again, this time with more authority, but Ant did not open the door. A stubborn silence prevailed. I was not prepared to plead with him through a wooden door. I stamped back upstairs. I felt so annoyed at his obstinate behaviour, his petty refusal even to speak with me, that I decided to meet Carson just to spite him.

I could see Carson waiting when I got out of the taxi. He stood, set against the vast swell of the harbour, the waters flushed lavender by the fading evening light. The other theatregoers swarmed away from him towards the theatre entrance in a buzz of anticipation. There was something undeniably melancholy about his solitary figure – leaning heavily on the railing, a slump to his shoulders, staring down into the harbour waters – which made me feel ashamed of my intention to stand him up. As I walked towards him, I could hear the bell chiming, indicating the start of the performance. I had decided to play it cool with him and then confide once the play was over that I was entangled with someone else. But when Carson turned and saw me, the relief on his face and in the slow dawning of his smile chastened me. He kissed me hello and then stood smiling at me with such open pleasure, I couldn't help responding. My recent days had been so morose and strained as I brooded over Ant's behaviour.

'I bought you a glass of champagne but I'm afraid I drank it waiting for you. I'm sorry.'

Carson was like a naughty schoolboy, confessing a misdemeanour to a master. He barely looked old enough to order a glass of champagne as he stood there before me, twisting his fingers, his white shirt billowing in the harbour breeze, his fringe dangling boyishly in his sheepish eyes. He was years older than me, but in fact he seemed, if anything, younger. Over dinner I'd noticed a childish enthusiasm to his nature, but this quality was much more pronounced now. Perhaps it was our situation: we were on a date. He seemed almost beside himself with delight that I had finally arrived.

'I was nervous that you weren't going to come,' he admitted. 'That Ant had managed to talk you out of it.'

'Ant? I haven't even seen Ant the last few days.'

'Oh. He's been phoning me. He's rung three times. In fact,

he asked me out tonight and I had to tell him a little lie.'

I was incensed. While I had been trying to relinquish Carson of my own volition, Ant had been secretly pursuing him. That charged the spark of competition in me. The urge to win had been bred into me by Elisabeth, and Carson was my new challenge.

'I can't believe it,' I said indignantly. 'Really?'

Carson nodded, his eyes wide at my sudden vehemence.

'I can't believe he'd do that to me.'

'What?' asked Carson, all concern.

'Ant has so many men, I can't believe he'd actively butt in on the one guy I finally feel attracted to.'

'Really?'

I winced and nodded reluctantly. 'I'm afraid Ant's going through a slutty phase—'

'No, no,' said Carson, interrupting, 'I didn't mean that. It was the other thing you said. That you were attracted to me.'

His hand slid cautiously along the railing and wrapped over mine. We stood smiling at one another for a moment, then Carson glanced around surreptitiously, and I knew he was going to kiss me. But when he turned back to face me, he grinned like a naughty schoolboy again. 'Oops,' he said, his grip on my hand tightening. 'We should take our seats or they'll start without us.'

The promenade outside the theatre was deserted. We dashed across to the entrance, ran through the foyer to the theatre doors which the ushers were preparing to close. Perhaps it was the acoustics, but somehow the tone of the bell which sounded to advise patrons to take their seats seemed louder, more frenetic, in the deserted foyer. As we were shown to our seats, it continued to echo in my head, and I had a sudden premonition that the bell had been spelling out a warning – *danger! danger! danger!* – which I should have heeded.

When we slid into our seats, having negotiated the obstacle course of knees, Carson turned to me and smiled, dispelling all my misgivings. The lights dimmed and Carson's leg came to rest against my own.

I bought the champagne at interval and we walked outside sipping it. I made a remark about the play but Carson didn't hear it or chose not to. Instead, he brought up the matter of Ant sleeping around. I affected a show of reluctance but finally narrated the story of his birthday dinner, which even without exaggeration was damning enough. 'He has a healthy appetite for sex. You can't criticise a guy for that. It's just not my style.'

'Nor mine,' said Carson quietly before returning to the subject of the play with great enthusiasm.

He talked almost constantly and I realised that at dinner he had been inhibited, out of nerves or shyness. I was surprised and impressed by the intelligence and perception of his criticism. He was very astute and informed, knowledgeable not only about the particular play we were seeing and its author, but also about contemporary theatre in general. From a couple of other remarks he made, it was clear his knowledge wasn't limited to theatre. Carson had a shrewd grasp of current political issues, or at least read the newspaper more thoroughly and frequently than I did. When I complimented him on his erudition, he passed it off as insignificant. 'It comes from having had a boyfriend twenty years older than myself and being forced to mix with all his friends.'

For some reason I had dismissed Carson as being not that bright. Maybe it was the haphazard nature of his education: dropping out of school early, the protracted time it seemed to be taking him to complete his degree, which I suspected meant failed papers.

Not that I could afford to be judgmental about failed papers. I had failed Legal I. Of course my father had been furious when I told him my result and very reluctant to continue paying my rent. I blamed my poor performance on my tutor – 'I think he was homophobic' – and my father seemed to accept that. Early in the new year he announced that I deserved a fresh shot at law: he would continue to pay my rent, if I repeated Legal I. I agreed. I had no inclination to get a job to support myself. But my own self-image had been tarnished. The golden boy did not fail, even if he had no interest or aptitude for the subject. It was a setback that had shaken my faith in myself.

By the time we returned to our seats, I was a touch spellbound by Carson: his looks, his eloquence and his enthusiastic spirit were beguiling. I returned the pressure of his leg against mine during the second act.

After the play had finished, I suggested a stroll around the promenade of the Opera House. Carson agreed. He had been talking quite animatedly about the conclusion of the play and I expected the two of us to slip into a flirtatious banter as we strolled away from the other theatregoers. But instead, to my surprise, he fell silent. We wandered around the west wing of the Opera House without speaking. The north-facing promenade was completely deserted. We walked halfway along it, then stopped and looked out across the harbour waters to the lights of the North Shore. By chance, I noticed his hands. They were clenched tightly around the harbour railing, the knuckles white from the tension of his grip. I glanced up at his face. His stance was very stiff and he stared across the harbour with a studied intensity. He seemed distant. I had noticed that same look several times the night of his dinner party when a topic of conversation was broached that he didn't care to discuss.

I was curious at this abrupt change in his mood. He had been such an engaging companion all evening. Was it significant that he had frozen up when the atmosphere had turned more intimate? I remembered Ant's description of his chaste New Year's morning with Carson. Was it the effect of his lover's death even after all this time, or was there some other problem? There had been some substantial gaps in the conversation the night of his dinner, things left unsaid, which hinted at other dark clouds in Carson's history besides the death of Stewart.

After some minutes, the silence between us began to seem oppressive. I used the breeze that was ruffling our hair and shirts as a pretext to leave. 'Are you cold?' I asked gently.

'A little,' he replied uncertainly.

'Should we go back . . . ?' I began to suggest.

It was then that Carson's fingers, tentatively, ever so tentatively, unclenched and stole along the railing to cradle mine. I turned to gaze at him, willing him to turn too, but he kept staring out steadfastly across the water. When I noticed him shiver, I gently pulled him against me and folded my arms about him. Carson didn't resist, but he didn't exactly relax in my arms either. It was like embracing a child who has become embarrassed by such demonstrations of affection but submits to them out of politeness.

I'd soon had enough of this awkward embrace. 'I really should be getting home,' I whispered in his ear. 'I have to get up early tomorrow.'

Those were the magic words. At that moment I distinctly felt Carson relax. It was like a sigh, a letting go of tension. He turned and the expression on his face was curiously radiant. He closed his eyes and sought my mouth with his. We kissed very slowly and tenderly and I noticed when we finally drew away from one another that Carson had begun to shiver again.

'You're cold,' I observed. 'We should walk back now.

Carson nodded and slipped his hand into mine. We walked towards the bus stop holding hands. Tourists stared. An Asian couple took a photograph of us. When a Newtown bound bus rumbled past us, Carson sprang free of me. 'That's my bus,' he yelled back over his shoulder. 'I'll run for it. Thanks for tonight.'

'I'll ring you,' I called after him, but Carson was sprinting away from me, his arms waving at the bus driver.

Carson phoned me the next day and caught me by surprise. I hadn't even had time to think about how I should proceed with him, if I should even see him again. I'd had no opportunity to talk to Ant. It was simplest to agree to what Carson was suggesting – seeing a movie together – and think about all that later. Once I'd hung up, I sat on the couch, thinking about Ant. I wanted to see him badly. I was accustomed to being privy to the minutiae of his day, so to be suddenly deprived of his company tormented my curiosity. But I felt slighted too. He had ignored me when I had knocked on his door. To my mind, it was now up to him to make an attempt at reconciliation. So I didn't seek him out. I left him to sulk and come to his senses. I went to the film with Carson on Thursday night and afterwards, when he suggested going to Opera in the Park together on Saturday, I agreed.

We met outside the Art Gallery midafternoon so that we could stake out a good spot. Even arriving that early, there was already a sizeable crowd there before us. We idled away the rest of the afternoon, sunbaking, reading the Saturday newspapers and starting in early on the champagne. We'd brought a picnic dinner which we began to eat around seven, but by that point we were both quite tipsy. When the opera finally began at eight, both of us felt too full and drunk to sit up and watch it. Instead we lay on our blanket, watching the sky darken and the stars emerge. When I snuggled up against Carson, he wasn't stiff and awkward. We cuddled while the arias rose all around us.

When the music finished, Carson pulled free of me, sat up and began to pack away the picnic things. It seemed so abrupt. I sat up, still a little dazed from the champagne, and watched him clear everything away with a startling efficiency. I suggested he come back to my place for a cup of tea, but he had a string of excuses. He didn't want to run into Ant; it was awkward to get back to Newtown from Kings Cross . . . 'You don't have to go back to Newtown,' I pointed out. 'You can stay the night if you like.'

Carson blushed and looked embarrassed. 'I should go home,' he said simply.

'Okay,' I said, quickly grabbing my belongings and stuffing them in my bag. 'See you.'

It was a petulant act on my part but it got a response. Carson came running after me, his hand pulling at my arm.

I turned and faced him coldly. 'Yes?'

'There's something I should probably explain,' he said breathlessly. 'I'm sorry. I don't mean to seem offhand with you. I'm just . . . a little nervous about sex. I've had some difficult times in the past . . . and I try to take things very slowly now.'

I softened a little. 'Because of Stewart?'

'Partly,' he said and sighed. 'To be honest, and this is embarrassing, the last time I tried to have sex, about six months ago, it was a disaster. I couldn't get an erection. I'd never had a problem before. Maybe it was a freak but it's just made me even more nervous about the whole thing.'

I thanked him for the explanation and tried to reassure him.

'Well, don't say I didn't warn you. You're dating a dud,' he joked as he turned and walked away.

Sass was fixing her make-up inside our foyer when I got home. 'You're home early on a Saturday night,' she observed.

'Yeah. Is Ant home, do you know?'

'He went out half an hour ago. Up to Oxford Street.'

I had been tempted to call in on him, but the fact that he was out on the town, on the prowl, hardened me against him.

Carson phoned the next day and invited me to dinner that night. It was such a sudden invitation and coming hot on the heels of our conversation the previous night, I felt certain it was significant. I suspected that Carson had got home last night, lain awake in bed with an erection and realised he was ready to try again.

However that evening, from the moment Carson answered the door, it was clear something was wrong. He was in a state. His smile was limp, his welcome distracted, and I could smell alcohol on his breath when I kissed him hello. When I walked through to the dining room, the table wasn't set. I went to put the wine in the fridge and noticed he hadn't even started preparations for dinner. Everything was still sitting in shopping bags on the kitchen bench. Carson followed me into the kitchen. I was aware of him loitering there in the doorway. When I turned to face him, his expression was contrite. He waved a hand at the shopping bags and laughed a little helplessly. 'I'm sorry. I'll have to buy you dinner. I'm not up to cooking tonight.'

'Are you all right?' I asked.

Carson sighed and looked troubled. I crossed to him and

put my arms around him, but he pulled away. 'What's wrong?' I asked.

Carson half turned away from me, hesitating. I was genuinely puzzled and concerned. I couldn't imagine what the problem could be. I stood there staring at him, struggling to comprehend, and finally he began to speak without looking at me. 'There's something I have to tell you . . . and I've been dreading it. Perhaps you've already guessed?'

I shrugged and Carson sighed.

'I'm HIV positive.'

It was something I'd never expected to hear.

I had managed so far not to think about AIDS much, except when Elisabeth gave me one of her lectures on the subject of safe sex, something that always made me squirm with embarrassment. She wildly proposed that it was responsible to have the HIV test every time I had a casual partner – a blatant attempt to curb what she imagined to be my rampant promiscuity. Even though I knew she was being extreme, she still managed to strike a chord of paranoia into me.

I had had the test soon after I came out. It wasn't only Elisabeth's influence, there was also an AIDS awareness campaign at that time which stressed how empowering the knowledge of your HIV status was. It seemed to be the correct thing to do. In retrospect, I can recognise that it was unnecessary. I'd barely done anything sexually with a guy at that point, but I was naive and increasingly paranoid. I felt compelled to take the test to put my mind at ease.

The week I had to wait for that test result to come back was so fraught with anxiety, I had difficulty sleeping. My appetite suffered; I barely ate for days. I was haunted by the memory of the two test tubes of blood that had been taken. I'd been surprised by how dark my own blood was and in my dreams it became darker still, almost black, glowing with the malevolence of the unknown. I couldn't shake that image out of my mind. When the afternoon of my appointment to be informed of my result finally came, I felt weak at the prospect of what I might be told. I had to climb the stairs to the waiting room supporting myself on the banister like an old man. When my name was called by the doctor, I was too scared to look up and meet his eyes in case I should see the bad news reflected there. I kept my gaze on the black and white chequered linoleum as I got to my feet. When it began to swim before my eyes, I panicked and then everything fell away before my eyes.

I fainted. I hadn't been able to eat that day and it was an oppressively hot afternoon. 'It's the heat,' the doctor explained, more to the other shocked patients in the waiting room than to me, as he and the receptionist helped me back up onto the couch and put my head between my legs.

They wanted me to sit there for five minutes but I couldn't wait any longer for the news. I insisted on getting to my feet and the receptionist helped me through to the doctor's room. 'All right now?' asked the doctor. 'Your test result was negative.'

That afternoon, leaving the surgery, I swore I'd *never* put myself in that situation again. It was simply too fraught with dread and the most excruciating tension, even when your common sense reassured you it would be fine. I couldn't imagine what it would be like if you had some cause to be genuinely anxious. I had always been careful, but from that point I became fastidious. I decided that being fucked was simply out of the question. Condoms could break and after that one sorry attempt with Reece (and Mike), I wasn't sure how keen I was to experience it anyway. I wouldn't allow anyone to even touch me back there. I slapped their hand away. I was nervous about oral sex – it seemed to be a grey area – but after discussing it with my doctor, I felt reassured that it was safe within certain limits. But I became paranoid about the state of my mouth. If my gums bled when I brushed my teeth, I felt that great tumour of trepidation turn over in my stomach.

I didn't have a problem sticking to my ground rules. Even if I'd had a bit to drink, my common sense always prevailed. Yet I was aware that I'd only had a few casual partners and I'd never felt utterly swept away by the intensity of the moment.

I'd never been in love. It would be different, I was certain, if something physical was ever to happen with Ant. *Then* I could imagine myself agreeing to whatever he wanted to do to me. That was undoubtedly part of the reason I never did talk plainly to him about my feelings. It wasn't only the possibility of rejection and perhaps the ruination of our friendship, there was also the knowledge that my feelings were too strong. That the potential was there for me, who had always been calculating and controlling, to be so overwhelmed by passion as to be made vulnerable. He was the man I would not be able to say no to, and that made me nervous.

When Carson made his confession, I felt that same awful waiting room dread turn over in my stomach.

Perhaps if I'd been more sincere in my pursuit of Carson, I would have guessed. There had been clues. His reluctance to have sex. The fact that Stewart had died of cancer, which I now realised was probably an HIV-related cancer. But I had never analysed Carson's conversation and behaviour too closely. I wasn't in love with him. It wasn't Carson I thought about at night when I jerked myself off. It wasn't his remarks I agonised over, searching for hidden meanings. It wasn't him I anticipated seeing throughout my days and who gave me such instantaneous pleasure when we were finally alone together. There was only one person who did all that for me: Ant.

Still, I couldn't deny that there had been moments, fleeting moments, when I had become caught up in the romanticism of our situation and felt something akin to the tug of desire. But I could never distinguish if the desire to kiss Carson, or even fuck him, was inspired by a genuine attraction or by more perverse and competitive motivations: to have for myself what Ant had wanted.

'I should have told you before now, but I was so scared of being rejected,' Carson continued a little plaintively. 'I wanted to give you a chance to get to know me first.'

I realised when he spoke that I'd failed to say anything in reply. I muttered an apology. I still didn't know what to say.

Finally I pulled him to me and held him, hoping that would suffice in place of reassurances. Carson began talking in a babble.

'I've avoided this situation for so long, getting involved with someone. It's just made it worse and worse, putting it off. I felt like I owed it to you to tell you before things between us went any further. Of course, there's no risk when you have safe sex, but I guess there's a psychological component.'

I did feel genuinely sorry for Carson and guilty for trifling with him, but it was also abundantly clear to me that relations between us had to cease. Carson was right. There was a psychological component and, in my case, I was irrationally paranoid. I managed to utter a few platitudes while my mind raced, trying to think how I could gently extricate myself without hurting Carson's feelings too badly. It was highly ironic. If I hadn't interfered, if I had merely let things run their course between Ant and Carson, then it would've been Ant in my position, trying to extricate himself.

'Perhaps you'd prefer not to have dinner at all,' Carson finally suggested. 'Maybe you'd rather just give yourself some time to think and we can see one another in a day or two.'

'To be honest, I think that's a good idea,' I said quickly, grateful to him for providing me with an escape.

His face was unreadable. I couldn't tell if he was disappointed. He led me to the door and I embraced and kissed him with what I hoped was as much conviction as I'd shown in the past. But I was relieved when he pulled back from me. His kiss, the probing of his tongue in my mouth, had seemed suddenly insidious. Invasive.

In the taxi on the way home, I told myself that Carson's silence had been deceitful. There had been more to our evenings together than merely getting to know one another. The holding hands, the lingering kisses, those dates, had all been calculated to make me fall in love with him, so that when the subject was finally broached, I would already feel bound to him emotionally. I decided to pound on Ant's door until he opened it and pour the whole sorry story out to him. I needed some support.

I ran up the stairs to his apartment with that thought in mind, but by some strange coincidence I met him on the landing. He had obviously come from upstairs and I wondered if he'd been visiting Strauss or been knocking on my door. My expression must've been agitated because the stiffness in his face melted and he asked me, with genuine concern, if I was all right.

'Can we talk?' I asked. 'I've had a helluva night.'

Ant nodded and unlocked his door. I walked into the room, turned to face him and blurted it out straight away.

'Carson told me tonight that he's HIV positive.'

Ant's expression was inscrutable. 'You've been seeing him?'

'He asked me out a few times,' I said casually, trying to make light of it. 'We saw a play together. Went to Opera in the Park yesterday.'

The concern in Ant's face was gone. He was looking particularly grim. I knew I would have to exaggerate the truth a little.

'I did try to ask you along, but you never seemed to be at home. Whenever I knocked on your door, I didn't get an answer.'

I expected Ant to make some weak excuse for avoiding me, but instead he ignored what I'd said and switched the topic back to Carson. 'You know that's not the sort of news you should go bandying about,' he upbraided me. 'I'm sure Carson would've told you that in confidence.'

I blushed. I hadn't given a thought to discretion. 'I think he'd understand that I needed to discuss it. I feel so wound up. And you'd never tell anyone.'

'No, I wouldn't. *I* can respect a confidence.'

We lapsed into silence.

'So?' asked Ant.

'It hasn't been sexual between us, if that's what you're asking,' I said quickly.

'I wasn't.'

'Oh,' I said. 'Well, it wasn't. I guess he thought it was heading that way. That's why he told me.'

'That was considerate of him,' Ant observed. 'No, Stephen, what I was wondering was, what do you intend to do?'

'I can't keep seeing him,' I cried. 'I'm just too nervous about the whole thing. If we did ever get into bed, I don't think I could relax, let alone get an erection.'

For an instant Ant's expression changed. A wave of emotion rippled across his face and then was gone, but it was so quick I couldn't ascertain whether it was disapproval, jealousy or relief.

'Look, I wasn't interested in him that way to begin with,' I defended myself. 'We had common interests. We got along. He kept asking me out and I kept agreeing. I don't know why. Maybe because you and I seemed to have fallen out and I was lonely.'

'Carson was the reason we fell out.'

'I'm not in love with him and I never will be.'

I hesitated. For a moment, I thought of telling Ant, then and there, the truth. That I was in love with *him*. But before I had a chance to decide one way or the other, he had begun to talk again.

'You must let him down gently then. He'll feel the rejection very badly.'

I pulled a face. 'I don't know if I can say it to his face,' I moaned. 'I'd feel so guilty. He's got such a little baby face, I don't think I could bear to see his disappointment. Wouldn't it be easier all round if I just didn't phone him? Let silence say it for me.'

'Silence can be very ambiguous.'

Our eyes met and for the very first time I was certain that Ant and I were both thinking of the same thing – our own unspoken attraction – but then he dropped his gaze and the moment was gone.

'You can't let it linger on not saying anything,' he said, his head still bowed. 'That would be even crueller.'

'You tell him for me,' I pleaded, suddenly seeing a way out.

'Please, Ant. I'd feel so guilty rejecting him, I don't know if I could get the words out.'

'You're usually rather good at padding the truth to your own ends.'

That was a slap in the face. I ignored it.

'Ant? Would you?'

Ant hesitated and I knew then that he'd agree.

That night I had difficulty sleeping. Even though Carson and I had done nothing more than kiss and I knew there was no risk, I still found myself fretting. When I finally did get off to sleep, inevitably Carson wound up in my dreams. We were having sex. Carson started to come, but when he ejaculated, he ejaculated blood, spurting out all over the sheets, all over me. Thankfully, somewhere in my consciousness I was able to recognise that I was having a nightmare and I forced myself to wake up. But it had been so vivid. My hands were pawing at my body, wiping the spots of blood off myself, like Lady Macbeth.

Ant came to my apartment the next night. He refused to come in, but stood in the doorway instead and told me it was done.

'Thank you,' I said. 'I really appreciate it. I think it was easier all round.'

'Easier on you,' said Ant brusquely and turned and walked down the stairs.

I worried that I'd disappointed him, but when I cautiously dropped in on him the next evening, he seemed to have regained his equilibrium. He was his old self and neither of us mentioned Carson. Gradually, over the days that followed, I began to feel reassured that, like me, he was happy to let the awkwardness of that situation be forgotten. So I was taken completely by surprise when he did bring the matter up, several weeks later. We were watching a video in my bedroom when, without any explanation, he paused the machine.

'What's wrong?' I asked. 'Do you want a cup of tea?'

'You never asked how it went with Carson.'

His voice was grim, laden with accusation.

'I s-s-suppose . . . I presumed . . . it w-w-went . . . okay,' I stuttered. 'Seeing as you never said anything.'

'You should've asked. Your silence has seemed uncaring.'

'But it went all right, didn't it? I mean, you would've said something otherwise.'

Ant sighed. 'No, Stephen, it didn't go all right. He was disappointed. Deeply disappointed.'

He paused as if waiting for me to respond. When I didn't, he continued.

'It was bloody awful actually. You were the first guy he's really made an effort with since his lover died. He said he told you that. He was too nervous of being rejected to even try before. He never went out, never put himself in the situation where he might meet someone he felt attracted to. Then when he finally did, he had the misfortune to get entangled with you. You've really shattered his confidence.'

'Okay, Ant. Spare me the lecture. I feel bad enough about the whole thing—'

'Do you?' Ant's voice was savage. 'I haven't seen any signs of remorse. You haven't phoned him or tried to see him, or even expressed anything to me.'

'Okay, I'll call him if that'll—'

'I think the time when he would've welcomed a call from you has passed.'

The pause button on the video ran out and the video began again. Ant let it play on. I felt thoroughly reprimanded. I couldn't concentrate on the television.

When the video finished, Ant sprang up off the bed, but I seized his arm.

He turned to me in surprise.

'Thank you,' I said.

'What for?'

'For dealing with Carson for me. I'm sorry. I behaved badly and I know it. But I learnt something. I think next time, if there was a similar situation, I would know how to do better. Next time.'

I meant every word I said. I felt genuinely contrite. But Ant didn't seem to be particularly impressed. He shrugged and left.

Carson weighed on my mind after that. I started writing a letter to him, apologising and explaining, and wished I'd thought of doing that in the first place and kept Ant out of it. It was not an easy letter to write. I made several false starts and found myself going over and over what I should say at all times of the day and night. So it was coincidental that I happened to see Carson then, at a time when he was constantly on my mind.

I'd been for a drink with Elisabeth and Uncle Vic at the Bayswater Brasserie one evening. I left them to have their dinner, walked out onto the street, turned to walk towards Darlinghurst Road, and there he was. Carson. Sitting at the window table of the Thai restaurant next door. I'd have looked twice even if I hadn't recognised him, he looked so handsome, his white shirt a striking contrast against the vibrant pink decor of the walls. His face was aglow, burnished perhaps by the flame from the candles burning in front of his table. I paused for a moment. I didn't feel confident enough to duck in and say hello and, of course, he wasn't eating alone. There was someone seated opposite him and it was with a jolt that I realised just who that someone was. I didn't need to see his face. Even from behind I could recognise him, the cut of his hair and the sports jacket that he wore only on special occasions. Ant wasn't one for dressing up unnecessarily. Not unless he wanted to impress.

I jerked my eyes away and hurried past the window. I'd only seen Carson for a moment, but it had been long enough to ascertain that the look on his face had not been that of someone suffering from my rejection. He had been smiling with blissful abandon, his face flushed with pleasure. I would've liked to have been able to believe that the reason he looked so radiant was that he was drunk. Or perhaps thrilled to be dining at one of the most chic restaurants in Sydney. But I knew, in my heart of hearts, I knew the real reason. His pleasure derived from his companion for the evening. The person seated opposite him, whose face he looked into so happily. I recognised that look on

Carson's face. I had seen it once before, when he had turned and looked at me, as he plucked up the courage to kiss me, that first time down by the Opera House.

I darted across the street. I could not go home without reconfirming what I thought I'd seen. I sidled back down the street, nervous even with the safety of that distance between us, but I needn't have been. I could've had my face pressed up against the glass and the two of them still would've been oblivious to me. Their eyes didn't leave one another's faces. They spoke intently. Smiled. Laughed. When the waiter presented them with their food, Ant drew his hand back and I realised they had been holding hands across the table.

It wasn't until I got home that I realised the significance of the day. There was a card in my letterbox and I opened it climbing the stairs. It was a Valentine's Day card. It was no mystery as to who it was from, although it was unsigned. I had recognised the writing on the envelope. It had even been written in pencil, exactly what he had used to write his secret gushing remarks upon my English essays. More than a year had passed since I'd left school, but Mr Preston was still thinking of me and had somehow managed to obtain my address. I tossed his card on the table as I entered the flat.

I wedged open my door so that I would be able to hear anything that happened downstairs, grabbed a glass and the open bottle of red, and sat down on the couch. I drank a toast to Valentine's Day. Then another. And another. I played no music. I kept the television switched off. I stared out at the darkening sky, my ears strained for the sound of footsteps on the stairs. When they finally came, I didn't need to slip out and peer down the stairwell to check. Ant's voice rose as he mounted the stairs and I realised with a pang that he was not alone. He was talking to Carson as they climbed the stairs together.

I went out that night. I could not stay in my own bed knowing what was happening in the apartment beneath mine. Sass caught my eye as I was leaving and from the gravity of her expression I knew she had witnessed the amorous arrival of Ant and Carson.

'I'm going out,' I called out defiantly, and she whooped her approval.

I went to the sauna. I wanted sex and I didn't have the patience to stand around in a bar playing eye games. I had never been before, but from all that I'd heard, it was exactly what I needed. Uncomplicated, anonymous sex. But though it was relatively busy and there were plenty of handsome, well-built guys prowling the corridors, none of the ones I indicated my willingness to gave me a second glance. Maybe there was an etiquette which I was unaware of as a novice, or maybe my face showed me to be as forlorn as I felt. Whatever the reason, after hopelessly circling the corridors for over an hour, I finally gave up, went into a cubicle, locked the door, jerked myself off and wept.

CHAPTER EIGHT

It was on the 326 bus one afternoon that it struck me: in trying to distract myself from the blissful union of Ant and Carson, I had become something of a slut. The driver of that bus was someone I'd had sex with recently. I had been very surprised to board the bus and find him there, behind the wheel. He appeared to be as startled as I was and forgot to give me my change.

I'd met him, as I'd met so many of the others, at the Oxford Hotel. We never discussed his occupation. In fact, we settled upon one another without exchanging a word. I noticed him standing against the wall, glowering his intent, and signalled my interest in return. I downed my drink, gave him a look and sauntered out of the bar. Of course he followed me. Trailed me for two blocks down Forbes Street but was too timid to approach me. Finally I stopped and pretended to do up my shoelace. When I stood up again, I felt his breath on my neck.

I noticed now, that he kept glancing back at me in the rear-vision mirror of the bus and I felt irritated that he wasn't keeping his eyes on the road. The bus was full and his passengers' welfare should have been his primary concern. When the bus reached Watsons Bay, he beckoned me up to him and reluctantly I complied. 'I always do this route. Drive right past your front door,' he said in a wistful way.

I wondered if he was hinting that I could ride free in the future. It wasn't the greatest of inducements. In fact, it was rather shabby when considered alongside Strauss's situation. He had a longstanding arrangement with a middle-aged, married taxi driver. 'It's so Hollywood,' Strauss often bragged. 'He's fascinated by me and will take me wherever I like, whatever the hour. I recline in the back seat, give directions and call him Driver.'

The arrangement wasn't quite as glamorous as Strauss made it out to be. According to Ant, the taxi driver charged a blow job for his services.

'I've picked up your neighbour from that stop a few times now,' the bus driver continued. 'The blond guy. He remembers me. We always have a bit of a chat.'

Of course Carson remembered him. He would take a malicious pleasure in remembering. I stepped smartly out of the bus without replying. I'd only walked a few steps when I felt a hand on my shoulder. I spun around, startled, and the bus driver leered his face into mine, quivering with anger and emotion. 'You're not as hot as you think you are,' he spat at me. 'Your dick was a total disappointment.'

He turned and ran back to his bus, apologising to the passengers, who stood in a queue, grumbling, waiting for him. I was so shocked at what he had said, I stood rooted to the spot. It was only when I noticed him glance over at me as he retook his seat that I felt spurred to walk away towards Lady Jane Beach. But my afternoon had been spoilt. I couldn't enjoy myself there, where nudity was sanctioned. Men strolled about or lay supine, sunning themselves without shame, their genitals gloriously, abundantly displayed. Even with my Speedos on I felt vulnerable. I was aware of how little I tested the stretch of the lycra. I lay back, placed my open book over my crotch and tried not to think of the bus driver.

The two of us had encountered Carson and Ant the following morning when I had been trying to rid myself of him. I tried to avoid those two at the best of times, so to run into them at such an inopportune moment was deeply embarrassing. It wasn't that the bus driver was a mistake, although in the blunt light of day he wasn't as sexy, nor as young, as I had thought him to be. It was more that our night together seemed tawdry and second-rate when viewed alongside the early-morning domesticity of Ant and Carson.

We ran into them outside their door: Ant was on his way out for the newspaper and pastries and was instructing Carson to make the coffee and squeeze the oranges for juice. Carson was wearing Ant's white fluffy robe and looking as pleased as a bride on her wedding day – I'd like to have poured a pot of coffee down his immaculate front! They said good morning brightly in unison, and I muttered a reply to their slippers (which I noticed were matching). I pushed the bus driver forward, perhaps a little more forcefully than was necessary. He had hesitated and half turned round, as if he expected to be introduced. We continued down the stairs and I told myself that I regretted nothing, that the night before had been exactly what I needed. And in a way it had been. Not the sex, but what he'd said to me. The bus driver had seemed awestruck to find himself in bed with me. He kept mumbling compliments, which were all the sexier for their banality. 'You could have anyone you wanted,' he'd whispered before he went down on me, and I'd liked that better than anything he did with his mouth or fingers. Even if the presence of Carson in Ant's bed in the apartment below did contradict his words. At that moment, drunk as I was, and being blown, I felt them to be resonantly true.

Out on the street I farewelled the bus driver passionately, as I knew Ant would be a witness to it. I heard the door open behind us as we kissed. I hoped it might stir something in him. I couldn't hope for jealousy, but thought it might at least spark a sense of nostalgia for the fleeting pleasures of the single lifestyle.

I hurried back upstairs, intent upon a return to my bed, only to be waylaid by Carson. His head popped out of Ant's door as I passed by. 'Come in for breakfast. We haven't seen you for ages.'

I mumbled an excuse, something about not getting much sleep and needing to go back to bed.

'I can imagine,' said Carson, arching his eyebrows. 'Oh well, some other time.'

I was in no mood for Carson. I wished he wouldn't make such an effort. I would've infinitely preferred him to bear me a grudge, to ignore me, then I would have the justification to ignore him in return. But he was always charming, always so chirpily charming. I was sure he only did it because he realised it killed me having to reciprocate in kind. I stamped up the stairs, feeling more convinced than ever that it had to be an act. Deep down, behind his enthusiastic 'good mornings' and invitations for croissants, had to be a noxiously fermenting resentment of me. He had to be bitter and vengeful. Anything else just wasn't human. Unless . . . unless he was so utterly happy with Ant that it had overwhelmed any ill feeling he bore me. That was an explanation that made me feel even worse.

I had a headache by the time I got back to my own flat. I blamed Carson for it, rather than my own ingestion of alcohol and lack of sleep. I took two Panadeine and two sleeping pills and fell into bed. I wanted nothing but to sleep. A chemically induced sleep, free of obsessive dreams about the darling domicile beneath me. But instead, Carson's words, that dry tone of voice – '*I can imagine*' – resounded in my ears. His remarks began to seem loaded with unspoken recriminations. He had raised his eyebrows at me in a manner that on reflection seemed condescending and superior. I knew what he had to be thinking. He had been a witness to the departure of the bus driver. He knew what had gone on between us. He must've been struck by the contradiction of the situation: that I would have sex with a stranger I knew nothing about, when I had rejected him, Carson, who had merely been honest with me and provided me with the opportunity to practise more care than usual during sex.

It had been some time before Ant had got round to telling me that he was dating Carson, and when he did, there was nothing embarrassed or apologetic about his confession. His attitude had been quite defiant, braced perhaps for a protest, but if he had been hoping for a rise out of me, I disappointed him. I'd had several weeks to grow accustomed to the horror of the match and managed to lie convincingly of my enthusiasm for them being together. It was only later that I realised this tactic was a grave error. Ant took me to be as nonchalant as I pretended to be, and continued to treat me as his confidant. I was privy to all his hopes and doubts for the relationship with Carson, as well as the most intimate details of their sex life.

Ant, whom I'd never known to buy a book – 'That's what libraries are for' – suddenly bought three. Their titles were a torment to me. *Permanent Partners. The Male Couple. Intimacy between Men.* He always had his head in one of them or was wanting to discuss with me a particular point the authors had made. I tried to borrow them from him with the intention of losing them, but he wouldn't lend them. 'That's what libraries are for,' he said indignantly. 'I *bought* these.'

My one consolation, when Carson and Ant got together, had been the hope that Carson would continue to be as chastely hesitant with Ant as he had been with me. But Ant quickly destroyed that illusion. According to him, Carson had gone without for so long that he was a very willing and enthusiastic participant. Ant admitted they'd done it on the night of their first date, the Valentine's Day dinner. He went on to brag about how often he and Carson had sex: twice a day, before sleeping and upon waking, and innumerable times on the weekends. It transpired that Carson had gone along with Ant when he visited the bookshop and he'd bought a book as well: *The New Joy of Gay Sex.*

'Carson has an interactive approach to reading that book,' Ant chuckled.

If it wasn't bad enough hearing it all direct from Ant, I then had to endure Strauss and Blair going on about the two of them, which they did endlessly. Both of them were perpetually single and studied and reported on Ant and Carson with such fervour, it was as if they hoped some secret might be gleaned to remedy their own failure to find someone. I could've given them both the same advice: stop wearing so much make-up and get realistic about your sexual expectations.

They were both hopeless cases. Strauss was desperately attracted to straight, rough ethnic boys who were more likely to laugh at him than to love him. His attempts to butch himself up were futile, as he himself acknowledged. Occasionally he'd venture out to the Bottoms Up Bar, having borrowed Ant's leather jacket, donned his one pair of Levis and left his face and hair bare of product. But he never made any conquests there. 'You can't make a boulder out of a diamond,' he admitted to me sadly.

And Blair had hung out with gay boys for so long, she'd practically become one by osmosis. She went to gay dance parties and to gay bars and picked up there more often than any of her gay friends ever did. She never showed any concern as to what a straight boy might be doing in a gay bar to begin with. 'I suppose, like me, they enjoy the atmosphere,' she shrugged.

But no-one could accuse Blair of converting lads who were wavering over their sexuality. If anything, she converted them to homosexuality. She not only had a fondness herself for anal sex, but she also liked to introduce straight boys to the pleasures of their own prostate gland via her vibrator. 'It's doubly satisfying taking their virginity when they're completely ignorant that it even existed.'

She was simply too 'out there' for many of the boys she bedded. Despite all their swagger, many took offence the next morning when she referred to them as trade.

It was the two of them, Blair and Strauss, endlessly speculating and sighing over how Ant and Carson had found true love, that finally pushed me to speak my mind to Ant. And I spoke out of genuine alarm. Ant had made it clear that his and Carson's roles were 'versatile' within the relationship, an admission that horrified me. It just seemed inevitable that sooner or later, especially with them at it so often, a condom would break and there would be a terrible mishap. Once that scenario had occurred to me, it preyed on my mind incessantly. I couldn't put the thought aside. But it was such a delicate subject to broach. I knew how it would sound, especially coming from me. But finally, one evening, I couldn't contain myself any longer.

'I've never felt this strongly about someone before,' Ant had said. 'Everything is so much more intense between us.'

'Because it has the potential to end tragically,' I sniped back at him, and then I surprised myself, and Ant, by bursting into tears.

I regretted my words. They resounded in my mind as I sobbed, sounding more and more callous with every passing moment. I had meant to say something caring about Ant's welfare, but his declaration of love had provoked something vindictive in me. When I finally glanced up at Ant, he didn't look angry. More surprised. I felt a rush of tenderness for him and I threw myself against him. Awkwardly he enfolded me in his arms. 'I worry about you,' I sobbed into his chest. 'I'm scared . . . you'll have an accident. You and Carson. I couldn't bear anything to happen to you.'

I meant you in the singular, not the plural, but Ant misunderstood me. He patted my back. 'You don't need to worry about us. We're very careful.'

I wiped my tears away, embarrassed by my emotions.

'But what about later on . . . if he falls sick?'

'I don't believe that will ever happen to Carson. I think if anyone can beat Iris the Virus he can.'

I knew what he meant. I'd had a lecture from Carson on the benefits of a natural approach to living with HIV, a viewpoint I was highly sceptical of. However, I had to concede that Carson had educated himself thoroughly about HIV and AIDS and was better placed than I to draw his own conclusions. He read everything he could on the subject. That night of the dinner, when I had inspected his house, I hadn't bothered to peruse the titles in the study bookcase. If I had, I would've discovered it was entirely given over to such books. I only noticed later when I was called upon to help him move some of his belongings into Ant's. Carson corresponded with a group in America who were convinced of the benefits of natural therapies and were constantly sending him updates about new treatments and advances. There was always one of their pamphlets or some new book on Ant's bedside table that Carson would be reading.

I couldn't imagine how Ant could bear to have them lying around. It wasn't exactly bedtime reading, certainly not an overture to intimacy. Rather, it was a visible reminder of what must already have been paramount in both their minds.

But in addition to his own research, Carson had also had the experience of nursing Stewart. He'd watched him decline and had come to the conclusion that, though the cocktails of drugs he was taking were inhibiting the virus, they were harming his body irrevocably in the process.

'He was part of a trial. He didn't know exactly what pills he was taking. He had different pills to take countless times a day. Two of this one. Nine of another. But Stewart had absolute blind faith in those pills. He insisted that the doctors must know what they were doing, when of course they didn't. It was a trial. They were hoping to find out. But to point that out would've broken Stewart's spirit. So I said nothing and he took the pills, even though the side effects were awful. They were so strong they made him haemorrhage whenever he had to go to the toilet. I'd help him off the toilet and just the sight of that blood splattered round the bowl convinced me that I'd *never* take anything that would do that to me when it was supposed to be healing me.'

I thought Carson's abhorrence of drugs a little extreme, and probably short-sighted, but I had to admire the way he applied himself to nurturing his health. He treated it as if it was his paid employment. His inheritance from Stewart meant he didn't have to work, and avoiding that potential stress was as fundamental to Carson's routine as taking AZT was to so many others living with HIV. His days were full. He had a routine. He meditated for half an hour once he'd woken up. Then he showered, had breakfast, sat down at his computer and wrote until lunchtime. In the afternoon he might do a yoga class, have an appointment with his naturopath, indulge himself at the Korean bathhouse, shop for organic produce for dinner or simply read or take a nap. He did all the cooking and often invited me to join Ant and him for dinner.

At first I resisted Carson's dinner invitations, but when he continued to ask me, I finally acquiesced. It was a lonely, depressing task cooking for one, especially when I'd grown accustomed to cooking for Ant and myself. It was the time I missed his company most. Carson's meals were always very wholesome and bland, rather like Carson himself. When I joined them, I always took wine downstairs with me, refused their offers of apple juice and insisted the bottle be opened. It helped me endure the domestic scene if I was a little drunk. I suppose I must have drunk most of the bottle myself the night I complimented Carson on his meal (poached skinless chicken breast on organic greens) and caused offence. 'Well, Carson,' I said, 'if I'd known what a sensational cook you were, I would never have given you up so easily.'

It was the first time either Carson or I had made mention of what had happened between us. It had been meant as a joke, but neither Carson nor Ant laughed or even smiled. There was just a silence, then Carson rose to clear away the plates and Ant steered the conversation in a different direction.

The next day Ant told me off. 'Carson has forgiven you. That must be obvious from all the effort he makes towards you. But how you treated him was very cruel and it's in poor taste to try to make a joke of it now.'

I resented Ant's tone but pretended to be remorseful. Though the incident clearly demonstrated that I hadn't been forgiven, nor would I be permitted to ease the tension between Carson and myself by making light of it. My guilt would not be dismissed that readily.

I began to feel more and more aggrieved by Carson and his constant insinuating presence. He was *always* at Ant's place. Carson's house in Newtown was so large and spacious and modern, Ant's apartment was a shoe box by comparison, yet they never seemed to spend any time there. The only reason I could see for Carson residing at William Street was to irritate me. He obviously relished tormenting me by rubbing my nose in their affair. He was like a ghost, with his pale skin and penchant for wearing white, always leering up in front of me, haunting my every turn. I decided it was high time he was exorcised back to Newtown where he belonged.

I mentioned the incongruity of their spending so much time at William Street to Ant. 'Too many memories in Newtown for Carson,' he explained. 'It was Stewart's house and even though he's dead, it's still his house. All his possessions are still there. Everything's the way he arranged it. It's like a museum to Stewart with his ashes as the main exhibit.'

I was intrigued. I could not recall seeing Stewart's ashes the night of the dinner. I thought I'd had a good poke around, but I'd missed both Carson's library of AIDS books and his boyfriend's remains.

'But it's a very stylish museum,' I argued, not even convincing myself.

'I can't sleep there. I've tried a couple of times, but that bedroom gives me the creeps. I can't help thinking about the fact that I'm lying in Stewart's bed, the bed he died in.'

I was aghast. 'What? Are you sure? Wouldn't he have died in the hospital?'

'He wanted to die at home. He *arranged* it that way.'

There was something in Ant's face that made me pause. 'What do you mean exactly?'

'He self-delivered.'

It took me a moment to take in the expression. 'Did Carson find him?' I asked tentatively.

'Find him! Carson had to help him. Sit there and make sure it worked.'

I was revolted. I felt my face screw up in distaste. 'Couldn't he at least get rid of the bed and buy a new one?'

'It doesn't bother Carson and it is a very expensive bed. It's very nice to lie on, if you can get past what happened in it. Which I can't.'

There wasn't much else I could say really.

Carson more or less lived with Ant and in May he was moving in officially. I had already helped with the transfer of his essential belongings. But then Carson went on to announce that he was selling Stewart's house. Suddenly the situation seemed horribly permanent.

'Actually, it was you that put the idea in my head,' Carson told me. 'That night when you came for dinner and spoke your mind about Newtown. It got me thinking about living over in the Eastern Suburbs and what a good change it might be for me.'

All I could do was try to smile and say how lovely and how delighted I was to be an inspiration for change.

Having interfered once to my own detriment in the Carson-Ant romance, I was reluctant to meddle again. But that the Newtown house was to be sold, and Carson in permanent residence beneath me, galvanised me into action. That was too intolerable to allow to happen. I skipped a class and called on Carson when I knew he would be at home working at his computer. I reminded him about his offer of breakfast. 'Sure,' he said, but his smile was uncertain and I could tell he was nervous, even suspicious, that I was finally responding to his efforts of hospitality.

It was the first time we'd been alone together since the evening of his confession. I walked into the apartment and stopped in front of the computer, scanning what was on the screen as quickly as I could. 'Oh, I'm sorry,' I said. 'I've interrupted your writing.'

'That's okay,' said Carson, stepping in front of me to block my view. 'I'd only just gotten started.'

I hadn't managed to read much. I had been scanning through for Ant's name but there had been no sign of it. Stewart's name hadn't jumped out at me either. Though there had been enough ripe language to make it clear that I was reading some sort of sex scene.

'I do hope your writing's not going to suffer when you move in permanently,' I remarked.

Carson was occupied saving the document. He switched off the computer and turned to face me. 'It's reasonably quiet here during the day, when I work, if that's what you mean,' he replied coolly.

'Actually, I was thinking more of the fact that you won't have your own space, your own study. If Ant's at home, you won't be able to work.'

I could tell by the look that flickered over his face that he hadn't considered that. 'I write during the day, when he's at work,' he said, a note of defensiveness creeping into his voice.

'Oh well, that should work out fine,' I said breezily, hoping Carson caught the undertone that I was certain it wouldn't.

'Coffee?' asked Carson, determined to change the subject.

'Thanks.'

While Carson was in the kitchen grinding the beans, I glanced around the desk. There was a black bound notebook open alongside the computer and I ran my eyes down the page. I'd thought, with a jump of excitement, that perhaps it was Carson's little black book, his index of past lovers, but it proved to be only a jumble of notes. The writing was very careless, almost impossible to read, and I wouldn't have strained to do so if my eye hadn't happened to catch on my own name. Stephen Spear. There was a note alongside my name, which I had to peer at very closely to decipher. I realised, with a start, that it said *HIS BETRAYAL!* The two words were capitalised and punctuated with an exclamation mark.

I became aware that Carson had stopped grinding the coffee beans. He would be back at any moment. Quickly I scanned through what else was written on the page, but most of it was illegible or made little sense. The notebook was obviously where Carson jotted down his lines of inspiration for his memoirs. I turned away from the desk. I wasn't that surprised I'd found my way into his book. What writer wouldn't feel inspired by the golden boy? Though I really did feel that I ought to be the main protagonist and not sidelined as some minor character. But that phrase attached to my name concerned me. Betrayal? That was an utterly overblown view of what had happened between the two of us.

Carson returned from the kitchen and I pretended to be looking at the photos on the noticeboard. He began making conversation about his plans to rearrange the flat once he'd moved more of his belongings in. I wasn't really listening. I was preoccupied by the realisation that Carson was fashioning me into the villain of his melodramatic memoir. Suddenly I became aware that he was waiting for me to reply to something he'd said. I had no idea of what the question had been so I just plunged straight into what I had to say to him.

'Well, to be frank, I'm surprised that you'd even consider moving in here.'

Carson looked startled. 'But we want to live together,' he said firmly.

'Yes, and you must. But it's important that it's in a space which is liveable. Carson, you're used to a two-storey terrace all to yourself. It'll drive you mad living here. It'll be so constricting. It's all right for one person, and maybe for two temporarily, but not long-term. Your relationship will suffer. I really think you should look for something larger. A two bedroom, somewhere with an outlook. A water view would be soothing for a writer. Perhaps Bondi?'

Bondi would be the perfect place for the two of them. It was far enough away from Kings Cross that I need never see them unless I chose to.

I could tell that Carson was suspicious of me. A caution had crept into that eager face of his, but I knew my argument was persuasive and that he must recognise the sense in it.

'Look, Carson, living together can be the kiss of death for a relationship. If you're going to do it, make sure you're in a place that is large enough and nice enough to make it workable.'

Carson looked thoughtful.

A few days later Ant popped up to my flat, his face flushed with excitement, to thank me for my advice. 'Carson and I have decided to look for a two bedroom apartment to *buy*,' he announced.

He stood there grinning at me, enjoying the look of shock

on my face. I was completely staggered. I couldn't believe it. Ant who fussed about the rising price of cappuccinos was buying *an apartment*. I opened my mouth to protest, but Ant quickly began to speak, rationalising their extraordinary decision. He was very casual about it, playing down the commitment it signified and trying to make it sound like a merely practical arrangement. 'It's dead money, renting. You see no benefit from it, but it's too much of a strain buying a place that's at all decent on your own in Sydney. The property market is so expensive. But for two people it's quite affordable. We realised if we were going to live together we might as well pay off a mortgage and get some benefit out of it financially.'

'But Carson doesn't have any money,' I argued.

'He'll have plenty once he sells that house in Newtown.'

That stumped me. 'And . . . and you have that sort of money for a deposit?'

'I have some savings,' said Ant evasively.

I was in shock. This was completely ludicrous. They barely knew one another.

'Is this a late April Fool's prank?' I finally asked.

'No,' said Ant indignantly.

'Well, it's a joke,' I snapped, unable to stop myself. 'I'm sorry but *really*. You've only known each other a couple of months. How do you know if you're even compatible to live together? It's an enormous step to buy an apartment together. A more sensible approach would be to try renting together first.'

Ant dropped his casual manner. Stopped acting so cool and clinical about the plan. 'We know it's ambitious but it's going to work out,' he confided with a girlish coyness. 'We love each other.'

That was the last thing I wanted to hear. 'Well, I'm glad you're so confident,' I retorted. 'Because I have premonitions of disaster.'

'We want to make a commitment to one another. A big commitment.'

'Why don't you commit to not cheating on each other?

Surely that would be a big enough challenge.'

Ant's face coloured. 'We've already discussed that. Look, Stephen, I know from your perspective it might seem premature, but our situation is different. We may not have the luxury of years and years together. We don't want to waste any time.'

With that sentence he revealed exactly how powerless I was to dissuade him, let alone compete. There was no possible rebuttal to that argument. Carson had used it to set his trap, and what a trap. Financially they would be bound to one another. There was nothing I could say. I let Ant rattle on about their plans, nodding and smiling as best I could.

I went out for a drink with Strauss that night. I had to have someone else agree that what Ant was planning was preposterous. 'Oh, the impetuous nature of love,' Strauss sighed. 'The foolish, foolish things it leads one to do, and of course queens are the worst. The absolute worst. They scoff about love, disclaim it, disown it, but as soon as there's the slightest scent of it, they seize it and try to preserve it with property settlements and joint savings accounts.'

I echoed his sentiments.

'But then who would have thought Antonio was the marrying kind?' said Strauss with a piercing look at me. 'If I'd had the least notion, I'd have offered myself up to him along with my glory box a long time ago. I wonder what dowry that sly little Carson had to offer besides his cute little butt and that air of innocence.'

I could've told Strauss then and there about Carson's status, and it crossed my mind to do just that. But Ant's reprimand – 'that's confidential' – came into my mind. He was right. It was not something to be gossiped about lightly.

'It's no act,' I said instead. 'I dated him briefly and nothing happened between us. He may not be innocent, but he's kind of frigid.'

'Hmm, that's not what I've heard.'

'*What?*'

'That boy has a past,' said Strauss authoritatively.

'Really? Who told you that?'

Strauss paused, enjoying himself. 'Ginger. Do you know her? She works William Street now and again. I was chatting to her one night when Carson and Antonio arrived home from somewhere. Ginger recognised him, though she said back when she knew him, Carson was his surname.

'Did he recognise her?'

'Hardly. She knew him before she started wearing dresses. She used to work as a boy at one of the agencies, before she realised she looked better and could make more money by putting a dress on. She knew Carson back then.'

'Are you saying Carson used to be a prostitute?'

'*I'm* not saying it. Ginger's saying it.'

My excitement must have shown on my face because Strauss cautioned me. 'Now don't go running off saying anything to Antonio. Ginger's addled her brain over the years. Some mornings she can barely recognise herself in the bathroom mirror, so I wouldn't go taking anything she said as gospel truth.'

'But she knew his name,' I pointed out. 'I won't say anything to Ant but I will ask Ginger a few questions next time I see her.'

I excused myself from Strauss soon after that. I *had* to talk to Ginger immediately. This was information that Ant ought to know about before he embarked on this folly of home-ownership. But Ginger wasn't around when I got home. Sass wasn't there either. I asked one of the other girls if she knew Ginger but she just shrugged and walked away from me. I decided to ask Jo-Jo. She was standing at the top of the Chard Steps, surveying the square and street below her. I wasn't on speaking terms with Jo-Jo the way I was with Sass. She wasn't the type to wave hello and ask how things were going or even to acknowledge me with a smile. But I had walked past her so many evenings, she had to know my face. Jo-Jo was conferring with her crony, whom Strauss had christened Suzy Sixty-Nine. Not in reference to the sexual position, but because he reckoned that was her age. Neither of them even bothered to give me a glance as I walked up the stairs towards them. It was only when I stopped next to them that Jo-Jo turned to look at me with an enquiring gaze.

'Excuse me,' I said. 'I'm looking for Ginger.'

Jo-Jo's eyes showed a spark of interest. 'What'd ya want with her?'

'I've just got something to ask her.'

Jo-Jo turned back to survey William Street. 'She's not around.'

'Has she been here tonight?'

Jo-Jo didn't bother to answer. She was occupied lighting herself a cigarette.

'She's gone north, hasn't she?' put in Suzy, but Jo-Jo ignored her as well.

'Is she on holiday?' I asked.

At that Jo-Jo began to laugh and Suzy joined in. 'A working holiday,' Jo-Jo finally cackled.

'Is she coming back?'

'I hope not.'

It was clear that was all Jo-Jo had to say on the subject. I muttered my thanks and trudged back down the stairs. I couldn't believe my bad luck. To have had this opportunity waved in my face and then snatched away again. All my enthusiasm seeped away. It was late, almost two in the morning, and suddenly I felt very tired. I felt as if I barely had the energy to walk up the stairs to my apartment.

I was passing Ant's door when suddenly it occurred to me. Carson's memoir. There had to be mention of his prostitution days there. That would have to be the heart of his book. From what I'd learnt of his life story, there was nothing else that could possibly be of interest to a mass readership. I hurried up the stairs to my flat and ran to the kitchen drawer. It was still there of course. Where I had hidden it. My copy of the key to Ant's apartment. I clutched it in my hand. I could barely wait to put it to use.

But I was obliged to wait. Several days. Until I knew for

certain that their apartment would be empty. On Thursday afternoon Carson did a yoga class in Newtown. I waited until then, skipped my afternoon lecture and let myself into their apartment. I didn't feel at all nervous about trespassing. I felt perfectly justified in looking through Carson's writings. After all, I had seen evidence that he was incorporating me into his story and, what's more, painting me in an unflattering light. It was only fair that I should learn exactly what he was saying about me. However, I didn't rush straight to the computer. I knew that I had plenty of time and could have a good look around for any other interesting evidence.

I hadn't really noticed on any of my previous visits how astonishingly orderly the apartment was. It was almost as if they were expecting guests, everything was so neat. It wasn't merely that the bed was made, the dishes done, the fridge stocked; there were signs that care had been taken to make the space homelike. It was this evidence of a shared life that wrenched at my heart. The two coffee cups upside down, side by side, on the dish drainer. The way they had their clothes arranged in the wardrobe: left side for Carson, right side for Ant. The framed photographs of the two of them together that were already positioned throughout the house in almost every room. When had they had time to have so many photographs taken? There was one on top of the television, another on Carson's desk, another on the bedside table.

Seeing all these photographs reminded me of the picture of him and me Ant had pinned to his noticeboard. Strauss had taken it the night of Ant's birthday dinner. The noticeboard sat on the desk, propped against the wall, but this space had been commandeered by Carson as a study. His computer took up most of the desk. The noticeboard was still there but my photograph was not. Carson had redecorated! The noticeboard had become a sort of shrine to him and Ant. There were all these photographs of the two of them and other significant mementos pinned to it: a glossy advertisement for the New Year's Eve party where they had met, a business card from

Darley Street Thai where they had celebrated Valentine's Day.

I went through the drawers of the desk. I looked in Ant's photo album. The photograph of the two of us together was not in either of those places. I couldn't believe that Carson would've had the gumption to throw it out, but it didn't seem to be in any of the obvious (and not so obvious) places. I began to wonder whether Carson had more spirit than I'd given him credit for.

One thing I did come across in the desk drawer was Ant's financial records. I was staggered by what he had in savings when all the time I'd known him he'd cried poor. He had a term deposit of twelve thousand dollars and four thousand dollars in his savings account.

That discovery prompted me to search the bedroom. I don't know exactly what I was looking for. Porn magazines. Sex toys. Handcuffs. Evidence of some kinky fetish of Carson's or perhaps even some clue that the sexual side of their relationship was already failing. But if there were any such aids, they were well concealed. The only testimony to their sex life was the inevitable Wet Stuff by the bed.

I turned my attention to the computer. I switched it on and brought up the directory of files. There was a series of files titled 'Memoir' and numbered. I retrieved 'Memoir 1' and quickly scanned through a few pages to ascertain if it really was what I was after. It was. Carson was indeed writing his life story, labouring under the illusion that his misfortunes were the stuff of literature. I had brought a floppy disk with me and I copied the files onto it.

There was a copying shop on William Street and I took the disk there and had the files printed out. I couldn't risk Carson noticing that the paper in his printer had suddenly been depleted. There was almost fifty pages of it. Five chapters.

I went home, settled myself on the sofa with a strong coffee – I was certain I was going to need some stimulation to get through it – and began to read the manuscript. Carson's story.

part two

I should never have been on the beach after midnight. Should never have lingered when I saw the figure silhouetted in the moonlight, standing on the northern headland, staring out to sea.

But I did linger. I waited there. Just out of reach of the breaking waves. My eyes fixed on the man – somehow I knew it had to be a man – and willed him to notice me.

I've often thought back on that moment and puzzled over my behaviour. I was very young, too young to know what a man loitering in a public place after midnight might mean. Yet somehow I did know. Instinctively. I felt compelled to wait there and be noticed. It was rather like finding myself in a well-known play, something we'd studied at school, and realising once it began that I did know the lines and the actions after all. When the man on the headland did finally notice me, he stood transfixed, and I understood that he too knew the play by heart.

It's difficult to explain but it's how I imagine hypnotism works, although obviously in the dark and at that distance, I couldn't look into his eyes. But that's how it felt. That I was being commanded by the force of that man's will to wait for him and I knew I must obey. I watched him walk towards me, his gait loaded with intent.

I was drunk. Joanne and I had shared a six pack in the back seat of Kerry's brother's Torana, though she barely bothered to sip at her can. Joanne had other things on her mind, namely me. I still clasped the final can from that six pack in my hand, even though I'd finished it some time ago. That's how drunk I was. Too drunk to think to drop it. But at that moment, watching the man approach, I felt completely lucid. I had no sense of danger. I crouched down to wait for him. It didn't occur to me that perhaps I should stand poised, ready to run if necessary.

I glanced about. The beach was utterly deserted. Sometimes there were boys hanging round outside the surf lifesaving club, drinking illicitly, but not tonight. They were all at the disco. No cars passed by. Even most of the houses up on the hill were in darkness. It was well after midnight and this was the quiet, posh part of town. Beyond those shadowy houses the escarpment loomed, shrouded in mist, looking all the more forbidding because it was half hidden. The road would be tricky, under mist, in darkness, and I hoped Kerry wouldn't hare off up there drunk. Suddenly something caught my eye, to the south, and I turned sharply. A sudden flash of flame from one of the factory smoke stacks and then, just as quickly, it was gone. A plume of white smoke billowed luminous in the moonlight for a few moments, then faded into the gloom.

I said 'Sure,' when he stood over me and offered me a cigarette. He crouched down beside me, grinning, and somehow I knew from the way his eyes raked over me that I was saying yes to more than just a cigarette.

'Perhaps you're too young for me to go offering cigarettes to? You too young to smoke, son?'

'Reckon I'm old enough to try whatever I like,' I said boldly.

'Guess if you're old enough to get yourself drunk, you're old enough to smoke,' the man laughed.

'I reckon.'

The man's hand moved swiftly. His fingers cradled my jaw. His face loomed close, searching mine in the dim light of the moon. The beers had numbed any sense of caution. I stared right on back at him. I could feel the pressure of bone hard upon bone as he tilted my face this way, then that. Then his fingers relaxed and playfully tickled my jawline. 'You even shaving yet, son?'

'I've been shaving for years,' I replied hotly. 'I could grow a moustache like yours, except I don't want to look stupid.'

The man chuckled and let his fingers drop away from my face. I could tell he wasn't from round here. That he didn't work locally. He looked down at the sand for a moment, tracing his finger in it, straying close to my own clenched hand, then retreating again. I could smell the apple scent of his shampoo in his hair as he bent towards me. Beyond him, there was another flash of flame from the steelworks.

'So how about that cigarette then?' I asked.

The man grinned and looked up. 'Sorry. Distracted.'

But the way his eyes lingered on me as he said that word let me know for certain that I was the distraction. I knew then that we both had the same thing in mind.

He started slapping at his jacket pockets. 'Damn. You know, I think I must've left my smokes back in the car. Damn it.'

But he didn't look annoyed. He was still grinning at me. I wondered if there really had been any cigarettes. If he even smoked. He was still crouched down close to me. His breath was in my face. It smelt of mint, not of nicotine.

We studied one another in silence. The smile slipped from his face. His eyes were no longer so knowing. They were asking silent questions. I realised I had to give him a sign. He had mentioned my age several times. It made him nervous.

'You sure they're not in your pockets?' I said lightly, reaching a hand out to pat the left-hand pocket of his jeans. I could feel the rhythm of the man's breath change in my ear. 'Not there,' I observed.

The man eased himself to his feet. 'I think . . . you'll find something . . . if you try the other pocket,' he whispered.

I could see it before I touched it. It jutted out from his fly at an angle. When my fingers touched the top of his right-hand pocket, it was there, prominent through the denim. The head of it peeked over the rim of the pocket. That's how big it was. I clasped it as best I could through the denim. I had never touched a man's penis before. Other boys', sure. On school camps we all got them out and played around with each other, trying to work out whose was the biggest. But that had been years and years ago, before puberty.

The man threw his head back and thrust his hips forward, which made it seem even bigger, straining against his jeans. 'Take it out,' he said softly.

His jeans were so tight it was difficult manoeuvring the buttons on the fly, but once I'd finally fiddled one free, the remainder sprang open readily. I tugged the jeans down his hips. He wasn't wearing underwear. His cock sprang out towards me as if it was introducing itself.

'Put it in your mouth.'

That made me hesitate. But the man's hands grasped me either side of my head and began to gently press my face forward, his voice wheedling, pleading. 'Just for a second. Put my cock in your mouth for just a second.

You don't know how much it would turn me on. Just to see your lips around it for a second. Just a second. Please. Please.'

I opened my mouth to say, 'No way' and the man nudged his cock into my mouth. I let him push it round in there for a while and then I pulled back from him.

'Good boy. Good boy.'

The man's hands were in my hair, patting my head. 'You liked sucking on that, didn't you? You liked having it in your mouth?'

I was afraid to say anything in case he took the opportunity to put it back in again. I nodded dumbly. He pulled me to my feet effortlessly and I was amazed at the strength of him. It should have been scary that he was so much stronger, that I was physically at his mercy, but it wasn't frightening. It was thrilling.

'The things I could do to you, sonny,' he whispered in my ear and his hand slipped down the back of my pants.

I undid the button on my jeans by way of reply and let them fall.

His mouth sealed over mine. His moustache was rasping against my lips and his fingers began delving into a place where they shouldn't have strayed and I began to squirm a little in protest. But his grip was so commanding, I gave in. 'You'll like this,' he whispered in my ear and after a little while I found that he was right.

He kept repeating something which I couldn't understand. I thought he was saying, 'So long' and every time he said it, I gripped him tighter, not wanting him to go. But eventually I realised he was saying, 'So young.'

He pulled my T-shirt over my head and then knelt down in the sand. I began to feel a little unsteady on my feet. I could feel his breath against the back of my legs, rising higher, coming faster, panting. His big hands encircled my legs, gripped them hard, then eased them apart. His breath was hot, so hot that it almost felt wet. It took me a moment to realise that something had changed. Something wet was burrowing, searching between my buttocks, and I thought it must have been his hand until I felt the unmistakable bristle of his moustache.

My instinct was to pull away when I realised what he was doing back there and in a public place! *His grip on me had relaxed and I realised I could wrench myself free of him if I'd wanted to . . .*

I didn't. The sensation refuted everything else. After a while my legs simply melted beneath me and I toppled over onto the sand. His tongue danced up the backs of my legs, mounting higher and higher. My chin sank into the sand. I was oblivious to everything. The chill of the evening air, the possibility of strolling holiday-makers, the frothing waves cresting and creeping steadily closer.

I must have been practically delirious not to have noticed immediately when he entered me. He must have been astonishingly gentle. But it was such a gradual transition that I truly couldn't pinpoint the moment. When it did begin to hurt, he whispered reassurances in my ear, told me to relax and the pain would ease. He grasped my penis and that seemed to help me forget the other. Still I was shocked when I felt his thighs pressed up against my haunches and I realised he had all of that well and truly pushed up inside me.

The first thrust of his hips rattled me. My entire body tensed from head to toe. My face pined forward towards the sea. My breath gasped loud in my ears, but it was a sigh more than a protest. The waves crashed and he thrust again and again in time with them. My breath quickened and I knew I was going to come too quickly and spoil everything when it had only just begun, but I couldn't speak to slow him down, to stop him. I began to thrash upon the sand like a landed trout and his breath was in my ear, hoarse and ragged, whispering encouragement. I gave a final gasping sigh and as if on cue, as if it knew there would soon be something that needed to be washed away, the sea swirled beneath my chin and filled my gaping mouth with foaming salt water.

I had been grateful when Kerry had asked me to join him for a night out. 'Go down the beach. Have a few beers. Maybe go to the blue-light disco if we're pissed enough to bear it.'

I agreed eagerly. It had been a long time since we'd done anything together on a Saturday night.

Kerry and I had declared ourselves best friends back in year eight. We sat beside each other in class, ate lunch together and mucked around together out of school. But by year ten things had changed significantly. We were no longer so sure of each other.

Slowly, the 'best' in 'best friend' fell into disuse. At first it was merely a slight hesitation. Then it became a mumble so that the word was indistinct, until finally 'best' was omitted altogether. It was too awkward to say. Introductions became precarious and tentative. 'This is me . . . mate.' That hesitation said it all. A pause of regret or respect, nostalgia perhaps, for our old intimacy. That unspoken word and all that it signified continued to hover ghostlike between us.

The differences between us had begun to mount up with every year that passed. At first they were trivial: arguments over which pop star was the coolest or which of Charlie's Angels was the least angelic. I had to lie about 'Charlie's Angels'. It was one of the many television programmes Mum considered unsuitable for me to watch. But gradually our clashes assumed greater significance. Kerry couldn't understand why I still bowed to my parents' wishes. In particular, why I wouldn't rebel over attending church on Sundays with my mother. He often stayed over on weekends, which obliged him to come along with us too. Finally, one Sunday morning over breakfast, he told Mum that he was going skateboarding instead of praying. Mum was annoyed but her good manners wouldn't allow Kerry to perceive that. 'Very well, Kerry. But Robbie will still be coming to church as usual. What will you do? We'll be late if we have to drop you home.'

Kerry stared at me, waiting for me to announce my defection too.

When I failed to, he lowered his eyes over his bowl of cornflakes. 'I can walk,' he mumbled.

My superiority at school became another point of contrast as examinations and tests began to assume a greater importance. At some point during year nine, in an unspoken agreement, we stopped comparing marks. The difference between our scores had become embarrassing. At the beginning of year ten, I was upgraded into the top-streamed class while Kerry was left where he was. 'Don't go,' he said to me plaintively, clutching my arm, his eyes very solemn. He hesitated, searching for a compelling enough reason to keep me at his side. 'I won't have anyone to sit beside any more,' he finally mumbled.

His argument was feeble, but the look on his face said what his dignity wouldn't allow him to say aloud.

But to me it wasn't even a choice. There was no question. The promotion was what I had striven for. 'We'll still see each other,' I said. 'In between times.'

'It won't be the same,' said Kerry.

And he was right. It wasn't.

I had disappointed him and made him acutely aware of his own intellectual inadequacies.

It was these incidents that began to create a distance between us, small antagonisms that Kerry complained of openly and which I tried to gloss over as insignificant. But then I committed the gravest crime I could in Kerry's eyes and stretched that distance between us out into a yawning gap, a breach that could never be bridged with platitudes.

I gave up playing rugby.

As far as Kerry was concerned, the only reason for giving up rugby was if you sustained an injury that left you maimed for life. I wanted to get out before that happened. I'd had a scare. Someone had raked my face with their sprigs during a match the previous season. Mum said I was lucky I didn't lose an eye. When the time came to sign up for the new season's trials, I didn't do it. Kerry, of course, noticed. He came up to me in the schoolyard, all smiles, pleased with himself. 'They're workin' ya brain so hard in that top class of yers, y're forgettin' about the important things.'

'Yeah?'

'The rugby trials, man. Ya didn't sign up. I had to do it for ya.'

I was too scared of his reaction to tell him then and there. All I could do was mutter, 'Thanks.' But he must've suspected something. My reaction was so muted. He stood there looking at me, hands in his pockets. 'We gotta get in trainin' for them.'

'Okay,' I nodded, managing a grin.

It was the least I could do. Help him train. To make up for the fact that I was going to be letting him down again. Kicking a ball round with Kerry, just the two of us, had always been the part I liked best anyway.

Before I went home from school that day, I went to the noticeboard and scrawled over my name so that it couldn't be read.

The trials were scheduled a week later after school. When I walked out of my final class that day, Kerry was waiting for me in the corridor, his rugby boots tied together by their laces, draped over one shoulder. 'I came to collect ya,' he said firmly.

I hesitated. Already, being in different classes meant we saw a lot less of one another. Once he was going to rugby practices and matches and I wasn't, we would practically never see each other. I wondered if he'd seen my name crossed out on the list. He knew. I could see it in his face but hope glimmered there too. That there'd been some sort of mix-up and I would have the explanation to set it straight. I closed my eyes. The look on Kerry's face was making it so difficult to stick to my decision. If I was selected for one of the top teams, and during our training sessions Kerry kept insisting I would be because I was so fast, I'd be playing against guys who were two or three years older, heavier and meaner. The grit and fury of such opponents was simply too daunting.

I opened my eyes and spoke. 'My parents don't want me to play any more.'

There was some truth in that. Mum had demanded that I give up when she saw those scratches on my face, though she hadn't mentioned it since.

'So?'

Kerry never paid any attention to his own parents.

'I'll come to all your games. I'll watch you score the tries,' I said quickly.

Kerry's face became heavy and suspicious. 'Yer name was crossed out.'

Slowly I nodded.

'I wrote it up again,' said Kerry defiantly.

'You shouldn't have,' I said.

Kerry had one hand slid inside the boot that dangled over his shoulder, as if it were a pocket. As we talked he pressed harder and harder into that boot. The sprigs pressed into the flesh of his thigh so that it puckered and swelled red. Kerry's face was as red as that worried skin. He was on the verge of saying something.

'Ya've got scared in that poofter class of yers,' he suddenly jeered.

Our eyes locked for a moment. Then Kerry snatched up his duffel bag which lay at his feet and stalked off down the corridor.

'I'll come and watch you try out,' I called out after him, my voice quavering.

Perhaps he didn't hear me. He didn't turn and wait for me to catch up. He kept walking. I didn't feel welcome after that and decided it might be better to stay away. I walked home, stung by Kerry's words. He'd hit upon the truth with his taunt. The other reason I could no longer play rugby. The real reason.

The previous season I'd gotten an erection, in the showers with my team mates all around me. I'd had to turn and face the wall and wait for it to subside. Luckily the water ran cold and everyone scrambled out. In the evacuation, I got to my towel without anyone noticing. Or at least without anyone saying anything aloud. I was too scared to meet anyone's eye until I was out of the changing room. The showers after the match were obligatory. The coach took that time to go over the match with us. You had to be there. It would be peculiar to excuse yourself as soon as the match finished.

I'd been looking at Kerry when I'd gotten hard.

Kerry was selected for the first fifteen and I did go to watch all his matches. I'd wait around for him afterwards and he'd acknowledge me with a wave or sometimes come over to talk if they'd won or he'd scored a try. His conversation always aimed to make me feel that I was missing out. He bragged about the parties he was going to with his team mates. Wild parties, where the women were as plentiful as the beers. I hoped that was just talk, but several times I noticed him waving and grinning at girls on the sidelines.

He was the youngest on the team. Fifteen. I was never invited to join him and his new mates. I noticed when he was obliged to introduce me to some of them that I'd become not even a mate, but merely 'someone who used to be in me class'.

Even though his friendship had become so grudging, I still went every Saturday to watch him play. I hoped to impress him with my faithfulness. I noticed that the girls he was friendly with never turned out if it was raining. I hoped that when the rugby season finished, things might be able to revert to the way they'd been before. But in fact it was worse. At least when the games were on I got to see him every Saturday, even if he didn't always talk to me or acknowledge me. At school I rarely saw him. Even at lunchtimes he never seemed to be in the cafeteria or hanging out anywhere. I figured he was probably off having a cigarette somewhere, but a boy from my old class mentioned that Kerry was cutting classes.

I was shocked when he did finally make the effort to seek me out. It was so unexpected. I walked out of church one Sunday and there he was, sitting on the brick fence across the street, swinging his legs and smoking a cigarette. He waved casually when he saw me and I hurried over. 'Hi,' I said eagerly. 'What are you up to?'

'Jus' on me way home. I was walkin' along this street and then I recognised the church and I thought, hey betcha old Robbie's inside there prayin'. So I figured I'd wait and see, check ya hadn't turned into some old heathen, but sure enough, here ya are. Still yer mother's son.'

Kerry's breath was rank. It was midday and it was obvious that he hadn't been home yet. I didn't know what to say. His words and the tone of his voice had an insulting edge to them, but the very fact of his presence, that he had sought me out at all, seemed to indicate something.

Suddenly Mum was at my side. 'Why, hello, Kerry. We never see you any more. Too busy being a rugby star, I hear.'

'Yeah, somethin' like that, Mrs Carson,' Kerry mumbled.

'What are you doing? Perhaps you'd like to join us for Sunday lunch, or is your mother expecting you?'

Kerry grinned sheepishly. 'She's been expectin' me for the last twelve hours. Guess a few more hours won't hurt.'

I looked at the ground. I could imagine the disapproval on Mum's face.

'She'll be worried about you then. We'll drop you home.'

'I can phone her from yer place.'

'I'll drive you home, Kerry, and you can ask your mother's permission.'

'Forget it, forget it.'

Kerry sprang off the wall and started slouching off down the street. Mum stood there hesitating. Finally she turned to me. 'Well! I can understand why we no longer see anything of that young man. I'm relieved that you're sensible enough to recognise a bad influence and avoid it.'

We drove home. Mum wondering aloud at the state of Kerry all the way. Over lunch she informed my father that Kerry had become a delinquent and that his parents must be at their wits' end.

Later, when my parents went out for their usual Sunday afternoon drive, I rang him. His mother answered and brusquely said he was asleep. She hung up before I could ask her to pass on a message.

The next morning I loitered around the school entrance waiting for Kerry to arrive. I felt quite desperate about seeing him. I had convinced myself that it was a sign, his turning up to see me at church. Kerry wanted me back as his best friend. But when he finally did stroll through the school gates, five minutes after the bell for the first class of the day, he didn't seem touched to find me waiting for him. He lowered his sunglasses and studied me quizzically. I felt stupid.

'I was just wondering if you were okay,' I said.

'I'm fine,' said Kerry. 'Jus' late for class. As usual.'

'I phoned you yesterday.'

Kerry shrugged. 'And?'

'I dunno. I guess, I thought you wanted to hang out or something.'

Kerry said nothing.

'We could do something on the weekend like we used to.'

'Play cards with yer parents?' Kerry sneered. 'Get real.'

Kerry kept walking and I followed him silently. When we reached the maths block, he turned. 'Y're late for yer poofter class,' he said.

'So?'

That made Kerry grin. 'Okay, Robbie. Y'can come out with me if you like. Next Saturday. We'll go down the beach. Have a few beers. Maybe go to the blue-light disco if we're pissed enough to bear it.'

'Great,' I agreed.

Kerry walked into the maths block. As soon as he was out of sight, I started to run to my English class.

Kerry had his older brother's car on Saturday night. I met him at his place. I was surprised when we stopped outside a house on Sutton Street and Kerry honked on the horn. I felt a surge of disappointment. He'd evidently invited some of his new friends along as well. The door of the house opened and I recognised the figure that stepped out onto the porch. Her long hair was illuminated, made golden by the light from the room behind her. Sonya Beck. There was someone else with her, another girl I vaguely recognised as being in the same class as Sonya. The two of them flounced down the garden path towards us, giggling and clutching one another as if they were unused to their high-heeled shoes.

'Hi, guys,' cooed Sonya as she approached the car.

'Jump in,' said Kerry.

I was disappointed when Sonya got in the front seat with Kerry. I'd been captivated by her for some time. She was one of the prettiest girls at our sister school, with her pert little face and long brown hair that she swept into so many different styles, altering her appearance every time. Her hair was her mystery. You never knew how it was going to be the next time you saw her. I would've liked to call for her in the mornings, help her decide on a style, watch her fix it that way, then escort her to school.

'This is Joanne,' said Kerry as the other girl climbed into the back seat.

We exchanged hellos but I barely glanced at her. I was intrigued to notice that Sonya had kissed Kerry on the mouth before settling back in her seat and putting on her seat belt. We drove to the beach. Kerry and Sonya were laughing and talking in the front, but it was impossible for me to hear and join in the conversation. The music on the stereo was turned up too loudly.

We parked up on the hill, above the surf lifesaving club. Kerry jumped out immediately to grab the beers out of the boot. 'Pa-a-arty,' he crowed as he passed a six pack over to Joanne and me in the back seat.

I was relieved to see that they were cans. I had never mastered the technique of flicking the caps off bottles using another unopened bottle. It seemed like every other kid at school could do it, even most of the girls, but it was beyond me. I had practised at home for hours and hours using a couple of bottles of Coke, but I could never get the hang of it. I had never been game to ask Kerry or anyone else for lessons. Admitting to such an inadequacy would only result in weeks and weeks of teasing and humiliation. When I went to parties, which wasn't very often, I carried a bottle opener in my pocket and hoped that I'd be able to use it discreetly.

I cracked open a can and handed it to Joanne. 'Thank you,' she said in a voice that was more of a whisper.

Her fingers encircled mine as she took the can, and I looked at her in surprise. Her smile seemed awfully exaggerated, but maybe it was her lipstick. It looked peculiar, so brashly red on someone so young. I smiled back at her as I eased my fingers out from underneath hers. 'I gotta open one for myself,' I mumbled.

'We can share this one,' Joanne said lightly.

'Yeah?'

I wasn't too sure about that. I imagined that her lipstick would end up all over the can, she had applied so much. 'Actually I'm feeling pretty thirsty. Think I need one all to myself.'

'Oh, you boys. There's more to life than drinking beer,' Sonya protested from the front seat.

'Don't I know it,' growled Kerry, lunging at her and rolling round on top of her.

Sonya screamed. 'Kerry! Not yet. Not with the others . . . Kerry!'

But her protestations were pretty feeble. They had that air of ritual about them, as if they'd been voiced many times before and ignored then as well. The resignation in her voice made me wonder anew if Sonya did deserve the nickname she had round our school. On Ya Back Sonya Beck. Through the gap between the front seats I could see a lot of Sonya's legs and even a glimpse of her panties. Her skirt had ridden up or Kerry had pushed it up. That sight reminded me that Kerry had commented on that skirt and on Sonya's legs when she and Joanne had walked towards the car. It struck me as more of the macho swagger he must've picked up from his team mates. I didn't even attempt to play along. I knew it wouldn't sound convincing. My voice would never carry that same brute enthusiasm that came so naturally to Kerry.

Not that I was entirely indifferent to girls. I did have crushes on certain girls occasionally. But my obsessions were so innocent: vague and fanciful. I fell in love with them from the neck up. Their faces. Their hair.

Their personalities, which were so much kinder and more generous than the guys'. I had no comprehension of what lay below the neck and felt intimidated rather than interested in ever finding out. I couldn't imagine doing anything with Sonya other than kissing her and becoming lost in that long hair of hers, which I imagined would cascade over the both of us, shielding us as we kissed

My interest in Sonya went unspoken. She saw Greg Arthur for years and when that broke up, I had a brief flare of hope. Sonya was my dream date for our high school formal and suddenly that actually seemed possible. I imagined her on my arm, in a dazzling new dress, with her hair piled up high on her head and kissing her at length when the night was over. Meanwhile, guys like Kerry and Jed Morgan were loudly announcing their own plans for the formal night. They'd booked a room in a nearby motel where they could sneak their dates off to during the course of the night. What they had in mind could not be achieved in dark corners of the school assembly hall.

I was devastated when I learnt that Sonya had agreed to go to the formal with Jed. Especially as I knew what he had in mind. If she hadn't disappointed me, I might've warned her.

Afterwards I felt guilty that I hadn't. Jed circulated stories that Sonya had gone all the way, and for a while Sonya and her coterie of girlfriends ignored every boy on principle for spreading such a slur. But whenever I witnessed Sonya and Jed encounter one another, at some place like the milkbar or the movies, I'd watch her closely. Her cheeks would flush pink but she'd raise her face and stare at Jed Morgan with a haughty grace. It was always him that ended up shamefully looking away.

Sonya announced that she had to go to the toilet block. 'Kerry, I have to,' she said, an edge creeping into her voice.

Kerry seemed to recognise that tone of voice because he retreated across the gear stick to the driver's seat. Sonya sat up straight, rearranged her skirt and patted her hair back into place. 'Come on, Joanne,' said Sonya.

Joanne smiled helplessly at me. 'Sorry,' she murmured.

It was as Joanne got out of the car that I noticed she was wearing a skirt even shorter than Sonya's.

Kerry cracked a beer in the front seat and gulped at it greedily. 'Wow! That Sonya. Jed told me she was a goer. Sure works up a thirst in a guy.'

'Yeah,' I said dispiritedly.

'How were ya gettin' on in the back with Joanne? Sonya tells me she's got the hots for ya.'

I got a lurching feeling in my stomach when Kerry said that. I hoped he was just teasing, spinning bullshit as he usually was ninety per cent of the time. But somehow I knew this had the ring of truth to it. The short skirt. The hand encircling mine. The shy, hopeful smiles. It all made sense in a very unsettling way. I felt trapped. Meanwhile, Kerry kept talking about his hopes for the evening with Sonya and instructed me to make Joanne and myself scarce if things started hotting up in the front seat. 'I reckon she's gone to the ladies to put her diaphragm in. That means I'm in tonight, matey. Maybe y'are too. Maybe Joanne's putting hers in too. You know she really likes ya.'

I reached for another beer. I had only the vaguest idea of the purpose of a diaphragm. The thought of yet another unknown added to all the other mysteries of Joanne's body only made me feel more nervous and uneasy. I skolled that beer. By the time Sonya and Joanne returned, I had almost polished off my third can. As soon as Sonya slid back into the front seat, Kerry climbed on top of her. 'Kerry,' she protested.

'I missed ya, darlin',' said Kerry, before sealing his mouth over hers.

I was watching his hand manoeuvre down the front of her shirt when suddenly I became aware of Joanne sitting beside me, her eyes fixed reproachfully upon me. I felt obliged to do something, so I put my arm around her. Joanne grasped me around the waist and rested her cheek against my chest. I was surprised how nice that felt and began to feel a little more relaxed. I stroked her hair, or at least tried to. It wasn't really the sort of hair you could run your fingers through. It was short and spiky and stiff with gel, so I sort of patted it as best I could. I didn't look at her. I was aware that she had twisted her head back and was looking up at me. If our eyes met, I would be obliged to kiss her. I kept looking ahead at Kerry and Sonya and what was going on in the front seat. Sonya's hands were kneading Kerry's butt. I couldn't see exactly what he was doing to Sonya but from the murmurs and grunts he was making, it sure sounded like he was enjoying himself.

Suddenly, unexpectedly, the passenger seat reclined back and with a whoop from both of them, Kerry and Sonya plopped down alongside us.

Joanne squealed and pressed herself even closer to me. I could see that Kerry's hand was down the side of the seat. He had released the lever. He stopped kissing Sonya for a moment and looked up at me with a big grin on his face and winked. Then he began to kiss his way down Sonya's neck to her breasts. She was supine, her eyes closed, throat trembling and her hair, her splendid hair, splayed across the back seat. Kerry's jeans had ridden down on his hips. I could see the waistband of his Jockeys and the sight of Sonya's hand clasped there on his buttock made me begin to grow hard.

Joanne and I were wedged up in the corner together and I guess her face was so close to my crotch that I shouldn't have been surprised that she noticed what was going on down there. But I almost jumped through the roof when I felt her fingers on my fly. Her hand jerked back as if she had been stung and she whispered an apology, but I was already reaching for the door handle and half falling out of the car.

Once I was outside, I felt better. It had been so close and claustrophobic in there. I sat on the gravel, leaning back against the car, almost panting. I felt thirsty. I had lost my beer.

The back seat door beside me creaked open as wide as it could. Joanne clambered out, a beer in each hand, smiling broadly. 'That's better,' she said approvingly. 'Not so cramped.'

She held out the fresh beer to me. As I took it, her fingers encircled mine but this time with more force. She gripped my hand against the icy can. 'It's more private too,' she whispered and she seemed to flow towards me in one sudden motion, so that she was pressed against me, sitting right on top of me. 'Now, where were we?'

That fiercely reddened mouth — she had reapplied it in the public toilets — was descending upon me, her lips parted. She closed her eyes and it was easier then to push her aside.

I sprang up and away from the car and ran down the road towards the beach. I was fast. I was renowned for my speed. There was no chance of her catching me in those heels. I could hear her calling my name, begging me to wait, but I kept running and didn't stop until my feet sank into sand. I stopped there, bent over, hands on my knees to get my breath back and then walked down to the water. I didn't care that my shoes and the bottoms of my jeans got wet. The lap of the waves would wash away the evidence of *my footprints. Somehow I imagined that Joanne might go to the extraordinary length of trying to track me down by my footprints.*

The moon was hanging out over the ocean. The crests of the waves were starkly illuminated as they swelled. I saw the big rock on the headland up ahead of me in the distance, one of the few landmarks on the beach. I was too far away and it was too dark for me to notice the figure that lingered there, staring out to sea, waiting.

That encounter on the beach did more than confirm my suspicions about myself. It awoke in me a sexual desire so voracious that, after a few days of being in thrall to it, I began to wish it had been left to slumber. Not that I could ever regret that initiation, but the feelings aroused in me were so strong, so demanding, they frightened me. Practically any man became a target for my sexual speculation. Even the Brothers at school. I was constantly erect and masturbated furiously at every opportunity. My penis became tender from the thrashing I gave it. Yet despite being so over abused, it continued to swell at the least provocation.

Coupled with this sexual agitation was the knowledge that I was a homosexual, and this pressed upon me every moment of the day and night. I couldn't concentrate at school, I couldn't sleep. I had a constant headache which no medication seemed to numb. After a week of this turmoil, with no hint of relief, I began to fear I'd go mad if I didn't do something to alleviate either the physical frustration or the emotional burden.

I began to haunt the beach in the evening. I wanted him to be there so badly, I could almost make myself believe he would return. Even though he lived in Sydney. It said so on my only souvenir of that night, the business card he had pressed into my hand before we parted. 'If you're ever in Sydney,' he said before he kissed me goodbye. He had only been visiting. Staying at the big hotel downtown for his company's national convention.

I kept that card in the inside pocket of my school uniform. I liked the notion of having it there, pressed close to my heart.

Those evenings on the beach became my tribute to him. I always took his card along with me and I would sit there at 'our spot', staring out at the darkening sea, my fingers tracing the embossed letters of his name on the card. Before returning home, I'd jerk off behind a rock.

Then one evening, when I was doing exactly that, my pants around my ankles, I heard a voice calling out what sounded like my name. I yanked up my pants, scrambled round the rock, and there he was. Standing *in exactly the same place that I'd been that night, down at the water's edge. He was staring back at me and calling out to me. I began to run towards him, my heart racing, a tremor of nervousness in my bowel; but I'd only gone a few paces when I realised there was something at my heels. A dog. Where had that come from? The man on the beach was walking towards me, calling, and suddenly everything fell into place. It wasn't him. I was now close enough to see that it was someone much older, more Father's age. He hadn't been calling me. He'd been calling his dog. I felt acutely foolish and stopped in my tracks. The man kept walking towards me, patting the dog as it leapt about him. 'Nice night for a walk,' he remarked.*

I was too aware of how odd my behaviour must have seemed to reply. I kept my eyes downcast. Though I watched the man once he walked on and noticed that he turned, several times, to look back at me. My cock was erect. I found myself staring after him with a mounting desperation, willing him to turn again, to stop walking altogether and then slowly but deliberately to wander back towards me.

But he didn't turn again. He quickened his pace. I watched him leave the beach.

I felt ashamed then. How could I have even considered it? Another man. In the same place. But I had done more than consider it, I had hoped for it. If the man had turned back to me, I had no doubt that I would have led him up to the place I had made for myself behind the rock.

I ran home spooked by the knowledge of what I was capable of. Somehow I believed if I ran fast enough, I could leave the extremity of my desire behind me. That man had not even been attractive. I'd been too embarrassed to look him in the face but I'd noticed his pot belly and cheap clothes. Yet the place and the atmosphere had been enough to make me want him. That night in bed, I masturbated so many times I lost count. My theory was that if I did it enough, I could wring my perverse desires out of myself along with every last drop of semen.

I felt like howling when I awoke. A dream was dwindling out of my consciousness. I let it slip away. I didn't want to remember. It was enough to know that it had featured Kerry and that my cock was hard. Nothing had changed. My hand clutched my erection automatically. But it stung! The few strokes I gave it stung. I kicked back the bedclothes and examined my cock. There were two big red blisters on the shaft. Even though it hurt,

I still had to do it. In fact, the need to ejaculate was made all the more urgent.

The attempted exorcism of my homosexuality had been an utter failure. So I continued to roam the beach at dusk, driven by a confused mix of romantic nostalgia and the crasser but more urgent pulse of what I might find there. But as the nights passed and the beach remained empty of opportunity, only strolling couples hand in hand or gangs of drunken louts ever passing by, my anxieties throbbed in my head more unbearably. Increasingly the only means of relief seemed to be to confess aloud what consumed me. To someone. Whatever the consequences.

But whom to tell? Was it a subject for the confessional? Perhaps, but I knew that would be a pointless exercise. There would be no solace offered there. No discussion or attempt at understanding. I would be warned that it was the most flagrant of sins. The Bible declared it as such. A penance would be demanded of me and somehow that was supposed to end the matter. I had no faith in such a scenario.

I wondered about approaching one of the Brothers at school. There were rumours about two of them, Brother Angelo and Brother William. It had been remarked upon that they volunteered to supervise the swimming pool at lunchtimes more than any of the other teachers. Those suspicions were made concrete one afternoon when a boy cramped in the pool and needed assistance. Brother William flapped uselessly above the boy. He couldn't swim. It was left to one of the older boys to come to the rescue. Both Brothers avoided the pool after that, but the ridicule and nicknames had already taken grip. I did not want to be seen having an intimate chat with either of them, and it was impossible to find a private moment.

The other known homosexual in the town was Colin, who ran the hair salon in the mall. In a desperate moment I rang him and made an appointment for a cut. But afterwards, when I got off the phone, I knew I wouldn't keep it. Not only was I scared of being seen in his salon by someone I knew, but his voice had sounded so effeminate and braying that it would negate any words of consolation or advice he might possibly offer.

The one person I really wanted to tell was Kerry, though my common sense told me that would be a critical mistake. Nevertheless, I longed to. For it would not merely be a confession of my suspicions about myself, it would also be a declaration of love.

In the past, if I had a serious personal problem, I usually brought it up with my father. In fact, some months back I did speak to him, in much vaguer terms, about my anxieties. It was round the time that Kerry began to boast about his exploits. I couldn't bear to hear his bragging. I hoped he didn't really do the things he claimed, that he was merely repeating the stories of those older boys on his team and claiming them as his own. His stories unleashed a panic in me that I had failed to notice what he drooled over so verbosely. Once he'd pointed certain things out, I looked and willed myself to feel something akin to desire. I never did. It was only when I imagined Kerry into the equation – his hand snaking up a girl's jumper or his fingers spread upon her thigh – that it stirred anything in me.

'Father.'

He liked to be addressed as Father. I found it slightly embarrassing – it sounded so affected – but I had to admit that it suited him. He had never been a Dad or a Daddy. Father had aristocratic pretensions. His accent was more English than the English, although he had never even visited there. He'd been born in Liverpool, Sydney, not Liverpool, Great Britain, and his great-grandfather had been a convict, not a lord. But he knew Great Britain intimately (he always emphasised the 'Great' with some ardour) through the thousands of novels that he had read. He read nineteenth century authors exclusively and I think he liked to imagine that Great Britain was almost unchanged today. He had no interest in its current affairs, though he admired Margaret Thatcher for no better reason than the fact that 'her diction is superb'.

Mum had her own explanation for Father. 'He's obsessed with the English because they're a nation of eccentrics. They make him feel at home.'

I was always nervous about interrupting Father when he was reading. It was a little like rousing the sleepy from their beds. You might be ignored or you might be snapped at. But the fact that he might not be paying attention made it easier for me to speak. 'Father. I'm a bit worried that I'm, like, such a slow starter. Compared to my friends. You know.'

Father looked up at me from his book, his eyes alert. He studied me for a moment, then took his bookmark from the arm of his chair and marked his place. He closed his book and clasped it upon his knee. His attention was focused upon me exclusively, an indication of the gravity *with which he regarded my words. It was very intimidating.*

'Is your meaning that you feel backward in regard to your relations with girls?'

I hesitated. Relations wasn't exactly the right word, but Father's way of speaking had been shaped by his reading and tended to be a little old-fashioned. It was unthinkable that I say something like 'girls don't make me horny', though that was the crux of my problem. Father would regard such a phrase as vulgar, would perhaps be more shocked by my use of the English language than by the implications of my words. He was very much the English teacher he'd been all his life, even outside school hours. So I nodded reluctantly to Father's question and hoped that he had perceived my meaning.

It was always to Father that I went when I needed advice, never Mum. She always offered a predictable solution, one I'd already considered myself and rejected. She also had a habit of discussing the more personal of my problems over the telephone with her friends. These women would then approach me themselves after church 'to offer their own words of comfort' or, as I saw it, to make it plain that they knew everything. I will never forget the most devout of Mum's friends, Miss Stroud, telling me in all earnestness that she had said a prayer requesting respite for me from my acne.

Father was a man of few words. 'Your mother talks enough for both of us,' was his excuse for his reserve. 'There's no need for me to go putting my two pennies' worth in.' But when he did say something, it was considered and often perceptive.

My problem clearly troubled him. He took some time before replying and when he finally did, he measured what he said carefully. 'In my opinion, the youth of today are far too impatient and impetuous. Relations between the sexes can arouse very powerful emotions, emotions that a young mind and heart are ill prepared to cope with. You have plenty of time before you need embroil yourself in that carry on and I sincerely believe you would be doing yourself a favour to wait until you are more mature both physically and intellectually. You shouldn't feel alarmed that you have a shyer and more gentlemanly approach. You are the product of your upbringing and as such are a credit to your mother and myself. It would pain me to see you rebel against that upbringing, to turn wild and uncouth, merely to imitate the behaviour of your peers. For I suspect that they may regret shrugging off their youth so quickly. It's a common mistake to attempt to dance when you've barely learnt to walk.'

Father studied me intently to ensure that I had paid attention, and waited for my response. When none came, he picked up his book from his knee, opened it to the page marked and returned his concentration there.

Father's book was omnipresent. He carried it with him everywhere and availed himself of its contents at every possible opportunity. At mealtimes. Upon the lavatory. Even during church services. 'I'm obliged to seize my opportunities when I can,' Father said in defence of his behaviour. 'The fact that they wrote at such length in the last century means there's a lot of pages to get through.'

Mum put up with his antisocial behaviour in most circumstances, but she drew the line at his reading in church. He became the scandal of the congregation over his blatant disregard for the service. He neglected to rise and join in the hymns. He rested his book upon the pew in front during the Holy Communion and turned the pages in what Mum described as 'a provocative insult to the Lord'. But his most grievous crime was laughing aloud at some passage that amused him during the priest's sermon. All eyes turned in our direction, but it was Mum and I that had to endure those stares of disbelief and affront. Father was oblivious, embroiled in his book.

'Everyone could see,' Mum railed at him once we were in the car. 'If it had been the Bible you were engrossed in, then perhaps it might have been excusable. But no, all you ever read is that old-fashioned nonsense. I suppose it makes you feel superior that no-one's ever heard of all these writers that you alone find so fascinating. In future, you must leave your book at home.'

'Or leave myself at home with my book, dear,' said Father mildly.

Mum snorted with laughter. She presumed he was joking. He wasn't. He didn't attend church with us again.

His books were his sanctuary from Mum and her constant prattle. Perhaps even a vain attempt to lull her into his state of quietude and contemplation. They were not compelling those books of his. They did not demand the devotion that he bestowed upon them. I knew, as he had pressed his favourites upon me.

Father was older than Mum by ten years. They both married late.

Father had been thirty-nine, so by the time I was sixteen, he had begun to look quite elderly. His hair was entirely grey and he was obliged to wear his reading glasses all the time. It was embarrassing to attend school events with him as he was mistaken for my grandfather. I don't know whether he overheard someone say something or whether, after all his years of teaching, he was sensitive to the cruelties of teenagers, but one day he took me aside and gave me permission to pass him off as my grandfather to my classmates. 'I know what boys are like. If it makes it easier for you, tell them your father is dead and that I'm your grandfather. The truth is I'm almost old enough to be that.'

The generosity of his words moved me but also sparked a terrible guilt in me. For I had already been engaged in what he had given me permission to do. Not actively. Quite reluctantly really. I never claimed Father was dead, but if someone noticed him and asked if 'the old man' was my grandfather, I had nodded my agreement to avoid the inevitable ridicule.

Father knew schoolboys all too well. It was their ways that defeated him. He had been an English teacher for most of his career, though with every passing year he complained that the boys became brasher and more impossible to manage. He rejected the use of the cane; but, instead of respecting Father for his principles, his students pressed home their advantage, knowing that his use of discipline was severely hampered. He was relegated to the junior classes but eventually even they became too boisterous for him to control. Finally the headmaster retired him from the classroom to the school library to serve out his final years there. It was an ignoble finale – the library was considered women's work – which rankled Mum. For years she had been claiming that her husband would one day become head of the English department. She invented a heart complaint for him as the reason for what was, in effect, a demotion and Father allowed her this small lie.

Father would not have me attend 'his school' though it was considered the best in the town. 'I have no doubt that your days there would be made unbearable once it was known that you were my son,' he said.

Mum had been pressing for me to be sent to a small private Catholic college and Father agreed, although he voiced reservations over the academic standing of the school.

That action, saving me from the tyranny of his pupils, was typical of Father. He possessed the qualities that would have made him the perfect confidant to all my anxieties: insightful, kindly, considerate. But there was a compelling reason why I could never be entirely candid with him. It was probably a totally irrational theory, but once it had entered my mind I could not dislodge it. Rather, evidence began to gather that supported what I would have preferred never to have thought of.

I feared that I had inherited my homosexuality from Father.

He was so different to other fathers. He showed no interest in sport or cars or drinking beer. He never watched the football on television. The only thing he watched were BBC adaptations of historical novels. 'The Forsyte Saga'. 'The Pallisers'. 'War and Peace'. He attended my rugby matches but it was only out of a sense of duty. He didn't follow the game. He stood on the sideline and read his book. Our family car was an embarrassment. It was a Morris Minor, at least thirty years old. All my friends' fathers drove Jaguars. I was deeply embarrassed to be seen in that car by anyone from school. Throughout my high school years I pretended that riding in that car made me feel ill, which gave me the excuse to lie on the back seat and not be seen. Father didn't even drink. He was more of a teetotaller than Mum, who might at least be persuaded to have a Pimms and lemonade on a special occasion. Father drank Coca-Cola. 'We didn't have this when I was a boy,' he would say. 'It's rather good.'

His long bachelorhood and late marriage were also damning. I half suspected that Mum must have proposed. I couldn't imagine Father relinquishing his book for long enough to utter the words. While she was almost thirty and no doubt made more assertive by the prospect of the shameful spinsterhood that loomed ahead of her.

I was terrified that if I confessed I was gay to Father, I might hear the same confession in return. 'Now that's a coincidence, my boy . . .'

As for Mum, I could never expect understanding from her. She had made her position on the issue of homosexuality very plain to me, Father, the broader community in our town and even to the State Government of New South Wales. Mum had been actively involved in protesting against the law reform which planned to decriminalise homosexuality. She and other members of the church had organised a petition against the reform. Flushed from the success of signing up the entire congregation of the church, it was Mum who suggested they commence a doorknock campaign to obtain even more signatures. 'But would we want the signatures of non-believers on our petition?' someone at the meeting queried.

Mum considered this thoughtfully. 'Is it not possible that this might be an issue upon which we could unite and draw them into the faith?'

The crowd about her erupted into spontaneous applause.

I had been obliged to accompany her on her doorknock campaign. She had a well-rehearsed little speech and routine, of which I eventually realised I was a part.

'I thank the Lord that we live in a Christian town,' she would begin. 'Nevertheless, we can't ignore the fact that a hotbed of sin is positioned practically on our doorstep. In times such as these we must do all we can to defeat the immoral threat of Sydney. Can you imagine what such a change to the law would mean? It would become legal for these homosexuals to prey upon our sons. Our sons!'

At that point, her arm would creep around me and she would hug me to her fiercely. 'It is our duty to protect them.'

I refused to participate after she had finished doorknocking the opposite side of our street. It was too embarrassing being thrust forward as some sort of symbol of unsullied youth before people I knew. When, in fact, I had fooled around with several of those people's sons, years and years ago. Something I had quite forgotten until that moment.

Mum trumpeted the achievements of her 'petition pilgrimages' over mealtimes. Father was always absorbed in his book. It was up to me to provide the congratulations and encouragement she considered her due. I tried to keep my mouth full at times when a response was expected.

'But you know there were several people who refused to sign. Refused to sign it point-blank. I beseeched them but it was in vain. One of them uttered a profanity and shut the door in my face. And can you believe that our butcher refused me? I told him then and there that I'd be taking my business elsewhere and he said, "Good ruddy riddance." It makes you suspicious when they won't sign as to what their motives actually are.'

'I haven't signed it,' said Father abruptly, without looking up from his book.

We both stared at him in surprise, but he said nothing further. His face remained bowed.

Mum was nonplussed. She didn't know whether Father's comment was a complaint that he had been overlooked or whether it was an assertion that he didn't intend to sign. I began to feel extremely nervous. I didn't want to know either way.

'What's for dessert?' I asked.

'Apricot jam steamed pudding,' replied Mum, but her eyes were on Father, regarding him suspiciously.

'With custard?'

'I have to make it,' said Mum, rising from the table.

'I'll help,' I offered, quickly gathering the plates from our roast dinner. And in that way, the moment passed.

I doubt that the matter was raised again in the privacy of their bedroom; I noticed that the petition was left lying around the house in obvious places, as if to rebuke Father into signing. Whether he took the hint or not, I never knew. I was not prepared to look through it to check. I preferred not having my suspicions confirmed.

I avoided Kerry after that night on the beach. Went out of my way not to go to places where we might encounter one another. But he sought me out. He turned up outside the church again two weeks later. 'I'll walk home with Kerry,' I called back over my shoulder to Mum when I spotted him.

'But lunch will be ready.'

'We'll walk fast.'

And we did, until we couldn't hear her protests calling after us.

'Joanne's bin askin' after ya,' was the first thing he said to me. 'A lot,' he added, when I failed to respond.

I shrugged.

'What am I s'posed to tell her?' Kerry demanded.

'Tell her I'm gay,' I blurted out.

'Yeah? She'd bloody well believe it the way y've been actin' towards her. Christ, Robbie. You'll even have me wonderin'.'

I couldn't reply. I couldn't believe what I'd actually said. I hadn't meant for that to come out.

A long silence stretched out between us. 'Robbie?' said Kerry in an uncertain voice.

I ignored him and kept walking, my eyes fixed ahead. But he grabbed me by the arm, forcing me to stop and turn to him.

'It's no fuckin' joke sayin' that sort of shit,' he said, his voice rising, taking on a slightly hysterical pitch.

I still couldn't say anything. Nor could I look at him. It was all wrong. This wasn't how it was supposed to have come out.

Kerry gripped my shoulder with his other hand and began to shake me. 'Say somethin',' he entreated me. 'Stop foolin' round. Tell me it's a joke. A lousy fuckin' joke.'

I opened my mouth to reply but found myself crying instead, tears pouring down my face. Kerry's grip on me weakened and then his hands fell away. He began to back away from me. I watched his sneakers retreat. Slowly I lifted my gaze to him.

His face was all red and puffy. He looked like he'd just come off the rugby field after a loss, all puffed and exhausted but with the aggression of the game still pulsing through him. I took a faltering step after him, but his eyes widened and he clenched his fists as if he intended to hit me if I came any closer.

'Keep away from me,' he said fiercely. 'I don't wanna hear about it and I never wanna see ya again either.'

'Kerry.'

My voice came out all high and twisted and pleading. But he whirled away from me and began to sprint back the way we had just come. He couldn't get away from me fast enough. In a few moments he had rounded the corner of the street and was gone.

I stood there stunned. I was aware that a car had pulled up alongside me but it wasn't until Mum emerged out of the driver's door that I comprehended it was our car. 'Stop daydreaming and get in,' she commanded me.

I lay down on the back seat and cried all the way home. After Mum had parked in the garage and turned off the motor, she could no longer ignore the fact that I still hadn't stopped crying. 'Did he hit you? Hurt you in some way?' she finally asked.

I just sobbed louder. She stared at me for a moment, searching for something else to say. Finally she got out of the car and excused herself. 'Your father will be burning the roast vegetables if I don't get myself inside.'

Perhaps she didn't mention it to Father, or perhaps his current novel *was simply too fascinating to put down, but he failed to come out to the car to ask what the matter was. If he had, I was so upset I probably would have told him. By the time Mum called me inside for lunch, I had composed myself, dismissed my parents in my mind and settled on a plan for my future.*

That afternoon, when Father took Mum out for their usual Sunday drive, I packed an overnight bag and hid it outside in the garden shed. I didn't go to bed that night but sat up at my desk, trying to write a note of explanation to my parents. In the end I left them no note. My attempts were screwed up in balls in the wastepaper bin and I decided they were explanation enough, while also being a testimony to my distress. I had no doubt that Mum would go through that bin the next morning when she found me gone.

I stayed up all night. I was too scared that if I went to sleep, everything would seem different when I woke up and I'd lose my resolve. Finally, at four o'clock in the morning, I stole out of the house and collected my bag from the shed. I walked to the nearest phone box and called for a taxi to take me to the main road out of town. I had expected the taxi driver to be suspicious of me, but he was new on the job, didn't even know the way to the main road and was grateful that I was able to guide him there.

I'd never hitchhiked before and I was nervous. But a guy stopped for me after about fifteen minutes. He'd been driving all night and wanted someone to help keep him awake on the final stretch through to Sydney. I asked him lots of questions and didn't give him the chance to ask me any. All the way I clutched that business card in my hand. I was going to be with him in Sydney.

The man dropped me at Parramatta train station and I got out of the car, feeling light-hearted. Maybe from lack of sleep or the thrill of my adventure. I took the train into the city but I was dismayed when I glanced down at that business card I was clutching. I must've been more agitated than I realised. I had scratched the embossed letters off the card without even realising it. Not that it mattered. I knew his name by heart. Raymond Price. But I couldn't shake the feeling that maybe it was a bad omen. I began to feel nervous about our reunion.

I found my way to the address on the business card. His work had their offices on the fifteenth floor of a skyscraper. I was there at seven-thirty.

There was no chance that I had already missed him arrive for work. I positioned myself in a nearby seat and waited.

By eight-thirty people were entering the building and I was feeling very unsure of myself. Would I even be able to recognise him? It had been dark that night on the beach. I rose out of my seat and moved closer to the main doors.

At first I did fail to recognise him. Maybe it was the business suit. It made him seem older and I dismissed him. But something compelled me to take a second look and it was then I recognised his way of walking. I had watched him approach me in that exact same purposeful way that night on the beach.

His eyes flickered up a couple of times and noticed me, but glanced away again just as quickly. When he was only a few metres from me, he looked straight into my eyes but there was no spark of recognition. His gaze was cold, impatient, unseeing. He walked straight past me. I wanted to call out but I felt awkward. We hadn't exchanged names. I'd only learnt his later when I got home and looked at his card.

I watched him stride away from me, feeling certain that at any moment he would turn back for a second glance, his mouth curving into a wondering smile as he recognised me. But he didn't turn. He kept walking. As he got closer to the door, I began to panic. My opportunity was about to disappear. I ran after him. I burst through the doors. He stood waiting for the lift and he turned at the clatter of my shoes on the marble floor.

His expression was quizzical. I lifted my hand in greeting but he merely frowned as he scrutinised me. I hurried over to him but I was so breathless, from the run or from nerves, I was unable to speak. I stood there in front of him, panting.

He was staring at me uncertainly, even edging away from me a little, when suddenly he realised. 'You?' he said in wonder.

I nodded.

'What are you doing in Sydney?'

'I've come to see you.'

'But how did you find me?'

'You gave me your card.'

'Did I?' he said in a disbelieving tone of voice.

I showed him the crumpled card in my hand. He looked at it. 'I guess I must have,' he said, though his voice still sounded unsure.

Two women walked up to wait for the lift. He glanced at them and then beckoned me to follow him around the corner. 'This isn't a good place to talk,' he whispered and I followed him out of sight of the lifts.

He set his briefcase down on the floor and stared at me. I noticed his eyes taking in my overnight bag. 'I can't believe you're here,' he said.

'I've run away from home,' I burst out.

Raymond looked very startled. 'You're very young to be leaving home,' he observed.

I shrugged. 'I can't go back now. Mum wouldn't have me.'

Raymond raised his eyebrows. 'But what will you do here?'

I couldn't believe that he had failed to understand. I looked at him, willing him to grasp my intentions, but finally I just had to say it. 'I've come to be with you.'

I couldn't believe it but Raymond began to laugh. My face must have shown my distress because the laughter faltered quite quickly and the look of concern on his face became even more marked. 'You're serious?' he said in disbelief.

'You said . . . if I was ever in Sydney . . .'

'Did I? Look, you're a sweet kid, but I never imagined I'd see you again. You should go on home to your parents.'

'I can't go back,' I said and now I was fighting back tears.

A man in a suit rounded the corner. His eyes swept over us, disapproval in his expression, before he backed away. Raymond looked worried and he continued to stare after the man. He glanced at his watch and I could tell all he wanted to do was get away from me.

'Couldn't I stay with you just for a couple of days?' I burst out.

Raymond laughed again nervously. 'That would take far too much explaining.'

I stared at him blankly.

'I have a lover,' Raymond elaborated, avoiding my eyes. 'We live together. I couldn't take you back there.'

I was having difficulty understanding. 'You . . . and another man?'

Raymond nodded. I started to protest. How could that night on the beach have happened if Raymond already had someone? How could he have done those things and said those things to me? But Raymond picked up his briefcase and interrupted my stuttering. 'I have to go to work now. I'm sorry if I misled you. I never imagined you'd see it for anything more than it was.'

I didn't understand what he meant by that but it was too late to ask him to explain. He'd already turned away from me and walked swiftly back around to the lifts. By the time I'd picked up my bag and followed him, all I caught was a glimpse of him darting between the closing doors of the elevator. He was gone.

I went back outside and retook my seat. I would wait until he came down at lunchtime. By then he would've gotten over his surprise, had time to think about my situation and begun to regret his hasty retreat from me.

Raymond did emerge from the building at lunchtime, but he wasn't alone. He was with a woman. He saw me, looked away immediately and the two of them walked off together. I couldn't follow. He was with a friend and I knew it would embarrass him if I was to run after him. Ten minutes later he returned alone, carrying a sandwich bag. He walked straight up to me and handed me fifty dollars. 'Here's some money to get yourself home and to buy yourself something to eat on the journey. You've misunderstood me and I at least owe you the train fare home. But you can't keep hanging around here. It's embarrassing me. Okay?'

I didn't have time to answer. Raymond was already walking away. But it was plain. I'd been paid to go. But where? I could not go home. Mum would have found my attempts at explaining my disappearance in the rubbish bin. In one of them I had said that I was running away to be with the man I loved. How could I return the same day, dismissing it as a mistake? I couldn't bear the look of righteous triumph on her face that it had been such a disaster, so quickly. That is if she would even look at me or speak to me. It was quite likely that I had been disowned.

After two weeks in Sydney, I was ready to retreat home and ask my parents to take me back. I'd found a job in a restaurant but the work was exhausting and the money never seemed to stretch far enough. My excitement at venturing out on Sydney's Oxford Street had been dampened when I was refused a drink in one of the most popular bars and told not to come back until I was eighteen. But the clinching factor in my disillusionment was the house I had moved into. I was becoming increasingly uneasy about the attentions that the owner and 'mother' of the household directed towards me and 'his other boys'.

Initially I had dismissed Fergus as harmless. Eccentric but harmless. When I first visited to inspect the vacant room, he had answered the door dressed in a kaftanlike robe which gave him the appearance of a benign shepherd from a Christmas nativity play. All he needed was a crook. He was middle-aged, tall, rotund, balding and bearded. He swept me into his sitting room for the 'interview', yet failed to ask me any questions about myself, even my ability to pay the rent. Instead he insisted on doing my astrological chart to ascertain my compatibility with himself and the other members of the household.

My stars were deemed exquisitely harmonious. I was shown the room.

But within a week I had begun to have misgivings. Fergus had three other tenants. They were all blond and of a similar age to myself. I began to suspect that our youth and colouring were the true criteria upon which we'd been judged and not the elaborate analysis of our zodiac. We were all strays, estranged from our families and, like the shepherd that he so resembled, Fergus had gathered us in. He tended us, 'his little flock', rather too slavishly. It put me in mind of the fattening of the lamb . . .

When Fergus showed me the vacant room, he told me that he strove to create a warm family atmosphere in his house. But I never imagined the lengths he would go to playing mother. He cooked all the meals. He cleaned and tidied all of our rooms and even made our beds. He did our laundry. I came home from my job one evening, doing dishes and preparing vegetables at a restaurant in the city, a week after I had moved in, and came upon him folding my laundry with such tender intensity that I felt repelled. My underwear was in a separate pile on the ironing board and Fergus's hand rested upon that little mound as we exchanged pleasantries. 'I can finish that off in my room,' I said abruptly, making a lunge for my clothes.

But Fergus shooed me away. 'It's a pleasure to help you out, Robbie, when you work so hard during the day. You get enough menial tasks to do there. I'll bring this to your room when it's all ironed and folded.'

I had no choice but to murmur my appreciation.

'I changed your sheets today too,' Fergus said, and a look that was both coy and sly slid across his face. 'I had to get out the stain remover.'

I could feel myself blushing. I bolted from the room.

When Fergus came to my bedroom with my laundry, he set the folded pile down on the bed, then sat down next to it and sighed. 'I hate to think of you washing dishes all day and coarsening your lovely skin,' he said.

I shrugged. 'It's okay.'

'But you're meant for better things, Robbie.'

'I like it,' I said firmly. 'It's my first job. I like the people.'

'Oh, I see,' said Fergus, his tone becoming nettled. 'Fixed your eye upon one of the waiters, have you?'

I hesitated. I didn't know whether it would be better to say yes or no; which would be most likely to deflect his attentions.

'You'd prefer not to confide in me? Oh well. Perhaps when we know one another better. I hope you'll come to trust me. If you have a problem, I'd like to help. Whether it's a dilemma of the heart or some financial trouble, I think you'll find me very understanding.'

I thanked him for his offer and picked up my clothes to put them away, turning my back on him. Fergus took the hint and heaved himself off the bed and waddled to the door. But he paused there and turned. 'You will have your bond to me soon, won't you, Robbie?'

I nodded.

'Just come and see me if it's a problem. I deal with my accounts in the evening. After nine.'

Fergus swept out the door and dread began to tie knots in my stomach.

The bond was four weeks' rent and it was a problem. I didn't have it and couldn't realistically see how I could get it. But I had an inkling of the circumstances under which Fergus might choose to waive the debt. Something I had witnessed on my first night in the house. I'd been restless and had woken at some point in the middle of the night. I got up and slipped out of my room to use the toilet. On my way back, just as I was about to enter my own bedroom, a door further along the hallway opened and Fergus emerged, his robe flaring out behind him as he glided down the hallway towards his sitting room. I thought nothing of it, taking it to be his bedroom. It wasn't until several days later that I learnt it was Benjamin's bedroom he had slipped out from. Benjamin who did not appear to work at all. That was obviously how his account had been dealt with.

I might have been able to dismiss that had there not been another incident which confirmed the designs Fergus had on us all. I walked out of my bedroom one morning and found Fergus kneeling in front of the bathroom door, his eye to the keyhole. I could hear the shower running from where I stood. He was too intent to notice me and I slipped back into my room. I made a point after that of plugging the bathroom keyhole with toilet paper before I showered.

When I found my little plug of toilet paper lying on the bathroom linoleum one morning, I resolved to ring my father at his work and find out whether I would be welcomed home or not. But that phone call was when everything began to unravel horribly.

There was a silence on the other end of the phone when I asked for my father. When the librarian finally spoke, it was to say that Mr Carson no longer worked there. 'He was working there two weeks ago,' I pointed out, unable to believe that something so fundamental could have changed so quickly.

'Yes,' said the librarian reluctantly. 'But . . . unfortunately Mr Carson suffered a heart attack ten days ago.'

I was trying to get the words out to ask if he was all right, when the woman filled in the blank for me.

'He died in hospital.'

It was strange walking through my neighbourhood having been away. I noticed things I'd never noticed before; how different it was to Paddington where Fergus had his terrace. Street upon street of cheap fibro houses with their peeling paintwork and feeble attempts at landscaping. How forlorn the local park was; a few shrubs, a set of swings and the grass brown, wilting and overdue to be mowed. It was a place to take the dog to relieve itself and that was all. I saw for the first time how awful that new modern home up on the hill truly was. Everyone had thought it so daring and longed to see inside. People went out of their way to drive past, to admire its amazing wave-shaped roof and port-hole windows. But I could see now how squat and ugly it was, and what a mistake it had been to paint it fawn. On the corner stood the A-frame church that soared so dramatically skyward, all sharp angles and sheer roofing. It had excited my mother so much when it was built she'd confessed to me one day that she felt tempted to change denominations.

It felt very peculiar to be ringing what I'd always considered to be my own doorbell. Aunt Adele, Mum's sister, opened the door. She didn't say a word to me, merely stood there in the doorway, a sorrowful look upon her face. Finally, she said that she would tell Mum that I had come but she continued to stand there hesitating, her fingers pulling at the sleeve of her floral blouse. 'She's been very upset, Robbie. She may not be ready to see you,' she finally blurted out, before turning and disappearing back into the house.

I could hear the rise and fall of Adele's voice and then Mum's voice replying, but I could not distinguish the words. Suddenly Mum raised her voice and I wished I hadn't been straining forward to catch what was being said. 'Are you mad? Of course I don't want to see him. I never want to see him again. Send him away. It was him *that killed him. Broke his poor fluttering heart . . .'*

I couldn't bear to hear any more. I dropped the wreath of flowers I'd bought and ran all the way down the street. There seemed nothing else to do except catch the train back to Sydney.

I couldn't face going back to Fergus's house. I dreaded his sympathy. If he noticed me looking unhappy, he would press and pry to worm my problem out of me, his arm stealing about me, his voice soft in my ear. I went to the pub instead. I peered through the windows of the door. The barman who had refused me a drink did not appear to be working. I walked in and noticed Benjamin slouched against the wall. I went over to him but he barely responded to my greeting. 'He's got his eye on someone,' said the blond boy standing next to him. 'He's oblivious to everyone else. We were supposed to be having a drink together . . .' The boy shrugged and grinned. 'I'm Aaron. Perhaps you'll have a drink with me instead?'

I nodded and Aaron insisted on buying. I was grateful. It would've been too humiliating to have been refused a second time. I also had very little money left after paying for my father's wreath. Aaron was very entertaining. He indicated the man who was cruising Benjamin and in a whisper began to list his flaws. Benjamin excused himself to go to the toilet and a few seconds later the man followed in his wake. We didn't see them again after that.

Aaron's eyes roamed about the bar and he began to remark about some of the other people there, relating amusing stories or intimate details that really ought not to have been repeated at all. I was struck by how confident and worldly Aaron seemed and I asked him how old he was. Aaron winced. 'Bad question,' he reprimanded me. 'Old enough to feel that I've been coming to places like this for far too long.'

He seemed reluctant to talk about himself, preferring to ask me questions, but later he admitted to being twenty-one. He worked in a nightclub. Tonight was his night off.

Suddenly I noticed the barman who'd refused me had appeared behind the bar. When I said I had to leave, I was surprised when Aaron said he'd come with me. He suggested we go back to his place and I agreed.

I was unsure what he had in mind by asking me home. In all the time we'd talked together, his manner had never strayed towards flirtation. But in the lift to his apartment, his voice suddenly softened and he reached out to me and drew me to him. 'I like you, Robbie,' he murmured. 'You're very sweet . . . and refreshing.'

He kissed me, then abruptly pulled away and slapped himself on the cheek. 'What a ridiculous compliment! I make you sound like a soft drink.'

We laughed together, the doors of the lift opened and we seemed to float into his apartment on the wave of that laughter. Any awkwardness or timidity that I might have felt slipped away. Aaron's hand strayed over my groin as he guided me into the bedroom and he remarked that what he'd found was the size of a Coke bottle.

Afterwards I felt guilty. It was the day I had learnt of my father's death. My conduct had been no tribute to him.

The next morning, while Aaron made us breakfast, I wandered around admiring his apartment. It was large and modern, bright and clean. Aaron asked me about my own situation and I explained about Fergus's household. He seemed to understand straight away that there was a problem and he pressed me to tell him more. I mentioned the incidents I had witnessed and my growing feeling of unease.

'I'm dreading going back there already,' I admitted. 'Fergus will know I didn't come home last night.'

'Don't go home then,' Aaron offered. 'Come back here after you finish work.'

'Really?'

Aaron nodded. 'I'd like that.'

I stayed another couple of days, during which Aaron wheedled all the details of my story out of me. After hearing it all, he offered me his spare room. 'You don't need to go back there if you don't want to.'

'Really?'

Aaron nodded. 'Not that I actually want you to sleep in the spare room,' he added. 'I want you to sleep with me. But it's up to you. No pressure.'

When I went to collect my belongings, Aaron came with me. I had hoped to slip in and out discreetly and leave a note on the bed, but of course Fergus found us. 'Robbie, I've been terribly concerned,' he began as he barged into the room, but then he noticed Aaron packing my clothes into a bag and he stopped mid-sentence.

'What's this?' he exclaimed, folding his arms and pursing his lips with disapproval. 'Surely you're not leaving us?'

I couldn't meet his eyes. I nodded and held out the envelope to him with the money that Aaron had lent me. 'It's two weeks' rent,' I muttered.

Fergus opened the envelope and I sneaked a glance at him. I wished I hadn't. Disappointment was stamped plainly across his face as he fingered the banknotes. I expected him to rant at me but instead he simply said, 'We'll miss you,' and retreated out the door. I was relieved. But then as we were manoeuvring my bags out of the front door, Fergus reappeared, in the doorway of his sitting room, clutching his robe to his throat. 'I'll take you back, Robbie, if things go badly,' he quavered. 'You mustn't feel proud about coming back. I'm forgiving of my boys and their follies.'

Aaron snorted and held the door open for me. I hurried outside. Fergus's expression was almost tearful.

It was that night that Aaron told me, after I'd arranged my belongings in his spare room.

'There's something I should have mentioned before you moved in,' he began ominously, his face clouding over, 'but I thought it might shock you. I wanted to get you out of that house, away from that dreadful man, but of course it should have been your choice. You may feel like you've gone from the frying pan into the fire.'

What I felt like doing was putting my hand over his mouth and silencing him. I'd had more than my share of shocks and upheavals and felt that I simply couldn't bear to be subjected to yet another one. I tried to hush him but Aaron talked over me. 'I don't work at a nightclub,' he said, pausing for a moment before he continued. 'I'm a sex worker.'

I didn't understand. I stared at him blankly and Aaron laughed. 'Robbie, you're such an innocent. A prostitute.'

I still didn't understand. 'But women are prostitutes,' I protested.

'And boys,' Aaron assured me.

'Really?'

Aaron nodded. 'Are you shocked?'

I nodded and we both laughed nervously, suddenly unsure of each other. Aaron began to speak quickly. 'I don't like to tell people straight away. They can be very judgmental and I like to give them a chance to get to know me first. But you do have to know if you're going to stay with me. I do a lot of out calls, but sometimes I have a client who prefers to come to me and you'd have to make yourself scarce then.'

I barely comprehended a word of what he said. I was still grappling with the initial revelation and hadn't been able to take in everything else. I was shocked by his profession, but more shocked by the sheer sordid scale of his infidelity to me. We'd had sex together a lot over the past few days. I'd presumed it was the start of something, that we were falling in love with one another. Now I understood that in the evenings when Aaron had been at 'work', he'd been having sex with other men and was paid for it. It was like the Raymond situation, only much, much worse.

My voice came out kind of strangled. 'You've been . . . doing it with other guys?'

'Only clients,' said Aaron swiftly. 'No-one else.'

He said it as if there was some distinction, as if his clients didn't count somehow. That he'd been unfaithful didn't even seem to occur to Aaron. He didn't offer any apology.

I excused myself. 'I want to go for a walk.'

'I do want you to stay,' Aaron called after me as I walked out the door.

I longed to snap something cutting back at him but I couldn't think of anything. Later I was glad I hadn't. I realised as I thought everything through that I had little choice. I had no money. In fact, I owed Aaron one hundred and fifty dollars and had nowhere else to go. He was my only friend in a city where I knew no-one. I had also come to rely on his superior knowledge and decisiveness. To be practical, I couldn't afford to have any scruples over Aaron's line of work.

When I returned to the apartment, he seized me. 'Robbie, I'm sorry. I've hurt your feelings. I forget what an innocent you are. Do you forgive me?'

I said yes automatically, without meaning it.

'You will stay, won't you? Let me make it up to you.'

'Okay,' I agreed.

Aaron was relieved. We smiled at one another, the matter settled. But there was something that had occurred to me on my walk that I had to ask. 'What do you do if someone turns nasty on you? What if a guy got violent or tried to make you do something you didn't want to?'

'I haven't had a problem yet,' said Aaron in a rush to reassure me. 'I have very good instincts about clients and a set of ground rules that I stick to. I tell them at the outset what I'll do and what I won't do, so they're not expecting anything they're not going to get. I won't go with a client if he's been drinking a lot or has taken drugs and I won't take an out call unless I know the client or they're staying at a major hotel. I'm careful, Robbie. I don't take risks. I've seen other boys who've been reckless and lived to regret it. Truly, Robbie, I'm careful.'

Aaron laid a hand upon my arm. I gazed down on it for a moment, then gingerly pulled away from him. 'There's one more thing, Aaron,' I said *slowly to keep my voice from giving out. 'I think I should sleep in the other room from now on.'*

Aaron's face fell. 'Of course,' he said, struggling to recover his composure. 'That'd be for the best.'

The more I learnt about how Aaron operated, the more I found my expectations confounded. He had never touted on the street. He told me horror stories about boys who worked 'the wall' in Darlinghurst Road. He'd gotten into sex work three years earlier via Nick, his first serious boyfriend, who was a prostitute. 'He was a very smart operator and he taught me a lot of invaluable lessons,' Aaron explained. 'The first thing he made me do was set myself a goal. What I wanted to achieve financially from working. Then he made me promise that once I'd reached that goal, I'd get out. I had to write that pledge down and then we both signed it.'

'So what's your goal?' I asked.

'To own my own place and to have travelled wherever I want to in the world. I own this apartment, so now I'm saving for the trip.'

I was amazed that Aaron owned the apartment outright. He shrugged as if it was nothing. 'I don't fritter my money away like a lot of those other boys who work and I've steered clear of drugs.'

One of Aaron's clients was an accountant and he gave him some financial advice. He invented a profession for Aaron and ensured that he paid tax like any other worker. 'This way, if I ever get investigated by the tax office, at least I have a record of paying tax. There might be some awkwardness over how the money was earnt but really, as long as the tax is paid, they don't care. It means I can have a mortgage and a bank account and can actually save. Most guys are so intent on hiding their money from the government that they end up spending it all.'

'What happened to Nick?' I asked.

'Oh, Nick set himself a goal too,' said Aaron, a bitter tone creeping into his voice. 'And he achieved it.'

'What was it?' I asked.

'To meet someone who was rich enough to look after him and who he felt enough for to make a relationship feasible.'

There was a long silence. Finally, I asked if he still saw anything of Nick.

'He lives in Los Angeles now, Hollywood Hills, with this executive. He phones me occasionally. On the business phone just to check if the line is still connected, to see if I'm still working.'

There were two phone lines into the flat, one for personal calls (the cream-coloured phone) and one which had its number advertised in all the appropriate places (red). Aaron had a different name when he answered the red telephone. Jason. 'Not a name I like much,' he said. 'But it sounds young and blond and sweet and that image is very popular.'

I ended up acting as receptionist for 'Jason' when he couldn't come to the phone. I still had my job in the restaurant, but I worked the day shift, which meant I could take appointments for Aaron in the evening. I had plenty of money as Aaron wouldn't allow me to pay him any rent. 'You make it up by answering the phone for me,' he insisted.

He wrote down his description, what I was to tell any callers. Eighteen. Blond. Green eyes. Slim build. Eight and a half inches. Versatile. When I queried the lie about his age, Aaron laughed. 'You have to embellish a little, to sound as good as the competition. I can get away with a little exaggeration.'

Sometimes the calls were cranks. Men who just wanted to talk dirty down the phone to me. Then there were others who seemed more interested in hearing about me than about when Aaron had time to see them. 'But you sound real nice. What's your name? Maybe I could come over and see you instead if Jason's not at home.'

I was too embarrassed initially to tell Aaron about these calls. It seemed a slight to him that I was attracting the interest of his clients. But when it kept happening, finally I asked his advice on what to say to them. 'Oh, it's easy to fix guys like that. Just tell them you do usually work but you've got a small medical condition at the moment that's preventing you from taking bookings. They'll hang up so fast and won't pester you again.'

Aaron was right. It worked.

I rarely saw any of Aaron's clients. He insisted I go to my bedroom if he was expecting a client. Though there were occasions when I was obliged to receive them if they arrived early or Aaron couldn't come to the door because he was in the shower or getting ready. Some of the clients I met confirmed my idea of why they would be obliged to pay for sex. They were unattractive, overweight, old or all three. One arrived in an electronic wheelchair. But Aaron never made fun of them or said anything derogatory. Generally he wouldn't discuss his clients, although he couldn't help confiding in me about Gavin.

Gavin had been born with Down's syndrome. His parents were wealthy and Gavin had his own apartment in Bellevue Hill and a private live-in nurse, Marjorie. It was Marjorie who made the arrangement for Aaron to visit once a month. 'He repels me,' Aaron admitted. 'But Marjorie's told me all the problems they've had finding any boy who will see Gavin. I'd feel guilty if I refused to see him. But it's not really the sex. I can cope with that. It's the fact that he doesn't understand the business nature of our appointments. I'm the only sex he ever gets and he has this idea that we're like boyfriends. He cries when I leave. He wants to come and see me all the time. Thankfully Marjorie won't allow it. She knows once a month is almost more than I can bear. She lets him watch porn for the rest of the month. But he sends me cards and drawings he's made of him and me together and it makes me feel like I'm fucking a ten year old.'

Occasionally there were clients who didn't fit the 'have to pay for it' stereotype. Like Stewart. It was an accident that we even met. I woke up one night, needing to urinate, and staggered sleepily across the hall to use the bathroom. I turned on the light and found myself confronted by a naked man washing his penis in the basin. It was so unexpected. I was half dazed from sleep but that sight shocked me wide awake.

'So?' said Stewart, raising his eyebrows as he brazenly turned to face me, his hand still upon his lathered penis. 'Is there a special on tonight? Two for the price of one.'

He was powerful looking: tall, bearded and muscular. Someone I would never have picked as gay. He had a direct stare which was very knowing and sexy. His eyes seemed to intimate that he could guess all my secrets.

I was like a rabbit, trapped by the sudden blaze of a car's headlights on a country road at night — inert when I should have been fleeing. All I could do was stand and stare as his penis began to grow before my eyes. He strode the two paces across the tiled floor that separated us and slid his hand into the gaping fly of my boxer shorts. He kept his eyes on my face and smiled his satisfaction as he fondled my genitals. His penis had transformed itself into a powerful erection. He saw my eyes on it and smiled in an amused, knowing way as he removed his hand from my shorts. Slowly he eased himself forward until his cock was pressed up hard against my abdomen. I closed my eyes, but the image of it against me was as vivid in my mind as if I was staring down at it.

I knew he had just been with Aaron. It was that thought that spurred me to pull away from him and scamper back down the hall to my bedroom. I locked the door, but a few moments later, when I saw the doorhandle turn, part of me wished I hadn't. I sat up in bed, watching the doorhandle turn fruitlessly, my hand upon my own erection.

When I arrived home from work the next day, Aaron mentioned the incident immediately. 'I hear you encountered Stewart last night.'

I was embarrassed that he had told Aaron and wondered what had been said. 'I bumped into him in the bathroom,' I muttered.

'Well, he enjoyed the bump,' said Aaron, his tone sarcastic. 'He came back to me visibly excited. It was the last thing I felt like. Having to endure that enormous cock of his all over again.'

'I'm sorry.'

I could feel Aaron's eyes studying me keenly. 'He kept suggesting that I ask you to come and watch us. But I knew you wouldn't want to get involved in my game. Even in the capacity of spectator.'

'No, I wouldn't,' I agreed automatically, meeting Aaron's gaze and hoping my face didn't betray the agitation his words had excited in me.

Aaron didn't say anything for a minute or two, then he continued. 'He asked a lot of questions about you. Naturally I said as little as possible.'

I couldn't help asking a question of my own at that point. 'Why would someone like him have to pay for sex?' I asked.

Aaron hesitated. 'There are some things Stewart likes to do in bed which a lot of guys wouldn't be into. If he's in the mood for what he likes, it's easier just to pay someone like me.'

That made me very curious. 'What sort of things?'

But Aaron wouldn't say. 'Robbie, that's why my clients pay me. To do what they want willingly and cheerfully and then to be discreet about it afterwards. I can't tell you.'

I felt embarrassed by my own curiosity. I could feel myself blushing.

We sat in silence until the red telephone rang and Aaron arranged an overnight with a South African businessman. I felt relieved that he was going out. I didn't like the way he seemed to relish this episode, seeing a kind of weakness in me exposed.

The red phone rang again soon after Aaron had left. The man asked to speak to Aaron. I began to explain that he wasn't available, when suddenly I realised I was talking on the wrong phone for an Aaron call. Aaron's personal calls came through on the cream phone. The calls on the red phone should only be for Jason. I stopped talking mid-sentence.

'So, Aaron's busy. Never mind. Why don't you tell me about yourself, Carson?'

I began to feel extremely nervous. I had not identified myself when I answered the phone.

The man laughed heartily. 'Hey, talk to me. This is Stewart. We met last night. In the bathroom. Remember?'

'I remember.'

'I was hoping you would,' said Stewart, and then his voice dropped into a quieter, confiding tone. 'I've been thinking about you all day today, Carson.'

'That's my last name.'

'I know that. But I like it better than Robbie, so that's what I'm going to call you. You don't mind if I have a special name for you?'

'No.'

'Good. You know, I wanted you to come and join Aaron and me last night but he wouldn't allow it. He was very strict with me, which was something of a role reversal. Usually it's me who's very strict with Aaron.'

'You know his real name,' I observed.

'Aaron and I have a very special relationship,' said Stewart, a bragging tone creeping into his voice. 'Has he told you about me?'

'Aaron won't discuss his clients with me.'

'Ah! So you asked and he wouldn't tell you.'

I felt caught out then.

'He's a good boy, Aaron. Good not to tell. I wonder if you're a good boy, Carson. I can't decide. Of course we only met briefly but I got the impression, the distinct impression, that you had the potential to be rather wicked—'

I hung up.

Stewart called several times that week. The conversation tended to run along the same lines. He always paid me a few compliments initially, how nice it was to talk to me, how politely I answered the phone; then gradually his voice would drop and the tone of the conversation would become more and more suggestive. But I never allowed him to talk for long. Sometimes he called when Aaron was at home but with a client and I had to cut him short. But I was also conscious of tying up Aaron's business phone. I knew he would not approve of me talking to Stewart at all, let alone allowing him to talk dirty to me when his clients could be trying to make appointments. If he was on an out call he would often phone in when he was finished to check for messages. He complained once that he had been unable to get through for ten minutes and had finally called me on the other line, demanding to know who I was talking to. I lied and said it was a troubled teenager from the western suburbs who thought he might be gay. 'I'm not in the counselling service,' yelled Aaron. 'Have him make an appointment. He can make up his mind about his sexuality after I've shown him a few tricks.'

I found myself answering the phone with a new anticipation. When it wasn't Stewart on the other end of the line I was disappointed. Every time Aaron got a hang-up when he answered the phone, I was certain it must've been Stewart wanting to speak to me.

It was about two weeks after our first meeting that the invitation from Stewart arrived in the post. Party *was printed across the front in silver lettering on heavy black card. On the back an address in Birchgrove and the date were given. There was a number in the bottom corner. Alongside it read that prizes would be drawn after midnight. A note from Stewart accompanied the invitation.* My friend Ken is hosting one of his famous parties next weekend. Do come if you're free. *Then I thought to check the envelope. It was addressed solely to me. Aaron had not been included and there was no matching envelope amongst the other mail. I had been invited alone. I did not mention the invitation to Aaron. I recognised its implications. Naturally I intended to go.*

When the night of the party came, I told Aaron that I had been asked out on a date by one of the waiters at work. Aaron's smile had a forced optimism to it when I left. I realised that it hadn't been a very considerate lie. Aaron probably hadn't had a proper date in years.

I arrived soon after eleven. I was about to walk up to the front door when I noticed a policeman lurking on the porch of the house. I whirled back around and walked on, hoping I hadn't attracted too much attention to myself. A policeman? What was he doing? Was he going to raid the party? I stopped outside the next-door neighbour's house where I was out of sight and checked the number on the invitation. I was at the right house. I was pondering what to do, if there was some way of warning Stewart and Ken of the impending danger, when to my astonishment two men sauntered past me, holding hands, turned into the house and entered, seemingly without any problem whatsoever from the policeman. Was it possible that he was acting as doorman in his off-duty hours? I stole back to the edge of the house and glanced up at the porch. He was still standing there, only this time he was staring back at me. I started back out of sight.

I was still debating what to do when another guest arrived. A boy of a similar age to myself, invitation in hand, who frowned when he noticed me hanging about so helplessly. He withdrew his gaze and pointedly ignored me as he sailed up the path and into the house, addressing the policeman by name as he entered. The policeman turned to watch the boy's retreating figure and it was only then that any lingering doubts were entirely banished. There was no way this was a policeman. No policeman would dress in such a fashion. He had no backside to the pants of his uniform. His buttocks were exposed, wantonly white against the dark leather of his uniform.

I walked up to the door and offered my invitation. The policeman raised his eyebrows at me. 'I was beginning to wonder if you were trying to lure me behind the garden hedge with you,' he said.

I was too surprised to reply.

'Maybe when I finish up here in an hour or so,' he grinned, opening the door for me, but not very widely, so that I was forced to brush against him as I walked by.

Down the hall, light and music spilled out from a doorway off to the right. I walked with a clip, an anticipation to my step, but the closer I got to that doorway, the less sure of myself I began to feel. There was a knot of men clustered together there, a barricade of muscle, moustache and leather, laughing and sipping on their drinks. Their conversation died as first one and then another and another turned in my direction to look me over with appraising eyes. The excitement curdled in my stomach. I began to deeply regret what I had chosen to wear, a blue and white seersucker shirt that I had often been complimented on. My favourite shirt was a big mistake here alongside these bare chests, leather vests and straining singlets. I knew I must look like a small-town hick. I squeezed past them, apologising. 'No trouble,' remarked the one with the moustache. 'I'll look forward to you passing back this way.'

I hoped that in the main room I wouldn't prove to be so conspicuously overdressed. But I was. Most of the men were bare chested. Several were dressed in the style of the policeman at the door. A boy of about my age danced by himself in the middle of the room, in his underwear, his head thrown back, his hands flailing round in the air above his head. I was grateful for his spectacle. He had usurped everyone's attention and no-one noticed me and my John-Boy Walton shirt as I sidled into the room.

Except Stewart. Suddenly he was at my side, his mouth curled up in a satisfied smile. He was wearing only a pair of snugly fitting leather trousers which emphasised his crotch. He kissed me hello, his mouth smothering mine for a brief, exhilarating moment. 'I didn't realise it was dress-up,' I said to him, trying to keep the distress I was feeling out of my voice.

Stewart shrugged. 'It's more like dress-down,' he said. 'Or even undress.'

But he must have noticed my discomfort, as he quickly added, 'I like what you're wearing. You look very nice. Have a drink and don't worry about it.'

Stewart steered me over to the bar. There was an Italian boy behind the bar wearing what at first I took to be the traditional waiter's uniform – white shirt, bow tie – and I was relieved to find someone dressed more formally than me, even if he was staff. However, as I drew closer, I saw that the shirt had been ripped across the midriff. White cotton threads dangled across his brown hairless belly. Instead of black pants, he wore only a black G-string. His thick black hair was slicked back with gel that had begun to lose its grip. The ends of his hair curled up at the back. The boy winked at me and ladled me out a glass of punch from the bowl on the bar. I was embarrassed and complimented by the implication of his wink. I hoped

Stewart hadn't noticed. Flustered, I turned away from the boy to survey the crowd.

There was not one woman in the room. It was entirely men. No-one was dancing except the boy in the underwear and he was indicating a willingness to discard his briefs if he was given enough encouragement. The music changed to a disco hit and the boy lolled there for a few moments, then walked off the dance floor to a round of applause. The next time I noticed him he was sitting on some man's knee and his underwear was around his ankles.

Men in pairs began to sidle onto the dance floor. I had never seen two men dance together before. At first I felt like laughing — it seemed so clumsy and ridiculous. But after a minute or two, I was riveted. I noticed a different waiter, in the same brief outfit, sandwiched between two men, all three writhing in unison. The music soared. The scent of male sweat tinged the air. My senses were borne up. I wanted to be in the midst of it all. I turned to Stewart, who raised his eyebrows and suggested we dance. His style of dancing was to pull me against himself and run his hands over me. I became erect in an instant. I could feel the bulge of his crotch against my navel. He wasn't hard but I was very aware of the lolling, indifferent mass of it pressed against me. After a few songs, he began to unbutton my shirt. 'You're working up a sweat,' he whispered in my ear.

At first I felt conspicuous that he was undressing me in public. Some of the men nearby actually stopped dancing to watch. Then I realised I didn't care. I'd felt idiotic in the shirt. The solution was simple: take it off. My shirt was whipped off from behind, whether by Stewart or one of the onlookers, I wasn't sure. I'd been gazing upward at the pulsing of the disco lights at the time. There was something quite hypnotic about them, a fact I'd never noticed at the blue-light discos back home. Someone ran a hand over my chest and I was startled when I looked over and discovered it wasn't Stewart. He had disappeared but I didn't feel too concerned. I turned to the man who'd fondled me and danced with him instead. When the song finished, I smiled at him and turned to walk off to find Stewart. But the man caught me by the hand. 'I'd like to be your daddy,' he whispered in my ear, his beard rasping against my cheek. 'And I think you'd like that too.'

Daddy. Daddy.

'My father's dead,' I cried abruptly, jerking my hand free of his, reeling off the dance floor towards the bar.

I didn't understand the man on the dance floor but he had turned my thoughts to places I had been steering them clear of for weeks. I felt anxious. Atremble. The solution, I decided, was to get drunk and forget myself. I slipped back through the crowd to the bar. The Italian boy had vanished. Instead there was a muscular, tanned man with grey hair ladling punch into glasses. He complained to me as I took one that the party had only been going for an hour and that his bar staff had run off with the guests already. This was evidently Ken. I introduced myself. Ken's eyes ran over me. 'Well, I can see why Stewart insisted you be invited.'

I blushed and turned away, taking a large gulp of my drink to cover my embarrassment. I moved away and began to wander around the room, looking for Stewart. I couldn't find him. But without my shirt and with a drink in my hand, I felt more confident and at ease. A lot of men smiled and said hello to me. Ken passed by with a tray of punch and I snatched another glass. I took a large gulp and the boy next to me frowned. 'I'd go easy on that,' he advised. 'It's not just alcohol and orange juice, you know.'

'I can handle it,' I replied in a suave manner, walking away from him.

But it began to make sense. I'd assumed there must be some exotic combination of spirits in the punch, things I'd never had before, because I'd never felt drunk in quite this way before. That it wasn't alcohol at all hadn't occurred to me. I began to feel anxious about what I'd swallowed and what was going to happen to me. I looked around for Stewart, he would know what was in the punch, but I couldn't see him anywhere. More than anything I felt like some fresh air. That would bring me back to my senses. But I was wary of encountering the policeman at the front door. I decided to find the bathroom instead. Splashing some cold water on my face might slow down the effects of the punch. I wasn't sure where the bathroom was but I plunged decisively through the door, ignoring the men who were still clustered there and who all groped me as I walked through. Up ahead of me, I caught a flash of white shirt as I fended off their grappling hands. It was the waiter who had winked at me. I felt sure of it. He would know what was in the punch. He had probably mixed it. It was the uncertainty of what it might do to me that was the worst.

I followed the waiter. I turned the same corner he had and found myself at the top of a cramped, unlit staircase. I hesitated. There was something ominous about its steep descent into darkness. I knew I wasn't going to find a bathroom at the bottom of that staircase but I crept down it anyway. I came up against a single doorway. I pushed it open slowly, but the room on the other side was also in darkness and I hesitated. Suddenly I heard footsteps on the stairs behind me and I slipped quickly into the room. The door closed behind me automatically. Or did someone close it? I thought I could sense someone standing behind me. A few moments later it opened again and the person whose footsteps I had heard entered the room. I moved away across the room, worried the man from the dance floor or one of the gropers had followed me. I trod on someone's leg and the person cursed me. I was not alone in that room.

Gradually my eyes adjusted to the darkness. I could vaguely make out clusters of men standing together. I became aware of someone close behind me, his breath on my neck. Then a hand reached out and ran across my stomach. Was it the waiter? I hoped it might be. I turned and reached out my hand to where I expected to find his head, anticipating that my fingers would encounter that stiff helmet of slicked-back hair. When I encountered a bald pate instead, I jerked my hand back in surprise. I dropped to the floor to avoid the outstretched hands of the man as he frantically searched for me. Keeping low, I slithered away from him.

I'd only gone a few feet when I came upon the waiter, or one of the waiters. He lay on the floor, his hands above his head, his white shirt ghostlike in the dark. He was not without company. There were two men, one on either side of him, with their backs to me, huddled over him. I knew what was being done to him and it excited me. I felt a little afraid, but it was a fear that thrilled, like driving too fast in Kerry's brother's Torana with the windows wound down and the wind whipping through the car. Or watching a film move towards its inexorably murderous climax, a scene you didn't want to watch but which you couldn't close your eyes against. Too scared and thrilled to resist.

I was at the waiter's head, looking down upon him. After a while he seemed to recognise me and his hands stretched up towards me. I drew back. I felt guilty. But he was persistent. His hands kept reaching for me, entreating me. I was erect. I wanted him to touch me. It was so easy in the dark to let myself sink towards him. The darkness was like an eraser, extinguishing all the evidence. No-one was ever going to know that I was there and what I did there.

His fingers were eager and I moved closer to make it easier for him. He ran his hands over my chest, his fingers searching for my nipples, pinching when he found them. My breath resounded loudly in my ears, fast and furious in that silent room. When his fingers trailed slowly down my stomach, a deliberately grudging progress, I pushed my hips forward. I began to shiver as his fingers toyed with my zipper. Then my teeth began to chatter. I had to clench them together as hard as I could to stop that ridiculous noise, but even then, exerting all my force, they still gave out an occasional involuntary convulsion.

Suddenly he was there. Standing over me. I recognised his profile, looking down at me.

The worst thing was that it was too dark to make out the expression on his face and read his mood. It made everything twice as ominous. I wanted to babble out my excuses, but the silence of the room was too intimidating. Instead I clambered to my feet, although the boy on the floor grabbed me by the hips and clung to me. 'Please,' he hissed, his voice shocking in that silent room.

Stewart took my hand and led me out of the room. I was certain once we were out the door he would reprimand me, maybe even hit me. He had the justification. He'd invited me and I'd betrayed him. I knew I would never have behaved in such a way if he hadn't disappeared and the punch hadn't been laced, but they seemed feeble excuses, hardly worth giving voice to.

But Stewart didn't yell at me. Instead, he told me very casually that something was about to happen upstairs. 'That's why I came to find you,' he said. 'I didn't want you to miss out on the show. Shall we go up?'

I nodded and walked up the stairs in front of him. 'Run away from you, did he?' one of the men in the doorway remarked as we passed through.

'Maybe you should tie him up so he doesn't do it again,' said the one with the moustache.

'Maybe I will,' Stewart chuckled slowly.

There was something slightly ominous about his laugh and the sudden tightening of his grip upon my hand.

The music had been turned down in that main room. Ken was perched on the bar and everyone had clustered around him. I noticed him exchange a look with Stewart, a quick nod, and then he began to speak. 'I hope you've all kept your tickets because one of you is going to win a very special prize to take home with you tonight.'

There was a punch bowl filled with small cards alongside him on the bar and Ken's hand delved into it. He grinned and winked at the crowd as his hand roamed around. Finally he plucked a card out and held it up before his eyes with a flourish. When he lowered it, his eyes scanned the crowd. He waited, letting the anticipation build. When his eyes settled on me, I began to feel uneasy. I knew from the way he looked at me that I was going to be declared the winner.

He called out the number. I knew it was mine without checking, but I didn't move forward to claim the prize. I dropped my gaze away from Ken's and stared at my feet. I was too shy to come forward in front of all those watching men. Whatever the prize, it wouldn't be worth the embarrassment of having to stand up there in front of them all. I felt sure there would be some sexual innuendo to the prize. I imagined something weird and extreme from a sex shop, which I wouldn't understand. My ignorance would be hugely entertaining for everyone watching and excruciating for me. But there also seemed something deeply fraudulent about the entire situation. How had Ken recognised the number as mine? It had to be a set-up. I stared at my feet and waited for Ken to give up and call out a new number.

But Ken was persistent. He called out the number a second time and urged everyone to check their invitations. Beside me, Stewart swore softly, screwed his card up and dropped it on the floor. Then, before I could stop him, he had pulled my invitation out of my pocket. 'Hey, we've got the winner here!' he yelled out. 'Carson, you've won. Go on. Go collect your prize.'

He began to push me towards the stage but I resisted. 'What's the prize?' I asked suspiciously.

Stewart shrugged. 'It's a surprise.'

Still I held my ground.

'It'll be something highly desirable,' Stewart said. 'Ken spares no expense with his parties.'

Now I was being pushed forward not only by Stewart but by all the other men around me.

'Our winner's a little shy,' murmured Ken. 'Come and sit up here beside me.'

Someone hoisted me up onto the bar.

'Bring the prize!' Ken called out and there was a stir of anticipation through the crowd.

The lights dimmed. The music swelled. One of the waiters appeared in the doorway, then another by his side. They were holding something high above their heads. It was only as they drew closer to where Ken and I sat that I could see they were carrying an enormous silver tray with a purple velvet cloth draped over it. Beneath that cloth was something very large. I forgot my earlier qualms. I was intrigued. The waiters held the platter up before Ken and me. Abruptly, the music stopped.

Ken leant forward, seized a handful of the covering cloth and whisked it away. Everyone gasped, then burst into applause.

My prize was a boy. A naked boy. He was curled up on the silver platter. His knees pulled up to hide himself. His blond head bowed and tucked into his chest. Slowly, as if in a ballet, the boy began to unfurl his limbs with great delicacy. First one of his long tanned legs stretched out and then the other. The watching crowd roared its approval. That was enough for me. My instincts had been right. This was some horrible exercise in mockery which I had to escape. I slid off the bar, but just as quickly Ken was beside me and had seized me by the arm. My position was even worse. The boy was there just an inch or two from my eyes. I couldn't avoid staring straight at him.

He had his face hidden, tucked against his chest. All I could see from where I stood was blond hair and the nape of his neck. Slowly, ever so slowly, he tilted his head to one side and then to the other, then he began to lift his face to me. But I didn't need to see. I knew. I closed my eyes. I couldn't bear to see the expression on Aaron's face when he saw who had won him.

I only opened them again when I felt a reassuring hand on my arm. Stewart. He was gazing at Aaron, that amused smile of his playing upon his lips, quite unperturbed by this unfortunate twist of events. I glanced at Aaron but he was staring at Stewart with a look of fury on his face. I began to feel embarrassed. I could imagine the assumptions Aaron must be making about us. I began to wish Stewart could have been more discreet and avoided Aaron seeing us together.

Stewart nudged me gently. 'We can leave if you like, Carson,' he said quietly.

'I suppose this is your twisted idea of a joke?'

Aaron addressed Stewart quietly so no-one but us could hear, but the sharpness in his voice was chilling. Then his eyes took me in and his expression softened a little. 'And I thought you would've known better,' he chided me in a sharp whisper.

That annoyed me. His tone of voice. Reprimanding me? When here he was in this sordid situation. Raffled off like a meat tray in a public bar. It was me who had the greater reason to feel injured. His deception had been the greater. He had made himself out to be so selective and careful about who he went with. How naive I had been to believe his rose-coloured view of his occupation.

'Do you like your prize?' asked Ken, running an admiring hand across Aaron's buttocks. 'He is quite a prize, I can assure you of that. You can take him home or, if you prefer, there's a room I can put at your disposal.'

'Let's have a runner-up's prize of watching the two of them together,' someone called out, and a roar of laughter and approving cheers rang through the crowd.

I was relieved when Stewart took control, clasped my hand firmly and led me out of the room. 'I'm sorry, Carson,' he said when we were out in the hallway. 'Aaron is a big favourite of Ken's. I had no idea he would want to use him in such a way.'

What Aaron had said to Stewart had been circling in my mind. I had been about to accuse Stewart of somehow contriving the entire situation along with Ken, but his expression was so sincere, his words so heartfelt, that I felt sure he couldn't possibly have set me up in such a way.

'Is that the sort of thing that usually happens at his parties?' I asked instead.

'Well, there's never been such a nasty coincidence before, but yes, there's always some sort of entertainment.'

'Was it a coincidence?' I asked sharply, looking at him closely.

Not a trace of guilt or guile crossed Stewart's face. He shrugged. 'Ken would never admit to orchestrating such a situation, but it's the sort of perverse thing he would do. Look, I'll just grab my jacket.'

Stewart excused himself and pounded up the stairs, leaving me to brood over what the truth of the situation was. Gradually I became aware of Ken's voice fighting to be heard over the hubbub of conversation. 'I've got an unclaimed prize here,' he called out. 'Any takers?'

There was a unanimous roar of yes.

'Well, well. With so much interest, it seems only fair to take bids.'

'Fifty dollars,' someone called out immediately.

Thankfully Stewart began to thud down the stairs at that point. I looked up at him, stricken. 'What are they doing?'

Stewart stopped and listened. Another bid was called out. He laughed. 'It's just a game, Carson.'

'It doesn't sound like it.'

Stewart hurried down the remaining stairs and put his arm round me. 'It's just something to get the boys worked up.'

'But it's not very nice for Aaron.'

'I'm sure he's been in worse situations.'

'He hasn't. He's very fussy. He won't even go with anyone who's drunk.'

'Is that what he told you?' Stewart laughed, loud and long. 'I don't think any hooker can afford to be that discerning.'

Someone called out a bid for two hundred dollars. 'Look,' Stewart continued, 'Aaron's going to make a lot of money out of tonight for not doing much. You rejected him. This little auction is just something impromptu to keep the atmosphere up. So Ken's guests don't go home feeling cheated. Knowing Aaron, he'll be enjoying all the attention. Everyone vying for him. He knew what he was letting himself in for tonight. It's unpleasant for you to have to witness, but this is the sort of thing he's paid to do.'

I wanted to protest that Aaron wouldn't normally do such a thing, but I realised what a waste of words it was. The fact was that Stewart undoubtedly knew much better than I did exactly how Aaron conducted himself and his business.

'Come on,' he whispered in my ear. 'Let's go. We'll go to my place.

It's probably simpler not to have to see Aaron tomorrow.'

In his car, on the way to his house in Newtown, Stewart began to tell me other things about Aaron, things he had kept hidden from me, and I began to feel a little better about abandoning him.

part three

CHAPTER NINE

I must admit, when I read those first chapters of Carson's memoir, I was moved. I could almost concede that perhaps Carson deserved Ant after his disappointment with Kerry and having to suffer a religious extremist for a mother. I felt a little ashamed of stealing his work and reading such personal revelations without permission. After the third chapter, I put the manuscript down, having resolved to read no more.

That resolution was short-lived.

I was in thrall to my own curiosity. I had to know what happened next. I picked the manuscript up again and continued to read. When I'd finished, I was mighty glad I'd given in to that urge. Carson had gone too far. He might have successfully manipulated me for the first three chapters, but what he expected me to swallow in the fourth and fifth was simply too preposterous. I did not believe for one minute that Carson had merely acted as receptionist to his prostitute friend. It was the biggest cliché out. If the number of prostitutes who claimed to be the receptionist were indeed the receptionist, brothels would have more phone lines than multinational companies. I felt like going through those next chapters with a red pen, underlining and deleting, then handing it back with *rewrite* scrawled across the top.

Yet despite this glossing over of the facts, I was still dying to know what happened next. It was frustrating that the narrative halted just as the revelations were tumbling out thick and fast. But when I'd copied the files, there had definitely only been five chapters. Evidently that was as far as Carson had got.

I let myself back into Ant's apartment the following week on the day of Carson's yoga appointment to check on his progress. I called up the directory of files on his computer with anticipation, only to find that there was still no Chapter Six. I couldn't believe it. Carson hadn't written a sentence all week. What had he been doing with himself? I felt like giving him a good talking-to, taking him aside and bluntly pointing out that he didn't have the luxury of frittering away his time, that he needed to be disciplined and concentrate on his writing at the expense of everything else.

Of course, what he'd been neglecting his writing for was house hunting. Carson spent his days doing the rounds of the real estate agents and looking at properties. When he confided to me how difficult it was trying to decide on somewhere, I longed to tell him to make up his mind or stay put and get back to his writing. Instead, I encouraged him to look for somewhere quiet, with a good study where he could make fast progress on his book. 'You know how much I'm dying to read it when it's finished,' I added, hoping the prospect of fans and fame would spur him on.

Carson looked startled and I realised in the past I'd been snooty and disparaging about his writing. I decided to repair that damage by reiterating my enthusiasm for his memoir and its progress as often as possible.

After a week of this encouragement, Ant took me aside for a quiet word and tactfully advised me not to ask Carson about his progress. 'He's feeling pressured. He's at a delicate point apparently and is having a lot of difficulty proceeding. I know you're only trying to be interested, and I appreciate you making the effort, but Carson doesn't. He feels like you're pestering him deliberately.'

I began to protest but Ant interrupted me. 'I know, I know. Look, he's just very sensitive about his writing. He'll barely discuss it with me. As for reading it, whenever I suggest it, he goes ballistic.'

'He doesn't have writer's block, does he?' I asked, genuinely concerned.

'Maybe he does,' shrugged Ant. 'Maybe that's why he's so moody about it.'

So I was obliged to halt my genuine support. The last thing I wanted was to aggravate Carson's writer's block. Occasionally I'd ask Ant what progress was being made, but he never seemed to know. Once he had been impressed by Carson's writing ambitions and had bragged about his book to me, but increasingly he seemed to resent 'The Book' and Carson's dedication to it. 'I'm always made to play second fiddle to that stupid book of his,' he complained, when he appeared at my door one night, evidently at a loose end. 'Lately, he's been working till all hours of the night instead of coming to bed with me.'

'Well, he's busy during the day looking at apartments,' I pointed out.

'But what about me?' moaned Ant. 'He should be paying more attention to me in the present, instead of moping over his past, writing about his old boyfriends. That's what he's doing. Writing about Stewart. Not that he's told me, but every time I've gotten out of bed and tried to persuade him to come and join me, it's Stewart's name I see all over the computer screen in front of me.'

I was doubly delighted. Firstly that Carson was writing furiously into the night – there would be chapters and chapters for me to read – but more importantly that his relationship with Ant was suffering *already* as a result.

'Now, Ant, you have to be more understanding,' I lectured him. 'Carson's future is . . . a little uncertain. It's natural for him to want to preserve his past, examine his mistakes and misdeeds, try to make some sense of his life, find some purpose or achievement in it.'

Ant nodded sheepishly and tried to reply, but I interrupted him. I had something candid to say. 'If you feel lonely and left out, you can always pop upstairs and see me. You know, I've been feeling quite forsaken since you two got together. You and I used to spend a lot of time together, and I miss that. I'd be very happy to keep you company any time of the day . . . or night.'

We were sitting side by side on my couch. I laid my hand on his to emphasise my words, expecting him gently but pointedly to pull away from my touch. But he didn't. Instead he slid his arm around me and pulled me to him. 'You feel left out?' he asked softly.

'I miss those evenings we used to have together like this,' I said, looking into his eyes and feeling that same glorious frisson I'd experienced the very first time our eyes had met. 'Just the two of us.'

Ant nodded. We were practically embracing. I let my head slide down so that it rested on his shoulder, and then gently I wormed my own arm around behind him. We simply sat there, in silence, huddled against one another for about five minutes. Finally Ant sighed, pulled his arm free of me and kissed me tenderly on the lips. 'I should go home,' he whispered.

I nodded. I didn't mind. The intimacy of merely being that close to him had been enough. The kiss, the perfect finale. I had no doubt that it was only the beginning. There would be plenty more evenings like this to follow.

But there weren't.

The very next evening I got dragged into Ant's flat by Carson as I walked up the stairs after my day at uni. 'I found the perfect apartment for us today,' he crowed, his face ecstatic with excitement.

I'd seen him in this state of happy agitation before, like a little boy on Christmas Day. 'I saw it this morning and I knew as soon as I walked in the front door. I called Ant and he came and saw it during his lunchbreak. It was scheduled to go for auction but we made an offer in advance. They turned it down, which we expected. So we've made a new offer. We could get the call at any moment, letting us know. Ant's gone to buy champagne.'

His news was like a late frost nipping at the bud of my fondest hope. A bud which only last night on my couch had begun to shiver and stir from its enforced hibernation. During the course of my day that hope had unfurled and bloomed, nourished by the optimistic anticipation of my imagination. But now, under the surprise assault of Carson's triumphant announcement, it cowered, shrank, then began to shrivel in despair.

I knew my smile would be limp but I tried my best to raise one. 'Congratulations,' I managed to say. 'Where is it?'

'Onslow Avenue, Elizabeth Bay.'

Elizabeth Bay. Betty Bay. Not William Street, Betty Bay, the illusionary address that Strauss had invented for us all, but the real thing.

'Stephen, you don't look very pleased for us,' Carson upbraided me. 'Don't worry. We'll still see you. We'll still be very close by.'

Carson's words were like a cloak, kindly meant, intended to warm and comfort me, but instead they were smothering, suffocating. Elizabeth Bay was the worst possible location. Not close enough for Ant to pop up in the evenings when Carson was otherwise occupied, but too close for me to shut him out of my life altogether and forget him. If he was to move across the other side of the city, instead of merely over the hill, the enforced separation would surely have made forgetting him a little easier.

Carson began to rave about the apartment: its location, its features, his plans for renovations. When Ant arrived with the champagne, I was in great need of a drink and insisted they open it, even though the phone call hadn't come. 'Somehow I just know you're going to get it,' I said, and I was right.

With such an enormous change to their lives looming, Carson's routine fell into disarray. I never knew when he was going to be at home and when he wasn't. There was no opportunity to sneak a look at the new chapters he had allegedly been writing. I was horrified when I went down to their flat only a week after their offer was accepted to find the computer disconnected and packed up in its box. 'What about your writing, Carson?' I protested. 'It's at least a month before you can move in. Why are you packing up already?'

'There's so much to do and think about,' said Carson

quickly. 'I can't really concentrate . . . and, to be honest, I was kind of stuck anyway.'

With the computer disconnected there was no possibility of me reading anything new. Then, when they finally did move into Onslow Avenue, I no longer had access to their apartment. My spare key became redundant. I hinted to Ant what a good idea it would be to entrust someone with a key to their new place in case they locked themselves out. I even feigned locking myself out of my own apartment and told Ant what a locksmith charged to break in, hoping the price would shock him into providing me with a spare key immediately. But my plan went awry. Carson gave their new next-door neighbour, Margo, a spare key instead. Margo was middle-aged, lived alone, seemed almost always to be at home and took a keen interest in 'the boys'. 'It's so wonderful having a neighbour like Margo,' Carson gushed to me when I visited for the first time after they'd moved in. 'She buys us things on special at the supermarket which she thinks we'd like. She's taken up a hem on a pair of trousers for Ant. She's even offered to sew us outfits for Mardi Gras next year.'

That was the last thing I wanted to have to witness. Ant and Carson in matching sequin shorts, with Margo the doting mother figure admiring her handiwork before waving them off for the night. The very thought of it made me wonder about gaining access to Margo's apartment as well and snapping the needle on her sewing machine in two.

It was this frustration at having Carson's book locked away from me that led me to do a little investigative work. If I couldn't read his new chapters, I decided to try to verify just how honest the previous chapters had actually been. I conducted some simple little check-ups, such as examining Carson's hands. Had they been coarsened from a career of washing dishes and peeling vegetables, the job he claimed he'd been doing when he first came to Sydney? I complimented him on his hands one day. 'You could be a hand model, Carson,' I suggested, giving myself the pretext to seize his hands and scrutinise them.

They were pale and smooth, not rough and red. I checked

for scars from a slipped vegetable knife. There were none. Even if Carson had started out washing dishes, I was certain when his eyes were opened to the lucrative nature of Jason's trade, he had quickly thrown in his pot scrub.

My next tactic was to try to get Carson to admit to turning tricks by casually bringing up the subject in conversation. It was a lucky coincidence that Blair's financial situation had reached an absolute crisis point at that time, and she had begun to complain that the only option left to her was prostitution. I narrated Blair's misfortunes to Carson, hoping it might encourage him to open up about his own experience.

Blair had always been notoriously bad with money. She was nonchalant about letters of demand from credit card companies and department stores that had been foolish enough to grant her an account. 'They'll never proceed. The sum they're seeking to recover wouldn't come close to covering their costs.'

But it wasn't the credit card companies or David Jones that finally defeated Blair and forced her to deal with her debts. It was a small travel agent she bounced a cheque on. She had frivolously taken herself off on a package holiday to Noosa. 'I'm so stressed by my debts,' she said by way of justification. 'I have to take myself away from all this pressure and try to think what I can possibly do.'

Blair returned with a vague resolution to find a weekend job, only to find her travel agent waiting at the airport to greet her. 'Have a nice time in Noosa, *bitch*?' he snarled.

Blair was stunned. Of course the travel agent knew her return flight details but she had never considered he would go to the extreme lengths of confronting her over her worthless cheque at the airport. 'Enjoy your holiday?' he asked again.

Blair managed to nod.

'Good. Now you can pay me for it. You owe me four hundred and fifty dollars, plus the bank's nine dollar fee for your dishonoured cheque, plus my expenses in having to come out here to get *my* money.'

The travel agent gripped Blair by the arm and steered her

over to the ATM. Despite her protests of poverty, he made her get out her wallet, insert her card and punch in her code. He selected a balance, studied the slip and then punched in a withdrawal. 'What are you doing?' cried Blair in alarm.

'Taking a part payment on what you owe me. Don't worry, I'll post you a receipt.'

He withdrew the one hundred and twenty dollars in the account and refused to return the card. 'I want you to come and visit me later this week with the balance of my money. I'm open late Thursday evening. You'll get your card back then. I know you don't have it, honey, but you'll have to get it. Borrow it. Just don't fuck with me or you'll regret it.'

But Blair disregarded his warning, cancelled her card, applied for a new one and figured she'd seen the last of him. She was wrong. He was waiting outside her door when she got home from work on Friday evening. Blair had forgotten that she had written her home address on the back of the cheque.

'This is harassment,' she protested.

'No, this is called collection. Do you have three hundred and fifty dollars for me?'

'Fuck off.'

It was at that point that the travel agent had turned nasty. He pushed Blair up against the wall and jammed his forearm up against her throat. 'It's me that should be swearing at you, you cheap, cheating bit of trash.'

He released her and Blair doubled over, wheezing and gasping. She'd been holding her keys when he seized her and they fell from her hand. The travel agent picked them up and proceeded to open her door.

'You . . . can't,' Blair wheezed.

But he ignored her and entered the apartment. 'I'll just take a few things as collateral, until you honour your debts,' he said.

'I'm reporting this theft to the police,' threatened Blair.

'Fine. They can come and arrest you for fraud.'

The travel agent was very clever. He didn't take the typical objects of value, such as the television set and stereo. He took

Blair's disposable contact lenses, her Lady Shave, her Alessi coffee maker, her alarm clock and all the make-up in the bathroom cabinet. He packed everything into Blair's Samsonite suitcase, pulled out the retractable handle and wheeled his booty out the door.

Blair had come pounding on my door as soon as he'd gone, desperate for advice. She wept as she acknowledged how impossible it was for her to function without these basics. 'The only make-up I have is the lipstick in my handbag. I have to throw these contacts I'm wearing out on Monday and I don't have a replacement pair. I can't go to work wearing my glasses and no make-up. I'll be sent home or fired. I have to make some money, and fast. I think . . . I'm going to have to work William Street over the weekend.'

She wasn't joking. That night Blair borrowed one of Strauss's drag dresses and had him do her make-up. However, when she timidly made her appearance on William Street, she was chased back upstairs by the prostitutes. Even Sass didn't intervene on Blair's behalf. 'We can't have real girls flogging it down here,' she explained to me the next day. 'The customers would be bewildered.'

'But don't they think you're real women?' I asked, quite bewildered myself.

'Darling, they pretend to think that. They might tell their mates that, even try to believe it themselves, but they still keep coming on back for the same ole thing. I guess they just love a chick with a dick.'

Blair went round the bars in Kings Cross the next day and landed herself a job at a club called Fizz. 'It's not what you think,' she assured me a few days later. 'There's no sex involved. I just have to wear a skirt halfway up my arse and chitchat with these hideous old men and ensure they keep buying me bottles of French champagne at one hundred dollars a pop. Which I have to throw back by myself, because the men will scarcely take a sip in the hope that they'll get away with only buying one bottle. But I have a quota to fill. Two bottles per client. I have the most terrible hangovers the next day. Monday morning, all I could think was how much easier it would be to go to some agency where all I have to do is fuck the clients. It's such a strain having to pretend to find these vile men attractive and interesting and talk to them, as well as knock back all that champagne. Yes, I'm going to be able to settle my bills but I'll end up a lush in the process.'

I related all of this to Carson, then added in a conspiring tone, 'There's probably more to it than she's letting on. There always is.'

Carson shrugged. 'I tend to believe what people tell me,' he replied primly. 'Except you, Stephen. I always take what you say with a pinch of salt.'

I pretended to treat that as a joke, but inwardly I was fuming. 'I think the secrecy around prostitution only adds to its mystique,' I persisted. 'If it was legalised and discussed, it would be a lot healthier all round.'

'No doubt,' said Carson and he hesitated before continuing. 'But I also think a person would have to have a very strong sense of self-worth not to feel degraded by that sort of transaction. It would have to have an impact on your ability to form a relationship, or even to have sex that wasn't work sex.'

Suddenly Carson's expression changed and I realised that my own face was no doubt reflecting the glee I was feeling. But I couldn't help myself. It all made such perfect sense. Carson had been sexually frigid when he first met Ant, and with me as well, and he had just explained the reason why.

My next step was to try to find out if Carson had confessed his past to Ant or whether he had merely been fed the official authorised version. But when I brought the topic of prostitution up with Ant, he wasn't at all forthcoming. 'I'd never pay for it,' he said bluntly and couldn't be prodded into elaborating.

Ant's attitude was no surprise. He was reluctant to spend money on the bare essentials of life, so naturally he would baulk at paying for what he could obtain for free. However, I couldn't help wondering whether his penurious ways were so extreme that he would knowingly form a relationship with an ex-prostitute and derive satisfaction in getting for free what so many others had paid for. He was so stingy that once that theory had occurred to me, I couldn't discount it.

I was very tempted at that point to tell Ant what I knew, but I hesitated. Carson hadn't confessed anything outright. If I had somehow got it wrong, I would never be forgiven by either of them. I needed some conclusive evidence. I took myself off to the State Library to do some research. I went through the old issues of *Campaign* and *Outrage* magazines looking at the sex workers' ads. I found the ads for Jason first and then ads for Jason and Hunter working together. Initially I was very excited, thinking this was the proof I'd been looking for, but after reading the description of Hunter (tall, top, muscular, moustache) I began to have my doubts. I couldn't imagine Carson as a top and he definitely wasn't capable of growing a moustache you would want to boast about. I realised that Hunter had to be Aaron's boyfriend, the guy who'd introduced him to his profession and then found a sugar daddy in Los Angeles. I tried the issues a year from that date, but although there was still the occasional advertisement for Jason (according to his copy, he had become a year younger rather than a year older), there was no buddy advertisement with Carson. There were lots of other single ads which might have been Carson – slim, blond, smooth prostitutes were plentiful – but there was nothing distinctive about any of those ads, nothing which might have confirmed that the boy behind the fake name and credentials was Carson. I gave up on that line of investigation.

My other potential lead, Ginger, was a complete dead end. Ginger had disappeared in Queensland. She never returned from her 'holiday'.

'Either she's making a fortune,' pondered Sass when I questioned her, 'which can't be right because she's such a dog these days. Or she's gotten out of the game, which isn't likely either because she's accustomed to the money and what else could she do? My guess is that she's done something stupid, gotten on the wrong side of someone, and is in hiding. That'd be typical of old Ginge. Always did have a mouth on her. I warned her. Keep it shut, honey, or you'll find someone sticking a gun down your throat instead of a cock.'

I protested that this seemed a bit far-fetched but Sass was convinced by the likelihood of her own theory and insisted she wasn't exaggerating. 'Discretion is everything in this game. Clients pay for sex, but what a lot of them are paying for is a confidential transaction. Ginge was always gossiping about her clients, and not just with the other girls, which always happens, but with friends and even other clients. With the type of men old Ginge was attracting, sooner or later she was going to piss someone off in a major way.'

There were no other avenues of investigation I could think of. All I could do was wait for the reclusive Ginger to reappear on William Street.

I turned my attention to another aspect of Carson's book which had intrigued me. It had been hinted in Chapter Five that Stewart was into something kinky in bed, something that he had to pay Jason to perform. Which begged the question: what depraved things was Carson introduced to when he and Stewart became a couple? Of course my imagination went wild. Bondage? Fisting? Dress-ups? Role plays? I reread that chapter several times for clues, but the only concrete detail was that at Ken's party Stewart (and many of the other men present) had been dressed in leather. Had Carson's relationship with Stewart been that of master and slave? It seemed highly likely.

One thing I knew for certain was that if Carson did secretly delight in being tied up, spanked or menaced by a leather-clad daddy, he would *not* have confessed such desires to Ant. Ant was very middle of the road sexually. Leather, dildos, even amyl nitrate, anything which was really only adventurous sex, Ant was appalled by. His Presbyterian upbringing asserted itself and he became quite puritanical. 'Call me old-fashioned, but all I want to do is suck a cute blond boy's cock and fuck his butt. I don't know why some of these gay extremists are so disparaging of that. It's not considered tame where I come from. It's kind of revolutionary actually.'

I tried to worm details of their sex life out of Ant but I didn't get very far. In the past Ant had been, if anything, too forthcoming about the nitty-gritty. He'd confided unbearably frank details of all his one-night stands and even narrated his early trysts with Carson. But lately he had become circumspect and discreet. Could it be that he was too embarrassed to reveal the rites and acts that Carson had lured him into? Or, alternatively, were they bored in bed with one another already? Had their sex life palled, lapsed into a once-a-week ritual?

Having failed to wheedle anything out of Ant, I decided to quiz the neighbours. I befriended Margo, their self-appointed mother. Surely if Margo heard one of her boys cry out in the night, she would whip out of bed and have her ear to the wall in a trice. I took to sunbathing in the little park next door to Carson and Ant's apartment block when I knew they weren't at home. I was aware that Margo considered this park her own backyard and was often to be found sitting out there with a book or merely keeping an eye on the visitors, whom she had no qualms about reprimanding if they left litter in their wake or exposed more of their bodies to the sun than Margo felt was necessary. One afternoon I introduced myself to Margo as Ant's closest friend and mentioned that, up until they moved, I too had been their neighbour. 'I do hope they're not too noisy for you,' I said. 'They used to live beneath me and though I never mentioned it – you mustn't say anything – there were occasions when I'd be woken in the middle of the night by them.'

Margo was intrigued but she assured me that she enjoyed the sleep of the dead and had never heard a peep from 'her boys'. After a few minutes of conversation I realised why she slept so soundly. Margo was a little deaf in one ear. She kept twisting her body round towards me and asking me to repeat myself as we chatted. Margo would be a dead loss as a spy.

My other motivation in befriending Margo had been the thought that I might be able to 'borrow' the spare key from her at some point in the future. However, I quickly gleaned that she would not part with that key readily. She proudly informed me that this was the first time any neighbour had ever bestowed such a trust upon her. She took the honour and the responsibility it entailed very seriously indeed.

When Margo failed to confirm any extreme sexual acts occurring nextdoor, I turned up on Carson's doorstep unannounced one Saturday in what even I had to admit was a last-ditch attempt to obtain some proof of his proclivities. 'Hello, Carson,' I said brightly. 'I've come to borrow some rope.'

'Some rope?' Carson repeated, doing a good job of looking utterly mystified.

I had been hoping he would blush or hesitate, show some signs of guilt or complicity. Or else shamelessly usher me through to the bedroom and retrieve a length of it from beneath the bed. But Carson merely looked put out. I was obliged to provide some kind of an explanation. 'Our clothes line broke on the roof and I've got a basket of wet laundry. I need a rope urgently.'

'Then you should have gone to a hardware shop,' said Carson tersely.

I noted that Carson wasn't his usual agreeable self. He was positively surly with me. Had I struck a guilty nerve?

'Yes, of course, I did think of that. It's just that I had this recollection of Ant saying that you had some rope somewhere.'

'Not that I'm aware of,' said Carson brusquely. 'I'll ask him when he gets home. He's at the gym. Sorry, Stephen, but I've got to get back to my writing. I'm in the middle of something important. I can't ask you in.'

I had to enquire. 'What chapter are you up to?'

'I'm *trying* to work on Chapter Eight,' said Carson and closed the door in my face.

I might have felt offended by his rudeness if I hadn't been filled with a wild joy at the progress Carson was making. There would be lots of chapters for me to read when I finally managed to get my hands on them.

Walking home, I decided to give up on my investigations. Every ingenious plan I'd tried had provided only inconclusive results. I was getting nowhere.

That evening Ant was dispatched to have a word with me. 'Carson thinks you're deliberately out to sabotage his progress on the book,' he sighed, sounding infinitely weary of Carson, his book and the message he was obliged to deliver.

I was incredulous. I did my best impression of Carson's innocent act. '*What?* Why does he interpret everything I do as some sort of elaborate scheme to undermine him?'

Ant refrained from pointing out that my past behaviour was reason enough to make Carson highly suspicious of me. 'Apparently you interrupted him at a crucial moment with some nonsensical request and he couldn't write another word all afternoon.'

'Your boyfriend is so paranoid,' I protested. 'Honestly, Ant. He's got writer's block and I get blamed because I pay a neighbourly visit. It was you I wanted to see anyway, not him.'

I made a point of interrupting Carson the next day by phoning to apologise for the previous day's interruption. I also had something else I wanted to ask him. 'By the way, how autobiographical is your autobiography?'

That question had been bothering me ever since I'd read the beginnings of his book. Writers were like actors. They tended to be vague and elusive about facts. Some were simply outright liars. I knew from a lifetime's experience of Elisabeth how capable she was of embroidering unpalatable truths. Writers were the same, possibly even worse. Reinventing their life histories and portraying themselves in more glorious lights. Recalling the worst moments of their friends' and families' lives, then exaggerating them to even more grotesque, unflattering extremes. They were not to be trusted.

But Carson would not be drawn on that subject. He thanked me for the apology and excused himself without answering the question.

I would not be put off that easily, however. I simply bided

my time and chose more suitable moments to pose my question. For instance, when Carson had had one of his rare glasses of champagne. Or when he let it slip that he'd had a good day at his computer and was feeling elated by what he'd written. Yet even at those prime moments Carson remained guarded and evasive. He would sigh and look pained, then complain that he didn't like discussing his work, at least not until it was complete. Given his ponderous progress, that point in time seemed very remote indeed. After much persistence on my part, at a cocktail party (where even he was completely smashed), Carson finally, grudgingly, admitted that what he was writing was an autobiographical novel.

'Well, what in the fuck is *that*, besides a contradiction?' I couldn't help blurting out.

My remark offended Carson and he refused to discuss the matter any further. I was forced to draw my own conclusions. Autobiographical novel, I decided, was merely a grand name for an autobiography but with the added bonus of an escape clause. It permitted Carson the luxury of disowning any exploits he might have second thoughts about. He could claim they were fictitious, adornments to make for a more compelling read.

'I'm having to put my book aside for a while,' Carson said to me later. 'My deadline for my thesis is the end of this year. I'm going to have to concentrate on that from now on.'

The months slipped by and I gave up even asking about the book. By the time the opportunity to take another look at it finally dawned, I'd almost forgotten about it. So much time had passed, almost a year.

When Ant told me he was taking Carson back to Dunedin to meet his family – 'I refused to come home for Christmas unless Carson was welcome too' – I felt too depressed by the news to consider that there might be an opportunity in their absence. Another landmark stage in their relationship had been reached: meeting the in-laws. It made me intensely jealous and vindictive.

'Well, Carson will *love* meeting your father,' I sniped. 'A headmaster. You won't be able to keep him out of your father's office, away from all his instruments of punishment.'

'What on earth are you talking about?' asked Ant, genuinely puzzled. 'Now look, do you think you could water our dope plants while we're away? Carson said not to trouble you but we can't ask Margo to do that. Not that she'd know what they were anyway.'

I was touched. 'Ant, you'd trust me with your plants after last time?'

Ant's expression grew wary – 'I'd forgotten about that' – and he began to prevaricate. It was infuriating: to have had the opportunity I'd once been desperate for offered to me, then snatched away again immediately on account of my own hasty words. Naturally the desire to read Carson's manuscript and have a good poke around their apartment resurfaced with ferocious intensity. I *had* to have that key.

Finally, thankfully, the day before they were due to leave, Ant dropped over with the keys and typewritten watering instructions. 'Read these and don't forget,' he commanded me. 'We've told Margo a little white lie. That you'll be popping in a couple of times to reset the video to tape some shows for us.'

But even after Ant and Carson had flown out, another obstacle remained. Margo. She considered neighbourhood watch a matter of twenty-four-hour surveillance. What's more, unbeknownst to me, she had finally invested in a hearing aid and she caught me fumbling outside their door on the eve after their departure. She startled me terribly, sweeping silently out of her apartment and accosting me with a loud, 'And what, may I ask, are you up to, young man?'

I was so startled I couldn't come up with a decent excuse. I stood mute while Margo surveyed me suspiciously. 'Anthony told me to expect you, but not this soon. They've only just left. They're probably still in the air. You can't have to reprogramme that contraption already, surely?'

I stuttered and then thankfully a likely lie occurred to me. 'You've caught me in the act, Margo,' I smiled helplessly. 'You see, Ant said they'd left a Christmas present for me on the kitchen table. I'm so impatient, I was creeping in to open it early.'

Margo chuckled with delight, then shooed me away from the door. 'You're not allowed it,' she insisted. 'Not until Christmas Day. Just think of the pleasure of anticipation if you wait. I'm going to commandeer that present myself and keep it for you until Christmas Eve. I can see you're a young man who is not to be trusted.'

Margo wouldn't permit another word on the subject. 'I'm on a red alert with my boys away. A red alert,' she assured me as she saw me out the front door onto the street.

I was forced to retreat home and proceed more cautiously. Even if I did visit the flat legitimately, Margo would be suspicious. I could imagine her barging in on me if she considered that the time I was spending in their apartment was excessive. Were she to catch me at the computer, she would of course tell 'her boys' when they returned. I decided to wait for an evening when Margo was not at home. I walked round to Onslow Avenue every night and checked to see if the lights were on in her apartment. They always were. She was on red alert all right. It was frustrating, but I knew the closer it drew to Christmas, the more likely it was that Margo would take herself off to spend time with her family. Finally, on Christmas Eve, I found Margo's apartment in darkness.

I'd had copies cut of the keys and I used them to make sure that they worked. I needed to know that I'd still be able to gain access after I'd returned the keys I'd been given. I didn't turn any lights on. I went straight to the second bedroom, which Carson had made over into his study. I turned on the desk lamp, switched on the computer, brought up the directory of files and scanned them eagerly. I was appalled by what I found. Carson had barely made any progress. Despite all the leisure hours he had at his disposal, during the past year he had only written two more chapters. Seven and eight. I was about to open the file for Chapter Seven when I realised. There was a chapter missing. The last chapter I had read had been number five. Chapter Six wasn't there, unless Carson had made the extraordinary mistake of misnaming his file. I stabbed at the keyboard to open the Chapter Seven file but Carson had another surprise in store for me. The computer screen demanded a password. I checked all the other book files. Carson had put password protection on all of them. Why? Was it to keep Ant out? Or me? Had Carson worried that my interest in his book over the last year might lead me to do exactly what I was now doing once I had access to their apartment?

It was a setback, but I was confident I could crack the code. Carson might consider himself a writer, but in my opinion he didn't have much imagination. It only took me ten minutes to discover his password; by monotonously entering all the obvious combinations, I finally hit upon it. Anti. His nickname for Ant.

Chapter Seven blinked onto the screen. I scanned through it, then scrolled down the page. It was all about his trip to Europe with Stewart. I scanned right through to the end and then moved on to Chapter Eight, hoping there was going to be some sort of flashback to Aaron and Ken and what had transpired after that party in Birchgrove. I skimmed through the pages, but neither of those names jumped out at me. It was all Stewart, Stewart, Stewart and domesticity in Newtown.

Finally I had to accept the evidence before my eyes. Carson had cheated and skipped Chapter Six and continued at Chapter Seven. But what was that unwritten chapter to reveal? I remembered now Carson's complaints of being stuck and Ant saying that he had writer's block. What had happened when he moved in with Stewart that Carson had such difficulty in relating? Something so sordid, so extreme, he couldn't bring himself to write it down. I was certain of that.

I copied the two new files onto the floppy disk I had brought with me. Then I began my search of the bedroom. I was looking for ropes, handcuffs, rubber gloves, dildos, pornography. I went through the boxes in the top of the wardrobe, thinking that perhaps Carson kept his old equipment hidden up there, away from Ant's eyes. But I found nothing. There were no leather garments hanging in Carson's wardrobe either. No photographs of him and Stewart dressed in leather in the old photo album I came across. Nor was there anything particularly masterful about Stewart. He was a handsome, amiable-looking, middle-aged man, whose ready smile faded as the photo album progressed. His appearance grew more and more wan until it seemed he could barely raise a smile for the camera. I had to stop looking through that album. Those photographs disturbed me and for the first time it struck me, the intrusiveness of what I was doing: wilfully trespassing. I replaced the photo album, quickly surveyed the apartment to check that it was as I had found it, and let myself out.

But there was one thing I had noticed during my search which nagged at me as I walked back up the hill towards Kings Cross. There had been no condoms anywhere. Not in any of the bedside drawers nor in the bathroom cupboard. There was lube by the bed but no condoms. I knew they couldn't be having unsafe sex. Given Carson's status, that was inconceivable. Had they stopped fucking? Had Ant finally become nervous about the risk of being fucked by Carson and put a stop to it? Was Carson in turn retaliating by not obliging him, and was that why Ant never boasted about their sex life any more? Had it deteriorated into nothing more than lots of hugging and kissing and the occasional bout of mutual masturbation? Of course, it was also possible that they might have taken all their condoms to Dunedin with them. Even if they had been assigned to separate bedrooms, as Ant joked they would be, they would still find a way to have sex. That they'd taken their supply with them was probably the truth of the matter, but I preferred to believe otherwise. I wanted to believe that the lack of condoms was a sign that all was not well in their marriage bed.

It was in my own bed that night, on the brink of sleep, when the thought flashed through my mind and I knew it had to be correct. What it was that Carson couldn't bring himself to write in Chapter Six. It wasn't sordid or extreme, simply the most devastating event in Carson's life. Chapter Six had to contain the revelation that Carson had sero-converted, that he'd had the HIV test and discovered that he was positive.

I couldn't sleep after that. I couldn't stop thinking about what that must have been like, how young Carson must have been when he found that out. He had been in year ten at school. He would only have been sixteen when he came to Sydney and got mixed up with Aaron and Stewart. Back then, in the early eighties, AIDS was still an unknown quantity. Safe sex guidelines probably didn't even exist. For the first time I realised how dreadfully unlucky Carson had been. If he'd only been a little slower to acknowledge his sexuality and act upon it, he might well have avoided what had befallen him.

I took a couple of sleeping pills to knock myself out and to stop dwelling on Carson's misfortune. I had to sleep so that I would be alert and appreciative for Elisabeth's Christmas celebration the next day. Christmas Day was one of her favourite performances. We all knew our roles by heart. Elisabeth: the noble, weary martyr who had been making preparations for weeks and expected applause and compliments throughout the day. My father and I: humble and grateful for her efforts and praising her after every mouthful swallowed. While Uncle Vic would be drunk and at his most queeny as he frolicked from kitchen to dining room, assisting Elisabeth, fussing and gushing over the lengths she had gone to. For once, my father and I would be grateful to him for his excesses. The more he carried on, the less was expected from us.

While I waited for the pills to work, I realised I was relieved Carson hadn't written Chapter Six. I had no wish to read about that aspect of his life – it made me feel so deeply uneasy. When I recalled my own machinations against Carson, my attempts to come between him and Ant, I began to feel genuinely ashamed of myself; an emotion I was very unfamiliar with. Carson had endured enough. I made my New Year's resolution then and there, a whole week early. I would stop prying into Carson's past. It was not my place to reveal to Ant that his new boyfriend was even more immoral than his first one. He must discover that for himself.

I felt much better having decided that. I rolled over, certain that now I would sleep. I didn't.

There was something else that kept niggling at me. The thought that my resolution ought to extend a little further, that I should also resolve to try to stop desiring Ant. My eyes blinked open in protest at the notion. How could I stifle what I desired most? What most certainly would have been, were it not for that series of unfortunate circumstances and the inopportune intrusion of Carson between us. How could I temper my animosity towards Carson when he had what I wanted, even if he was more deserving and scored full marks in the sympathy vote?

I didn't honestly believe I could, but I grudgingly conceded to try to forsake Ant. I knew how difficult that would be. I would need a major distraction like an overseas trip or an exciting new career path to placate myself. Unfortunately, neither of those was particularly probable. I had no money to go overseas and no likelihood of persuading my parents to pay for me to do so, especially as I had failed Legal I for the second year in a row. A new career path was a certainty but it was unlikely to be glamorous and exciting. I was going to have to get a job to pay my rent. My father would refuse to keep paying it when he learnt my university results. The problem was I had no idea what job I could possibly do. The golden boy, who had been assured of so much, surely couldn't end up as a waiter, but I couldn't think of any other job I could possibly hope to get.

The new year was already looking thoroughly depressing. How could I possibly renounce Ant, my one joy, when life was so bleak?

Then it occurred to me. The perfect distraction. A boyfriend. But he would have to be very handsome and very eligible. Although I knew it was wrong, that it opposed the virtue of my newly formed resolution, I couldn't help considering that my new boyfriend would not only have to dazzle me, he would also have to make Ant jealous.

CHAPTER TEN

Having resolved to find an eligible boyfriend, I began to feel anxious about how achievable that in fact was. The few men I had met over the past year did not augur well. Paulo-Henrique was a prime example. He was Brazilian, gruffly masculine and with the sexiest accent. I was so enchanted by his looks, it took me several weeks to realise that his dark mood was not the after-effect of too many drugs at the Mardi Gras party where we'd met, but his permanent state. He confided to me that he'd been diagnosed as clinically depressed and had been on anti-depressants for two years, ever since his first boyfriend dumped him. At first I was flattered that Paulo-Henrique confided his intimate problems to me so candidly. But after a couple of weeks, I realised he was merely desperate for a sympathetic ear. And his sexy accent could not disguise the fact that he was whingeing. Paulo-Henrique had always been slightly indifferent to sex. Increasingly, he would only submit his flawless body to me after I had endured a long evening of listening to his woes. But even the sex began to fail when he started doubling the dose of his medication on the advice of his GP. The change did lift his mood but also caused a deflation elsewhere, somewhere much more vital. Paulo-Henrique could no longer maintain an erection.

Roger seemed to be the opposite to Paulo-Henrique. He was a loud and effervescent Sagittarian I met at the Hand in Hand dance party and went home with. However, lying in his bed the next morning while he slept on, I noticed his clothes rack. I was shocked to realise that he had more dresses hanging there than shirts and jackets! Raising my head off the pillow, I saw a line of high heels and a pair of knee-high leather boots arranged neatly below the dresses. I escaped while Roger slept.

I had no wish to linger and discover what outfit he would choose for the coming day.

The boy I'd liked the most, Liam, was fresh out of the closet. He was so sweet and timid and tender, I couldn't help falling in love with him instantaneously. But after only one night together (his first time), he confided that he was still confused about his sexuality and didn't want to see me again. I preferred to believe that it was meeting both Sass and Strauss when I brought him back to my place that had driven him back into the closet posthaste. But I couldn't discount the possibility that there was something about me, something I'd said or perhaps done to him in bed, that had repelled him, not only from me, but from the entire homosexual lifestyle.

It was Warren, however, who had been the most seriously fucked up of them all. His boyfriend had ended their four-year relationship to take up with a bear. 'It's obscene. He left me for someone who's fat, furry and forty. He dumped me for that! I just can't believe it. I can't accept it. I'll never accept it. It's so demeaning.'

Warren was seeing a psychiatrist and a counsellor recommended by his doctor, as well as someone who advertised in the gay press as a Positive Self Image Counsellor. But all that therapy didn't stop him earbashing me. 'What does his choice say about me? Okay, I have some hair on my chest but I don't have it on my back and bum, thanks to electrolysis. And I'm not fat. No-one's ever called me fat. This is muscle. And I've just had my thirtieth birthday. I'm ten years away from forty. I'm not a bear, but I'm beginning to think that bastard considered me to be a cub. And now he's graduated to a grizzly bear! Oh, it's so humiliating.'

I dumped him myself after that speech. Once he'd pointed it out, I realised he was a bit plump, and he was indeed waging a battle against body hair without achieving much of a victory. But the last straw was his age. He'd claimed to be twenty-five when we first met.

So I wasn't feeling confident about my prospects when I

went to the New Year's Eve dance party. I also ended up going by myself. Ant and Carson were away; Blair had sworn off dance parties and was working the night at Fizz, and Strauss had been invited to an underwear party which was reputedly going to end in an orgy. 'My resolution for 1995 is to have sex and lots of it,' Strauss confided to me. 'I've unwittingly become the Doris Day of Darlinghurst. Things have to change.'

I arrived at the Hordern in time for midnight, but afterwards I wished I hadn't. It was downright depressing. Everyone around me seemed to be in couples, hugging and kissing and laughing. No-one wished me Happy New Year, let alone kissed me. I felt deflated and it was a struggle to dance on the crowded dance floor. I went and sat down, eyeing the boys who strutted by, hoping to catch the interest of someone I liked the look of. I was so preoccupied cruising an Italian boy, who was dancing by himself in front of me and steadfastly avoiding my eyes, that I didn't pay any attention to the guy who sat down next to me. When he tapped me on the arm after a few minutes and asked me a question, I turned around startled.

'Sorry?'

'Would you like to dance?'

I was very surprised by his request. I couldn't recall anyone asking me to dance at a dance party before. In fact, I didn't think I'd ever been asked by a *man* to dance. There was something familiar about this guy. I was certain I'd seen him before somewhere, but I couldn't place where.

Perhaps he thought I still hadn't understood him because he repeated himself. I realised how much I liked being asked. I grinned. 'I've never been asked for a dance at one of these parties.'

'I find that hard to believe. I'm Shaun.'

I introduced myself and we shook hands. Shaun stood up, still holding my hand, and pulled me to my feet. He led me onto the dance floor and we danced a few songs together. I scrutinised him whenever he affected to look away and he grinned widely every time he caught me staring. He had an open face, a ready smile and playful eyes. He was tall and had a sturdy, lightly muscled physique. He was dressed simply in jeans, dancing with his shirt off, the band of his Versace underwear on display. When he turned away for a moment I was impressed to notice that the jeans were by Paul Smith.

It was beginning to irritate me that I couldn't remember where I knew him from. It made me worry that perhaps my drinking was actually a problem. Then, as one song merged into the next, Shaun leant forward and kissed me. 'Happy New Year,' he murmured in my ear as he drew back.

'Where do I know you from?' I finally had to ask.

'We saw each other here last year,' he revealed, smiling slyly.

I felt a flush of relief. 'You should've said hello,' I reproved him.

'I did, and I've been thinking about you ever since,' said Shaun. 'For an entire year.'

I liked that. I liked to think of someone pining after me.

'You probably don't even remember,' Shaun continued. 'You were kind of out of it or distracted. You didn't seem up to conversation. You were sitting outside by yourself when I said hello and it was as if you didn't even hear me.'

That stirred a vague memory. A boy in silver shorts saying hello to me when I was sitting outside, on the lookout for Ant.

'You were wearing silver shorts,' I said.

Shaun blushed with pleasure that I had remembered.

We spent the entire party together. Whenever I excused myself to go to the bathroom or to buy a mineral water, he would accompany me and wait. When I returned to his side, his face would light up with that smile and win me over anew.

When the party finished, he offered me a ride home. I was surprised he had a car. None of my friends had cars. I was even more impressed when I actually saw it: a black Saab convertible. We drove back to Kings Cross with the top down, the wind whipping through our damp hair and drying the sweat on our bodies. It felt reckless and exhilarating. I invited him up to my flat for some breakfast and truly had only that in mind. The last thing I felt like was sex. I didn't know that I even had the energy to grind the coffee beans.

But Shaun had other ideas. Halfway up the stairs he pressed himself against me. He was erect. His hands slid around my waist, over my abdomen and rested on the waistband of my shorts. Clasped against him, our ascent up the stairs became cumbersome, but by the time we reached my door, he had me hard too. While I slid the key into the lock, he slid my shorts down my thighs. I opened the door, my shorts fell around my ankles and I stepped out of them. I walked through to the kitchen in my underwear – I was dying for a glass of water. I'd just turned on the tap when he seized me from behind. He pulled me back against him, hard, kissing and nibbling at my neck, his hands grasping insistently at my chest, buttocks, abdomen, before finally delving down the front of my underwear. At first I felt like telling him to hold on a minute – I hadn't had a chance to fetch a glass – but his hands running over me felt so good, I didn't want him to stop, even for a moment. The water was gushing out of the tap and I felt thirstier than ever. Gently I pulled myself forward, away from Shaun, and put my head under the tap. I gulped down mouthful after mouthful of water, delighting in the sensation of it splashing all over my face. I was aware that Shaun was murmuring something (sexy talk? compliments?) as he peeled my sweat-drenched underwear from my buttocks, but I couldn't distinguish the words for the noise of the water beating against the steel sink. I turned my face away and let the water run through my hair and over my neck.

When I pushed away from the sink and straightened up, I threw my head back and the water ran down my back and buttocks. Suddenly I looked down to see Shaun take my cock in his mouth. He had been too impatient for me to turn and offer it to him, so had dived between my legs and claimed it himself. Cramped up against the kitchen cupboards, his knees two islands in the puddle that had formed on the slate tiles of the kitchen floor, he worked my cock ferociously. I had to grasp the kitchen bench again so I didn't lose my balance. No-one had ever managed to make me come just from sucking my cock

– either they didn't possess the technique or the persistence – but after a couple of minutes, Shaun had me swooning and moaning. I blew all over his Paul Smith jeans.

He half carried me into the bedroom from there and together we collapsed on the bed. After five minutes of lying clasped against each other, his erection showing no sign of dissipating, I couldn't escape my obligation. I owed him a blow job. It was the last thing I felt like doing, but once it was done, we could both get some sleep. So I slithered down, took it in my mouth and lolled it around a little. My indifference must have been apparent because, after a minute, he stopped me. 'Come up here and kiss me instead,' he commanded.

He pumped some lube out into his hand from the bottle by the bed and began to jerk himself off. I kissed him, pinched his nipples and he came very quickly in great heaving pants. He wiped the come off his belly with some tissues, then cuddled up against me. 'You owe me,' he whispered in my ear. 'When we wake up you're going to have to fuck me.'

We dozed off. When I woke up, Shaun was lying beside me, staring at me with big surprised eyes. 'It's kind of unbelievable to be lying here next to you,' he whispered. 'I've had a crush on you all year.'

It was the second time he'd mentioned something to that effect. We began to kiss and cuddle and before long he was ripping a condom out of its wrapper and sliding it over my erection. He had discovered where I kept them while I was asleep. 'Fuck me,' he whispered.

I was a little shocked by how into it he was, how abandoned he could be. I'd only ever fucked two other guys before (sweet little Liam had been one of them) and both of them had been so cautious and strained that I couldn't be sure if they were even enjoying themselves. There was no such ambiguity with Shaun. He was clearly having the time of his life. He was thrusting back against me, moaning and sighing, encouraging me, begging me. When he finally came, his whole body began to twitch as though racked by demons, and his moans were loud enough to awaken Blair and Strauss in their nearby apartments, no matter how many sleeping pills they'd taken.

We showered together afterwards and then I made us some breakfast. While I did that, he smoked a cigarette and gazed down at the laneway. The cigarette made me wonder what other weaknesses he had. Over the food, I gently quizzed him, expecting a major flaw to be revealed, but his answers were all very impressive. He lived in Woollahra. He worked as a human resources consultant in a bank. His parents lived in Rose Bay and also had a small farm near Bowral. The only thing I could fault him over was that he was perhaps a little older than I would've liked: he was twenty-six.

He excused himself once we'd finished breakfast. He had to go home and get organised for a seminar he was presenting at work the following day. But once he'd got up from the table, it was as if all his confidence had evaporated. He stood over me, fumbling nervously with his car keys. 'I'd like to ring you later tonight and see how you're recovering,' he said tentatively. 'That is . . . if you'd like to give me your number.'

It was another sweet, sincere request, like asking me for a dance, and it touched me. I went over to my desk and wrote it out for him.

After he left I began to clear the plates from the table, but the sight of the two coffee mugs side by side made me pause. It was the same sight that had irritated me in Carson and Ant's apartment, one of those many signs of their status as a couple. It made me realise that Shaun could indeed be the one for me. In addition to all his admirable credentials, he was clearly obsessed with me. Which meant I would be in charge, exactly the way I liked it. The question wasn't so much as to whether I was attracted to him, but whether he was good looking enough for me? Handsome enough to make Ant jealous?

The odd thing was that Shaun had a slight physical resemblance to Ant. They were the same height and their build was similar – solid and masculine, though Ant was more muscular. They both had dark brown hair cut short and green-grey eyes. Of course, they were nothing alike in the face, and if you judged them side by side, it was Ant who would always be declared more handsome, but Shaun possessed something else. His good nature was reflected in his face. He had a classic nice-guy demeanour and a ready smile, while people often remarked that Ant seemed aloof, even morose. 'He's creepy,' Warren had said after meeting him several times. 'I can never tell what he's thinking. It's unsettling.'

Shaun wasn't necessarily the kind of guy you'd turn around in the street to get a second look at, but the more you gazed into his eyes, the more you found yourself returning the smile that was always playing round his mouth.

When he rang that evening, we talked for about ten minutes, but when it got to the point of saying goodbye, I was surprised that he'd made no attempt to invite me out. After I'd hung up, I regretted taking the call. I should have let the machine pick up and make him wonder where I was.

But the next day he sent me flowers. I cursed the fact that Ant was still away and not there to witness this evidence of my new beau's ardour. The flowers created a small sensation amongst my neighbours. Blair saw them being delivered, phoned Strauss immediately and the two of them came knocking on my door, demanding to know who had sent them. On the note that accompanied the bouquet, Shaun suggested dinner at Paramount on Friday night and provided his phone number. Of course I accepted.

Dinner began awkwardly. Shaun was like a completely different person. Tongue-tied, nervous and obviously intimidated by me. The spell that the party drugs had woven was well and truly broken. Our weekend together was like a dream, distant and strange. We polished off a bottle of Croser champagne before our entrees had even arrived: Shaun out of nerves, and me to help myself endure what seemed set to be a torturous evening. But the alcohol seemed to help Shaun relax. He began to talk more freely, his hesitant smile gradually became bold and by the end of the meal he was pressing his leg against mine under the table. My resolution not to encourage him had been forgotten several glasses of wine back. I found myself returning the pressure.

He also insisted on paying for dinner, which charmed me even more.

He walked me back to my apartment where he'd left his car and I was curious as to how he would go about trying to seduce me. I expected him either to get all nervous and deferential again or simply to seize and molest me. But I was surprised. 'I'd very much like to spend the night with you,' he said politely, the only sign of his nerves being the formal construction of his sentence.

It was direct and ingenuous. 'Okay,' I agreed. 'You've had too much to drink to drive yourself home anyway.'

When he left the next morning, I suggested an afternoon at the beach on Sunday and his face lit up. He seemed so pleased I was reciprocating his interest that I didn't have the heart to point out that it had merely occurred to me how much easier it would be getting to the beach by car. I loathed going there on public transport.

He picked me up at midday on Sunday and we had a late breakfast at a cafe in Bondi, then walked round the clifftops to Tamarama Beach. Lying on the sand, looking out to sea, I noticed the planes flying in and out further down the coast. Which reminded me that Ant and Carson were due home that evening from New Zealand. The thought of having to endure hearing what a wonderful impression Carson had made on the Tallantire family gave me an idea. I leant over to Shaun, pinched his nipple and suggested we have dinner together. He would be my excuse to avoid that smarmy story. Shaun opened his eyes and gave me such a heartfelt smile, I felt warmed through at making him so happy.

We stayed late at the beach, then on the way home drove via Surry Hills and picked up some takeaway Thai from a favourite restaurant of mine which was usually too far out of the way to go to. On the drive back to my place I began to worry that things were becoming too serious too quickly. I tried to make light of our day together. 'You know I only love you for your Saab,' I teased him, only half mockingly.

'That's okay. I only love you for the way you look. It's an equally fatuous reason,' he replied easily.

It was not the reply I'd expected and I found myself brooding over what he had meant. Was he suggesting there was something deficient about my personality?

There was a message on the machine from Ant when we got in but I put off calling him. Dinner would get cold. But Ant called back again when we were in the middle of eating.

'Hey, we're back. Didn't you get my message?' he complained.

'*We* just got in. Sorry.'

'That's okay. It's just Carson and I thought you might like to have dinner with us and we could all catch —'

'I'd love to, but in fact *we*'re right in the middle of dinner *ourselves*,' I said, rather enjoying the use of the plural pronoun.

There was silence from Ant for a moment. 'We?' he queried.

'Yeah. I have someone here with me. Someone I met at the New Year's Eve party.'

'Oh.'

'We've been seeing quite a lot of each other while you've been away.'

I was choosing my words carefully. I wanted to arouse some jealousy in Ant but I was also aware of Shaun, sitting at the table, listening to every word. I didn't want to give him too much encouragement. I could hear Carson complaining in the background that the plants didn't appear to have been watered recently. To my delight, Ant told Carson to stop whingeing. 'Stephen's met someone. He's obviously had more exciting things to do than fuss over your plants.'

'Who's he met?' I heard Carson demanding.

'Look, Ant, I can't really talk now,' I said. 'We can catch up tomorrow night. Okay?'

'Okay,' said Ant, but the excitement that had been in his

voice when he'd announced his return had disappeared altogether.

I put the phone down with a sense of triumph. I had succeeded in unsettling him.

Later, lying in bed while Shaun sucked me off, I wondered if it might have been better to save the news and tell Ant face to face. What would that inscrutable face of his have revealed? Would it have clouded over with jealousy?

Carson and Ant came over the next night. I picked out the few blooms that had wilted, then placed the flowers Shaun had given me in the middle of the kitchen table where they couldn't possibly be overlooked. Both Carson and Ant admired them and admired them anew when I airily mentioned that Shaun had sent them. 'I can't recall you ever sending me flowers,' Ant complained to Carson.

'He must be keen,' said Carson, his eyes calculating the scale of the arrangement.

I told them about our first dinner date and the fact that he had paid for it. 'We should have dinner,' said Ant quickly. 'The four of us. We'd like to meet him. Carson can cook.'

Carson gave Ant a look, but the next day Ant did phone to confirm the dinner invitation.

I asked him then how it had gone in Dunedin. Ant wouldn't give much away, though he did say that Carson being such a fussy eater had caused a few tensions.

'For Christ's sake. Couldn't he eat your mother's roast if she could pretend to enjoy having a faggot come to stay?' I said hotly.

'You'd think so,' Ant said disloyally, with a sigh.

The dinner was a success. The only awkward moment of the evening came when Shaun teased Carson about not working and being a 'housewife'.

'Well, actually, it's for health reasons that I don't work. I thought Stephen would have told you.' A supercilious tone had crept into Carson's voice. 'I'm HIV positive.'

But Shaun wasn't at all fazed by the revelation. He didn't look awkward or pained or say, 'I'm *so* sorry.' Instead, he praised

Carson for not being secretive about his status. It reminded me that before I fucked him that first time, Shaun had told me he was HIV negative and reminded me not to come inside him and to be alert to the sensation of the condom breaking. I'd never had sex with anyone before who'd announced their status like that and it had surprised me. I'd muttered that I was negative too. I hadn't wanted to think about the fact that two years had passed since I had had my only test.

Shaun then mentioned that he was a volunteer for Ankali, something he hadn't told me, and Carson said that Stewart had had an Ankali carer towards the end. From that moment the two of them conversed in an almost conspiratorial manner which excluded Ant and me for the rest of the meal.

That dinner was the first of many the four of us shared. Shaun reciprocated the hospitality and had a dinner party at his apartment in Woollahra the following week. I'd only been there once before. Shaun had a flatmate and he preferred to spend the nights at my place where we could be alone, or perhaps where he could be as noisy as he liked during sex without having to consider a flatmate or risk disturbing his discreet neighbours. I was as surprised as Ant and Carson were when Shaun revealed that he wasn't renting the apartment but was, in fact, paying off a mortgage on it. 'How can you afford it?' asked Ant.

I could see Ant and Carson were impressed and looking at the apartment anew. There was no comparison. It left their apartment in Elizabeth Bay for dead.

'I have some family money. An inheritance from my grandmother. And I work for a bank, so my mortgage is very cheap. I wouldn't have been able to buy in Woollahra otherwise. And of course I do have a flatmate who pays rent.'

When Shaun was in the kitchen, making coffee, Carson remarked what a catch I'd made. I nodded. I was only beginning to realise myself. 'I predict that you won't be living so close to us for much longer,' laughed Carson.

'*I* won't be rushing into anything,' I replied pointedly, and both he and Ant looked a little abashed.

There was something undeniably cosy about the friendship that developed between the four of us. Shaun brought a balance and symmetry to our group. Two couples. Two sets of friends. For Shaun and Carson quickly established a friendship and saw each other independently, without Ant or myself. From a couple of casual remarks Shaun made, I realised that he had become Carson's sympathetic ear.

'But why doesn't he discuss his health anxieties with Ant?' I protested to Shaun.

He shrugged. 'I don't know. Maybe Ant's not ready to think about some issues just yet, whereas because I've done the Ankali course and I know about all that stuff, it's easier to discuss with me. I guess Carson doesn't want to burden Ant, the way he felt burdened by Stewart. But it's good for Carson to have someone other than his lover to talk things through with.'

Our dinners became a regular weekend event. We rarely went out to the Oxford Street bars. Instead, we'd choose somewhere new or fashionable for dinner on Friday or Saturday night. It was on one of the very first occasions the four of us went out together that we encountered Elisabeth. She and Uncle Vic happened to have chosen the same restaurant as we had. She rose from her seat as soon as she spotted me and came over to be introduced. Luckily, she didn't linger. Her entree arrived at the same moment and she went back to her own table. But later, after we'd had our main courses, she beckoned me over for a chat. I could tell she'd had a bit to drink.

'Your Uncle Vic and I can't decide which one of those boys is yours. Tell us. We've got a bet on it.'

I knew if I refused to tell her she would only raise her voice and embarrass me. I indicated Shaun to her.

'Oh,' she said in surprise. 'Neither of us picked him. I thought it was the blond boy and Vic thought it was the surly one. Hmm. Why haven't you mentioned him to me before?'

I explained that we'd only just met. 'But you never introduce your boyfriends to me,' Elisabeth complained. 'Why not? Are you ashamed of me?'

'Of course not. I mean . . . this is really my first relationship and it's in the very early stages—'

Elisabeth interrupted me. She was outraged. '*This* is your *first* relationship? I can't believe it. I presumed you must have had several by now but weren't prepared to have any of them meet Mother. Does this mean you've been trolling round Oxford Street all these years?'

I knew what was going through Elisabeth's mind. That I was indeed a younger version of Uncle Vic. I had to restore my reputation.

'There has been someone,' I admitted in a low voice. 'But it's been unrequited. It's dragged on for a couple of years.'

But that only served to stoke Elisabeth's fires of indignation. 'What do you mean, unrequited? Who wouldn't want you? Who? They must be mad. You're very eligible. Young, smart, handsome. What more could they want? Who is this person who has been toying with you?'

I could see Ant and Carson turning round in their seats. Her voice had been trained to carry. I excused myself from her and Uncle Vic, but as I walked back to my table, I overheard her urging Vic to find out what had been going on. 'Of course you can find out,' she declared. 'I know what queens are like. Impossible gossips. Someone must know something.'

It was obvious whom I had inherited my scheming, interfering ways from.

On their way out, Elisabeth and Vic stopped by our table. Elisabeth was at her most charming as she discreetly quizzed Shaun. Her smile grew broader and broader as he revealed his address (Rosemont Avenue, Woollahra), his employment (Citibank) and his family (his late grandmother had been one of the Willoughby sisters of Bowral). Throughout this I was frantically making pleading eyes at Uncle Vic and finally, after several failed attempts, he succeeded in steering Elisabeth out of the restaurant. As she left, she smirked at me. She approved wholeheartedly. Shaun was politely waving as she departed and unfortunately caught her look. When he turned back to me, there was a gloating smile on his face. He had guessed from Elisabeth's behaviour that he had been described to her as my boyfriend, but now he also knew that he had her endorsement.

Everyone expressed their delight at meeting my mother but for me the meeting was extremely ill-timed. Elisabeth had obliged me to put a name to my relationship with Shaun and it felt premature. Neither Shaun nor I had described ourselves as boyfriends or lovers before. It also bothered me that both Elisabeth and Uncle Vic had failed to pick Shaun as my partner. It made me worry that he wasn't handsome enough and that I could do better. But I had also loathed that expression on Elisabeth's face as she'd left. I could read her mind. Her smile was triumphant. 'I've taught you so well,' it declared.

I regretted that meeting, but I became downright annoyed with a remark that Carson made only a few minutes later. 'For God's sake, Stephen, help your husband decide on a dessert if you're going to share one.'

My husband. It was Ant I thought of and I looked to him instinctively. Ant regarded me from across the table, his expression grave, unreadable. Meanwhile, Shaun was nudging me with the menu to get my attention. Of course it was Shaun Carson was referring to. His arm slipped round the back of my chair at that moment, his fingers resting upon my shoulder. I felt like shrugging him away but we were in company. Instead, I turned to face him and he proffered the dessert menu to me. I hesitated. The intent in his face loaded his gesture with significance. It wasn't merely the menu that was being offered, it was Carson's words as well. I was very aware that, across the table, Ant and Carson were watching us. What else could I do but smile graciously, accept the menu and allow Shaun's fingers to curl around my hand? The grip of his other hand on my shoulder tightened – the clamp of possession. But I could not have embarrassed Shaun by refuting that moment. He had been too kind and considerate for me to disappoint him in front of our friends. But inwardly I fumed at Carson for drawing us – no, dragging us – to that moment.

Later, when we'd left the restaurant and I'd calmed down a little, I realised it was the first time I'd felt my old antagonism towards Carson in weeks. The tension which had tended to prickle between him and me had eased. Shaun had become like a buffer, smoothing over our rough edges with a quick, soothing remark.

The following weekend the four of us went away together. Shaun drove us down the coast to his father's beach house at Hyam's Beach. The house was nothing grand. I noted the thin walls and took great pleasure in fucking Shaun our first night there, knowing Ant and Carson were in the next room and couldn't help but hear us, even though Shaun buried his face in the pillow to try to muffle his enthusiasm. I also insisted that we do it again the next morning before we got up.

When we finally emerged from our bedroom, the two of them were sitting quite primly at the breakfast table, showered, fully dressed, drinking coffee and reading yesterday's newspapers. Shaun went to shower and I marched into the kitchen wearing the expensive designer underwear Shaun had bought me recently.

I relished the opportunity of flaunting myself in front of Ant. 'Sleep well?' I asked brightly.

Both of them looked up, but the sight of me seemed to freeze any answer upon their tongues. I knew exactly how hot I looked. I wandered round the kitchen and took my time, preparing myself some breakfast. But every time I glanced back at the two of them, Ant was steadfastly studying the newspaper. Instead, it was Carson I caught stealing glances in my direction.

Later, down at the beach, I was walking down to the water for a swim when I had a sudden provocative impulse. I stopped and slipped my Speedos off. Wolf whistles and whooping erupted behind me. I glanced back. Shaun and Carson had jumped to their feet and were cheering me on. Ant lay on his towel, his hand on his sunglasses, which he had slid down his nose, as he watched me. Assured of my audience, I turned back and ran, bare arsed, down to the water. Once I was knee-deep,

I dived forward and soared right over the top of a timid wave. I knew Ant's eyes had to be fixed on me, my buttocks framed momentarily in the air, their whiteness startling against my tan and the cerulean sea. When I surfaced, I looked back to find Carson and Shaun running down towards me, both stark naked.

Ant could not be cajoled to join us. We stood in the shallows and wiggled our butts at him, but he continued to lie on his towel reading. He didn't even glance up from his book when the three of us walked back up the sand towards him. I had modestly put my Speedos back on by then. I didn't want him assessing the size of my penis, even if I did have the excuse of cold water shrinkage.

Or at least he appeared not to be looking. He was wearing sunglasses so it was impossible to tell. But after I'd been lying back down on my towel beside him for a while, I realised it had been a long time since he'd turned a page of his novel. For someone who appeared to be reading so intently, he had not made particularly fast work of those two pages.

That weekend away cemented our little foursome. It became natural if one couple was planning something, to invite the other couple along. We talked to one another on the phone every day. It was so cosy, so symmetrical, though privately I mourned that as couples we were mismatched. When I watched Carson and Shaun huddle together, talking intensely, I would turn to Ant and wonder if he was thinking the same thing I was – that we belonged together. But it was impossible to gauge Ant's thoughts. He seemed to have become even more taciturn since his trip to New Zealand.

Ant hadn't warmed to Shaun. In fact, there was often a palpable antagonistic tension between the two of them. I found it thrilling. I liked to imagine that I was the root cause of their antagonism – each wanted to have me wholly to himself – although logically it could more readily be attributed to the fundamental differences in their personalities.

Shaun was direct. If he wanted something, he said so. While Ant could be so cautious with his words that at times I wanted to poke him to prompt him to say something, anything. If he was displeased, he couldn't hide it. He was prone to moody silences, while Shaun was good humoured and agreeable. We had never had a fight because he was always so obliging and content to let me have my way. Ant was puritanical about alcohol, drugs and cigarettes, while Shaun indulged in all three, not excessively, but with relish. His attempts to ditch the cigarettes were always short-lived.

But it was their attitude to money that was the greatest point of contrast and conflict. Shaun was extravagant, Ant was frugal. Whenever we went out to dinner, Ant always seized the bill and scrutinised it for errors, behaviour Shaun found immensely irritating. On those occasions Ant did find a mistake, he reported it triumphantly. Ant also always insisted, against a chorus of protestations, that we must only pay for exactly what we had eaten. It would've been so much simpler to divide the bill in four, but Ant wouldn't hear of it. He would have a waiter bring him back a copy of the menu so that he could work out exactly who owed what. When the issue of the tip came up, he would contribute, but grudgingly, after a warning look from Carson. Evidently his disinclination for that practice had been discussed between them.

'Does he behave so boorishly when he takes Carson out for dinner on his birthday or Valentine's Day,' Shaun asked me after the first time the four of us ever ate out together, 'and completely ruin the evening?'

But Ant never seemed embarrassed by the situation. He considered his own thriftiness to be merely prudent, and Shaun to be a spendthrift. 'More money than sense,' he remarked of him several times.

In a way it was unfortunate that eating out became our weekend thing, because those dinners created other tensions too. The choice of restaurant became an issue. Shaun inevitably favoured somewhere new and chic, while Ant always wanted to go somewhere dependable and known. They often clashed. Ant would refuse Shaun's choice because the desserts were the price of mains, while Shaun would refuse Ant's choice because the chairs were ugly or the lighting overdone. They would mock each other to me. 'He wants to eat somewhere that's *value for money*,' Shaun would say scathingly, but Ant could be equally as sarcastic. 'We can't eat *there*! The waiters are wearing the wrong jeans label.'

Perhaps in reaction to each other, they both became more extreme. Ant more penurious, Shaun more extravagant. Shaun took to ordering expensive bottles of wine and would then tempt Ant with a glass. When Ant divided the bill, Shaun would watch with interest to see how he attributed the cost of his glass of wine.

They were the same with clothes. Shaun was often wearing something new to dinner and Carson would always admire it. 'Oh, this,' Shaun would respond. 'I got it at Barneys in New York/the Macy's sale/Jigsaw in Covent Garden/etc etc.'

'Do all of your clothes come from overseas?' Ant asked one evening, an edge to his voice.

'Most of them,' Shaun admitted cheerfully. 'Clothes are so cheap in America and I go into a frenzy if I come across a sale. Though actually this top is from Saba.'

'Do they produce lavender jumpers as well as cars?' Ant said to me, but so Shaun would hear.

'Sab*a*,' said Shaun loudly. 'They have a shop in Skygarden mall.'

'Oh,' said Ant.

Ant of course was wearing a variation on what he always wore. A black ribbed T-shirt and black jeans. It was simple, sexy and he looked very handsome. Shaun looked striking too, in his lavender knit top, but it wasn't a particularly flattering colour on him. I knew it would look a lot better on me.

Shaun was a label queen. It seemed to impress Carson who was always assuring me what a catch Shaun was, as if I needed to have his advantages, both financial and emotional, constantly pointed out to me. I appreciated his assets and liked him and, yes, there were even things I preferred about him to Ant, but there was no compulsion in my feelings for him. Ant could look at me, his eyes serious, his intent unreadable, and a delirious sense of wonder and hope would prickle up through me. Shaun never managed to stir that same depth of feeling. Nevertheless, he was attentive, devoted and generous. His wooing of me was so smooth and charming, it seemed wholly inevitable. Sometimes I fantasised about breaking free of it, for no good reason other than sheer perversity and a curiosity as to how he would react.

My major reservation about Shaun was that he was too slick. He'd brought a level of sophistication to his pursuit of me which I enjoyed and admired but which also highlighted the six-year age difference between us. He had evidently learnt how to behave, though he claimed his previous relationships had been brief and that he'd never been in love. 'Not entirely,' he claimed. 'Not like this.' His actions and words were always so assured. Everything had been carefully calculated to ensure that I was impressed: the flowers, that first dinner at Paramount, the spontaneous gifts. Sometimes it felt as if he was following, point by point, chapter by chapter, a guidebook on winning your man. It was a campaign – it felt – carefully orchestrated with Carson enlisted to promote Shaun's suit at every opportunity.

And I could see where his campaign aimed to claim victory. Valentine's Day would mark six weeks of serious dating.

Carson began alluding to a special celebration a week or so in advance. 'Why does Carson know what I'm doing on Valentine's Day when I don't?' I finally demanded of Shaun a few days beforehand.

But Shaun merely smiled mysteriously and assured me it would be worth the wait. When the day came, I awoke with the expectation of flowers being delivered and dinner somewhere special, with an intense declaration of love during the course of the meal. I sent Shaun some lilies to Citibank and, on impulse, for a stir, I sent Ant half a dozen roses with no card. I had them delivered to Onslow Avenue, knowing that Carson would be at home to receive them and would fume all day, wondering who they could possibly be from.

I was surprised when my anticipated bouquet didn't arrive. I had stayed at home deliberately to receive it, forsaking the beach. Nor did Shaun ring to reveal what we were doing for dinner. Finally, at five o'clock, the telephone rang. It was a Valentine's Day singing telegram. At the end of the song I was advised that I was expected for dinner at eight at Forty One and that Shaun would meet me there. I was impressed. It was the most glamorous place to eat in town. Nevertheless, I arrived late deliberately, leaving him to stew for twenty minutes. My entire day had been wasted because he'd kept me in suspense. After I joined him at the table, he thanked me for the flowers and complimented me on what I was wearing. I made no excuse for being late. Shaun apologised for drinking so much of the champagne, but there was an undertone which implied that if I'd been on time he wouldn't have had the chance to drink half the bottle. The champagne was Krug.

I had noticed the envelope placed between my cutlery as soon as I sat down. 'My card?' I asked.

Evidently there was to be no present, given that dinner would be expensive. I presumed that he didn't expect me to pay for myself. 'Open it,' Shaun urged me.

I ripped open the envelope and when I withdrew the card, a key fell out. I picked it up, puzzled. 'What's this?' I asked.

Shaun's smile was rapturous. 'It's the key to my apartment. Stephen, I want you to move in with me.'

He had succeeded in truly surprising me and I said as much while I grappled for a response. Meanwhile, in a rush, he told me that he'd asked his flatmate to move out. He pointed out all the advantages of us living together and the many drawbacks of my own apartment. However, he must have been able to tell from my face that he was failing to convince me. 'You needn't pay me any rent,' he said finally, desperately.

I picked up the key, leant across the table and dropped it into the breast pocket of his dinner jacket. 'What you wrote in the card was very sweet,' I said and picked up my champagne glass, which the waiter had just filled. 'But I think moving in together now would be premature.'

Shaun sulked. I imagined he wished he'd brought along his manual: what to do when your date does not behave according to expectations. When we finished the champagne, he complained that he was going to have to find a new flatmate or beg his evicted one to come back.

'Well, it's your own fault for being presumptuous,' I pointed out, not very tactfully.

'Why won't you live with me?' he moaned.

'Because it's too quick.'

I was determined to enjoy the dinner but Shaun seemed only to want to get drunk and brood. By the time dessert arrived, I was talking more to our waiter, whom I recognised from one of Strauss's parties, than to him.

When the bill came at the end of the dinner, Shaun refused to tip the waiter. 'You can leave the tip if you like, along with your phone number,' he said pettily, getting up from the table and walking off without me.

I left the tip and took the elevator down to the lobby. I couldn't see Shaun anywhere, although I didn't bother to look very hard. I hailed a taxi that was driving past as I emerged from the building. I jumped in and as we set off down the street I heard Shaun wailing in protest somewhere behind us. I didn't bother to look back. Twenty minutes later he began insistently pressing my doorbell, which I also ignored, and finally he gave up.

I expected him to ring the next day and apologise. But when the phone rang early, it was Carson, enquiring solicitously as to how our Valentine's Day celebration had been. I could tell from his tone of voice that he knew everything. Shaun had obviously been moaning in his ear. 'Well, I didn't get flowers, but we did have a lovely dinner. Did either of you get flowers?'

'Ant did,' Carson managed to say.

'Lovely. He was complaining, wasn't he, that you'd never sent him any before?'

I excused myself but once I'd hung up, it occurred to me that it wasn't a guidebook that Shaun had consulted, it was Carson.

Shaun was waiting outside my apartment. I happened to glance out the window and there he was, leaning against his car, parked in the laneway, looking up at my window. He gazed up at me contritely and then finally called out, asking if he could please be admitted to apologise. I nodded.

'I behaved badly,' he said in that direct sincere way of his when I opened the door to him. 'You're right. I was presumptuous. I guess I just love surprises and expect other people to as well.'

So I surprised him, undid the fly of his Emporio Armani suit and gave him an enthusiastic blow job.

I surprised myself a little too. I'd been toying with the idea of ending things between us, but lying there beside him on the couch afterwards, I acknowledged that there were too many pleasures in our relationship to consider renouncing them. Nor was there a compelling reason why I should, other than an acknowledged imbalance in our depth of feeling for one another. And that might easily change. It was perfectly possible that in time more of a balance would be achieved. His initial ardour would eventually cool a little and it was not impossible that I might manage to reciprocate some ardour of my own.

It was so much easier merely to coast along with what he offered so willingly. It would've been churlish to protest. I could even justify Shaun as what was due to me. I had spent two years pining hopelessly after Ant. I felt that I deserved to be in the position of being adored and indulged for once.

It wasn't difficult to say 'I love you' back to Shaun when he whispered those words in my ear that morning for the first time. It wasn't exactly a lie either. It was Ant I was thinking of when I repeated what was to become Shaun's catchcry.

CHAPTER ELEVEN

That Valentine's Day dinner set the pattern for my relationship with Shaun. Him trying to beguile me into some act of closer commitment. Me resistant and endeavouring to keep him at arm's length. To my surprise, he didn't nag me about moving in with him after I refused, nor did he enlist Carson to talk me round. He was much cleverer than that. He mentioned it only once again and that was to inform me that the invitation remained open. 'If and when the time feels right, you need only let me know.'

Then he set about speeding up the process of making it feel right by transforming his apartment into an even more desirable place to live. He decided to renovate. He rationalised the expense by saying that if he had a proper kitchen, he would regain his enthusiasm for cooking at home and wouldn't fritter so much money away by eating out all the time. 'Wouldn't it be cheaper to buy a couple of new cookbooks to revitalise your enthusiasm?' I enquired.

But no, that would only frustrate him more. Having elaborate recipes to try, only to be hampered by his kitchen. 'Cooking should be a pleasure, not a chore. I need a new kitchen. And a dishwasher.'

That was something of a masterstroke. Shaun knew I loathed doing the dishes.

Shaun's renovations required close consultation with me. He claimed to need a second opinion, but I knew what he was up to. He included me in the planning of the dream kitchen in the hope that I would get caught up in the momentum of the project and come to regard it as *our* renovations rather than *his*. Once it was complete, I would surely want to enjoy the improvements as much as possible and move in.

He had an architect friend whom we had several meetings

with. My opinion was sought endlessly. The plans were drawn up, then Shaun and I drove around selecting the fittings for the renovation. The cupboards he ordered were European beech, to be custom-made to the architect's plans. The bench top was six thousand dollars' worth of stainless steel to be lit by ten low-voltage halogen spotlights. The dishwasher was all gleaming steel and German efficiency. Instead of the ubiquitous polished floorboards, we decided on white terrazzo. Perhaps the most difficult decision was which shade of white to paint the walls. Finally, we agreed on 'birch'.

Predictably, the fit-out was a nightmare – protracted and problem-ridden. It had been estimated that it would take ten days but it ended up taking thirty. After three weeks I began to suspect that Shaun had deliberately hired the most inefficient tradesmen so that he had the perfect excuse to spend every night with me.

However, when the kitchen was finally finished, it did look spectacular. Carson and Ant were invited to a special celebration dinner to christen it. They bought Shaun a new cookbook as a gift and over the next month he made good use of it. He did cook more at home and I did end up staying over a lot more than I had in the past. But I knew with every meal he set down before me, it wasn't praise for his cooking that he was seeking. He was waiting for me to say that I wanted to come home to this every night, that I wanted to live with him.

As the weeks passed and I failed to give notice to my real estate agency, I noticed the meals becoming less elaborate and less frequent. Eventually they dwindled down to pasta and a five-minute tomato sauce a couple of times a week. The kitchen had failed in its main purpose. So Shaun announced stage two of his renovations: the bedroom.

I groaned.

'What's wrong?'

'No more tradesmen. I couldn't bear it.'

'No tradesmen,' he agreed. 'All I want to do is redecorate a little.'

His bed was a futon. Perfectly comfortable but he decided he wanted something more luxurious. We spent weeks trekking round the shops. 'It's your decision as well,' Shaun kept reminding me. 'You'll be spending a lot of time in it too.'

The bed he eventually decided on was magnificent and very expensive. In fact, it cost so much, Shaun conceded he would have to wait a while before he could afford new linen for it. But he was thrilled by his purchase and especially taken by the name of his new bed. It was called the Royal Splendour and once it was delivered, Shaun took great delight in announcing at bedtime that it was time we retired to the Royal Splendour.

The arrival of the bed coincided with winter. Those two factors were almost enough to make me give in. I had sworn the previous year that I would not endure another winter on William Street. My apartment was unbearably cold and damp in winter. It never saw any sunlight, except at midday when a shaft of light fell through the toilet window for ten minutes. Elisabeth visited on a particularly bleak day and declared that my apartment was like living in a fridge. 'Wonderful for preserving the complexion, no doubt,' she added. 'Not so good for one's health.'

The Woollahra apartment, in contrast, was always warm and cosy. Sunlight streamed in all day. Shaun even complained about it, as the sun bleached the colour out of a new rug he had bought for the living room at the start of summer. Originally it had been a deep plum colour, but it had faded to a hesitant red. To me, that rug was significant. I felt the same fate awaited me if I was to move in: that the energy and spirit would be leached out of me until I was a wan, colourless version of my former self. When I tried to explain this to Carson and Ant one night, Carson rudely insinuated that such a transformation would be a positive thing. 'You can't carry on being careless and callow forever,' he railed at me. 'People won't forgive you your bad behaviour on account of your youth and looks forever, you know.'

'Steady on,' Ant protested. 'That's a little harsh.'

Carson apologised, not very sincerely.

The other pressure pushing me towards moving in with Shaun was that I was having to pay my own rent. My father had refused to keep contributing after I failed Legal I for the second year. I had appealed to Elisabeth, but she informed me that my father had forbidden her from helping me out. 'I'll be forced to move in with Shaun,' I threatened.

'Well, I think Woollahra would be infinitely preferable to where you're living now,' Elisabeth answered.

I tried to shock her. 'Mother, we'd be living together. As a couple. Surely you don't approve of that?'

'He has a second bedroom, doesn't he? I remember you telling me that he had a flatmate. You can always sleep in there if you're concerned what people will think.'

'I'm not concerned. You are.'

Elisabeth shrugged. 'Am I? Oh no, I don't think so. I'd prefer to have you living in a nice suburb with a nice boy from a nice family than living in that squalid apartment on that disgraceful street, spending your nights goodness knows where.'

I was lost for words. I had never imagined I would have Elisabeth's blessing in this way, but after giving it some thought, her viewpoint began to make sense. It was the safe middle-class option and the suburb was the icing on the cake. Woollahra made it permissible in Elisabeth's mind. If Shaun's apartment had been in Darlinghurst, she would have been aghast at the proposal. Darlinghurst was suggestive of threesomes rather than a committed couple.

'Mother, Shaun doesn't want me to pay rent. I'd be kept.'

Elisabeth raised her eyebrows. 'Well, you can always insist on paying rent. I'm sure you'd gain Shaun's respect by doing that.'

'I don't have a job, so I can't insist.'

'Well then, you must earn your keep. Do the housework. Prepare the meals.'

I couldn't believe it. Elisabeth was suggesting I become a housewife.

'I can't do that,' I snapped tersely.

'Of course you can. You were always so helpful in the kitchen when you were younger. You'll do fine.'

I was speechless. Elisabeth studied me thoughtfully.

'Yes, darling, I know you think you're made for better things, but you'll have to hurry up and decide what those better things are. The world won't wait for you to decide. Perhaps you should consider your father's suggestion while you make up your mind.'

My father knew of a job going as a law clerk at a friend's firm. I mumbled to Elisabeth that I'd consider it, but I didn't. Instead, I began to think seriously about a career as an actor. I had put those ambitions aside to please my father and given law a try (a rather unmotivated try, it had to be admitted) but the stage was my destiny. That was what everyone had been telling me for years. Elisabeth had been discouraging in the past, but I presumed that was because she considered it the province of poofs. Given that I'd turned out that way regardless, I expected her to embrace the idea of me following in her footsteps.

When I broached it with her, she misunderstood me. Her expression froze in disapproval. '*Drag?*' she queried, her voice stiff with repugnance.

I realised she had taken me literally. 'No, no,' I laughed. 'In your footsteps – on stage or on television. I'm going to be an actor.'

'A most unsuitable profession,' Elisabeth said firmly. 'You should get a proper job and dabble in acting on the side if you still have the heart for it. You'll find it a lot less frustrating.'

'But I want to go to drama school. I thought perhaps I might go to your old school in London.'

I presumed she would like that idea but she dismissed it instantly. 'Out of the question. I'm not paying to send you across the other side of the world where I can't keep an eye on you.'

'I'll go to NIDA then,' I snapped.

'If they'll have you.'

'Of course they'll have me.'

'Well, we'll see. You should have applied straight from school. You'd have had more chance. You're older now and you've done no theatre work since school. That won't look very good on your application.'

'People never tell the truth in their applications,' I said. 'You're obliged to lie just to keep pace with the other liars.'

Elisabeth frowned and I frowned back. I had never considered that I wouldn't be accepted. I knew that I would have to do an audition, but I had thought it would merely be a formality. I was a name already, or at least I would be if I used Elisabeth's stage name.

'I'll do some work this year to impress them,' I declared. 'I'll get an agent. I'll give Anne a ring.'

Anne was Elisabeth's agent and I had known her since I was a child. She had even attended some of the school plays I was in. 'Don't do that,' said Elisabeth sharply. 'She couldn't possibly take you and it would only be embarrassing for her.'

'But she always used to say that she looked forward to representing me one day,' I protested.

'She was only being encouraging,' said Elisabeth. 'Or if she did mean it, she expected you to come to her when you were qualified.'

It was all so disheartening and so unfair. It wasn't how I had been led to believe that it would be. I had been assured so many times that I would be a star, but now that I had decided I was ready, everyone seemed to have gone cold on the idea.

I felt so depressed by Elisabeth's dampening attitude, I even tried to contact Mr Preston. It had been so long since anyone had sung my praises the way he once had and I craved hearing that exaltation again. Mr Preston would reassure me that I was bound for glorious achievements. But when I finally managed to find the correct D. Preston in the phone book, he wasn't at home. The boy who answered the phone was slightly aggressive and became very insistent about taking a message when I declined to leave my name. I hung up. Evidently Mr Preston had a boyfriend. I couldn't help feeling supplanted. I didn't try to ring again. I had a suspicion, which I had no wish to confirm, that Mr Preston might no longer admire my talents as effusively as he once had.

That winter was a time of self-doubt and indecision for me. I couldn't decide what I wanted. But I was obliged to take a job, any job, to pay the rent. Everyone told me that I would be dynamite in retail. 'You could talk a customer into anything,' said Carson. I wasn't sure if he was being encouraging or snide. But I was so desperate by that point, I took his advice. I responded to an ad for a position at a record shop and got the job.

Carson was right. Making a sale was a cinch for me. But there were other aspects of retail work, the unseen drudgeries and complexities, which quickly made every position I held untenable. I did not take well to receiving orders and lost that first position for declining to do some dusting when I was ordered to. Not that I refused point-blank. I simply said, 'I'd prefer to serve at the counter. Can't someone else do it?'

It seemed obvious to me that I was attractive and charming and outgoing, an asset behind the counter, and totally wasted with the duster. That was a task that befitted Sandra, a grungy, moody creature who looked like she could do with a good dusting herself.

'And I'd prefer to employ someone who can take instruction obediently and cheerfully,' the manager responded.

I was fired. Sandra snickered.

But I found another job that same day in a delicatessen. I saw a sign in the window as I was walking home. But I only lasted there the day. One of the first tasks I was given was to wash the sausages. I could not believe what I was being asked to do. I studied the sausages. They did look exceptionally slimy. 'They're perfectly all right,' the owner said haughtily. 'They've just been on display a little long. Give them a wash and they'll look super again.'

I was not prepared to wash the sausages. Nor was I prepared to eat them ever again after that insight into their merchandising.

Blair told me about a job going at one of the men's boutiques up in Paddington. I used her as a referee and got the job. That shop was more my style. I liked the clothes and got on well with the other staff. However, I could not get the hang of the computerised till. There was so much to remember. In the end I gave up and every time I had a sale to complete, I simply had one of the other sales assistants ring it up for me. At the end of the week I was hauled into the supervisor's office and told I was fired. I couldn't believe it. 'Why?' I protested.

'You haven't made a single sale in the entire week.'

It transpired that every sale was tagged to a sales assistant. My co-workers had stolen my sales. When I explained the situation, the supervisor remained unsympathetic. 'If you can't work the till after a week, you're still no use to me.'

All these frustrations and setbacks that I suffered, I took out on Shaun. I would push him away when he tried to console me. I'd ignore his phone calls until he worked himself up into a frenzy over my silence, or I might refuse to sleep with him after spending an evening with him. I would depart feeling triumphant, but my sense of victory quickly faded once I was at home in the Frigidaire. My apartment always seemed so grim after being at Shaun's: cold and dull and deeply ugly. There was no pleasure or comfort to be derived from being there. Of course that had not mattered when Ant was living only a few steps away. But now he was gone and my other friends in the building could not be counted on for companionship.

Blair was either at one of her jobs or at home suffering from a champagne hangover, while Strauss had a glamorous new career which came with a new set of friends and social schedule. Strauss had begun to get work as a *model*. I found it completely unbelievable. In fact, I refused to believe it until I saw the photographic evidence, his first fashion spread in *Oyster* magazine. Then he was on television, in a jeans advertisement for which he was paid a small fortune. It was totally improbable, but apparently Strauss's peculiar looks were now in vogue. He was considered versatile. He could do the geek look and the dandy.

What pained me most was that this was the career that I should have had. It was me who had the face. It was me who was always being told I should be a model. But when I went to Strauss's agency, I was told I wasn't tall enough. That was one of the most humiliating moments of my life. To be rejected by the agency that had Strauss on its books. I avoided him after that. His success aroused violent urges in me. I felt like taking him by his oversized ears and shaking him.

Even Sass wasn't around any more. She had given up the street. She'd been badly shaken when Ginger had turned up or, rather, when her remains had turned up. The badly decomposed body of a transsexual was found in a national park near Noosa at the beginning of May. The body was beyond identification; however, the 'woman' had been wearing some distinctive chunky amber-coloured costume jewellery. Sass had flown to Brisbane to identify the corpse by her baubles. On her return, Sass had endeavoured to keep the spirits of her girls high. 'Let Ginger be a lesson to you all. Dress impeccably. It's a dingy sort of finale to be identified by your lack of taste in jewellery.'

But she confessed to me later that same night how shattered she was by Ginger's fate. 'I'd read in the paper what they did to her, but it didn't sink in till I was shown the earrings and the necklace. There was blood all over them. Poor old Ginge must've suffered terribly. And been so terrified.'

I mourned Ginger's demise along with Sass quite genuinely. She had been the one person who might have told me the truth about Carson's past. Although I had vowed to cease my interfering, I hadn't been able to put what I'd already learnt out of my mind.

That was the last time I saw Sass. A few days later I noticed Jo-Jo and Suzy Sixty-Nine lounging on the bench in the Chard Steps square, toasting one another with Spumante in plastic cups. I thought it was peculiar and mentioned it to Blair. She knew all, having been present when 'the invasion' had taken place. She had been stopped in the square by a couple of Maori trannies she was friendly with who breathlessly informed her that Sass had allowed one of her regulars to set her up in an apartment in Bondi. But the news of Sass's retirement must have reached Jo-Jo at that very same instant, for suddenly she appeared at the top of the stairs, illuminated by the headlights of a passing car. She surveyed the square below with a triumphant toothless grin, then spread her arms wide in a ghastly imitation of Evita. She let out a screech of a battle cry and her troops, led by Suzy Sixty-Nine, streamed down the Chard Steps. Their only weapons were their foul, threatening mouths but that was all that was required to chase Sass's girls across to the other side of William Street. They fled screaming and shrieking. Even Blair was menaced. 'Shift your skinny arse,' Suzy screeched at her and Blair obeyed. Suzy was standing under a streetlight and she looked truly scary.

So I had no-one to hang out with. I couldn't even go over to Carson and Ant's because it would inevitably get back to Shaun that I'd been with them when I'd told him I needed time to myself. So, out of loneliness, I did begin spending more and more time with Shaun. I also lost faith in my own ability to find a suitable job and asked my father to arrange the position at his friend's law firm. 'I'll set up an interview,' he replied. 'But it will be up to you to make an impression. You will need to think of some credible reason for your appalling examination results, or pray that they don't ask.'

I performed well at the interview. I blamed my father for my poor showing at university. 'He put so much pressure on me to pass with distinction that I just froze up in the exam. I couldn't write a word.'

His friend, Mr Leckey, smiled sympathetically and phoned me that night to offer me the job.

I began staying over for entire weekends at Shaun's and a couple of nights during the week as well. I even began to keep some clothes there. 'These are your drawers,' Shaun informed me proudly one day, pulling them out and showing me my underwear and T-shirts which he had laundered and neatly folded away.

This was the sort of thing Shaun was always doing and which made me cringe and want to draw back. But this time I didn't. He was smiling at me bashfully, unsure of how I would react. I startled him even more than usual by saying thank you.

However, I was to regret encouraging him because later that night, after I'd fucked him, he brought something up which reversed the inclination I had been drifting towards. 'We've been together six months,' he began. I thought it was going to be a reiteration of the invitation to move in with him, which is why I was so startled by what came next. 'If we both had a blood test and tested negative, which of course we would, then we can fuck au naturel. Without condoms. Imagine!'

His words stirred something in me that had lain dormant for a very long time: that sense of dread I'd felt all those years ago in the doctor's rooms waiting for my test result. Shaun kept rattling on, listing the advantages. Suddenly I became aware that he was looking at me expectantly, waiting for me to reply.

'Sorry?' I mumbled.

He repeated himself. 'I said throwing away the condoms would signify a certain commitment.'

'Yes?' I said, unsure of what he was getting at.

'We would have to agree to be monogamous. Anything else would be too risky. I wouldn't feel comfortable to have you fuck me without protection unless I knew that you wouldn't have sex with anyone else.'

I said nothing in reply. 'Well?' asked Shaun.

'It's a big issue,' I said. 'I'll have to think about it.'

'But you're monogamous with me now,' said Shaun quickly. 'Aren't you?'

I nodded.

'So what's the difference?'

The difference was that it was a life and death commitment which could not be strayed from. I hesitated.

Shaun seized my hand. 'Stephen, have you got any idea of what it feels like *not* to use a condom?'

I shook my head.

'Fucking fantastic,' Shaun assured me, his eyes bright and wide, his head nodding.

'I'll think about it,' I said.

I could see that Shaun was dissatisfied with my response but he had the sense not to persist. He knew that to argue with me always meant that he lost. I said nothing more about it and hoped Shaun would refrain from bringing it up again. He didn't.

A week later he announced after dinner that he had made an appointment for us both at the doctor. My heart began to pound. I knew what he was up to. 'Why?' I asked shortly.

'So that we can both be tested. Remember we talked about it?'

'I remember you trying to talk me into the idea and me being noncommittal.'

'Oh,' said Shaun. 'Is it a problem?'

'Yes, it is a problem,' I snapped at him. 'I find that test and waiting for the damn result extremely stressful.'

'But you haven't been unsafe? You don't even get fucked. If anyone should be anxious, it should be me.'

I didn't answer him.

'Is there some incident, in the past, that you're worried about?'

'No,' I said angrily, annoyed that he would even make me start to think about any potentially problematic encounters. 'I just don't see the point in being tested.'

'The point is that if you have a test you can fuck me without a condom and I know you want to do that.'

'Don't make presumptions about me,' I snapped and walked out the door and went home to Kings Cross.

Shaun managed to keep quiet about the issue for a couple of weeks. Then he went and had himself tested, although he didn't tell me directly. He rang me at work one day to tell me he couldn't cook me dinner that night because he had something very important to do after work. He waited expectantly for me to ask. I didn't. A week later he asked me to come to the doctor's with him. 'I have to collect my HIV test result.' I agreed to accompany him, but said I wouldn't go into the surgery. I suspected that he and the doctor would try to ambush me into a blood test once he had received his result.

So I waited in the car while Shaun went in. 'It's fine,' he told me as soon as he slid into his seat. 'But you should have come with me and held my hand in the waiting room. That was the worst part.'

I ignored him. While I'd been waiting for him, I'd been working out what to say to avoid him placing further pressure on me. Once he'd pulled out into the traffic, I began. 'I've been thinking, Shaun, and I've decided I don't want to go placing limitations on our relationship.'

Shaun glanced at me, his brow furrowed.

'I don't think this monogamy idea is a good one,' I continued. 'Practically all the allure of having an affair is the illicitness of it. If sex outside the relationship is placed off limits, I know that I'm more likely to start wanting to do exactly that. It's the human condition to pine after what you can't have.'

'But if we weren't using condoms, you wouldn't want to have sex with anyone else because you wouldn't want to go back to safe sex,' Shaun insisted.

I was furious. 'Don't tell me how I'd feel. You have no idea what I think and what I feel.'

We had stopped at a traffic light and Shaun turned to me, his face twisted up in anger. 'This is not my idea of a relationship. Every time I try to seek a closer commitment, you back away. You won't live with me; you won't promise to be faithful to me, and you won't take a simple blood test which could revolutionise our sex life.'

'That's right,' I said. 'I won't. Finally I seem to have made myself understood.'

The conversation terminated there. Shaun didn't say another word. He drove me to William Street, let me out and drove off. I watched his car merge into the traffic and wondered if I'd see him again.

He sulked for a week. When he did finally ring, it was to remind me about his cousin's wedding on the weekend, which I'd vaguely committed to attending with him. But I knew what he was really saying: that if once again I refused to do something he asked of me, then it was over between us. Attending a wedding in rural New South Wales and being obliged to make conversation with all his family was the last thing I wanted to do. However, it was a lesser commitment than moving house and taking blood tests. I agreed to accompany him.

All through the winter, the issue of the blood test lay dormant and I figured we had reached an uneasy stalemate. But then, one night after sex, I discovered the condom had broken. I showed it to Shaun ruefully.

'Now you have to have that test,' Shaun insisted. 'I can't spend the next three months worrying over this broken condom. You could go for a test tomorrow and we'd know in a week that everything is okay, and it'd only be a week of anxiety instead of three months.'

'Calm down,' I said. 'You'll have forgotten about it in a week.'

A dark look crossed Shaun's face. 'Is that what you did when you did something unsafe? Forgot about it after a week?'

'I haven't done anything unsafe,' I said, feeling my cheeks growing hot. 'As you know, I haven't been fucked. There's no risk.'

'That's not the only way you can get it. There are cases of people getting it from oral sex. Last time I saw my doctor, he told me about a guy who sero-converted after having oral sex when he had a cold sore on his lip.'

I couldn't answer. What Shaun had just said made me feel sick with anxiety. Shaun pressed home his advantage. 'Then there's a guy in my Ankali group who sero-converted last month. He was sucking a guy off and the guy came unexpectedly and John got some come in his eye. The next time John tested, he was positive.'

'I don't believe that.'

'It's true.'

'In his eye?'

Shaun nodded. 'Stephen, I want you to do this for me,' he pleaded. 'To spare me three months of fretting. Is that too much to ask?'

I took a deep breath and looked Shaun in the eye. 'Yes, it is,' I said coolly. 'It's extremely manipulative. You've twisted this situation to suit your own ends and I won't do it.'

Shaun exploded. '*What* is your problem? I don't understand. If you haven't done anything unsafe, why is it so impossible to confirm that with a simple blood test?'

That made me lose my cool. 'Because it freaks me out,' I shouted back at him. 'Because it's life and death and . . . it scares me . . . and I swore after the last time that I'd never put myself through it again.'

It was the most honest I'd been with Shaun over the issue, but he failed to comprehend that. All he heard was no. He looked disgusted. 'Carson warned me you were hung up over this.'

'*You've discussed this with Carson?*'

Shaun nodded.

'This is personal. Confidential. How could you discuss it with him of all people?'

'Because he's our friend and I have to be able to confide in someone. And, in fact, he's a lot more understanding of where you're coming from than I am.'

'Well, maybe I should be having a relationship with him instead of you.'

'You had your chance once,' said Shaun quietly.

I was shocked. I couldn't believe that the two of them had discussed that too. I got out of the Royal Splendour and began to get dressed. Before I walked out of his bedroom, out of his apartment, I told Shaun it was over between us. To my surprise, he didn't plead with me or weep or beg me not to do this to him. Instead, he was very cool and bitter.

'Throughout this attempt at a relationship,' he said, 'you've shown a greater level of commitment to watching "Melrose Place" on television every Tuesday night than you've ever shown towards me.'

This remark really took me by surprise. It was so cutting. There was no possible retort. All I could do was walk silently out the door and walk home (which seemed defeating in itself – it was farewell to the Saab). It irritated me immensely that Shaun should have the last word, especially such a magnificent last word. It had been me who had ended the relationship, it should have been me who'd come out of it with the upper hand. But the unflattering truth of his words deflated my sense of power. Shaun had succeeded in making me feel rejected.

Two weeks later, when I realised he wasn't going to call me to try to wheedle his way back into my life, I began to wonder what he was up to. It was Carson who let me know. He came over with my clothes, the contents of those two drawers from Shaun's wardrobe. 'It's so cold in here,' Carson complained as he walked into my apartment. 'It's a beautiful day outside. How can you bear it?'

I felt irritated by Carson pointing out the obvious. 'Because I have permafrost of the heart and it suits me to live in an icebox,' I snapped. 'As I'm sure Shaun has told you endlessly. And why are you his delivery boy anyway?'

'Don't you know? Shaun's gone overseas for six weeks. I'm looking after his place while he's gone. He wanted me to make sure these were returned before he got back.'

I was surprised. Although Shaun had been talking about making such a trip ever since we had met, he had always talked of it as something we would do together. I hadn't expected him to take off so suddenly. Or to go without me.

'It's the best thing he could possibly do,' said Carson briskly and I began to suspect that it was he who had persuaded Shaun onto the plane. 'When he comes back he'll have you out of his system.'

I felt even more irritated. Not only by Carson's optimism

that I could be eliminated so swiftly but also by his assumption that Shaun had the monopoly on suffering over our break-up. I almost felt inclined to owning up to some of my own regrets, but Carson excused himself. 'I can't stay,' he said. 'Ant and I are going up to the mountains for the weekend. Shaun left me his car so we're taking advantage of it. I'd ask you to join us, but I can't. He left me the car on the strict condition that I didn't give you a ride in it anywhere. Sorry. You could always get the train up.'

I didn't even bother answering. Carson gave me a long, shrewd look and left.

His visit infuriated me. Carson had been my friend first. I had introduced him to Shaun. He should be offering *me* counsel and support, not Shaun. But Carson hadn't even enquired how I was bearing up. Out of loyalty and consideration to me, Carson ought to have gently but firmly refused all Shaun's overtures of friendship. He owed it to me to sever all ties.

I was so annoyed with Carson that I went down to his and Ant's apartment that night to see what progress he'd made with his book. Even though I'd sworn off prying, Carson's betrayal had spelt the end of my admirable restraint. I was delighted to find that he'd completed two new chapters. I printed them out, not caring if he noticed that his paper had run down inexplicably. While I was waiting for the printer to finish, my eyes fell upon two postcards from Amsterdam sitting on the desk. I knew they would be from Shaun. I turned them over and read them. They were written on consecutive days.

Thursday
Dear Carson
I think perhaps it was a mistake to come to Amsterdam first. So many attractive blond boys everywhere. Inevitably they remind me of Stephen. So far this expensive distraction has only made me feel even lonelier. I need company, not to be alone brooding, and now I'm thousands of miles from all my friends.
Love Shaun

PS. It's been raining so much, I'm sure the canals will start to overflow!

I felt a pang for him. I almost felt tempted to ring him at his hotel, but he hadn't given its name. However, I regretted that instinct once I had read his second card.

Friday
Dear Carson
I had to write immediately and reassure you after my first whingeing card. Not all blonds are cold and aloof. I've just spent the most wonderful night and day with this gorgeous boy, Jap (pronounced Yap). He has insisted that I move out of my hotel and into his apartment (overlooking a canal) and is already trying to get me to change my ticket and stay for longer. It's so refreshing after you know who. Trying to be his lover was like trying to sunbathe in Deepest Siberia!
Love Shaun
PS. Also thank you for trusting me to read that particular chapter. I read it on the plane. You were right. It made me feel better and you've captured him perfectly.

I felt like tearing that postcard up, but unfortunately it wasn't mine to dispose of. I was obliged to position it back where I had found it. I picked the pages up out of the printer tray and left the apartment. I rather wished I'd never intruded. It hurt that Shaun was getting over me already in the arms of some Dutch floozy.

I should've taken that second postcard as a sign not to pry further and put Carson's new chapters aside unread. But I had an inkling that it was me Carson had 'captured perfectly', and of course I couldn't resist reading about myself.

I was prepared for it not to be the flattering portrayal that I deserved. I knew Carson would be bound to mention a few of my bad habits – the golden boy was not without tarnish – but I expected the expansive descriptions of my looks and lively personality to balance out any negative remarks. So I was totally unprepared for what I read. The opening paragraph set the tone for the pages that followed. I read that paragraph then reread it and realised I was in for a character assassination.

Steven was like a knife. Sharp, slender, carefully wrought, even dazzling in certain lights. I recognised him for what he was – a young blade – but his youth reassured me. He was too young to have been ground upon by life. But that was where I misjudged him. He sharpened himself upon me, first one edge and then the next, then tested the blade upon me and found that, yes, it did pierce and wound, quite easily.

As infuriating as that paragraph was, I was at least reassured that Carson was no writer and that his memoirs would never make publication. What a ridiculous metaphor! How could he compare *me* to cutlery? For, as I read on, I found that this motif ran through the entire chapter. On the first page I was a knife, stabbing and scarring; then on the second page I had become a fork as well, always poking and prodding. It carried on in this laboured manner for ten pages, the cutlery toying with the food on the plate, until finally I made a meal of Carson, dissected him with the knife, mashed him with the fork, then took an enormous mouthful and spat him out. 'I was not to his taste after all.'

But it wasn't only that it was a one-sided diatribe with an idiotic metaphor woven through it, but the fact that the chapter dwelt upon that brief flirtation between Carson and myself. I had never expected that unfortunate episode to be revisited. Frankly, I was horrified and shocked at Carson's lack of tact. Surely it was understood between us that it was best forgotten? But Carson evidently had an axe to grind, and was unrelenting in overblowing the episode. No excuses were made for my behaviour – my youth, my inexperience – I was simply an uncaring bastard.

I also found it personally infuriating that Carson had

snatched my role from me – the golden boy – and made it his own. What's more, he had exalted himself to the angelic. You expected him to sprout wings and flap up into the clouds at any moment. Carson was naive, innocent, guileless, while I was artful, manipulative and selfish. He also failed to do my looks justice. The references to my appearance were brief and ungenerous. I was curtly described as 'cute with a Puckish charm', then later as 'pretty but cold, as frosty as the Arctic Blonde dye he used to colour his hair with'. I was particularly furious at that! How dare Carson tell the world that I dyed my hair, and how did he know what brand I used, unless he had been poking around in my bathroom cupboards? I was staggered by how vicious and exaggerated it was. I had never read such rubbish in my life. I threw it under the bed in disgust, along with the other unread chapter.

But what was worse, I was not the only person who had read this appalling slander. Carson had given this malicious, overwrought diatribe to Shaun, to make him feel better, and Shaun's spiteful response had been that it captured me perfectly. What if other people were to read it? What if Carson were to give it to Ant?

The thought of that was so unbearable that I stormed back down to Carson's place determined to delete the entire chapter from his files. I would type in some gibberish and he would presume it had been gobbled up by a computer virus. But as I approached their building, I noticed that Margo was at home. I couldn't run the risk of her catching me in their apartment. As I turned to walk away, I realised how hopeless the idea was anyway. Even if I did delete the original, Carson would undoubtedly have a back-up copy on disk, or even a hard copy hidden away somewhere.

My initial instinct was to exact some nasty revenge of my own. Redouble my efforts to discover Carson's past. But then I thought of something simpler and, the more I considered it, the more perfect it seemed.

Shaun was overseas. I would supplant him. I would become

Carson's new best friend. I would be so thoughtful, so attentive, so omnipresent that, out of guilt, Carson would feel obliged to rewrite that chapter completely in a new and very flattering light.

CHAPTER TWELVE

I saw a good deal of Carson throughout that spring of ninety-five and the summer that followed, as I endeavoured to convince him of my new caring and sharing character. I did everything I could think of to impress him, from becoming a volunteer for an AIDS charity (cutting up red ribbon) to baking and delivering him cookies ('A little snack for while you're writing!'). Initially he was highly suspicious, but when an ulterior motive failed to reveal itself, Carson slowly began to warm towards me and even conceded to Ant that I 'appeared to have matured a little'.

I also saw a lot of Ant. Possibly more than was good for me. We became gym buddies. I'd complained to him in October how self-conscious I'd felt when I went to Tamarama Beach on an unseasonably hot afternoon and no-one had given me a second glance. Which wasn't entirely true, as it was impossible to tell from behind the Ray-Bans that all the boys wore. But I had lain there, face down on my towel, not daring to turn over and reveal the extent to which I failed to fill out my Speedos. Ant presumed I was feeling inadequate about my body. 'Yes, it's about time you started going to the gym,' he declared with a brisk enthusiasm. 'After all, you are single and we both know that in this town no pecs means no sex.'

Ant had been going to Bayswater Fitness since he moved to Onslow Avenue. 'We could work out together,' he suggested. 'It's not such a chore if you have company.'

I agreed immediately. Too eagerly. Ant was startled by my enthusiasm. But his asking me felt as good as a proposal of marriage. I wanted to be his *something* – if not his boyfriend or bit on the side, then his gym partner would suffice. I was also terribly excited by the prospect of seeing him naked under the changing-room shower post work-out.

In fact, I never did. 'I shower at home,' Ant said firmly as we headed towards the changing room after our first session. 'After all, I am a married man. I can do without any distractions.'

But for a married man he still had a good look at what was going on around him. Occasionally I'd catch him watching someone in the shower and he'd grin and look abashed.

'Nice muscle definition,' he'd say.

'Nice cock,' I'd correct him.

Lifting fifty kilograms on the bench press almost killed me, but it was a huge incentive to be able to look up at the swell of Ant's crotch in his sweat pants as he stood over me, ready to rescue me if my muscles failed. Or, even better, to stand before him, gazing into his eyes as he urged me on with my bicep curl. But as much as I revelled in those moments, my pleasure was laden with pain. The physical torture – Ant's split programme of twenty exercises over two days – *that* was going to be good for me. His companionship was another matter. I'd almost forgotten how much I liked it when it was just the two of us. For we had drifted apart over the past year and even I could recognise that seeing him practically every day was unwise and likely to undo the good work, the sensible restraint of the previous year.

After he'd moved to Onslow Avenue with Carson, I'd only seen Ant on the weekends, and I rarely saw him alone. We had always been a foursome, the two couples. The ache of my desire for him had slowly begun to dwindle to the point where I began to congratulate myself that I felt nothing. But then some circumstance would undo me: I would be obliged to introduce Carson as Ant's boyfriend, or Ant would place a casual hand upon Carson. At moments like that, moments which spoke so poignantly of intimacies I was denied, I suffered. But with time, that pain had gradually become more and more muted. It was not so fierce that words failed me or I felt compelled to leave the room or avert my eyes. I could actually watch Ant's hand roam over Carson's thigh and consider my own reaction with an almost scientific detachment, measure my own distress against what I would have felt one or two years previously.

But working out with Ant made me acknowledge that my desire had only been tempered by time, not extinguished altogether. It was like a popular song from a few years ago. It would only take a few bars of the melody for the lyrics to come flooding back. My fear, now that I was committed to seeing Ant on an almost daily basis, was that I would find I still knew the song, in its entirety, by heart.

This particular point in time was bad for me. I was feeling bereft of company after the break-up with Shaun. I was vulnerable, although no-one else seemed to appreciate that fact. The general consensus seemed to be that I hadn't loved Shaun and people were amazed it had lasted as long as it did. It was presumed that I was out and about, doing the bars, and admittedly I had been initially. But somehow there wasn't the same erotic charge to going out that I remembered. Maybe it was my own state of mind, but I was finding those places smoky and loud and the people either aloof or drunk. Nor did I seem to attract attention the way I once had, or at least not from the men that I found appealing.

When I told Ant it was over between Shaun and me, despite myself, expectations began to well up in me. I don't know what I hoped for exactly: an expression of sympathy, then perhaps to be enfolded into his arms and comforted, and from there . . . anything might have been possible. But Ant barely raised an eyebrow, let alone a hand to comfort me. 'I'm not surprised,' he said curtly. 'It was always obvious to me that you didn't love him.'

His expression also stated quite plainly: 'And I never liked him.'

To my surprise I felt a sudden intense compassion for Shaun. Ant had dismissed him so thoroughly, almost contemptuously. Shaun was a nice guy. He deserved a better valediction than that.

This reaction of mine was in itself unsettling. For strangely, now that it was undeniably over between myself and Shaun, I had begun to feel for him something akin to my 'Ant ache'. It was difficult to discern whether those feelings were actual twinges of love, regret, or merely a perverse desire to possess what I no longer did. Or perhaps having become used to companionship, being single now seemed a lonely, desolate state.

That old melody was humming louder in my head every time I met Ant at the gym. I tried to resist. In a last desperate measure I even banned Ant from my masturbation fantasies. The thought of him fucking me had been my favourite bedtime lullaby for years. I'd always known it was a bad habit, only serving to fuel what ought to be on the wane. I bought some pornography in a conscious effort to distract myself but I grew bored with it after a week and had to buy some more. I realised this form of therapy could become expensive.

I'm sure I would've gone on in this manner, valiantly resisting my feelings, if Ant hadn't gone and done something thoroughly astonishing. He betrayed me! Betrayed us, I suppose I should say (Carson was also affected). Betrayed us with a careless disregard for the consequences.

Ant had been going to Bayswater Fitness for more than eighteen months before I joined, so he knew plenty of the regulars to chat to. I wasn't surprised when I arrived late one evening for our work-out to notice him talking to some guy as I dashed into the changing room. When I re-emerged, Ant was doing his bench press and the guy he'd been talking to was spotting him. But there was something in the way the guy hovered over Ant, something insinuating and almost predatory. I felt a twist of jealousy, so sharp, so vicious, my next breath came out half gulp, half cry of protest. I marched over to them. I was Ant's gym partner. I would *not* be supplanted. I stood at the foot of the bench press, my arms folded, waiting for Ant to acknowledge me. As I waited, it suddenly struck me. Ant's face was screwed up as he heaved the weight upward. His new friend was encouraging him in a low, intimate voice. Call it premonition, call it paranoia, whatever – I knew that grimace on Ant's face was exactly how he would look when this guy fucked him.

Ant finished his set. He exhaled loudly, sat up and turned around to beam at the guy behind him who was praising his effort. Neither of them paid me any attention. I couldn't believe how blatantly I was being ignored.

'Sorry to be late,' I said, asserting my presence.

Ant turned his attention to me. 'Oh, that's okay. I started anyway and Ellery has been helping me out,' he said, glancing up at the guy with a grateful smirk.

It was obvious that Ellery was American before he even opened his toothy mouth to speak. He had that classic American look: bleached hair, bleached teeth, tall, strapping, tanned and massively muscular. He was wearing sweat pants and a T-shirt from the Gap. He bounded around the bench to me and thrust out his hand with a flash of his winning smile. 'I'm Ellery.'

I took his hand and his huge fingers wrapped around mine and squeezed. His handshake inevitably made me wonder what it would be like to have all of him wrapped around me. 'I'm Stephen,' I said, responding to his grin despite myself.

'Nice to meet you,' said Ellery, but he had a way of saying those words that made them seem heartfelt and not a mere formality. Maybe it was the directness of his gaze as he spoke and that smile. He was forthright and courteous in a typically American way.

'You out for Mardi Gras?' I asked.

'Sure am. I'm here for the entire month. I hear it's some party.'

I nodded.

'Ellery lives in Miami,' said Ant.

'Great. What do you do there?'

'I have a little gift shop on Washington Drive, South Beach. I'm kinda new to retail and I'm enjoying the change.'

'Ellery used to be an actor. In Hollywood,' Ant chimed in again.

'Really?'

Ellery laughed modestly. 'It's no big deal.'

I was sure it wasn't. If he'd already given up on his acting career, he couldn't have been very successful.

'So,' I said to Ant, 'you going to give me my turn on the bench press?'

Ant hesitated for a moment and glanced at Ellery. 'You guys go ahead,' said Ellery. 'I was just filling in. I'll go do some legwork.'

Both Ant and I ran our eyes up and down Ellery's legs. Ant pulled up the hem of Ellery's sweat pants a little. 'They look like they've already had a lot of work.'

Ellery laughed and slapped Ant's hand away. 'Gotta keep 'em that way,' he said and strode off.

'Jus' holler if you need a helpin' hand,' Ant called after him in an attempt at an American accent. 'Someone to spot you.'

Ellery turned back, grinned and winked.

Ant's face was luminous as he reluctantly turned his attention back to me. '*He* is a god.'

I said nothing, just grunted.

'I couldn't believe it when he came up and started talking to me,' Ant continued in a wondering voice.

'Ex-actors need attention more than they need oxygen.'

Ant had begun to stare across the room after Ellery. 'Look at him.'

'Yes, it's a shame you're married and not available,' I said sliding in beneath the weight.

Ant didn't seem to hear me. He was still staring across the room after Ellery.

Throughout the rest of our work-out, I noticed Ant glancing in Ellery's direction several times. We had barely begun on our sit-ups when Ant suddenly got up and walked off. I presumed he must have gone for a drink or to the toilet. But after five minutes he still hadn't come back. I sped through my last set, then went to look for him. He wasn't anywhere on the floor downstairs. I went into the changing room to collect my bag and there he was, chatting to Ellery, who was sitting on the bench in his Tommy Hilfiger underwear, drying between his toes. Ant was pulling on a pair of cut-off jeans over his Calvin Kleins. They both glanced in my direction as I walked in.

'Hey, Stephen,' Ellery greeted me.

I felt like asking Ant what had happened to him. He who always made such a fuss about me doing every exercise of my work-out no matter how tired I was feeling. He who insisted that abdominals were the most important exercise of the work-out. But it was all too obvious what had suddenly taken precedence. Ant had been watching and waiting for Ellery to finish and as soon as he saw him head for the changing room, he had followed. I noticed Ant's hair was wet. He'd had a shower. Next to Ellery no doubt.

Ellery stood up, towering over both of us. I could see the outline of his cock coiled in his underwear. He pulled on his jeans and then a grey T-shirt.

'Tony and I thought we'd get a bite to eat across the road. Care to join us?'

I felt like saying yes. To spite Ant. Two or three years ago I would've done exactly that, but now I had the foresight to realise how painful it would be for me to sit across the table from these two and watch the attraction between them blossom. I shook my head and mumbled something about a prior engagement. The two of them sauntered out of the changing room and I sank down onto the bench. I felt totally deflated. I sat there for so long, someone kindly enquired if I'd strained something.

'Just my heart,' I muttered.

The guy misunderstood, and began babbling about his own heart rate and what he'd achieved himself on the bicycle.

The next day Ant showed up late for our work-out. I was halfway through by the time he arrived. 'Where have you been?' I asked curtly.

Ant didn't answer. He picked up a dumbbell and did a quick set of curls. I stood in front of him. He was avoiding my eyes. I noticed the ends of his hair were wet. He had presumably come straight from work but it was seven o'clock and he'd had a shower. When he put the weight down, I pounced.

'You've been with Ellery,' I accused him.

Ant looked at me with an expression of utter innocence.

'You have. I know you have. So don't deny it.'

I expected Ant's expression to crumple into a smile, for him to admit it and confess all the details. But he didn't. His face remained implacable. 'Don't be ridiculous, Stephen,' was all he said and he turned away from me to face the mirror.

But he hadn't denied it outright. Perhaps he felt ashamed at all the lies he was already having to tell Carson, and he didn't want to add to them. Still, I was disappointed, even hurt that he didn't confide in me. Didn't he trust me? Was he afraid I'd make some barbed remark to Carson?

The next day Ant phoned me to say that he wasn't going to be able to work out with me for a few weeks. 'I've taken on a private client who wants some figures done urgently. I can't make it in the evenings.'

I saw straight through that. It might be a story to satisfy Carson, but I wasn't fooled. However, I wasn't going to attempt to confront him again. 'That's a shame. Especially with Mardi Gras drawing so close,' I said as sincerely as I could.

Ant muttered something about getting into the gym when he could. Then a thought occurred to me, something to tease him, as he was being so evasive and secretive. 'You know, maybe I'll ask that American guy to work out with me while you're busy.'

'Who?' asked Ant, though the sharpness of his tone indicated he knew exactly who I was talking about.

'Ellery. The American god. I'll leave a message for him at reception for the next time he comes in. Unless you know where he's staying? Did he mention his hotel to you?'

'No,' said Ant curtly. 'I think he's probably left town.'

'I'm sure he hasn't. He said he was here for the whole month.'

Ant had fallen silent and I was grinning to myself when suddenly he lashed out at me. 'Don't even think of doing to Ellery what you did to Carson,' he warned me, his voice cracked with emotion. 'Stephen, I mean it. I won't stand for it.'

The line went dead. Ant had hung up on me. I couldn't believe it. I was shaken. I seemed to have wrung an indirect confession out of him, but at what cost? His tone of voice had been venomous.

I felt upset about our exchange all day. When I got home from work, I decided to phone him, but Carson answered and explained that Ant wasn't home. 'He's just called to say he's going to stay late at the office to do this work for his private client. He won't be home till ten or even later. The thing is, I've already cooked. I don't suppose you feel like coming over for dinner?'

I couldn't help feeling sorry for Carson, believing Ant's lies. I accepted the invitation.

I walked over to Elizabeth Bay. It was Margo who opened the door when I knocked. 'Carson's busy,' she explained, ushering me in.

He was standing on a chair in the middle of the living room in a T-shirt and his underwear. 'I'm being measured,' he explained. 'For our Mardi Gras costumes which Margo the Marvel is making for us.'

Margo blushed with pleasure. 'Your arrival is very timely,' she said, handing me a pencil and notebook. 'You can take down Carson's measurements as I call them out. Right, waist first.'

Carson lifted up his T-shirt. I was struck by how childish he looked, standing there with his slim, hairless navel exposed. Even his underwear seemed charmingly juvenile. Not the ubiquitous Calvin Kleins but white Jockeys, the brand Elisabeth used to buy for me fifteen years ago. His hair fell into his eyes as he looked down at Margo. She was readjusting the measuring tape. 'Twenty-seven? Is that right? Yes. Twenty-seven. I suppose you boys are metrified and don't understand what I'm talking about.'

'We know what eight inches is, don't we, Carson?' I joked.

'I'm glad to hear it,' said Margo, failing to comprehend. 'But you are too skinny, young man. Twenty-seven inches round the waist. And these legs. Sticks!'

Margo was fumbling her tape measure round one of Carson's thighs. She didn't notice that her remark had wiped the serene smile off Carson's face, but I did. Our eyes met for a moment and Carson looked abashed, before looking away. Had he lost weight? I couldn't bear to look and have it confirmed.

'Carson's lucky to be so lean, Margo,' I said brightly. 'Not like Ant and me spending all our time in the gym trying to keep our tummies tight.'

Margo merely grunted.

'Were you at the gym tonight with Ant?' Carson asked.

Carson had said, over the phone, that Ant was working late. Evidently he didn't believe him either.

'He told me he's not going to be able to work out with me for a few weeks because of his private client,' I said.

Carson nodded but his eyes lingered on me, as if he suspected a lie.

'You'll have to send Ant in to see me before he goes to work tomorrow,' said Margo firmly. 'I'll be telling him that he needs to fatten you up a little. Twenty inches upper thigh.' Margo glanced at me sternly. 'Have you been writing these down?'

I hadn't been. 'Yes, Margo,' I said, noting the measurements down, although once I had, I felt like scribbling them out again. Margo was right. Carson had always been lean but twenty-seven round the waist was a bit thin.

Carson got down from the chair and put on his jeans. Margo excused herself. 'I was going to cut the trousers out to the pattern but I can't do that now you have company.'

We assured her that she could, but she wouldn't hear of it. 'Oh no, these costumes have to be top secret. Top secret. Or it will spoil the surprise. No-one must catch a glimpse of them until the two of you arrive at the party together. Then they'll have the full impact.' Margo turned to me. 'You know, I got the last five yards of this material in the shop. It's sensational. Wait until you see it.'

Margo departed, insisting Ant come to be measured the next

morning. 'This is the fourth time we've tried to arrange it. Time is of the essence. He must come tomorrow.'

Carson showed Margo out. 'She's a sweetie,' he said when he returned. 'Making our costumes for us. The thing is, she's probably more excited about doing it than either me or Ant. Ant's gone right off the idea of going dressed identically.'

I tried to protest but Carson interrupted me. 'He told me quite bluntly a few nights ago that he thinks it's a naff idea, and I kind of agree. But Margo offered such a long time ago and has been so enthusiastic ever since, we can't tell her we've lost interest.'

'I'm sure once it's all finished and he sees how good it looks, he'll want to do it.'

Carson didn't look convinced. 'He's talking about taking along a pair of shorts to get changed into at the party. He'll just put this outfit on for Margo's sake, so she can take some photos.'

Carson changed the subject after that and started organising dinner. But as he set my plate down before me at the table, he sighed. 'I don't know why Ant doesn't just come home, have a proper dinner and then work in the study.'

'Probably because he'd end up in front of the television, instead of in front of the computer.'

Carson shrugged. We ate dinner and then watched some television. But I could tell Carson was distracted and by ten o'clock I was feeling agitated by Ant's absence too. Finally I suggested the two of us go out for some cake. Carson refused at first, but eventually I persuaded him. 'Margo would approve,' I pointed out and he laughed and agreed to come.

We went to Moran's and by the time we'd finished, it was well after eleven. We kissed goodbye, and I paused for a moment on the corner of Macleay Street and Challis Avenue and watched him cross the street. He was only wearing a T-shirt and a stiff breeze had sprung up. He was hunched over from the cold, which made him seem a rather forlorn figure as he made his solitary way home. I hoped vehemently that Ant was home when he got back there.

The next day Elisabeth had invited me for lunch at the Bayswater Brasserie. She'd been a little mysterious when she rang to make the arrangement, but had implied that she had some exciting news for me. As soon as I sat down she blurted it out. 'You'll never guess. I'm going to march in the Mardi Gras parade, darling,' she gurgled at me. 'Such fun! I can't wait.'

I stared at her in disbelief. 'Are you trying to come out to me?' I finally asked, though the thought of Elisabeth as a lesbian was beyond belief.

'Don't be ridiculous,' Elisabeth tittered. 'I'm going to be marching with the P-Flag group. Parents with gay children.'

'I know who they are,' I said. 'But you don't belong to their group.'

'I do now,' said Elisabeth triumphantly. 'And they're very excited about having me as a member because of my high public profile. Already the ABC, who are televising the parade, have approached me about an interview on the night.'

So that was Elisabeth's motivation. Of course if there were television cameras involved, she would find her way in front of them.

'Actually, they want to interview both of us,' Elisabeth continued. 'They'll film us walking up Oxford Street together with the P-Flag group and then they'll whisk us aside and ask us both a few questions.'

'I am *not* going in the Mardi Gras parade with my mother.'

'Why ever not? Don't you want me to publicly embrace your sexuality and inspire other parents to do the same?'

'I'd rather you embraced it sincerely in private.'

'I have,' said Elisabeth indignantly.

I felt like reminding her of her long laments about how she would never know the pleasure of grandchildren. Or how whenever there was a family wedding or reunion I was never invited with a partner, although my cousins were welcomed with their junkie boyfriends, illegitimate children and Thai mail-order brides and then fawned over by Elisabeth. Her attention was pointed. My cousins were a little disreputable, but at least they were heterosexual.

I knew it was pointless to get into an argument. Elisabeth would simply refuse to listen to anything she didn't want to hear and repeat her own point of view with increasing stridency. We discussed safe topics over lunch instead, and then when the time came to part I said simply that she was more than welcome to march with P-Flag but not to include me in her plans. Elisabeth was all smiles. She kissed me goodbye and I had the distinct feeling she was, as usual, choosing not to hear what had just been made plain to her.

I was correct. A few days later I had a phone call from a researcher at the ABC to confirm our interview on the night of the Mardi Gras parade. I told him firmly that I had no plans of marching with P-Flag and my mother.

I was expecting an irate call from Elisabeth but instead, the next day, Jane Sykes, the coordinator of the P-Flag float, phoned me. She was soothing, persuasive and armed with facts and statistics. 'Stephen, I wonder if you realise what it would mean to have a woman of your mother's stature publicly endorsing our group and embracing her own gay son's sexuality on prime-time television? For mothers and fathers in the suburbs or in small towns or in the country, seeing your mother would be a revelation. It would help to break down their own sense of discomfort and isolation. Make them understand that they're not the only one with a gay child.'

Jane continued on in this vein for ten minutes, illustrating her argument with case histories, tragic stories of teenagers kicked out of their homes after coming out. Battered by their fathers. Insulted by their mothers. Forced onto the streets, into prostitution. By the time she began to relate a recent case which had culminated in suicide, I found myself agreeing to march with P-Flag, agreeing to the television interview and even agreeing to wear a rainbow leotard which would match Elisabeth's outfit. I regretted my capitulation as soon as the words were uttered, but it was too late.

I didn't complain to anyone about how humiliating it was going to be. I was vainly hoping that none of my friends would bother to watch the parade or, if they did, that they would be too drunk or out of it to recognise me. I kept up my gym routine, spurred on by the necessity of my body outshining the sheer hideousness of a rainbow leotard.

I learnt from the boy on reception that Ant was still coming to the gym, at times I wasn't, with Ellery. 'He's traded you in as a gym partner for that big American,' the boy teased me.

I felt discomforted throughout my work-out. The thought of Ant with Ellery stirred up a flurry of agitated feelings. Anger, rejection, frustration. I did my work-out automatically, without thinking, and was surprised to find myself finished twenty minutes earlier than usual. I decided to call down to see Carson. I was curious as to how much he knew. As I suspected, I found him home alone.

'How's Margo getting on with the costumes?' I asked.

'Oh, good,' said Carson. 'And Ant has agreed to wear it.'

'I knew he'd come round to the idea—' I began, but Carson interrupted me.

'But only on the condition that we don't spend the whole night hanging round together "looking ridiculous",' he added bitterly.

I was a little shocked by that. I tried to suggest some more optimistic interpretations of this statement, but to Carson it was a very clear sign of rejection.

'I'm sure once Mardi Gras is over with, he'll be back to his old self,' I suggested.

Carson fixed his eyes upon me grimly and I knew then that he didn't know as much as I did and expected me to enlighten him. I was saved by the doorbell.

'Perhaps that's him,' I said hopefully.

'He does have a key,' Carson said scornfully. 'He does still own half this place, even if he chooses not to be here very often.'

It was Shaun at the door. He was wearing a new suit, one I hadn't seen before, and I felt a little pang at how handsome he looked in it. Carson had mentioned a month or so ago that Shaun was dating someone new. But seeing me seemed to discomfort him for he immediately reached for his cigarette packet. Carson had also told me that he'd given up cigarettes. I made an excuse to leave.

I was so busy in that week prior to the Mardi Gras parade, I didn't get to see Carson again. What with work and going to the gym every night and Elisabeth nagging at me daily over our impending television appearance. She even insisted we have a rehearsal and I was obliged to go all the way out to Wahroonga one evening. Basically all she wanted was an audience. She had obtained a list of the questions that would be asked and had formulated elaborate answers not only for herself but for me as well. She practised her own lines – she already knew them by heart – and then she tried to instruct me in how I should deliver mine. I managed to avoid that by suggesting I learn them first. She agreed and I was allowed to go home. She rang me the next night to test me on them over the phone. I hadn't even looked at them. I'd gone home via Oxford Street. All the bars were jumping and so packed with Americans (variations on the general look and dimensions of Ellery), you could be forgiven for thinking you were in California.

On Mardi Gras evening, Strauss held his annual pre-parade drinks on the roof of our apartment block. It was packed as usual, although Strauss was curiously absent. Finally, after a quarter of an hour, I spotted him. He had been there all along but he was in drag and quite unrecognisable.

'Why have you been ignoring me ever since you arrived?' Strauss demanded when I went over to compliment him.

'I didn't recognise you. You look . . .'

'Immaculate. I know.'

I had been going to tell him he looked better than he did as a guy.

'I had a professional do my make-up for tonight,' Strauss boasted. 'It makes the world of difference. Darling, what's the worst thing about having a party? Being the host, of course.

But I've escaped that drudgery by transforming myself for the night. I've never enjoyed myself so much at one of my own parties before.'

'Everyone is wondering where you are.'

'Let them wonder. I'm incognito and I'm adoring it.' Suddenly, Strauss exclaimed, 'Good heavens! *What* are they wearing?'

Ant and Carson had arrived in their top-secret outfits. They were dressed as space-age cowboys in slinky silver chaps and matching cowboy hats. I noted with annoyance that they had also brought Shaun with them. They saw me and hurried over. Carson did a twirl. His chaps had no arse in them. 'What do you think? We're Butch Cassidy and the Sundance Kid.'

Strauss and I mumbled something which could be construed as admiring.

'I'm sorry about bringing Shaun,' whispered Carson in my ear. 'But otherwise he would've ended up going to the party alone and you know how hard it is to meet up with your friends there.'

'I thought he was seeing someone.'

'It broke up. The guy wanted to be single for Mardi Gras.'

Ant kissed me hello and began to chat as if he had never hung up on me. We hadn't spoken since then. Not in three weeks. At first I was pleased at the warmth of his greeting, but it didn't take me long to realise that he must've taken some speed. He was babbling. There was no sincerity to what he was saying. Everything coming out of his mouth, his elaborate excuses as to why he hadn't seen me or phoned, was bullshit. I interrupted him. 'I'm sorry. I have to go. I'm in the parade.'

Everyone chorused their astonishment. I had told no-one what I had been coerced into. Ant turned his attention to Strauss. 'Who are you? Do you work downstairs?' he asked.

'I beg your pardon, Butch,' Strauss protested shrilly. 'I have a respectable profession. I'm actually something of a supermodel.'

I winked at Strauss and hurried downstairs to change into

my leotard. It was truly awful, something Uncle Vic would wear to the gym and think was fabulous. It had P-Flag spelled out across the buttocks in pink lettering. Thankfully I managed to leave the building without anyone seeing me.

When I arrived at the float's assigned position, Jane was furious. I was almost an hour late and Elisabeth had turned up not wearing her rainbow costume. We were both in disgrace.

'Mother, where is your lovely frock?' I asked her.

'It wasn't at all flattering,' said Elisabeth dismissively. 'I decided it was a mistake and that black would be much more decorous for someone of my years.'

'I would've been happy to wear black too.'

'Well, they went to so much effort making the outfits, I thought one of us should take the trouble to wear them.'

At that moment an out-of-it drag queen approached Elisabeth squealing with delight. 'Darling, you look fabulous. You look just like her. Brilliant. Absolutely brilliant,' she declared as she swept on by.

Elisabeth's expression became quite stricken and she clutched my hand.

'It was you who insisted on doing this,' I couldn't help pointing out to her.

She pursed her lips. 'I didn't realise there would be all this waiting round,' she complained. 'Now I'm told we're number fifty in the parade. I expected to be at the front.'

The next half-hour while we waited for the parade to start was one of the longest of my life. Naturally every man I'd ever slept with walked past. Some were content just to wink at me, others felt the need to French kiss me. Warren the bear cub decided to kiss Elisabeth as well. And because of the party atmosphere of the night, a lot of guys I knew only by sight, from the gym or from going out, came up and said hello to me. I could tell from the look on Elisabeth's face that she presumed I had slept with every single one of them. 'What a lot of friends you've made,' she observed. 'Though it's odd so many of them don't recall your name.'

After a while I gave up caring what she thought. After all, it was Mardi Gras and I was still a little drunk from Strauss's party. I decided just to enjoy all the attention and began to smile and flirt and joke with the guys that passed by.

But then someone seized me by the shoulders, someone who did remember my name, or at least the name I had given him. It was Bern, the Dutchman I had taken back to Ant's apartment.

He greeted me with such enthusiasm, throwing his arms around me and kissing me four times, twice on each cheek. 'Oh Ant, Ant, Ant, Ant,' he cried in delight. 'I am so happy to have found you again. I have looked for you in all the bars where we first met. I have been to your apartment, but you have moved. Your name is not known there. Oh, I am so pleased to have found you. As you see, I have returned to Australia for the Mardi Gras, though also I returned with the hope of finding you single and available.'

I was aware of Elisabeth, her eyes running up and down Bern, taking in his black shorts from which protruded a pointed metal codpiece which looked highly treacherous.

'I believe you've mistaken me for someone else,' I said firmly, relieved he was using the wrong name. 'My name is Stephen.'

Bern looked perplexed. 'There is no mistake. I could not forget a face as beautiful as yours. Three years ago your name was Ant.'

'My *mother*,' I said, with much emphasis upon the word, 'will vouch for me. My name is Stephen.'

Bern turned to Elisabeth, his mouth agape with surprise.

Elisabeth nodded and gave one of her stiffest smiles. 'Stephen,' she confirmed in a terse voice.

Bern blushed, mumbled something in Dutch and fled into the crowd.

I avoided Elisabeth's interrogating stare. Thankfully, by that point, the parade was under way and our group was soon called forward. By the time we turned into Liverpool Street, Elisabeth's smile had slid back into place and it became quite genuine as she was recognised and photographed by people in the crowd. Lots of people wanted to shake her hand and say hello. By the time we were halfway up Oxford Street and the ABC cameras swooped down on us, her face was flushed with excitement. I'd already heard Elisabeth deliver her lines in a dozen different ways but that night, for the first time, what she was saying sounded sincere. With her face aglow, her eyes sparkling, one hand resting gently on my shoulder, she told the camera that of course she still loved her son and had joined P-Flag in an attempt to understand his lifestyle better.

Then it was my turn. 'And how have you enjoyed marching in the parade with your mother?'

Elisabeth had written my response to this question – how thrilled I was to be sharing this night with her, how much this public display of support meant to me – but somehow it went out of my head. I answered spontaneously, without thinking. 'Deeply embarrassed.'

But in a flash, Elisabeth had insinuated herself in front of the camera. 'My son may be a little embarrassed but I've seen a side of him tonight, and of the entire gay community, that I was ignorant of. The sheer fun they all have! When we as parents don't want to acknowledge our children's sexuality, that's not the only thing we're blocking out. We're not seeing them at their best. When they're with their friends and lovers and are happy and relaxed. We just see the misery and tension.' And she gave a winning smile.

The cameras and lights were whisked away. Elisabeth took me by the hand and we hurried to rejoin our group which had moved on ahead of us. But even once we had caught up, she continued to hold my hand, and I was surprised to realise that I didn't feel inclined to pull free of her. She probably hadn't held me by the hand for almost fifteen years.

Along the course of the parade, I was stopped so many times by gay boys and lesbians who told me how lucky I was to have a mother like Elisabeth, I was almost beginning to believe it. Perhaps her motives for marching weren't as selfish as I imagined them to be. When a middle-aged woman in the crowd stopped us, clasped me to her and told us we were her favourite float of the entire night, I felt unbearably moved. Elisabeth's smile was radiant. She had been waiting to be told she was the best all night.

I was sorry when we reached the end of the parade route and had to move away from the crowd. Elisabeth slipped her hand free of mine and turned to me. 'There,' she said. 'That wasn't such an ordeal, was it?'

'No,' I agreed quite genuinely. 'It was . . . kind of uplifting actually.'

Elisabeth smiled her approval. 'Yes. My only regret is that I wish I'd worn that gaudy dress. Black isn't really appropriate in such a carnival atmosphere. Never mind. Goodness, it's a long walk in heels. I don't know how all these drag queens do it and then go on and dance in them all night too. I'm afraid I really don't have the energy for carrying on to the party.'

I laughed. 'Mother, you need a ticket to go to the party.'

'I'm aware of that,' said Elisabeth haughtily. 'I have a ticket.'

I could *not* believe it. I insisted she get it out of her handbag and show me. When she produced a ticket, I was stunned. They weren't easy to obtain. Only members of Mardi Gras could buy them.

'How did you get that?'

'One of the fathers at P-Flag is a member. He talked me into going. But I'm too tired and I think I've realised it's your night, darling, not mine.' She handed me the ticket. 'You sell it for me, or give it to one of your *many* friends. I'm going to go home.'

I was touched by her words. I kissed her goodbye on the cheek.

'Run along. I can get a lift with Jane or someone.' She had turned away from me, but suddenly she turned back. She leant close to me and whispered in my ear. 'Remember, dear, if you can't be good, be clever.'

Her words resonated in my head as I joined the throng of

people walking towards the party. She'd said that exact same thing to me on my eighteenth birthday. But this time I understood what she was getting at. In her own discreet motherly way, she was telling me to be safe.

When I noticed Bern walking towards me, my initial impulse was to try to hide. But he looked so distraught, and was walking in the wrong direction, I felt compelled to stop him and ask what the problem was.

'I have come all this way to go to the party,' Bern wailed. 'And now I am told there are no tickets. Sold out. I do not understand. I have money.'

I gave Bern Elisabeth's ticket and his face lit up with joy and relief. He seized me, kissed me and almost castrated me with his metal crotch. He insisted on giving me one hundred dollars, which I refused to take. Finally he stuffed it down the front of my rainbow leotard, which I had rolled down into shorts. While he was down there, his fingers curled around my cock. He looked me intently in the eye. *'That* I remember,' he said emphatically. 'I think you have played games with me.'

I smirked and ran away from him. It was easy to lose him in such a crowd.

Once I'd gone into the party, I made my way to the main hall. I took my ecstasy as soon as I'd squirmed onto the middle of the dance floor. Half an hour later I was wishing I hadn't. I'd begun to feel nauseous. The guy I'd bought it off had tried to talk me into buying a second tablet and inserting it anally. 'You'll have spasms up your rectum like you wouldn't believe,' he'd assured me.

I'd ignored that sales pitch but now it made a cruel sort of sense. His ecstasy was shit. I wondered what it actually was that I'd swallowed. The dance floor was unbearably crowded and hot. I was slick with sweat from head to toe and ferociously thirsty. I was trying to ignore the heaving in my stomach, when suddenly, unexpectedly, I dry retched. It was so violent that the muscles in my stomach cramped from the force of the convulsion. My hands flew to my mouth. Luckily, nothing came out but I knew I had to get off the dance floor. I pushed my way through the crowd, one hand clutched to my mouth, the other massaging my aching stomach muscles. It was fast becoming one of those times when I wished I wasn't by myself.

I found my way to the bar and bought myself a bottle of water. I turned away to take a sip and the next thing I knew, I was throwing up. Not a lot of vomit came out but enough to make all the people around me aware of what I had done. I was being stared at with such disdain but there wasn't anything I could do to clean it up. If I'd been wearing a T-shirt, I would've thrown it over the mess. Finally I up-ended my bottle of water on it to try to sluice it away, which in fact only made matters worse. The vomit began to glide across the floor towards a threesome of very chic girls in black halter tops and hot pants. They stared at it in horrified fascination but seemed powerless to move away from its inexorable progress towards them. I yelled something at them about going to find a mop – an impossible quest – but I plunged frantically into the crowd and escaped their haughty, horrified stares.

Instead, I went to the toilets to rinse my mouth out and wash my face. Bern was hanging around in there and as soon as he saw me, he tried to whisk me into a vacant toilet cubicle. I told him I was feeling sick but he wouldn't listen. 'I cannot believe a word that comes out of your mouth,' Bern said to me sadly, his expression melancholy.

His grip upon me was very firm. In the end I pretended to agree to go into the cubicle with him. 'But you have to remove that metal phallus first,' I said sternly.

While Bern concentrated on dismantling it, he let go of me and I made my escape.

I went and sat down in the bleachers, my head between my legs. I wasn't paying any attention to who was sitting around me, although the guy next to me began to pester me as soon as I sat down. Moving his leg so it rested against mine. Offering me chewing gum. Finally he put his hand between my legs. I stood up to move and that was when I saw them. It was the cowboy hat that caught my attention. It was lying behind my seat. A silver cowboy hat. Then I recognised the legs, or rather I recognised the pants. The silver lurex pants. The last material in the store. Sewn by Margo for 'her boys'. One of Ant's silver-encased legs stretched out towards me, his boot resting on the back of the vacant seat next to mine. The mass of muscle in a pair of leather shorts writhing on top of him was, of course, Ellery.

I was too off-colour to feel jealous or vindictive. I just felt sadly resigned, that what I'd suspected had turned out to be true. I should have walked off then. If I had, perhaps I might have saved Ant. But as I wavered there on my feet for some moments, I realised I wasn't in a state to go anywhere. Then the guy who'd groped me gently helped me back down into my seat, his admiring hands sweeping over my buttocks.

'Sorry about before,' he muttered. 'Didn't realise you were so out of it. I thought you were coming on to me.'

I stared at him in amazement. This guy had to be really out of it himself, if he thought I was coming on to him when I was practically catatonic.

I was embarrassed to be sitting so close to Ant and Ellery but, after glancing back at them a couple of times, I realised they were oblivious to everyone around them. It didn't matter. They weren't going to notice me.

'Those two are hot stuff,' the guy next to me whispered. 'But then you're not bad yourself.'

I didn't see them coming until they were standing over me. By then it was too late. My admirer was asked to move along a seat. He gave me a pleading look, which I ignored. 'Shove over,' I said roughly, and he stomped off in a huff.

Carson and Shaun sat down on either side of me. Shaun's ecstasy was obviously far superior to whatever it was that I had taken. He kissed me, complimented me, and even told me my leotard was gorgeous (which reminded me that I had some shorts checked at the cloakroom that I had intended to change into). Then he began to rave on about how much he'd missed me over the last few months.

Carson, of course, never took drugs at parties and he noticed at once that I wasn't myself. 'Are you all right?'

'Actually, I'm feeling sick. I threw up.'

'You look pale,' said Carson.

I couldn't decide what to do. If we stayed there, eventually Carson was going to notice what was going on behind us, and part of me couldn't help wanting that to happen. Suddenly my stomach turned over and I dry retched again.

Carson put his arm around me. 'Are you all right?'

His voice was so gentle and concerned, I felt ashamed of myself. I shouldn't wish such a nasty scene on Carson. 'I think maybe I should go outside.'

'Good idea,' said Carson, standing up and helping me to my feet.

We still had our backs to Ant and Ellery. I thought I'd actually managed to avoid a confrontation when Shaun, who was leading the way back to the aisle, stopped to check how we were coming along behind him. At first, I was irritated by him, standing transfixed, with such an odd look on his face. I thought his ecstasy had suddenly compelled him to make a new declaration of love to me. It was only when I'd moved right up next to him that I realised he wasn't staring at me. He was looking beyond me, over my shoulder. He had recognised Ant's silver-clad legs. I turned Shaun around and pushed him forward, but it was too late. I felt Carson's comforting hand, which had rested on my waist, fall away. I knew he had turned back and seen what was behind us.

I was almost too scared to look back. When I finally did, Carson was pushing his way back down the row of seats from where we'd just come. People were swearing at him. 'Make up your mind.' He stood over Ellery and Ant for what seemed like forever. Just staring down at them. It seemed even worse that they failed to notice him. Finally Carson tapped Ellery on the shoulder. He glanced up at Carson, then went back to kissing Ant. Carson tapped him again and this time Ellery sat up. Carson looked down on Ant, the profile of his face not twisted with fury but pale and very solemn. From where Shaun and I stood, we couldn't see Ant, but I could imagine the shock, the guilt, stamped all over his face. Ellery's eyes were taking in Carson's costume, identical to Ant's, and realising who he must be.

The music was soaring around us – 'Missing' by Everything But The Girl – but there was a sudden lull in the song at the exact moment Carson turned on Ellery. Everyone nearby could hear him as he yelled, 'That's right. Help him off with that costume. He made such a fuss about wearing it.'

Carson stalked back towards me and Shaun. Behind him, Ant clambered to his feet, fumbling with the fly and button on his pants. He looked wild-eyed and dishevelled. Our eyes met. My instinct was to go to him – there was a look of such bewilderment on his face – but then here was Carson moving towards us, his face now cold with anger. 'Take this,' said Carson, handing me his silver cowboy hat. 'Feel free to throw up in it. I don't want it.' Carson pushed past me and flung himself upon Shaun. One desolate sob rang out and I felt a sudden tug of compassion for Carson. Shaun was looking even more bewildered than Ant. He was so wasted that even as he held Carson, he was still instinctively twitching to the dance music. I realised he would be of no use to Carson. I glanced back at Ant. Ellery was standing beside him, his arm around his shoulders in a protective manner. Ant looked dumbstruck, but I noticed he was leaning into Ellery. At this moment, with Carson so upset, he should have been pulling away from him, running after his boyfriend, begging his forgiveness. I turned away from them, took Carson by the arm and led him down the stairs. 'I'll take you home,' I offered.

'I don't want to go back there,' said Carson bitterly. 'I don't want to see him again.'

'Well, we'll go to my place.' I turned to Shaun. 'Now you go and have a good time and I'll look after Carson.'

Shaun protested and clung to us, telling us how much he loved us both. When we finally extricated ourselves I led Carson out of the hall and encountered Uncle Vic outside. He was too trashed to remember Carson from the one time he'd met him. He raised his eyebrows. 'That was quick work,' he said. 'That leotard must do something for you after all.'

Uncle Vic's own choice of costume was a jungle-print fake-fur g-string.

It was as we got into the taxi that Carson said it. I was so startled that I stood there and forgot to clamber in after him. He turned to me, wiping away his tears with his fists. 'I thought it was you,' he said. 'I thought you'd finally seduced him and that was why you kept coming round to see me, out of guilt, for what you'd finally managed to accomplish.'

All the way back to my place in the taxi, we sat in silence. I couldn't stop asking myself, if Carson had managed to guess my feelings, why hadn't Ant?

CHAPTER THIRTEEN

Ant blamed me for his break-up with Carson. He turned up at my place the following evening, still strung out on whatever he'd taken. He was emotional, aggressive and looked terrible. His complexion matched his inflammatory mood. His nose and cheeks were ruddy. Ugly patches of stubble burn had seared his chin and upper lip. Purple bags swelled beneath his eyes, which were bloodshot.

'Where is he? What happened when you took him away?' he demanded, his face contorted with emotion. 'I saw you leave together. I ran after you to talk to Carson and saw you with your arm round him. Did you bring him here? Where did he sleep? You've only got one bed and it's not even a queen. Did you take advantage of him when he was upset?'

This barrage of accusations, combined with the rankness of his breath, left me wilted. I didn't know where to begin to defend myself. But Ant gave me no time to respond. He exhaled deeply in my face and railed at me. 'You led him to me and Ellery. You were there. You'd been there for some time. I remember glancing to the side and seeing those awful psychedelic shorts, with the lettering peeling off. I didn't recognise them at the time, but later I realised. Somehow you lured Carson up to sit beside you, then pointed us out. You've been trying to ruin things between us since the day we met. I could see the look on your face when I sat up. You standing there with Shaun. Gloating.'

I was not going to stand for that. For once I was innocent of what I was accused. 'I can assure you,' I said indignantly, 'that was no look of triumph on my face. It was a grimace. I was sick. My drugs were fucked and I was trying not to throw up. I was in fact trying to lead Carson away from you and that pumped-up Californian queen. But believe whatever you like.

Blame me if it's going to help Carson accept you back. I don't mind. I want to see the two of you back together, whatever it takes.'

That last sentence wasn't strictly true, but I was playing the aggrieved innocent and got a little carried away.

Ant said nothing for some moments. 'Well, where is he then?' he asked finally.

Carson had gone to stay at Shaun's but he had made me promise not to tell Ant. I could have said I didn't know, but I felt like provoking him. 'He asked me not to tell you and I'm not going to.'

That infuriated him. 'You're supposed to be my friend. For Christ's sake, tell me where he is.' He stood there waiting expectantly. 'Well?'

'I promised.'

'I don't know why you've suddenly decided to act all honourable. You've never bothered to in the past. But I can guess where he is anyway.'

Ant stormed out and I phoned Shaun to warn him that Ant might be on his way over. 'We were about to go out for dinner anyway,' said Shaun. 'Why don't you meet us?'

We arranged to eat at Fez, the new Moroccan place. Over his vegetable tagine, Carson explained why he wasn't prepared to tolerate Ant's behaviour.

'It's not just the infidelity. I know the temptations. I can empathise with the urge. It's the fact that he lied to me over and over again. Him and his private client! If he'd simply told me what he was doing, of course I'd have been upset, but at least I would have felt informed rather than deceived. We could have discussed it and why he felt the need to do it. But to hide it from me and keep lying to me, I can't forgive that. From the start we said our relationship would be based on honesty. That was very important to both of us and it's why I feel so betrayed now. I can't trust him and I'm not prepared to give him a second chance. He doesn't deserve one. It's over. I don't want to be with him any more.'

Carson was adamant. He wrote Ant a letter expressing those feelings and enclosed a cheque to cover the mortgage for a month. 'I suggested he get a flatmate,' he told me. 'Or put the place on the market.'

Carson never spent another night at the apartment in Onslow Avenue. He moved his belongings into Shaun's spare room on the Tuesday after Mardi Gras when Ant was at work, and presented a 'don't care' attitude to the world. Whenever I saw him he seemed bright and happy. He was doing things he'd let slip over the past year: working on his book with renewed vigour (even submitting the first half to an agent – rather optimistically I thought), going to meditation and yoga consistently rather than haphazardly, catching up on his reading. It was implied that Ant was to blame for Carson lapsing out of his once regular habits and he resumed them with a vigour that bordered on the manic.

But I was dubious of Carson's claims that he was over Ant. It seemed to me that he never gave himself the chance to feel lonely and miss him, because he was always with Shaun. They became inseparable. You never saw one without the other. If I arranged to see Carson, Shaun always came too, even though I never invited him. If I ran into them by accident somewhere, it was always both of them. They were never apart. Except when Shaun went to work, and then Carson kept himself preternaturally busy. If he wasn't writing or reading or cooking or cleaning, he was meditating and off in some other dimension altogether, where thoughts of Ant couldn't possibly pursue him.

His closeness to Shaun irritated me. It reinforced my own sense of isolation – excluded by their intimacy and estranged from Ant by taking Carson's side. But I also felt vaguely supplanted. I had looked after Carson when he was at his most vulnerable, provided support, ruined my friendship with Ant in the process, while Shaun carried on dancing. When I took Carson home with me, I had expected he would want to sit up and talk. Berate Ant and reveal in the process all sorts of secrets about their relationship. But perhaps Carson had suspected me of having an egoistical interest in their problems. He scotched my hopes of intimate confessions by walking straight into my bedroom and flopping down on the bed. 'I just want to sleep and not have to think. Can I borrow some boxer shorts?'

Sleeping was the last thing I'd felt like doing. I still had traces of what I'd failed to vomit up pulsing through my system. I couldn't imagine that Carson would be able to sleep either, considering all that had happened.

But he did. Maybe he used some meditation trick to accomplish it. I lay beside him, preoccupied and restless, for hours.

We didn't wake until midday and that was only because the ringing phone shocked us awake. I jumped out of bed and answered it instinctively. I suppose we were both expecting it to be Ant and I felt suddenly, shockingly guilty to be lying in bed beside his boyfriend. But it was Shaun phoning. He had only just got home from the party, could not sleep and wanted some company. 'You should've picked someone up then,' I said tersely and was about to hang up when Carson appeared beside me and retrieved the phone before it was slammed down.

Carson began to chat with Shaun and I heard him offer to come over as soon as he'd had a shower. I went back to bed feeling disgruntled. I had expected to spend what remained of the day with Carson. I hated coming down off drugs, especially bad drugs, by myself. When he'd finished speaking to Shaun, Carson appeared awkwardly in the doorway of my bedroom, twisting his hands together, and asked for a towel. Suddenly our situation seemed implicitly sexual. Him standing there in my boxer shorts. Me supine amongst the rumpled sheets, an erection rising in my underwear. I was too embarrassed to get out of bed. I directed Carson to where the towels were kept and while he showered, I masturbated.

I lent him a T-shirt and a pair of jeans and he departed with a quick, brotherly peck on the lips. 'Promise me you won't tell Ant where I am if he rings,' he said and I promised.

I had kept my word and offended Ant in the process. He

didn't contact me again. At first I refused to take the initiative. I was adamant that it was up to Ant to make the overture. He had unjustly upbraided me. I was owed an apology. What's more, he had betrayed my love for him. Admittedly, he was unaware of my feelings, but I still felt betrayed. I had suffered over his infidelity just as much as Carson had. In fact, I had probably suffered more. I had to pretend to be unaffected, while Carson reaped the sympathy of everyone around him. I felt just as cheated and betrayed as he did, but I didn't even have the consolation of discussing that with anyone. However, after two weeks had passed, I relented. I phoned Ant at work, only to be told he wasn't in. When I tried him at home the machine was on and I didn't want to leave a message. I didn't phone again. I became nervous of actually catching him. I had tried; I could say in all honesty I had tried to ring, when we did finally see one another.

Nor was there any contact between Ant and Carson. Undoubtedly there was a time when their relationship could have been salvaged, back in the early days, in that first week of strained silence. But both of them failed to act. No doubt they recognised the opportunity but elected to wait for the other to take the initiative. Too quickly that moment slipped by and was lost. The only communication Ant made with Carson was eloquent in all that it failed to say: he sent him, care of me, a receipt for his cheque.

It was left to Margo to mourn their separation and I felt an almost elated relief when I ran into her at the supermarket one evening. Finally this unnatural code of silence could be broken and the circumstances discussed. I was longing to be told some shocking, revealing details. That was the heart of any normal break-up – the salacious slander revealed in its wake. 'It's a tragedy, a tragedy,' Margo kept repeating. 'Although I had my suspicions, I kept them to myself. He wouldn't come for his fitting, you see. He put it off so many times, I knew there had to be something more to it. But I never suspected infidelity. Never.'

It transpired that Margo knew nothing. In fact, she pestered

me for the dirt. 'I expect you know all the details. The dear
boys think that sort of thing's not for my ears.'

Margo would not let me continue with my shopping until I
had told her all about Ellery. 'Terrible, terrible,' she kept
repeating, but the delight with which she was listening
contradicted her words.

However, Margo did eventually prove to be an important
source of information. I ran into her again at the supermarket
two weeks later. She gently reprimanded me for being late and
I realised that it had been at this same time on a Thursday
evening, after I'd been to the gym, that we'd met the first time.
It was clear Margo had been loitering about in the hope of
encountering me again. There was very little in her trolley. She
was obviously missing having her boys to talk to.

'The apartment's on the market. There's a huge sign out the
front of the building and they're showing people through
already. I haven't liked the look of any of them. It's
heartbreaking to lose such good neighbours. I dread to think
who will buy it. Anthony doesn't care who he sells to. He said
as much to me. He wants a fast sale but at the right price.'

Margo began to complain about a young couple who'd
inspected the apartment twice. 'I overheard them talking as they
walked in the park afterwards and they mentioned it. Their
dog. They said how happy it would be to live right next to the
park. A dog! Imagine. The noise. The fleas. The smell. Oh, it's
more than I could bear. A dog in our building. It makes me
shudder.'

Finally I managed to excuse myself from Margo but only
after swearing faithfully to convince Ant not to sell to any dog
owners. 'You should take him out to dinner,' she said, as she
began to wheel her trolley away. 'He hasn't been eating
properly.'

The contents of her own trolley did not testify to particularly
nutritious eating habits. It contained only a can of baked beans,
a packet of instant cappuccino and a frozen steak and kidney
pie.

I abandoned my shopping and took a taxi to Shaun's to see Carson. 'You've put your apartment up for sale?'

Carson sighed and admitted that, yes, apparently they had. 'I can't believe he'd do something so drastic without even trying to see me,' he said.

'Well, officially, he doesn't know where you are,' I reminded him.

'Didn't you tell him?'

'No,' I said indignantly. 'You made me promise not to.'

'Oh,' said Carson, suddenly deflated. 'But you never keep your promises. Of course I thought you'd tell him as soon as he asked.'

That offended me.

Carson sighed a second time. 'So he's worked out for himself that I'm at Shaun's. He sent me a note here yesterday. A very formal note.'

He passed it to me to read.

In accordance with your wishes, I have advertised our apartment for sale. Garth from Richardson and Wrench will keep you advised of any suitable offers that are made. Ant

'Did you tell him to sell the apartment?'

Carson blustered. 'Well, yes, I suppose I did in the heat of the moment. But I never imagined that he would and I don't actually believe he will carry it through. I know what he's like. He can be so stubborn. This is just a ruse to try to provoke me into rushing to him, to beg him not to act so rashly. I know how he thinks and I'm not going to fall for it.'

I was impressed with Carson's twisted interpretation of Ant's motivations. It was exactly the sort of trick I would pull in Ant's situation. But I wasn't convinced that he was that devious. Money meant too much to him. The apartment was his investment. He wouldn't put it on the market and incur all those fees unless he was serious about selling.

'If it's a ruse, he's going to some lengths,' I pointed out.

'According to Margo, people are being shown through the apartment.'

There was a thoughtful silence. 'Look, Stephen, you go and see him. You need to make up with him. I know he was unpleasant and owes you an apology, but it wasn't really him talking. It was the drugs. You make the overture. It won't kill you, and you can find out where his head's at, then let me know.'

'I'm not going to act as your spy,' I protested. 'You should talk to him yourself.'

'Oh, Stephen, don't start developing scruples. It doesn't suit you. You wouldn't be spying, you'd be like a go-between.'

Carson began to apply some pressure, pointing out that it was four weeks since I'd seen Ant, stressing how abandoned he must be feeling. I didn't agree to do anything on Carson's behalf but I did concede that I'd think about phoning Ant.

It was so ironic. It made me grin to myself as I walked home. That I should be asked by my rival to resuscitate his relationship, the relationship I had wanted to ruin for years.

Ant weighed very heavily on my mind after that conversation. I had trouble sleeping and I couldn't concentrate at work the following day. When I went to the gym in the evening, I kept my usual sharp eye out for Ant. I'd dreaded encountering him there. I'd always planned to slip away if I saw him arrive for his work-out. But that night I had such a strong urge to see him. When it was time for me to leave and he hadn't appeared, I felt a wrench of disappointment. It would've been simpler to bump into him. It seemed like a defeat to be the first one to phone, but I did it when I got home. I was surprised when he answered. I'd hoped to get the machine. I was unprepared and hastily suggested dinner the following night. Surprisingly, Ant agreed warmly and we decided to meet at his place.

When I arrived at seven-thirty as arranged, I was a little shocked by the *For Sale* sign fixed to the building. It was so big and bold. It definitely meant business. I rang Ant's doorbell and he buzzed me in.

I studied him carefully when he opened his door. After

Margo's remark, I expected to find that he had gone to rack and ruin. For him to be thin and wan, brooding and depressed (the way he had been over Kip), but he looked the same as ever. In fact, he looked somehow better than usual. He was smiling shyly when he opened the door. 'I've missed seeing you,' he said simply and opened up his arms to me for a hug.

I fell into them awkwardly. I was deeply confused. I had expected him to be either withdrawn and melancholy or aggressively defensive and suspicious. He pulled back from me and gave me an affectionate kiss. I had not expected this – for him to be happy.

We pulled back from one another and I looked him over quickly. He didn't appear to have lost weight as Margo claimed. His biceps looked as ripe and impressive as ever. When he hugged me hello, there was the same hardness and mass to his body that there'd always been. Ant was returning my gaze and I realised I was staring, and that I'd said nothing in reply. 'I've missed you too,' I muttered. I felt very guilty about the number of weeks I'd allowed to pass without seriously trying to contact him. 'You look well. Very well.'

Ant laughed. 'You sound amazed. I can look after myself, you know. I'm not helpless just because I don't have Carson to cook me dinner any longer.'

'I feel terrible that it's been so long since we've seen one another . . .' I said as I walked past him into the apartment, but then I stopped in surprise. The living room was so changed. Ant had rearranged everything. Some of the furniture was gone, the pictures were different and he had even painted the walls a new colour.

'You've done some redecorating.'

'I had to paint it before I put it on the market. Spruce it up a bit.'

I realised what else he'd done. Everything that had been Carson's had been taken away. I was puzzled. 'Did Carson take all his pictures and furniture with him?'

'Oh no,' said Ant. 'I've packed all that up and stored it in the study. It's there for him to collect when he wants to.'

I was taken aback. It seemed rather premature to have packed Carson's possessions away. 'Perhaps you could mention it to him,' Ant continued. 'I presume you still see him. Tell him to arrange some removalists.'

'Couldn't you tell him yourself—' I began.

But Ant interrupted me. 'I don't really know where he is.' His implication was clear.

'You sent him a note to Shaun's,' I defended myself.

'I presumed he was there or that Shaun would know where he was.' Ant paused for a moment. 'Look, I tried to see him weeks ago. I think it's up to him now.'

There was a silence between us. 'Sit down,' said Ant. 'Would you like a drink? I bought some champagne. I know how much you like champagne.'

I was touched that he'd remembered. That sentiment faded a little when he produced the bottle. He had overlooked the fact that I don't drink cheap stuff. He poured us both a glass, then sat down opposite me on the couch.

'So are you here tonight because Carson sent you?' Ant asked, a twist in his voice.

I wasn't ready for such a question. He had disarmed me by being so amicable. I felt tricked. I looked down at the glass in my hands, feeling my face grow hot. I could tell his eyes were trained upon me.

'I'm here because . . . you've been weighing on my mind for a long time.'

'You could have called me much sooner than this.'

'I did. But you weren't in.'

'I didn't get any messages.'

'I didn't leave any. I don't know. I presumed we'd run into each other at the gym. I was going at our usual time, expecting to see you,' I finished, with a lame little lie.

'I had to change my routine at the gym,' said Ant. 'I go before work now. I've been working on the apartment in the evening, painting it and so on.'

A silence stretched out between us. When I looked Ant in the eye, he smiled warily. 'Perhaps I should explain why I haven't been in touch. It just seemed like you'd taken Carson's side. The way you led him away that night and then when you wouldn't tell me where he was—'

'It wasn't about taking sides—' I began to protest.

'It's *always* about taking sides when a couple breaks up,' Ant interrupted me firmly.

I was a little shocked by his resolute tone. It sounded so final.

Ant was waiting for me to reply.

'I didn't persist in ringing you . . . because you said some things to me that night . . . which I felt were unjustified.'

To my surprise, Ant laughed. 'I did, didn't I? It was the drugs. You know how it is. You can get so paranoid. Imagine all sorts of things.'

But he watched me very closely after he said that, as if searching for signs of guilt. I gazed straight on, back at him, all innocence. As I stared, I noticed the T-shirt he was wearing was new. It was an emerald green, a colour I'd never seen him wear before. His hair was different too. He'd had it cut, but not at Gowings. The cut was more sophisticated than that. I realised that Ant had made some effort for this meeting: his appearance, the champagne. No doubt it was designed for me to report back to Carson that he was in top spirits and looking great. Rather, *appeared* to be in top spirits. It had to be an act. He had to be hiding his remorse over what had happened.

But Ant had a further surprise in store for me. He jumped to his feet. 'Let's eat,' he announced.

'Okay, where shall we go?'

'Nowhere. I've cooked.'

I couldn't remember Ant ever cooking for me before. 'I'm impressed.'

'It's just chicken salad,' he said.

'Perfect!' I declared.

Ant beamed at me. He looked so pleased with himself. With

a start, I realised it was the happiest I'd seen him look in a very long time.

Over dinner he told me that he'd taken some time off work and gone away for a few days down the coast to do some thinking.

'It's done you good,' I complimented him.

'Yeah, and I've been having some counselling. Of course, I have my psychiatrist, but I decided I wanted to have counselling from someone who was gay too . . .'

I was bewildered. 'You have a psychiatrist?'

Ant nodded. 'You knew that,' he scoffed.

'No,' I said firmly.

Ant shrugged. 'I thought I told you. I guess I didn't. I was a bit embarrassed about it to begin with. But I started seeing him after the Kip episode. But actually it's with this counsellor my doctor recommended that I feel I've made real progress. He really helped me through this break-up with Carson and —'

This time I had to protest. 'But you haven't really broken up,' I said.

'Of course we have,' said Ant, nodding vigorously. 'He moved out. He left me.'

'You can't break up with someone without discussing it.'

'Carson was very blunt. He told me to get a flatmate or sell up. That doesn't sound like he's intending to come back.'

'It was the heat of the moment . . .'

'So was my little pash with Ellery.'

I sighed. I certainly didn't want to become trapped into pleading Carson's case for him. I changed the subject. 'So what happened to Ellery?' I asked.

'He's gone back to Miami, back to his gift shop. He was only here for a holiday. Maybe I'll visit him later in the year.'

I must've raised my eyebrows or looked disapproving, because suddenly Ant became heated. 'I wasn't having an affair with him. I know you think I was. Of course I was attracted to him. Who wouldn't be? You were. I saw the way you looked at him. But he has a boyfriend back home. That night at the party was the first time I'd ever kissed him like that, and it only happened because we were both on ecstasy and the atmosphere of the night was so sexual.'

I shrugged.

'You don't believe me.'

'I never believed your private client story because I know you hate your job and wouldn't take on extra work, as much as you might like the extra money. I think you were with Ellery all those nights you said you were working late. In fact, I'm convinced of it.'

Ant studied me. 'You're right,' he said evenly. 'The private client was a fib. But I had to have some excuse. I was spending time with Ellery but nothing sexual was happening between us. We were just talking. There were things he knew about . . . that I was very interested in.'

'Like what?' I asked, but Ant hesitated. 'Well, if it was so innocent, why didn't you tell Carson and me the truth? Why didn't you invite Carson along to meet him?'

'Because he wouldn't have approved of Ellery . . .' Ant began to flounder and then abruptly changed tack. 'Look, would you explain to Carson that we weren't having an affair? I don't want to see him but I'd like him to understand that I didn't cheat on him.'

I was bewildered. 'How can I explain that? It doesn't make sense. Ant, your story doesn't hang together.'

Ant blushed. He was hiding something.

'Talk to Carson yourself,' I said sharply. 'You know you could salvage things if you'd just talk to one another.'

'I don't want to salvage things. I've moved on. I've worked out some changes for myself with my counsellor. I don't want to see Carson and be talked out of what I've decided to do.'

I was surprised by his tone. This obviously wasn't an act. He was in earnest.

'Shouldn't you have been seeing this counsellor with Carson?'

'No.'

That one word was defiantly belligerent.

I began to wonder if Ant was drunk. He had polished off most of the bottle of champagne. I'd barely managed to drink my glassful, it was so sickly.

'I've realised what I had with Carson has run its course. I met him at a bad time, when I was very insecure and vulnerable, while he seemed to be totally together and focused. Those qualities were very attractive and comforting to me at that time.'

I cringed. Ant's recollection was so warped. I couldn't recall this vulnerable stage. The way I remembered it, Ant had been aggressively promiscuous up until meeting Carson and had revelled in his conquests.

'What about Carson's big blue eyes and blond hair?' I said, trying to tease him out of this territory we had strayed into, so serious and strange.

But my words came out wrong. I couldn't keep a twinge of jealousy from creeping into my voice. Ant looked at me sharply. He was perched on the edge of the couch. He started to say something, then stopped, then looked away from me, down at the polished floorboards, which had begun to lose their lustre.

'I've always liked your eyes better.'

He said it very casually and quietly and his words hung in the air between us, as shocking and unexpected as the manifestation of a ghost.

I swallowed. Had I heard correctly? Or were my long-held hopes deceiving me? But I wasn't overwrought. I wasn't drunk. I hadn't come to Ant brimming with my own desires for him.

Ant sat across from me. Hunched over. His hands locked together. He was clearly suffering as he waited for me to respond. I began to accept that I must've heard what I thought I'd heard.

I had so much to say. All these different speeches were running through my head, but it was like several records being played simultaneously, over the top of one another, all of them jostling to be heard. Then I knew. The simplest reply. What must be said first. I had been paid a compliment and, as

Elisabeth had taught me, I must acknowledge it graciously.

'Thank you,' I said quietly and Ant looked up at me, his face flooded with colour.

Slowly, ever so slowly, an uncertain smile began to pick at his mouth as we stared at one another.

'Sometimes you'd turn those eyes of yours on me in a certain way,' Ant said, his voice gruff and broken, ' . . . and I used to wonder . . .'

I rose from my chair, keeping my eyes fixed on his face. In my mind's eye I saw myself crossing the room to him as if in a trance, hypnotised by desire, to swoon into his embrace. Which wasn't quite how it happened. I fell at his feet instead. Quite unceremoniously and heavily. I failed to see the coffee table – it had been moved in the redecorations – and tripped over it.

It hurt. My knee and hip and elbow stung from the impact. I raised my face from the floor to complain and there was Ant's face, hovering just above my own, an adorable concern in his eyes. I pushed myself up on my good elbow and craned my face forward. His expression became wondering and awed as his mouth descended to meet mine.

It was so strange to be kissing him at last.

I wish I could describe that moment as being perfect and blissful. I felt I deserved perfection after my graceless stumble. But there was a small distracting flaw which prevented me from surrendering wholly to the moment. Ant's breath was sour. When I broke free of him for a moment, he gasped a big curdling breath in my face.

I wilted.

But it had to be endured.

I pulled Ant forward so that he toppled off the couch and fell on top of me. I didn't mind his breath so much then. I liked having him on top of me, pinning me against the floorboards. But we didn't stay that way for long. He rolled over and pulled me on top of him, so that our positions were reversed. That was completely wrong. He should've been on top of me!

But he seemed to like it. We kissed like that for a very long time. When he finally did roll me to the side, I felt a tremor of anticipation. Finally. I was going to feel him on top of me, all of him, bearing down on me. But instead, he got up and walked off without saying a word. I wondered, for a moment, if he might be going to the bathroom to gargle. But no, he paused in the darkened doorway of his bedroom and glanced back at me. I couldn't read his expression. It was so quick. Just a fleeting moment before he stepped through the doorway and then was gone, swallowed up by the darkness. I was left lying on the floor, my aches suddenly insistent again.

I was filled with uncertainty. Did he intend me to follow or had he suddenly had second thoughts and gone to his bedroom to escape me? Tentatively I stood and followed him. I paused in the bedroom doorway. It was very dark within. The blinds were drawn and night had long since fallen outside. I could only just distinguish Ant's figure lying on the bed. I took a few cautious steps towards him, intending to express surprise at what had just happened between us, to discern his state of mind, but as I sat down on the bed beside him, I realised with a jolt that he lay face down, naked.

There could be no ambiguity about what that meant.

I began to run my hands over him. His body felt magnificent. All the muscles in his back. The breadth to his shoulders. There was great power to that body, dormant now but which I wanted to awaken and feel bucking on top of me. Ant rolled onto his side and turned his face towards me. I bent down to him, anticipating a kiss, but instead he said something to me, something I never expected to hear.

'Fuck me,' Ant whispered fiercely.

If it hadn't been so dark, then he might have seen the astonishment in my face.

Every time I'd fantasised about having sex with Ant, I had always imagined that he would fuck me. That he would be the first.

I had never been fucked; I'd put it off for such a protracted time, it had become an embarrassment. When the topic came up in conversation, I lied, the way teenage boys do about their sexual experience. That first attempt all those years ago had been so off-putting, I'd avoided it ever since. My curiosity and desire did grow as the years passed, but so did my fastidiousness over who should do the deed. The fact that it was a high risk for HIV infection made me too nervous to give myself to a casual partner. Some gruff stranger who'd depart as soon as it was over, leaving me to fret in the dark as to the state of the condom we'd used. I developed the notions of a fifties debutante. I had waited so long, I wanted the first time to be with someone I trusted. Someone I loved.

Ant.

As the years passed, I'd become more and more obsessed that he had to be the one. His muscles, the hair on his chest, his butch inscrutable face. He was my perfect top. He would overwhelm me physically. The idea had become so embedded, it was like a promise, a betrothal. When Shaun had said he wanted to fuck me, I'd laughed at him. It had seemed so ludicrous at the time. It was only when it ended between us that I realised it might've been quite a sensible initiation.

I rolled Ant onto his side and reached for his cock, intending to whisper back that no, he must fuck me, fuck me with his big cock . . . but the words died away on my tongue. There was nothing big about Ant's cock. He was quite limp and shrunken.

I was taken aback. But I knew how to remedy such a setback. I began to kiss my way down his chest to his cock, but he stopped me when I reached his navel. He actually grabbed me by the hair to stop me. 'Don't bother. I haven't been able to get erections lately.' He showed no signs of embarrassment or concern. 'That's why I want you to fuck me. That'll make me come.'

He rolled back onto his stomach and lay there face down, waiting. I paused, assailed by doubts and confusion. Should this be stopped now, gently halted and laughed off as a drunken mistake? It was perverse to stop when this was the moment I had longed for, dreamt about for years, but so many things were wrong. I ran a comforting hand over Ant's shoulders, trying to think how best to phrase such a suggestion, how to prevent it sounding like a rejection.

As I stroked him, I decided to say nothing, just to hold him instead. He wasn't erect. Some affection, a nice cuddle, was probably all he really wanted. He just didn't know how to suggest it. I slipped out of my T-shirt and jeans, lay down on the bed beside him and put my arms around him. He pressed back against me and I let my hands drift over him: his thighs, his chest, his stomach. He twisted his neck back, offered me his mouth and we began to kiss again. My cock stiffened against him almost at once.

'Feels like you're ready,' he said, reaching behind to squeeze it appraisingly.

The touch of his hand upon my cock was all it took for my reservations to slip away. If the moment wasn't quite how I'd imagined it, that was the fault of my fantasies, I decided. I peered over the side of the bed, looking for some lube and condoms. There was none there, although I noticed a pill bottle, half hidden by the valance. It was too dark to see the label. I rolled over to look on the other side of the bed. There was nothing there either. Then I thought to look in the bedside cabinet and I found the lube. But there were no condoms.

'I need a condom,' I whispered to Ant.

Ant rolled over and laughed. 'Can you believe it? I don't know if I have any.'

I stared at him in disbelief. What gay man didn't have condoms? I wasn't sure what this implied. That he'd run out or that Carson had taken them with him? Or that their sex life had died some time back along with his erections?

'You must have one somewhere,' I said. 'In the bathroom maybe?'

Ant shrugged but made no move to go and look. I clambered off the bed and went into the bathroom. I snapped on the light and opened the cabinet by the mirror. There were so many pills. Bottles and bottles of pills. I glanced at a couple of the labels but they meant nothing to me. A lot of the bottles were vitamins and I was surprised that Carson hadn't taken them with him. I poked about gingerly.

Suddenly, out of the corner of my eye, I caught a flash of Ant, naked, heading towards the kitchen. 'I've remembered where there's one,' he called out to me.

I followed him out to the kitchen. He was poking around in the rubbish tin. 'I threw one in here the other day. Ah, here it is.'

He held it up to me triumphantly. It was a safe sex pack from a New Year's Eve party. It must've been handed out at the door of the party and kept as a souvenir. But suddenly I recognised that packet. It had been pinned to the noticeboard that hung above Carson's desk, along with photos and other memorabilia chronicling his relationship with Ant. That safe sex pack was from the New Year's Eve party where they had first met.

Ant was grinning at me. 'Isn't that lucky? I threw it out a couple of days ago.'

I nodded. But it didn't feel lucky. It felt wrong. To end up in bed with Ant when I was here on behalf of Carson was bad enough, but to use the condom he had saved for years as a memento, that was highly inauspicious.

Ant ran his hand over my chest and kissed me on the cheek. 'Come on,' he said, taking my hand and leading me back to the bedroom.

It was nice the way he kissed me and held my hand. It helped me relax a little. Back in the bedroom I sat on the bed, and watched him as he lit a row of candles that were lined up on the windowsill. Then he came towards me and I ran my hands over him as he lit one final candle which was sitting on the bedside table. 'There,' he said when he'd finished.

He lay down and pulled me to him. We kissed and my cock stiffened immediately. Our kisses became more passionate but it bothered me that his cock still remained limp. I could feel it, or rather I couldn't feel it, not the way I wanted to. I remembered Paulo-Henrique. Was Ant on anti-depressants too? He hadn't volunteered the information and it wasn't the moment to ask. He'd said that he hadn't been able to get erections in a while, so I knew it wasn't through any fault of mine. But after so many years of anticipation, I couldn't help feeling that with me it should've been different. His penis should have miraculously stiffened.

Ant rolled me off him again but we didn't switch positions as I'd hoped we might. Instead, he lay there, on his stomach, and looked back at me over his shoulder. 'I think you promised me a fuck,' he whispered.

I felt doubly cheated. If I was going to fuck him I wanted it to be face to face, so that I could see him, look into his eyes, kiss him. Not this way.

'Hey, I'd like to see your face,' I suggested tentatively.

His reply was muffled by his face being pressed into the pillow but it sounded like no.

No.

I ripped the condom out of the packet, irritated. Fuck him. If that's what he wanted, I would fuck him. A surge of anger, hard and mean, rose up in me. I slid the condom on, slapped some lube over it, then pushed my cock into him. I didn't warn him it was coming. I didn't take it slow. I wanted to hear him protest, and he did. He arched away from me, but I pushed in regardless and began to thrust.

It was then that I noticed the photograph. It was positioned there, in its wooden frame, on the bedside table, illuminated by the candle Ant had lit. A photograph of Carson. That was why he wanted me to fuck him this way. So he could gaze at bloody Carson while I did him. I leant forward and blew the candle out. But at that instant, I almost wished I hadn't. The photograph wasn't well illuminated but I realised I hadn't seen it before. I was curious for a moment as to where and when it had been taken. But it was too late to peer closer. The candle was extinguished.

Ant began to resist beneath me. Maybe he wanted to try a

different position or to relight that candle, but I wasn't having that. He had wanted it this way and that's how he was going to get it. I seized a handful of his hair, pulled his head back and rode him. I was determined to make him come. I surprised myself; the pleasure I took in dominating him and hearing him cry out. My body slapped against his with such force, the rhythm of my thrusts whipped along even faster by his moans.

I began to sense Ant stirring beneath me in a new way. His breath grew faster and ragged. He kept repeating something I couldn't quite hear. It sounded like 'kiss', but when I strained forward to reach his mouth he didn't turn his face to mine. He ignored me and stared straight ahead. When he came it was in great hoarse heaving sighs and then he tried to pull free of me. But I pinned him back down. 'Just a minute,' I breathed in his ear. 'I'm getting real close.'

For in that frenzy of driving him to orgasm, I had begun to feel a tremor of pleasure myself, even through the deadening rubber of the condom. I was determined to chase it. All the times I'd fucked Shaun, I'd never quite managed to bring myself to orgasm. The condom numbed a lot of the sensation. I'd always had to finish myself off with my hand. But this time it was going to happen. I gave a volley of quick thrusts and felt the orgasm ripple up in me. I pulled free of Ant, ripped off the condom and came.

That first spasm of come shot right up over Ant's shoulder and landed on the pillow. I was impressed. I rather wished I'd leant forward a little and aimed. I could have hit the framed photograph of Carson.

I collapsed on top of Ant. We lay like that for only a couple of minutes before he wriggled out from beneath me, clambered off the bed and went into the bathroom. The door closed resoundingly behind him. I listened to him use the toilet and then the sound of water running in the handbasin.

When he came back to bed, he snuggled up against me and put his arms around me. 'I never imagined you'd be so rough with me,' he complained, but I could see he was smiling as he said it. His teeth shone dully in the dark. 'I haven't had an orgasm like that in a long time.'

'Me either,' I said.

We lay clasped together like that and after a while I realised he'd drifted off to sleep. It was nice feeling him against me, though in the end, to get to sleep, I had to turn away from him to escape his breath. He had neglected to brush his teeth while he was in the bathroom.

When I awoke in the morning, Ant wasn't in bed beside me. I wondered how long he'd been gone. It made me feel anxious. It would've been much easier if we could've begun the 'morning after' by cuddling up together. Was the fact that he had slipped out of bed already a sign that he didn't want to cuddle up together, this morning or any other morning? Had he awoken with regrets? With a hangover?

I was lying there, feeling nervous about getting out of bed and facing Ant, when I noticed the framed photograph again. I started. Surely it couldn't be. I sat up and snatched the photograph off the table. It was Kip smirking back at me.

It was a photograph I remembered seeing in Ant's photo album. A close-up of Kip's devious little features. A knowing grin on his face. I fell back against the pillows and let the photograph fall to the floor. I just didn't understand.

But then something began to make sense. What Ant had been murmuring, when I was fucking him, just before he came. It hadn't been 'kiss me'. It was Kip's name. Kip. Kip. Kip. He'd been repeating it over and over.

Maybe he did like my eyes better than Carson's, I mused bitterly to myself, but apparently both of us lost out when it came to comparisons with Kip.

My anguish quickly gave way to fury. I threw the sheet off and sprang out of bed. I dressed, not caring that I hadn't showered or what I looked like. I just wanted to get out of that apartment as quickly as possible. I marched out into the living room. Ant was sitting on the couch in a pair of boxer shorts reading a magazine. He looked up and I could see he was nervous, but when he saw my face, bewilderment flooded his features. He rose from the couch, holding out his hands to me, but I looked haughtily away and walked towards the door.

'Where are you going?' he protested.

I didn't answer. He came after me. 'Stephen? What have I done?' he asked.

His voice was quiet but stricken.

I tried to open the door but unbelievably it was deadlocked. I felt panicked. Whatever I did, I didn't want to break down in front of him and give him the satisfaction, but I could feel an insistent hysteria rising up in me. 'Let me out,' I wailed.

Ant's eyes were beseeching. I couldn't bear to look at him. Then I spied the keys on the bookcase beside the door. I grabbed them, fumbling for the correct one. Fortunately, having entered their place illicitly several times, I recognised the key. I unlocked the door, opened it, burst through it and ran across the foyer to the front door.

Once I was out on the street, a great sob heaved through me. I turned back and caught a glimpse through the glass door of Ant coming after me. I fled down the street sobbing, trying to keep my hands over my ears as I ran, to block out his voice plaintively calling after me.

CHAPTER FOURTEEN

There was a message on my machine from Ant when I got home that morning. He sounded genuinely mystified as to what he had done wrong. His distress was slightly consoling. I replayed his message, relishing the shrill, frantic edge that crept into his voice. I wanted him to be hurting too.

Kip.

After all the time that had passed, was it possible that Ant was still hung up on Kip? Had Carson just been a distraction? And myself? From what he'd said last night, I'd begun to think he'd always wanted me, perhaps secretly loved me too. Had it only been that I bore a likeness to his precious Kip? Was that all he saw in me? The more I thought about it (and it was all I fucking could think of) the more sense it made. That was why he'd had the bedroom in darkness. Why he wouldn't look me in the face. He had wanted to imagine he was with Kip. It was *so* mortifying.

I began to screen my calls. I knew I wouldn't be able to cope if I picked up the phone and found Ant on the other end. I wasn't sure if I'd abuse him, be struck dumb or just break down and cry at the sound of his voice. But I didn't intend to put myself to the test and find out.

He called me several times that day and left messages. But by the following day, he'd tired of that and simply hung up when he got the machine. On the evening of the third day, there was a knock at my door. My visitor had not used the security system in the foyer. Evidently, they had a key. I felt certain it was Ant. I didn't answer the door and later, when I glanced out the window, I saw him in the laneway, looking up at my apartment.

The next night, at the gym, I spotted him hovering outside,

intending to waylay me when I left. I felt a fluttering of nerves. There was only one exit from the gym. It would be impossible to avoid him. I concentrated on my work-out and avoided looking out the window, so he couldn't catch my eye. But I had begun to feel nauseous at the thought of having to confront him. Then I noticed John on the pec deck. He was an older guy who was forever offering me training tips as a pretext for touching some part of my body. Whenever our glances happened to meet, he always winked. He noticed me staring at him and winked. I beckoned him over and suggested a drink after we'd both finished our work-outs. He agreed enthusiastically.

When we left the gym together, Ant was standing at the patio railing staring out over Bayswater Road. He whirled around at the sound of the gym door opening. His face fell when he realised I wasn't alone. But John's presence didn't stop him from approaching me. He walked over to us, obliging us to stop.

'Hello, Stephen,' he said, his face very grave.

I didn't want to look at him. The expression on his face, so sad and tender, had the power to manipulate me. 'Doing a work-out?' I asked, hoping I sounded breezy and indifferent.

'No,' said Ant, with a quick glance at John. 'I came to see you. I thought perhaps we could have dinner?'

'I'm having dinner with John,' I said, struggling for a moment to remember his name. 'Do you know John? He's my new gym partner.'

John offered his hand with a hearty smile, but Ant ignored him. He gave me a sharp look of reproach, then turned and walked off.

'Surly fellow,' John remarked as we continued to walk.

I couldn't reply. I was trembling from the emotion of the moment. I'd managed to keep myself together admirably, but now I almost regretted it. I glanced back in the hope that Ant, too, might have had second thoughts and lingered for a moment, but the patio was deserted. He had left a trail in the litter of leaves that crushed beneath his feet as he walked away.

'I've got such an appetite tonight,' said John, giving me a loaded look.

The last thing I felt like doing was having dinner with John, but it seemed too difficult to extricate myself. When we sat down at Fu Manchu, John began pressing his leg against mine. He sheepishly revealed that I'd got his name wrong and it was actually Jim. When the food arrived, I just passed my noodles over to Jim. I couldn't eat.

Ant gave up on me after that. There were no more phone calls, no further attempts to see me. His silence left me on edge. I told myself that I didn't expect to hear from him, but every time I arrived home, the flashing light on my answering machine fired a quick fierce flare of hope in me. Had he relented and given me one last try? No. He hadn't. It was always my mother or Strauss or Carson. I was crushed every time. I hadn't the heart to return those calls.

I kept expecting Ant to pop up and confront me somewhere. I found myself looking out for him, even in places that it was highly unlikely he would be. A week passed, then a second week passed and I began to concede that he wasn't going to seek me out, that it was up to me.

I was so relieved, when finally, more than two weeks later, another of those unannounced knocks came at my door one evening. It could only be Ant. I ran to the bathroom and checked my appearance before scurrying to the door. I opened it, my face radiant with grateful relief that he had offered me one last chance. It was a nasty shock to find Carson waiting on the other side. I could feel my face curdle with disappointment. Carson was someone I was still trying to avoid.

There had been a second message on my machine the morning I got home from that disastrous night with Ant: from Carson. He had wanted to know how things stood between him and Ant. I had put off phoning him back, although he left a couple more messages during the week and several more the following week.

Carson was highly aggrieved that I hadn't returned any of his calls. 'Why haven't you let me know what's going on?' he demanded. 'What happened when you saw Ant?'

The way he looked at me as he said that made me worry that he had his suspicions. I was at a very low ebb. I did not feel up to this conversation, but Carson kept firing questions at me.

'Okay, I have been avoiding you,' I admitted. 'I didn't want to be the one to tell you.'

I was struggling with how to phrase what had to be said, but Carson held up his hands to stop me. His face had crumpled. He looked infinitely weary. 'I'll go and see him,' he finally said quietly, a grim resolve tightening his expression.

'I think you should.'

Carson left, and naturally I presumed that he would ring me to let me know how things had gone. When he didn't, I concluded he was taking out a petty retaliation on me because I'd been slow to call him. But as more and more days passed, I began to grow anxious that Ant must've confessed what we'd done together. I wasn't game to ring Carson myself and risk being abused.

I tried to talk Strauss into finding out for me. Usually he delighted in prying into other people's affairs, but I asked him at a bad moment. A photograph of him (without make-up) had recently been run in the gossip column of the local gay newspaper. It was not attractive. 'I've forsaken gossip,' Strauss declared. 'Now that I've been the public victim of it, I can see how cruel it is. How it's inspired by envy and malice. I've lost all heart for it.'

I had no alternative but to confront either Ant or Carson myself. I decided to phone Ant. More than three weeks had passed since our night together. I dialled his number but, after a few seconds, a Telstra message informed me that his number had been disconnected. That did not bode well. He must be in a state if he was neglecting to pay his bills. It was Saturday. I decided to drop in on him. If he wasn't at home, it was more than likely that Margo could shed some light on what he'd been up to.

I walked down to Onslow Avenue. The *For Sale* sign was still on the outside of the building but as I drew closer I realised that *Sold* had been plastered across it in large lettering. A queasiness began to grow in my stomach. Sold? Was that why the phone had been disconnected? Had he already moved out? I pressed his bell several times but there was no answer. I tried Margo's button and she answered immediately. I identified myself and she released the lock on the front door. She was waiting for me in her doorway, her face grim.

'Where's Ant?' I asked.

Margo dramatically clamped her hands over her ears. 'Don't mention his name. I'll never forgive him for betraying me. Selling to the dog owner. He knew my feelings but he gave them no consideration. No consideration. He's gone and I was pleased to see the back of him.'

'Did he leave a forwarding address?'

'Not with me,' said Margo haughtily. 'But I haven't been home to him since he told me what he'd done.'

'He was depressed . . .'

'I won't hear any excuses for his behaviour. Can you imagine what I'll have to endure? That animal scrabbling about, scratching itself, barking at all hours. And the fleas. But I'm prepared.' Margo picked up a bright green stuffed snake and brandished it at me. 'I'll use this to seal the crack below the door. A defence against fleas.'

I apologised on Ant's behalf, excused myself and Margo closed the door (and no doubt sealed it with the snake). I decided to get a taxi to Shaun's and talk to Carson. He would have to know where Ant was.

Luckily Carson was at home. I studied him carefully when he opened the door, feeling I'd be able to judge how much Ant had told him from the look on his face. But he seemed quite cheery. He smiled warmly, apologised for not phoning me and ushered me into the living room. There had been some changes made there. The room was much sprucer than it had ever been before. Everything was neat, fresh flowers in the vases, magazines artfully fanned on the coffee table. I noticed there was a painting Carson owned hanging above the sofa and that the photograph of me Shaun had once kept on the bookcase had been banished. Even though I had refused countless offers to move into this apartment, it annoyed me to find Carson installed so cosily.

'Where's Ant?' I asked, failing to keep the irritation out of my voice. 'I've just been to your place and there's sold signs plastered all over it.'

Carson's tone was equally terse. 'Well, how do you think I felt when I turned up there to talk to him last week and discovered the same thing? I owned it.'

I gave a quick sympathetic smile. 'Where's he gone?' I asked.

Carson sighed. There was something about that sigh and the troubled look on Carson's face that made me feel extremely anxious. 'He's gone to New Zealand to see his parents.'

'Oh. When's he coming back?'

'I'm not sure. He was carrying on to America after that and it sounded like he intended to stay there for a while.'

Those words were like a physical blow to the head. My vision stuttered for an instant. I felt weak, unsteady on my feet; I needed to sit down. 'What . . . do you mean?' I asked in a voice strangled by my own crushing sense of regret.

Carson was bitter. 'Well, he's resigned from his job, put all his belongings in storage and left me to see the sale of the apartment through. He didn't say anything about coming back.'

'Of course he's coming back again . . .' I tried to insist.

Carson raised his eyebrows and sniffed.

'You don't think he's gone to America to be with Ellery?' I said, aghast.

Carson shrugged, but it was obvious that was exactly what he thought.

'Do you have a phone number for him?' I asked.

'No. We argued when I went round there. By the time I'd calmed down a few days later and felt like talking to him, it was too late, he'd already gone. But he'll be in touch. There's paperwork relating to the sale he has to sign. He'll ring me with the address to courier it to.' Carson suddenly looked at me keenly. 'But I can't believe he left the country without saying goodbye to you. Haven't you seen him?'

I grappled for an excuse. 'Yeah, well, we had a bit of a falling out too.'

Carson was waiting for me to elaborate. Instead, I excused myself to use the bathroom. I used the ensuite off Shaun's bedroom. I was curious to see whether Carson had established himself in there as well. There were no obvious signs that he had. None of his clothes littered the bedroom floor, no books of his were on the bedside table, no second toothbrush in the bathroom. I washed my face and walked back through to the living room.

Carson was waiting for me, the expression on his face strangely grim. I thought for a moment he was going to reprimand me for not using the guest bathroom, but to my surprise he presented me with a book. 'This is your copy,' he mumbled.

A bare-chested blond boy gazed out moodily from the cover. It took me a moment to comprehend that this was Carson's book, that it was his name printed on the cover. 'It's an advance copy,' Carson explained. 'It won't be in the shops for a couple of weeks yet.'

I looked up at Carson, my bewilderment rendering me speechless. Carson began to laugh. 'It's not *that* surprising that I've finally had my book published.'

But it was. It was utterly astonishing. The publisher's name on the spine was well known, an international company. I couldn't understand how he could possibly have had his drivel published by such a reputable company.

I forgot to offer my congratulations. 'You've been very cagey about this,' I accused him. 'You must've known for ages.'

Carson looked a little sheepish. 'I signed the contract September last year. I didn't make a fuss about it because I didn't want to be nagged by people wanting to read it before it was finished. It had to be edited and revised first.'

I began to flick through it while Carson kept talking. I was only half listening to him brag on. 'But I always wanted you to be one of the first to read it, Stephen,' I heard him say.

I was tempted to reply that I had taken care of that myself.

'Because in a way,' Carson continued, 'you inspired one of the chapters.'

That made me pause. It should have been my first thought when he gave me the book: was I still in it? Was I still savaged in it? I began to flick through its pages, searching for my chapter, my indignation mounting. Surely that slanderous diatribe had been cut or, if it was still intact, had undergone a major rewrite. Eventually I found it. I skimmed through the chapter to see if it had been toned down at all. It appeared to read exactly as I remembered it. I was still likened to a knife and fork.

'The thing you have to understand, Stephen, when you read it,' said Carson, a pleading note quavering into his voice, 'is that even though it says memoir on the cover, it is fiction. Of course, you and I know this particular episode has some basis in reality, but that was only a starting point. I've dramatised and amplified, changed everything around . . .'

'I can see you've made a massive change to my name.'

The character was called Steven.

'How did you find yourself so quickly?' he asked, his voice perturbed.

'Instinct,' I snapped back.

Carson began to bluster. 'I did try several different names but none of them had the same resonance. Nothing else was as good. I agonised a lot about the name being so similar.'

'Similar?' I spluttered. 'It *is* my name.'

'It's a different spelling.'

I snorted my contempt.

'No-one is going to know it's you . . .' Carson's voice began to whine.

'For Christ's sake, Strauss will know. He'll broadcast it all over Oxford Street.'

Such juicy news would rekindle his taste for gossip posthaste.

'I think you're doing him a disservice. Strauss can be very discreet,' said Carson.

'Well, he wasn't very discreet about you. He told me ages ago you used to be a prostitute when you first came to Sydney. Is that in here? I bet it isn't.'

Carson turned pale. '*What?* I was never a prostitute. I shared an apartment with a boy who—'

'Yeah, yeah.'

I had a string of insults poised to fling at him, but then I thought better of it. It would be more effective to play the suffering martyr than the hysterical shrew. That would work on Carson's guilty conscience more.

'You've made use of me, Carson,' I reproached him in an injured tone of voice.

Carson began to stutter. 'It's . . . it's an important issue. Relations between positive and negative gay men . . .'

'Unfair use of me,' I said firmly.

'I think you used me first,' Carson defended himself, his voice trembling. 'To make Ant jealous.'

We stared at one another. I was so surprised that he had worked that out. 'What a peculiar theory,' I said snappily. 'What vivid imaginations you writers have.'

But he had unsettled me. I marched out of the apartment, unable to endure his eyes on me for another moment. It was only when I was halfway down the street that I realised I was still clutching his book. I'd meant to stuff it down the kitchen sink and turn the waste disposal on before I made my exit.

I did my best to put Carson's treachery out of my mind. The matter of Ant was far more pressing. Unlike Carson, I didn't believe Ant had gone to Miami to be with Ellery. He wouldn't sell his house, quit his job and move to the States in the tenuous hope that Ellery would still want him. Ant was too cautious and sensible for that. It would be completely out of character for him to behave so recklessly. Everyone knew that long-distance relationships were doomed to failure, that they never lived up to all the anticipation and idealisation that being apart engendered. And hadn't he mentioned that Ellery had a boyfriend back home anyway?

Not that that usually meant much.

Despite myself, I began to imagine the worst. That Ant had felt so rejected by everyone he loved in Sydney, Ellery Queen had seemed his best option . . .

It was imperative that I speak with Ant as soon as possible. I tried to get contact details for Ellery from the gym. I thought that was an inspired idea. Ellery must've filled in some sort of form there. But the boy on reception found my request ludicrous. 'You don't know his surname but he worked out here casually in February. He was American and had a really great body. Do you have any idea how many men that description fits?'

When he put it like that, it did seem rather a long shot.

'But it's very urgent I contact him,' I protested. 'His name was Ellery. He was very striking. You must remember him . . .'

'Think of it as a lesson, honey,' the boy said smarmily. 'Next time, you'll pluck up the courage to ask for his phone number while you have the opportunity.'

I tried to contact Ant's parents next. I obtained a number from directory and phoned several times but they were never at home and, unbelievably, they didn't have an answering machine.

When I finally did get on to his father, after almost a week of trying, the conversation did not go well. I introduced myself, explained that I was a close friend of Ant's and that I needed his address in America.

'If you are the close friend you claim to be,' said Mr Tallantire frostily, 'then I'm surprised Anthony didn't entrust you with those details himself.'

I tried to argue the point, but Mr Tallantire wouldn't budge.

'I'll mention you rang next time I write to him,' he finally conceded. 'Then he can contact you himself. That would be best.'

'Couldn't you phone him? I need to speak to him urgently.'

'That would be a wee bit expensive,' said Mr Tallantire. 'As I'm sure this call will be for you.'

I tried to argue but Mr Tallantire insisted on terminating the call for the sake of my phone bill. 'I'll mention you called when I write next,' he said before hanging up.

There was nothing to be done but to wait. For Ant to contact me or Carson, or one of his other friends in Sydney. I knew I would be furious if someone else got a postcard before me. I deserved to be first.

I don't like to be made to wait. It was made worse by the fact that I had few distractions to help endure the process. No-one phoned me. No-one invited me anywhere. Even John from the gym ignored me when I went for my work-out. I felt friendless. Abandoned. I was grateful when the buzzer rang during another evening at home watching television.

'Yes?'

'It's Grant Kippax. Kip.'

I buzzed him in, though as soon as I'd done it, I regretted it. For a moment I thought he might know something, might have heard from Ant. But then I realised how unlikely that was. They hadn't seen each other in years.

If he hadn't identified himself over the intercom, I doubt that I would have recognised him when I opened the door to him. He looked so different. The blond hair was gone. I had never realised he dyed it. His hair was now entirely dark. He'd filled out a little and was no longer so lean. His eyes were still magnificent, and he hadn't forgotten how to use them to effect. When they turned upon me, for a brief moment I felt as though my heart had missed a beat. But there was an agitated air about him. He stood outside my door, wringing his hands nervously. I ushered him in.

'Some grumpy old guy is in Ant's flat,' he said with childlike indignation.

I pointed out that Ant hadn't lived in this building for a couple of years, that he'd bought an apartment with his boyfriend.

'Oh,' said Kip, digesting this information, then looking at me curiously. 'I thought you would've been his boyfriend by now. I remember you were after him. What's your name again? I've forgotten.'

I told him. 'And I wasn't after him,' I added.

'Oh?' said Kip, looking puzzled for a moment.

'No,' I lied. 'That was a whim of yours. You used to spy on us, from that cafe, and jumped to a few conclusions.'

'Oh well, it was a long time ago. Where's Ant? I have to see him urgently.'

'I don't know that I'd tell you even if I knew. But as it happens, I don't know. He's left the country.'

Kip's face froze. 'What do you mean?'

I quickly explained the circumstances of the last few months. His break-up with Carson. The sale of their apartment. But then I stopped mid-sentence in astonishment. Kip had begun to cry. The tears were slipping down his cheeks, which had become pink and feverish. I sat him down on the couch. 'What's wrong? Did you need to see him so badly?'

But Kip was crying too hard to answer. Finally, when his sobs had subsided, he reached for my hand and placed it on the left-hand side of his neck. It was extremely swollen. It was how I imagined a tumour would feel, beneath the skin. His beautiful blue eyes were filled with fear. His lip was quivering.

'What . . . is it?' he asked me.

'I don't know,' I said, quickly moving my fingers away from his neck. I felt squeamish feeling that mass beneath the skin. 'It seems worse than just a swollen gland. You should go to the doctor.'

'I'm too scared to go to the doctor,' Kip whispered hoarsely. 'What if he tells me I'm going to die?'

I felt like laughing. Kip had always seemed younger than his years, but at that moment he seemed such a child. I began to scoff at his anxiety, when suddenly I understood. Why he was crying. Why he was so scared.

Kip must've seen the light-heartedness drain out of my face. He realised that I understood. He began to talk. 'It's been like this for four days and I'm too scared to see a doctor. It's the first sign that anything is wrong.'

'Is it your lymph node?' I asked.

I felt panicked. I didn't really know where the lymph nodes were. In the neck? Under the arms? I just knew that in people with HIV they swelled up.

'I don't know,' wailed Kip. 'I never knew there was anything there until now.'

I tried to keep my voice soothing. 'Kip, I think it might be your lymph node. But I don't think you should get too alarmed. It's a common problem—'

'Has it happened to you?'

I hesitated and Kip's face fell. He began to cry again. 'I have to see Ant,' Kip sobbed. 'Ant will know what to do.'

Then a solution struck me. I would ring Carson and have him come over. I explained to Kip that I had a friend who knew a lot about these things. He nodded dumbly. I felt an enormous sense of relief as I dialled Carson's number. I could pass Kip over to Carson and he could deal with him. There was no reason why I should become embroiled in his problems.

Thankfully, Carson was home. When I identified myself, he started to apologise. I interrupted him. 'Not now. There's an emergency here. I need you to come over. Now. To my place. Just come. And don't bring Shaun. I'll explain when you get here.'

I hung up and turned back to Kip. 'That's fine. Carson's coming over.'

'Is he a doctor?' asked Kip.

'No but he knows a lot about . . . these things.'

'Carson?'

'Yes. He's Ant's boyfriend. Or used to be Ant's boyfriend. I told you before. They broke up . . .'

The words died on my tongue. Kip's expression had become so strange. He drew back from me, his eyes flickered about the room and he looked deeply, intensely troubled.

'Have you met Carson?' I asked, taken aback by his manner.

Kip hesitated. He glanced towards the door as if he was contemplating running out of it. 'He knows a lot about this?' he repeated slowly, and I nodded.

'So he's HIV positive too.'

I hesitated. 'It's not really my place to say . . .' I began to reply.

'But he is,' Kip insisted and he leant forward and seized my wrist, his fingers squeezing like a clamp.

I nodded and Kip released me. I was rubbing my wrist, wondering at the strength in his grip, when he spoke again. I wasn't really paying attention to what he said. His words shimmered there in my consciousness, slowly gaining meaning. I looked up at him and half snorted, half laughed. I knew I must have misheard him.

'What?'

Kip repeated himself.

'*Did he get it from Ant?*'

I had not misheard. I also knew that this was not one of Kip's lies or games. It made horrible, horrible sense.

I was aware of Kip physically, sitting beside me on the couch. I was looking at him. I could see his mouth moving but I couldn't actually hear his words. He was talking to me but it was as if my sense of hearing had shut down, had been numbed into a temporary deafness by the extremity of the revelation. The only sound I was aware of was the hiss of my own blood washing through my veins, and my heartbeat so loud it seemed my whole body must be reverberating from the sound.

A tingle danced across my neck, like the breath of a ghost behind me. Slowly, ever so slowly, the sensation swept around and rose up, cradling my jaw, then flooding up through my cheeks to my brow. My entire face felt peculiarly ablaze. It struck me that I was going to faint and then – *slap!* – an insistent clamour struck my ears, calling me back to reality. An alarm? A siren? Gradually, I understood that it was only Kip making a god-awful noise, wailing in my ear, gripping me by the shoulders. 'Forgive me,' he moaned. 'Forgive me.'

The tingling in my face had stopped, the heat run out like bathwater. I felt drained, unable to move a muscle and escape him.

He moaned with such anguish – a horrible, mournful, grieving wail – it made the hairs all over my body prickle. I tried to stand but Kip seized me by the wrist with both his hands. My legs buckled beneath me and I sank back down beside him. I tried to stand again. I thought to get something from the bathroom to calm him down: pills, a bucket of water, anything to stop this shrill keening. But Kip fell to his knees before me, still clutching my wrist.

'I did a terrible thing to Ant,' he gasped. 'Terrible.'

Instinctively I knew I didn't want to hear what Kip was intent on confessing. His face had begun to contort. His teeth were chattering. He released my wrist, his hand flew to his mouth, and he jammed his fingers in his mouth in an attempt to stop the convulsion. Below the ball of his fist, his chin shuddered.

I knew I must steel myself, bear up. There was more to be told and it would be worse. Much worse.

'I knew what I was doing,' he babbled. 'I could lie and say it was an accident but it wasn't. I made him turn on his stomach, away from the light of the candles. If I'd been looking him in the eye, I couldn't have done it to him.'

On his stomach. Candles.

What had my night with Ant been? A re-enactment? An exorcism? Something his psychiatrist suggested?

'I didn't want him to leave me when he found out. I didn't want to have to face it on my own. I thought if we shared it, if we both had it, then we would stay together forever. It sounds deluded, I know, but I think perhaps I had been driven mad, temporarily insane, by what the doctor told me. It seemed to make such sense at the time.'

Kip paused and swallowed. 'And ever since, it's seemed so unreal, almost as if it had never happened. It's only in the last few days, when I felt this thing growing on my neck, that I was forced to remember . . . and acknowledge the gravity of what I did to him.'

Finally he had finished.

Throughout Kip's confession, my body had been recoiling from him. My breath began to stutter, coming out in convulsing gasps. My throat had swollen up. I could barely swallow. A headache tolled in the depths of my skull.

His hands fell away from me. Everything in the room became very still, silent and tense.

It struck me how banal it was that a heart attack could be provoked by stress or a hereditary disposition or an excess of fats. How much truer it would be if a coronary was suffered when the heart was stricken with grief and longing. At that moment I longed to die. Kip's revelation was simply too cruel to bear.

I opened my eyes. I had closed them when he began his long speech and had kept them screwed shut, wincing from the effort. I thought, I hoped, that if I strained hard enough, I might close my ears to him as well. Blinking, I noted Kip crouched before me. On his knees. Gazing up at me so meekly. As if I should forgive him. The thought enraged me. His posture so contrite, so submissive . . .

As that word flashed through my mind, suddenly it struck me how sexually suggestive our physical closeness was. I sat on the couch, my legs apart. Kip knelt, his face close to my lap. If someone had walked into the room, they would have assumed Kip was about to suck me off. The image repelled me. I drew back from him, pressed myself back against the far end of the sofa. When he whimpered like a puppy and came after me, I threw back my head and howled, a scream of protest that filled the room.

Kip fell back on his haunches, shocked. The sight of him, his pitiful expression, made the anger surge up in me again.

How dare he even hope that the unforgivable could be pardoned? I sprang off the sofa and stood over him.

'What you've done is unforgivable. Unforgivable,' I snarled. I gritted my teeth, inhaled fiercely and raised my hand to slap him with all the power I could muster.

He knew it was coming. His eyes widened but he didn't recoil. Instead, he lifted his chin a little, as if offering his cheek for a kiss.

I was about to bring my hand down upon him when I glimpsed the lump in his neck. The fury coursing through me fell instantly away. My shoulders slumped and my hand dropped back to my side.

The buzzer sounded.

It startled us both. At first I couldn't think who it could possibly be. Then I remembered. My sense of relief was overwhelming. Carson was here. Carson. I was babbling his name aloud as I stumbled across to the security phone. I buzzed him in. 'Hurry,' I whispered into the phone.

I turned my back on Kip. I could not bear to look at him, even to be in the same room as him was almost unendurable. I thought if I didn't look at him, he might do us all a favour and heave himself over the balcony to fall two storeys into the gutter of Shame Lane. I opened the door and listened for the sound of Carson's footfalls. I prayed for him to take the steps two at a time, to run.

I could hear him coming closer, then I saw the cuff of his white shirt in the gloom, his hand on the railing where it twisted back on itself. My mouth trembled and I began to cry, my sobs resounding loudly in the stairwell. I was relieved to hush them, to bury my face against Carson's chest and quell them, feel his arms around my shuddering shoulders.

'Why didn't he tell me?' I wept into his chest. 'Why didn't he trust me to know?'

But Carson didn't need to tell me. As he held me and patted me on the back, I understood for myself. I had condemned myself by my own behaviour. The way I had treated Carson. If

Ant had ever had the inkling of an attraction towards me, if there was ever any chance of him loving me, I had ruined it.

I cried into Carson's white shirt as if it was my handkerchief. But I wasn't only crying for Ant and the monstrous thing that had been done to him, nor my own thoughtless mistakes, but for all those times when secrets might have been confessed but weren't.

CHAPTER FIFTEEN

Thankfully, Carson took control. He led me through to my bedroom and I felt better as soon as there was a closed door between myself and Kip. He put me to bed, then went back to deal with Kip. I lay still, unable to do anything except go over and over what I had been told. 'Has he gone?' I asked in a hoarse, urgent whisper when Carson finally came back to me.

Carson nodded and sat down on the bed. I didn't have to ask. He gently pushed me back against the pillows and began to explain everything Ant had kept from me. All the half-truths, evasions and deceptions that stemmed from his one fundamental secret.

Ant and Ellery had not been having an affair. Ant had told me the truth when he claimed they merely talked. It was what they talked about that he couldn't tell me or Carson. Drug treatments. Treatments that inhibited the progression of HIV.

Ant admitted to Carson that the first time he had dinner with Ellery, he was guilty of intent. He was hoping their evening together might lead to sex. But all that was forgotten during the course of the meal. When Ellery stopped eating to swallow some pills, Ant asked him what they were. Ellery casually explained he was HIV-positive and that he was on a new trial that was having amazing results. Ant didn't know whether he was more shocked or impressed that someone could be so up-front about having HIV and mention it so breezily to a person he barely knew. For the first time Ant didn't feel awkward and vulnerable telling someone his secret.

Ellery's reaction was nonchalant. He raised his eyebrows and kept eating. When he finished his mouthful, he asked Ant what drugs he was on. It was only when Ant said that he was on nothing that Ellery put his knife and fork down and stared at him in surprise. Ant quickly outlined the natural regime he was following. He was impatient to know what it was that Ellery was taking.

Ellery was in a trial which treated patients with a combination of D4T and 3TC. The effects had been dramatic. His CD4 counts had risen and his viral load had plummeted. This astonishing news kindled a glow deep within Ant, a warm comforting glow that unfurled and bloomed right up into his face. His cheeks were hot. His grin irrepressible. He felt an almost drunken elation. As Ellery elaborated, Ant began to realise there was an entire range of possibilities he knew nothing about. Not only had he never heard of the drugs Ellery was taking, but he knew nothing of the other trials happening all over the world. Ellery chided him for not educating himself and advised him to read the medical journals and browse the Internet for information. 'Your AIDS Council here does fantastic work,' Ellery had said, and Ant had felt too ashamed to admit that he'd never been there.

Ant walked home uplifted. Genuinely heartened for the first time since his diagnosis. Here was an alternative to that superficial 'think positive' optimism that everyone kept prescribing as being so vital to his wellbeing. For it didn't matter how many affirmations Ant recited, they could only cast the flimsiest of veils over the well of dread and fear that lurked deep down in him.

There was one thing about Carson's explanation that puzzled me. 'Why didn't Ant tell you about Ellery?' I asked. 'Why did he pretend to have a private client?'

'Because he assumed I would disapprove of Ellery and the drugs he was taking,' said Carson. 'And he was right. I would've been sceptical. That night he came back from being with Ellery and brought up that drug trial. I was very short with him. I told him I would *never* go on a trial. That I'd never put a drug in my body until there was indisputable proof that it worked and continued to work in the long term.'

Carson sighed. 'There was tension between us after that

but I didn't connect it with what I'd said to him. He was staying out late and, of course, my first thought was – he's having an affair. The truth was he'd begun to resent me and wanted to avoid me. The more time he spent with Ellery, the more convinced he became that I had been hiding things from him, keeping information about these new combination drugs from him and pushing my own views on to him.'

Carson began to admit to some regrets. He bemoaned avoiding Ant in those first few days after Mardi Gras. 'I should have seen him. That note I sent with the cheque was so dismissive. It hardened him against me. He didn't want to see me and he definitely didn't want to hear any argument against these new drug treatments. When I finally went to him and he told me what he was considering, I behaved exactly as he'd worried I would. I tried to change his mind. But I couldn't help myself. A lot of these drugs are toxic. I couldn't stand by and let him compromise his immune system. Even if the short-term indications are good, what about the long-term? Ant has no symptoms. Why jeopardise that?'

Carson was indignant with evangelistic conviction, his body taut with energy. I smiled to defuse the sudden tension in the room and he gave a sheepish smile. 'I have strong views when it comes to that subject,' he muttered.

That was an understatement. His fervour had unnerved me a little. I changed the subject. 'Why's Ant gone to America?' I asked.

'To get away from me, I think,' said Carson with a grimace of a smile. 'I don't know. For a holiday. To think his options over. Do a bit of personal research into Ellery's trial. He's been talking to our doctor and a counsellor at the AIDS Council about treatment options. He's trying to make a decision about starting on a drug therapy programme himself.'

'Do you have a phone number for him yet?'

Carson looked abashed. 'No. But he'll be in touch soon. You know what he's like with money and he has a lot of it tied up in our apartment. He has to contact me soon.'

We lapsed into silence. When I yawned, I realised how deeply tired and overwhelmed I felt. I had other questions, but the night had been so draining. I didn't have the emotional energy to give my mind more to worry over.

'I think I'll take some sleeping pills and try to sleep. I just want to knock myself out and stop thinking.'

Carson agreed that was a good idea. He fetched me a glass of water and my Normison from the bathroom. 'I hope you don't take these often,' he nagged, before kissing me on the cheek and leaving.

I took a second sleeping pill once he'd gone and lay back down, waiting for them to work. Inevitably my thoughts circled over what we'd been discussing. I began to appreciate why Carson had become so heated. After all, his health was at stake. He couldn't afford doubts to creep in and undo the psychological benefit of his affirmations and visualisations. For the first time I asked myself what I would do if I had to make the decisions he and Ant were forced to. I'd always assumed that you simply did whatever your doctor recommended. It had never occurred to me that different doctors might have different approaches. I began to appreciate how enormous and impossible deciding what to do was, when no-one knew conclusively what worked best. I hoped Ant was doing the right thing.

I awoke early the next day. I rolled over, hoping to reclaim sleep, but my mind had already begun to trawl over the events of yesterday. I glanced at my bedside clock. It was far too early to phone Carson and ask him to come over. I noticed his book beneath the clock. Up until now I'd been too irritated and jealous to look at it, but suddenly I was curious. Had he exploited what had happened between Ant and Kip for his book as well? I picked it up and started skimming through the chapters. It took me a while to find the relevant section. Ant's and Kip's names had been disguised more effectively than my own.

Something struck me as very familiar about the first paragraph of that chapter. I had a strong sense that I'd read it before. As I continued to read, this sense of *déjà vu* quickly fell away. I stopped, went back to that first paragraph, and then I realised. I *had* read it before. On the computer screen, as I waited for Carson's printer to print it out. It was the other chapter I'd swiped all that time ago, along with the one that so maligned me. I had been so furious at what Carson had written about me that I'd left the other chapter unread and then forgotten all about it.

What had I done with those chapters? I knew I wouldn't have thrown them out. I began to search my bedroom and eventually I found them stuffed under the bed, buried beneath a stack of magazines. I skimmed the first paragraph – it was identical – then kept reading. It was easier to read the draft as the names hadn't been changed. Not that it was at all easy to read. I wept all over it. Just seeing Ant's name linked with Kip's on the stark white page stung me every time I encountered it. I felt such a sorrowful, tender anger with Ant. He had been too trusting, too naive. That he could misplace so much love and faith in such a deceitful individual . . . But such was the effect of physical beauty. Common sense was easily dazzled.

But I was more angry and frustrated with myself. To think that the chapter which explained everything had been here all that time, beneath my bed, within such easy reach. Ant's secret had been right under my nose every night as I went to bed.

If only I'd read that chapter first. If only I hadn't allowed my sense of injured vanity over 'my chapter' to get the better of me. If only . . . but it was far too late for 'if onlys'.

Ant was gone.

I was startled when my eyes fell upon my own name in the last paragraph of that chapter.

Anthony felt ruined by love. When he saw Steven for the first time, he saw him as a test, an irresistible boy sent to torment him. For he had sworn only a few days before that he would never permit himself to fall in love again.

I fell back against the pillows and let the pages fall to the floor. Tears smarted my eyes. Shivers ran up and down my neck and face. If this was true, I had been cheated, most cruelly cheated.

But it made too much sense to be fiction. I remembered when I first met Ant: the attraction I felt and the vibe I sensed from him in return. Our attraction had been mutual, but he had checked it at every step.

Suddenly I was curious to know more. Surely I was more than just a passing fancy. Surely his feelings for me would've endured despite everything. I seized Carson's book and flipped through to Chapter Eleven.

It was a sobering read. I felt extremely contrite by the time I'd finished.

Ant had been appalled by the way I'd rejected Carson. Any tender feelings he might have had for me were obliterated by his shock and dismay at my behaviour. Carson intimated that he'd been wavering towards confiding in me what had happened between him and Kip. I stopped him dead in his tracks. Pushed him in another direction altogether. Into Carson's arms.

Ant had arranged to see Carson to cheer him up over his disappointment with me. They met for coffee one afternoon and talked. It was inconsequential, chitchat. It wasn't until they were back out on the street, about to part, that Ant caught Carson by the arm and mumbled that he had 'the same problem'. They returned to their table in the cafe and talked properly.

When they'd finished, Ant suggested dinner a few days later. 'So I can keep cheering you up,' he said.

But it had been obvious to Carson that Ant was the one in need of comfort. Carson was the only HIV-positive person he knew. He had confided his result to no-one. His doctor had referred him to a counsellor at the AIDS Council but he didn't go. He didn't want to be seen going into that building. A terrible thing had been done to him and he shared it with no-one. He'd been on a waiting list for six months to see the psychiatrist his doctor had recommended. When he finally started appoint–ments, Ant had found it very difficult to open up. Carson became his confessor and adviser. He was in the same boat. Ant shared things with him he'd told no-one else.

We became very close as we confided in each other. When the time came to part, our hugs drew out. We clung to one another. Both of us needed that physical comfort. We were both vulnerable. Both hurt. After Steven's rejection, I had drawn the conclusion that a relationship with someone who wasn't positive was too difficult, was simply untenable. To Ant, who couldn't even confide his status to anyone, I must have seemed like his fate.

But when I awoke beside him for the first time, I couldn't shake a nagging conviction that both of us had settled for second best.

I always knew Ant's heart was elsewhere. With Kip, with Steven, or maybe it was just too traumatised to try again with anyone.

I understand that you don't necessarily love the person who's good for you. You love and long for the ones who've hurt you.

When Carson dropped by to see me later that morning, I burst into tears as soon as I opened the door. I felt so remorseful at the sight of him.

'Hey, we did this yesterday,' Carson protested gently.

I nodded and laughed and lifted up the hem of my T-shirt to dab at my eyes. I apologised.

'It's all right. Don't apologise,' said Carson.

I took his hand and squeezed it. 'But I do have to apologise,' I said, trying to control my sobs. 'It's so overdue, I don't expect you to welcome it now. But I am sorry for how I behaved all those years ago. You confided something delicate and I freaked out. I didn't give a thought to your feelings. I wince every time I think of how I behaved. How lacking in empathy I was. It's my biggest regret.'

Carson blushed. He looked embarrassed, but gratified. 'You were very young,' he excused me. 'Because you're always so assured, I forget how young you actually are.'

We stood there shyly, both awkward, me still clutching his hand.

I was startled when Carson changed the subject to Kip. 'I'm going to try to arrange an Ankali carer for Kip. He needs someone to talk to.'

I felt like snapping that he didn't deserve any help, but my eyes met Carson's at that moment and I felt reproved.

'He's very scared,' Carson continued. 'He needs some reassurance. I won't do it myself. I feel too personally involved. But Ankali will find someone to help him.' He paused for a moment as he noted my expression. 'You know, Ant's counsellor has helped him express a lot of his anger and resentment and let go of it. If he can come close to forgiving Kip, it's not for us to judge him.'

I couldn't bring myself to agree with that.

Then a thought occurred to me. All morning I had been feeling so frustrated by Ant's inaccessibility. I longed to help him, demonstrate how much I cared for him, even just talk to him face to face. Being obliged to wait, to do nothing, was unbearable.

But there was something I could do. The most obvious thing in the world. 'Carson, I'm going to go to Ant,' I announced. 'I'm going to bring him home.'

Carson smiled and nodded, but I could tell he didn't think I was serious. He said something vaguely encouraging and then continued talking about Kip. I wasn't listening. The more I thought about it, the more fired up I became. Following Ant halfway round the world to tell him I loved him appealed to my sense of the dramatic. It was bold, epic, quixotic. I had to do it. I couldn't wait for Ant to decide to come home. His parting from both Carson and me had been fraught with animosity. This silence of his seemed like a deliberate ploy to make us worry about him. He'd felt neglected and abandoned when he left and now he was no doubt relishing the thought of making us anxious. It seemed a little petty, but it was exactly how I would've behaved if I were him.

I had to make Ant understand that there was something in Sydney worth coming back to – *me* – and I was determined to go to whatever lengths were necessary to prove it.

If I hadn't had this plan, something constructive to do, I think I would have gone to pieces. As it was, I was in a surrealistically heightened emotional state. I couldn't concentrate on anything. Certainly not work. I was constantly being scolded for being distracted and making mistakes. But even in my leisure time I had trouble relaxing. I couldn't even lose myself for an hour or two in a film or television. My attention always wandered. My moods swung from high to low. I'd become maniacally elated, my mind imagining my reunion with Ant as I made arrangements for my trip. Then when I ran up against an obstacle, I'd burst into tears and sob uncontrollably from the sheer frustration of it all.

I cried a lot at that time. In public too. After a while I stopped feeling embarrassed. It came upon me when I was made to wait or had nothing to occupy myself. My mind would turn to Ant; suddenly I'd be overwhelmed by his plight and would find myself weeping. People pretended not to notice – on the bus, in the supermarket queue, as I waited to use a machine at the gym. But bedtimes were the worst of all. Then I was utterly alone, in my bed, with nothing but my thoughts. Lying there, of course I could think of nothing else. Sleeping pills couldn't be relied upon. In the end I went back to my doctor for some Valium, which helped.

I booked my flight that same day I decided to go. Then I sought out Mr Leckey at work and resigned.

'And what are you leaving us to do, Stephen?' Mr Leckey enquired.

I hadn't been expecting that question. I floundered for a moment. 'I'm following my heart,' I finally said.

It was like a line from a Hollywood movie but it seemed appropriate.

'A foolish enterprise,' Mr Leckey scolded me. 'Your father will not approve of you giving up your career for some girl.'

'Oh he would, Mr Leckey,' I assured him. 'It would make his day, if I ever told him that.'

But Mr Leckey's words did strike a chord of trepidation into me. He reminded me that I had not yet obtained my airfare from my father and that it might have been smarter to secure that prior to resigning. My father had arranged my job. Quitting it for a girl would indeed be a slap in the face. Quitting for a guy might provoke him to slap mine.

I decided to ask Elisabeth for the money instead. Given her membership of P-Flag and the new closeness it had helped forge between us, I felt certain of success. I told her the whole story candidly, confident that its tragic twists and turns would stir pity in her. When I noticed tears well up in her eyes I felt certain of success. Rather than just the airfare, she might be good for some spending money too, now that she understood how much I'd suffered.

'No,' said Elisabeth firmly, once I had unfolded my financial predicament to her.

I couldn't believe it. I began to protest and threatened to expose her to Jane and the other P-Flag parents as unsympathetic.

'*Don't!*' Elisabeth cried out as if in pain, and to my surprise she burst into tears. 'How can you expect me to pay for you to be with someone who could be the death of you?'

I tried to talk over her but she wouldn't be silenced.

'Accidents happen,' she insisted. Her tears were suddenly gone, and her mouth set into a stubborn line. 'Condoms break or get forgotten in the heat of the moment. I know. It happened to many women of my generation and I don't believe it's a great deal different these days. Especially amongst boys like you. I couldn't do it, and it's not because I don't want you to be with a boy. It's this particular boy.'

'He needs me.'

'I'd spend all my days fretting that there'd be an accident. And if there was, how could I live with myself for bringing you together?'

'But it's what I want. I don't care —'

'You should care,' Elisabeth reprimanded me, her eyes flashing. 'It's irresponsible not to. You're lucky you have a mother who does care enough about you to be sensible. And don't bother asking your father. His answer will be the same as mine.'

I sat in silence, defeated.

'You can be a friend to him instead, Stephen,' Elisabeth suggested. 'From the sound of it, he needs you more as a friend.'

I stormed out of the room, furious tears stinging my eyes, my mind whirling with counter arguments. How could I persuade her? Then I thought of Uncle Vic. Perhaps he could do it for me? Talk her round or perhaps even lend me the money himself. Surely he would be touched (possibly turned on) by the tale of two young boys thwarted in love and would delight in playing the benevolent uncle.

I telephoned him. I was cryptic, knowing that would prick his curiosity. 'There's a crisis, Uncle Vic,' I informed him. 'I need your help.'

We agreed to meet at Cafe 191 in an hour.

Uncle Vic turned heads when he arrived. Finally he had undergone a fashion make-over. He'd been on a trip to London after Mardi Gras and was thrilled by the new citrus summer colours he found in all the shops. Uncle Vic had always adored vivid colours on himself. He bought up big, and with a blind enthusiasm. Gone were the bike shorts: Uncle Vic was resplendent in a lime-green muslin shirt, unbuttoned to where his stomach began to swell. A sarong knotted at the waist, dazzling to the eye with its vivid splashes of orange, canary yellow and aquamarine. While on his feet he wore lime sandshoes with orange laces. When he sat down at the table, he removed his cap (which coordinated with his shoelaces) to reveal that he had bleached his hair blond. Thankfully, I had taken a table outside and had an excuse for putting my sunglasses back on.

'I hope you're wearing underwear beneath that sarong, Uncle Vic,' I teased him.

'I don't believe in underwear,' Uncle Vic replied airily. 'I detest getting sweaty down there.'

I must've looked alarmed because Uncle Vic sought to reassure me. 'Actually, I did feel a little vulnerable when I put this on. But when I opened my underwear drawer with the intention of wearing one of the two pairs I own, neither pair was there. Stolen! By some light-fingered piece of trade I'd taken home. So I had no alternative but to go *au naturel*. Can you believe it?'

I couldn't.

'But enough about me. What's this crisis? I presume you want me to intercede on your behalf with Liddy. What do you need? Money?'

I was startled that Uncle Vic had guessed my motive. 'No, no,' I protested, mustering a show of indignation. 'I'm in love but it's become very complicated.'

That made Uncle Vic pay attention. 'Go on,' he urged me and I began to unfold the story.

Uncle Vic was not a passive listener as my mother had been. I had barely begun when he stopped me and insisted I describe Ant. Then he interrupted me again a few sentences later to exclaim that he had met him. 'When I was at dinner with Liddy. We ran into you. There were four of you. I knew he was your type. I just knew it.'

He carried on in this manner throughout my story. Interrupting to demand elaboration, motivation, explanation.

When I'd finally finished, Uncle Vic sighed and raised his eyebrows. 'Well, it's patently obvious you only want him because you can't have him. The allure of the unattainable is always the most piquant but it's also the most frustrating. You should be relieved this boy has taken himself off overseas. He's done you an enormous favour. Finally you can forget him and get on with your life. Trust me. Once you've had him, all desire will die.'

I protested, but Uncle Vic insisted it was true.

'I do love him and we have been together once anyway,' I

admitted, to prove how wrong Uncle Vic's theory was. 'Only that time doesn't count.'

Uncle Vic pursed his lips. '*You* have not been candid with Uncle Vic. How can I give you advice if you withhold things from me. Why doesn't it count? Because it was bad sex?'

I was surprised that Uncle Vic had guessed that too. 'Yes,' I finally admitted.

Uncle Vic insisted on a full recounting of that abortive evening. 'Hmm,' he mused when I'd finished.

'I *have* to get to America. I could bring you back some underwear if I went,' I added hopefully. 'Calvin Kleins are very cheap over there.'

'Yes, shopping,' Uncle Vic declared boisterously, rising from the table. 'That's the answer. Forget this boy and go shopping. It's fabulous therapy. Look at me. I've bought a whole new summer wardrobe and I'm a new man. Excuse me a moment.'

Uncle Vic strode across to a man sitting alone at the breakfast bar. At first I presumed it was someone he knew, but when I noticed them shake hands I realised Uncle Vic was introducing himself. I sat there, growing increasingly impatient that he had abandoned me at this most crucial of moments. I would have glared at him if he hadn't had his back to me. As the minutes passed, I felt more and more like tapping him on the shoulder and reminding him that we were in the middle of a very important discussion. But I was afraid of offending him. After all, I needed to get a couple of thousand out of him.

I couldn't believe it when Uncle Vic strolled out of the cafe with that man, without even saying goodbye. He gave me a quick conspiratorial wink and then returned his attention to his new friend. It dawned on me as they walked off to cross Taylor Square that Uncle Vic had picked him up. Had he even been paying attention to what I'd been confiding to him? Or had he been making eyes at that man throughout everything I had said? It seemed even more insulting when I got up to leave and the waiter chased after me. Not only had Uncle Vic failed to offer me a loan, he had departed without even paying for our coffees.

There was one last resort I could try. He had been my least favoured option, but the more I thought about it, the more apt it began to seem. Carson. He had just sold his apartment and had a book coming out. There was no way he could deny having the ready cash. There was also the consideration that he had used my character for his personal profit. For that, I was owed compensation.

I arranged to have dinner with him that night. When I arrived, he gave me Ant's address in Miami. I was thrilled. Then I glanced at it and realised there was no phone number. I asked Carson for it.

'He didn't give it to me. I think it's deliberate. He doesn't want either of us ringing him and hassling him. And I don't know Ellery's surname to trace him through directory either. Unless you know it?'

I didn't. It was a blow. My exhilaration fell away. But after a while I began to concede that perhaps it was preferable this way. Considering everything I wanted to say to Ant, it would be best done face to face. Now I had the address, I could go to him any time. Or at least once I got the money I could.

I told Carson that I'd quit my job and booked my ticket to Miami. He looked startled. 'I didn't realise you had any money,' he said.

'I don't,' I sighed. 'And my parents don't approve of my plan. Which is why I wondered if you might consider lending me some money. A loan against all those royalties you'll be pulling in soon.'

But Carson had reservations. 'How will you pay me back? You've quit your job. Maybe I'd lend you the money if I believed that you'd pay it back quickly, but I'm afraid I don't see how you could do that.'

I very nearly lost it. It was on the tip of my tongue to retort, 'Very well. I'll sell my butt, the way you did.'

But I refrained. I was trying to be nice to Carson. To start afresh.

Although I must admit, I had no intention of paying Carson

back. I'd have called it a loan, then when his book came out, defaming me, I'd have claimed the money as recompense.

But Carson must've been mulling over my request because suddenly he turned on me. 'You've got a hide asking me for money,' he railed. 'You just want Ant for yourself. That's why you want to go to him.'

It was so unexpected, I sat stunned, blushing, unable to reply.

'Well? It's true, isn't it?' Carson demanded.

I made myself stop and think, stop and search my heart before I answered that. Even though Carson's eye were on me, demanding an answer, I didn't give a quick glib reply. Or tell a lie in the hope of securing the money.

'That was my first impulse,' I finally admitted. 'I have feelings for him, Carson. I've had them for a very long time and never told him. But I've always been a friend to him, and it's as a friend I should go to him. I'm trying to suppress any expectations.'

The advice Elisabeth had given me had sunk in.

Carson didn't reply for some time. 'I don't even know if it's really over between us,' he finally said, a slight wail to his voice. 'We argued. So much was said in the heat of the moment. I don't know if he meant any of it.' He paused for a moment. 'Though it's been over between us sexually for a while. That's why I was so sure he was having an affair. We were intimate with each other, but we hadn't fucked in six months. Did he tell you that?'

'He mentioned . . . he had problems getting an erection.'

'I think his therapy brought back bad memories. A couple of times he mistook me for Kip. He'd wake up from a nightmare, think he was lying in bed next to Kip and start crying all over me. Once I woke up and he was hitting me.'

He changed the subject after that. I waited for him to bring up the matter of the loan again. He didn't. When the bill for dinner came and I offered to pay it all, he refused. 'You need to save all you can,' he reminded me.

I couldn't keep the disappointment out of my face.

'Stephen, you can't expect me to lend you the money. Really, you can't. If you want to go to Ant, you'll have to do it without my help. I'm not that big-hearted.'

The next day my bank turned down my request for a loan. It was beginning to seem that 'doing a Carson' was indeed the only way I could get the money quickly. I was despairing. I was feeling so overwrought and desperate, I was quite capable of doing something foolish.

But then the cheque arrived in the mail. A cheque for $2500 from a most unexpected source. There was a note that accompanied it.

Stephen – I've been asking Carson about Ant. I want him to come home too. Carson said you had plans to follow him and bring him home but couldn't afford the airfare.

I can lend it to you. I'd go myself if I wasn't nervous about my health. Though would Ant even talk to me now? I don't know. It's best you go. Pay me back when you can.

Kip

My initial impulse was to throw the cheque away. What Kip had done was unforgivable and any attempt to redeem himself should be rebuffed. I did tear up his note, but when it came to the cheque, when I held it in my hands, I hesitated. I couldn't bring myself to rip it in half.

I told myself it was curiosity that led me to bank it. That I wanted to see if it would bounce. I couldn't believe that Kip had the resources to write a cheque for that amount of money. I suspected a ruse, that he'd written the cheque knowing I would send it back but that his offer would win him brownie points. He probably only had twenty-five dollars in his account which was how much I was charged for the urgent clearance I requested.

The next day I rang to enquire. The cheque had cleared. The funds were available.

It seemed like fate. The money had been provided and should be accepted. Besides, it was too late for the cheque to be returned. Those were the justifications I made to myself when I wrote out my own cheque to pay for the airline tickets.

CHAPTER SIXTEEN

It was Carson's success that was my initial impetus for writing all of this down. His book was released a week before I left the country. It was absolutely everywhere. I couldn't believe it. I'd expected copies to be confined to the gay bookshop on Oxford Street, but no, it was on display in sizeable numbers everywhere, from the city chains to newsagents. At the launch, which I was foolish enough to attend, I was approached by a dozen people (including a prying journalist from the gay press) who'd read the book. They all crowed that they'd recognised me at once. Carson had made it easy for them. He'd listed me as one of the first thank-yous at the front of the book. He seemed to imagine this was some sort of honour, when actually all it did was signpost the fact that I was indeed the Steven he had written about so disparagingly. I irritably pointed out to all those people that Carson insisted his book was a *fictional* memoir. No-one listened. In his launch speech, Carson kept referring to it as his autobiography.

My hostility mounted with every glass of champagne I knocked back. Finally I could endure it no longer. I swept up to Carson's publisher and threatened to sue her for defamation. But she merely laughed delightedly in my face. 'Wonderful,' she gushed. 'Court cases are fabulous for publicity and of course you'd lose. Your claims are utterly nebulous.'

It was so frustrating to have been libelled, to be surrounded by lawyers but to be too humiliated to ask their advice. It was unthinkable that I should ask my father. I did not want him reading that book. Nor would I consult any of the lawyers at work and become the talk of the office in the process. I didn't have the money to consult a lawyer I didn't personally know.

I was so relieved to be going to America. The public scrutiny and speculation was punishing enough, but having to witness another moment of Carson's glory was simply unendurable. I was beginning to consider America a self-imposed lifelong exile rather than a mere holiday. Carson was simply becoming too famous. It was a particularly galling blow to the golden boy, who had always been destined for fame himself. Once it had seemed so assured; what had become of that glorious promise? Tossed into some astrological rubbish bin, my destiny had indeed become a *horror*scope. Rather than fame, I had gained a most unbecoming notoriety, thanks to Carson.

It was stumbling home drunk from the launch that I decided I would write my own book. If Carson could do it, I could do it too. Only my book would be far superior. I wrote the first line of my first chapter that night before I went to bed.

I was always the golden boy.

The golden boy would glitter again. What's more, he would outshine *and outsell* Carson.

Strauss consoled me through my hangover the next day. 'At least that Steven character is always mentioned in all the reviews of Carson's book,' he pointed out, trying to be consoling.

That was true. But none of it was ever flattering, never sympathetic but always excessively alliterative. I had been called 'a prissy, pumped-up prima donna', 'a quibbling, quarrelsome queen', and even 'a cutesy cad of the most callow and conniving kind'.

I'd expected to see a couple of reviews in the gay newspapers. Instead, they both ran full-page features on Carson, adorned with his photograph and bold headlines – CARSON'S CANDID DEBUT and BUY THIS BOOK. His publicist, evidently a genius, also managed to get him mainstream attention. I was shocked to open the *Sydney Morning Herald* on the Saturday morning before I flew out to find a sizeable review of Carson's book. What's more, the reviewer admired it. Excessively. In that review, and in every other that I read, the book was referred to as an autobiography. The fictional memoir label had been well and truly trashed.

I didn't phone Carson to say goodbye. It had been a monumental struggle to maintain my composure around him since his book had been released. Every time he opened his mouth, he had something new to boast about. That he had two television appearances to do in the same week. That there was interest in the German translation rights. That his publisher was considering a reprint already. But I had resolved after the terrible revelations of a few weeks ago to be a better, kinder, more sympathetic person. However, I had never expected it to be so hellishly hard. Carson tested me sorely, yet somehow I managed to maintain a saintly stoicism in the face of his immense provocation.

When he turned up at my place twenty minutes before I was due to depart for the airport, I felt touched that he'd remembered I was leaving, when his own life had become so busy and exalted. But to wish me bon voyage face to face was not the sole reason for his visit. He also wanted me to deliver a copy of his book to Ant. 'He only ever got to read the proofs,' Carson explained. 'I'd like him to have a first edition. You know it's gone into reprint already?'

I did know because he'd told me twice already.

'Are you all right, Stephen? You've gone very pale. Are you afraid of flying?'

I was on the brink of telling him to fuck off, that I was going to sue him for all the money he was making by defaming me and that I was delivering myself *and myself alone* to Ant. The new caring, sharing Stephen, and not any reminders (i.e. his bloody book) of that more callow version of myself. But I couldn't get a word in. Carson's concern was fleeting. He was soon babbling about film rights and the high hopes of his agent in London, and how I must tell Ant all his news, every single development and possibility. He began to recite them all again and finally I had to push him towards the door. He stopped talking and looked a little startled.

'You're making me late,' I said as neutrally as I could.

But he wouldn't leave until he had personally packed a copy

of his book into the bag I was planning to carry onto the plane. His action implied that he didn't trust me to remember to pack it myself. Then he insisted on helping me down to the street with my luggage and seeing me off in a taxi. I had the distinct feeling that he was more interested in seeing his book safely off to Ant in America, rather than me.

'See you,' he called out, waving.

'In court,' I responded gaily as the taxi pulled away from the pavement.

I even found his book at the airport bookshop. I walked in intending to buy something to read on the flight and was confronted by an entire shelf of Carson's book. That was the last straw. My public humiliation was not even to be limited to Australia but had already begun to extend worldwide. Copies of that book were being bought and transported to all corners of the globe. I'd endured enough. I swept all the copies from the shelf and tipped them into a nearby sale bin. I was rearranging some other titles in its place when a sales assistant approached me with a quizzical look on her face. I informed her I was the new merchandiser and was appalled by the state of the shelves. 'Go and tidy the magazines,' I snapped at her and she sprang away from me to obey.

I was so pleased with myself that I completely forgot my original purpose for entering the shop, and it wasn't until I was already seated on the plane that I realised I had nothing to read. I got up from my seat and snatched a women's magazine from the rack near the galley. I began to flick through it after takeoff but I couldn't believe what I found there. A review of Carson's book. Carson was being reviewed in *Cleo*.

Even at thirty-five thousand feet that book was inescapable. There were people on the plane reading it. When I went to the bathroom, I noticed not one but two passengers engrossed in it. A middle-aged woman was weeping over her copy. I felt like snatching it out of her hand. It was me who should have been weeping, the way I'd been portrayed in that thing.

Ironically, I had to resort to pulling the copy Carson had given me for Ant out of my bag, I was so bored. I'd already seen the film they were showing and I'd packed my sleeping pills in my suitcase by mistake. I hoped a few chapters of Carson's book might send me off to sleep. I'd plodded through the first chapter when suddenly I noticed a much superior distraction for the ten hours that remained of the flight. A man, a strikingly handsome man, walked past my seat and glanced back at me, twice, as he continued on up the aisle. While he queued for the bathroom, he pretended to ignore me, although he knew that he'd snared my attention. I studied him. He was tall, tanned and filled out his Armani jeans very nicely indeed. I was beginning to feel very excited about the prospect of America if all the men looked like this guy or Ellery.

When he emerged from the bathroom and began to walk back down the aisle towards me, he glanced at me. He smiled, his eyes sparkling their interest. 'Hi there,' I said, forgetting momentarily my own purpose for being on this flight, my reunion with Ant.

'How are you enjoying that book?' he asked, glancing at it discarded in my lap.

I was surprised to realise he was Australian. Everything about him – his clothes, his look – had convinced me he was American. I tossed the book onto the empty seat beside me, allowing my admirer a view of my crotch instead. I was irritated that his eyes continued to linger on the book.

'To be honest,' I said quickly, 'I'm about to give up on it. It's terribly self-indulgent.'

'You think so?'

I nodded vigorously. 'Yes. I wouldn't recommend it. Don't bother buying it.'

'Actually, I've already read it.'

That startled me. 'Oh well,' I said, floundering for a moment. 'Maybe I'm a bit critical because I happen to know the author.'

'Really?' The guy seemed very interested.

'Yes,' I nodded. 'It's being marketed as an autobiography, but it owes more to fantasy than fact.'

The guy nodded. 'Yes, that was my impression too.'

I can't describe the satisfaction I felt when he said that. Finally, finally here was someone who wasn't gushing over it, who had the sense to recognise how overwrought and exaggerated it truly was. 'You could perceive that just from reading it?' I asked excitedly. 'It just seemed totally far-fetched, right?'

The guy laughed. 'Well, not exactly. I happen to know the author too, indirectly. He's a friend of a friend. So I know that some parts of the story have been glossed over.'

That intrigued me. 'You know Carson?'

'Well, not personally. I've never met him, but a close friend of mine knew him very well once and has talked about him to me.'

'Who's your friend?'

The guy's attitude suddenly changed. 'It was a long time ago. Like about ten years ago,' was all he would say and then he excused himself and went back to his seat.

I was intrigued and puzzled by the sudden change in his manner. I mulled over everything he had said, trying to think who his friend could possibly be. Ten years ago. Then I realised. Who his friend was and who he must be and why he'd suddenly become so secretive. It all made sense. I was on a flight to Los Angeles, and that was where he had gone to live. It was mentioned in one of the early chapters. I picked up the book and searched through it, looking for the guy's name.

When I found it, I jumped out of my seat and hurried down the back of the plane after him. All those questions about Carson's dubious past were teeming through my mind again.

He saw me coming and pretended to be absorbed in a magazine. There was an empty seat across from him and I sat down in it. He glanced over at me warily.

'Let's have a drink together, Nick,' I said. 'I've got a few questions I'd like to ask you about our mutual friend, the author.'

At first Nick hesitated, as if he might deny his identity. That he was Nick, the prostitute who had been Aaron's boyfriend and mentor. Who had left Aaron for a rich client who lived in Los Angeles.

'Look, Nick, I wouldn't admit this to anyone else, but I'm in the book too. I'm the evil Steven. What's more, Carson didn't even bother to change my name.'

Nick raised his eyebrows and then a slow smile crossed his face. 'Okay,' he said. 'But my name's not Nick. He *did* change my name. I'm Rick.'

I pressed the button for a hostie to bring us some drinks and I leant across the aisle to Rick. 'So? Carson was nothing like the way he portrayed himself in that chapter with Aaron?'

'Darren,' Rick corrected me. 'His real name's Darren. Yeah, Carson really made himself over.'

I was jubilant. This was exactly the information I needed. It was payback time for the man who had smeared me so publicly. I would take great delight in revealing the truth about him in my book. 'So he was turning tricks along with Darren, working from the same apartment—' I began to babble, but across from me Rick was shaking his head.

'No,' he said firmly. 'Carson never worked.'

'What do you mean, he never worked?' I spluttered. 'You just said he made himself over.'

A steward turned up at that moment and I quickly ordered a gin and tonic. Rick ordered a mineral water and then turned back to me. 'He did. Darren was shocked at what he left out. But he could understand that Carson wouldn't want to admit to what he was like back then.'

'What? A slut? Insatiable?'

'Well, no,' said Rick with a sly grin.

I gestured at Rick helplessly. 'What?'

'Carson was religious.'

That was the last thing I expected to hear.

'Fanatically religious,' Rick continued. 'He was so straitlaced when Darren met him he used to take showers in his underwear. He was totally screwed up about anything to do with sex or nudity. He'd been completely brainwashed by his mother and was deeply, dangerously conservative. He was appalled by what Darren was doing, but secretly, subconsciously, he was fascinated. He kept hanging around Darren. His excuse was that he'd been sent by God to instruct him in the error of his ways. None of this is in the book of course. He'd be totally mortified to be reminded what he was once like.'

I understood what Rick meant. In inner-city Sydney, being religious was the last thing anyone would aspire or admit to. While being a prostitute was considered quite hip in certain circles.

'Darren used to ring me up in LA complaining about him. How Carson was doing his head in, always lecturing and rebuking him.'

'Why didn't he kick him out?'

'Well, he tried. But Carson wouldn't go. "Not until you're saved," he'd say. Darren's kind of easygoing. He figured that maybe he could save Carson from himself, open his eyes to the real world. So he put up with him. But then he found out that Carson was sabotaging his business. He was acting as unofficial receptionist when Darren wasn't around but, rather than taking bookings, he was turning clients away. Telling them that Darren had realised the error of his ways, that he'd stopped working. Then he gave the clients a sermon, told them they were sinners. Darren only found out about it when Carson gave Stewart this lecture and got him all excited by being so stern and chastising. Stewart rang back to make an appointment for a fantasy session with the choirboy.'

'I can't believe it.'

Rick shrugged. 'Carson was very young. It was all he knew. His mother always dragging him off to church and preaching to him. Anyway, when he wouldn't leave, Darren decided to try to evict him by shocking him. He had Stewart molest him in the bathroom one night. But that didn't work. Carson liked it, though he wouldn't admit it. As a last resort Darren got Carson invited to that party described in the book. The raffle did the trick. Carson considered Darren irredeemable after that, and Stewart pounced.'

'Darren set that up?'

'Yeah, and it worked. Darren never saw him again. Carson was exactly Stewart's type. He seduced him that same night and Carson ended up with a sugar daddy who had the patience to moderate his religious zeal.'

I sat across from Nick for the rest of the flight. He retold the early chapters of Carson's book from an entirely different perspective. Then he talked about himself and his life in LA. He was still with the same man he'd left Darren for. As for Darren, he now owned and ran a restaurant in Bondi. When we landed, Rick invited me to stay with him and his lover if I wanted to change my ticket and break the journey. I thanked him but declined. I had to get to Ant as quickly as I possibly could.

After we'd disembarked, Rick guided me through to the arrivals hall, showed me where to queue and gave me directions on how to get to the terminal for my American Airlines flight. Then he shook my hand and disappeared to join the queue for American residents.

I had a wait of several hours before my flight to Miami departed. I went to the bookshop to buy some magazines to read, but I was stopped in my tracks by the newspaper headline displayed on a board outside the shop. AIDS MEETING: SIGNS OF HOPE.

I felt weak with emotion, as if I might crumple to the floor. Was it merely some sensationalised story or could it possibly, finally, be some sort of breakthrough? I hurried inside and felt reassured that the story was on the cover of the *New York Times*. I quickly scanned through the report as I stood there in the shop. It had been announced at the international AIDS conference in Vancouver that combinations of new and old drugs promised to slow the progression of HIV and possibly even stop it in its tracks altogether. I bought that newspaper. I wanted to own it, to be able to brandish it at people and crow my delight to them. I stood outside the shop, newspaper in hand, grinning like a fool. A black couple walked by me holding hands, oblivious to anyone else. A very chic grandmother in a black jersey dress, professionally styled hair and Chanel jewellery frowned at me as she marched by. A couple of teenage boys wearing their baseball caps back to front screwed up their faces at me. Finally, after standing there for ten minutes, I spotted a guy I was sure was gay. I hurried over to him, smiling, waving the newspaper aloft. But the guy backed away from me. 'Fuck off,' he said. 'I'm an atheist and a homosexual. I don't want to buy your stupid newspaper.'

He fled. I had been mistaken for a Jehovah's Witness.

I felt very alone. I had no-one to share this extraordinary news with. I couldn't even phone home to Strauss or Carson. It was probably the middle of the night back there.

I went and sat down in front of the television and waited for the news to come on. While I waited I read right through the newspaper report which continued several pages on. What I read tempered my exhilaration. Although patients on the new drugs had suppressed the virus to undetectable levels in their bloodstream, it was still possible the virus might hide elsewhere in the body, in the brain or intestines. Also, as the research was so new, no-one knew how long the benefits might last. Some people couldn't tolerate the new drugs. Others found it difficult to adhere to a strict regime of twenty pills a day.

But I kept going back to a sentence at the beginning of the article – patients on the drugs had bounced back from their deathbeds. Those doctors and scientists had to be cautious in what they claimed, but to me that sentence sounded a hell of a lot like some sort of miracle.

I never did get to see the news. Some basketball game was on the television and when I suggested changing channels to CNN, I was stared down into silence.

When we finally got on the plane, I celebrated the good news with several drinks, which nudged me off to sleep. I awoke as we descended into Miami. Despite the long flights and the time change, I felt in top form. Positively serene at the prospect of my reunion with Ant. I floated through the rigmarole of disembarking the plane, locating my luggage and working out how to make my way to my hotel.

When I walked outside the airport terminal, the air was like someone's hot breath, slightly smothering and laced with odours that hinted of fast food. The shuttle bus I took turned out to be a mistake. Yes, it would take me to my hotel, but only after it had dropped all ten of my co-passengers at their hotels first. I grew more and more impatient as each hotel we stopped at turned out not to be mine.

'What about me?' I finally wailed, not caring what the couple seated behind me thought. 'I have an urgent appointment.'

'He has an urgent appointment at midnight?' I heard the woman behind me drawl to her husband.

'You're next. Next,' the driver muttered.

'I've come from Australia. All in one day,' I threw in, hoping the distance might impress him.

The driver answered me in Spanish, while the husband whispered back to his wife that I should go back there and learn some manners.

But the next hotel was theirs, not mine. Both husband and wife turned self-satisfied smirks upon me as they disembarked from the van.

'Yours next,' the driver reassured me redundantly.

When I finally got there, my hotel turned out to be a confection of pink, lemon and aqua. Across the street there was a chrome deco diner. But I had no time to admire the architecture – I marched into the lobby with my bags and demanded an express check-in. I had to see Ant *immediately*. That it was after midnight seemed completely insignificant.

Once I was installed in my room, I showered, shaved, and changed my clothes. Refreshed, but not looking as good as I would've liked, I went downstairs to the lobby and showed the boy at the front desk Ellery's address. He explained that it was only a fifteen-minute walk but I was too impatient to walk there. I took a cab.

Tremors of excitement tingled through me as I pressed the doorbell of Ellery's house and waited. I craned forward to listen. I could hear movement inside. I was so looking forward to the expression on Ant's face when he opened the door that I was startled when it swung open to reveal a man I had never seen before. I gasped my disappointment. The man, bleary-eyed, wearing boxer shorts, studied me quizzically. 'I sure hope you have a good explanation for waking us all up,' he said tersely.

I began to stutter and pulled the address from my pocket to check. Had I made a mistake? The man snatched the slip of paper from me, impatient for an explanation. Then a man's voice called out from within the house – 'Honey, who is it?' – and a few moments later, Ellery loomed out of the shadows. I was so relieved to see him.

'I have *no* idea,' Ellery's boyfriend said tetchily.

'Do you remember me?' I appealed to Ellery.

The boyfriend turned and fixed Ellery with a look of immense disapproval.

'From Sydney,' I added. 'A friend of Ant's. I've come to see him.'

'Yes, of course I remember,' said Ellery. 'But this is so unexpected. Tony didn't tell us you were coming.'

'He doesn't know. I just came.'

'Oh? A surprise. Joel, this is Stephen. You've heard Tony talk of Stephen.'

'Uh-huh,' said Joel in a voice that seemed laden with disapproval.

We stood there on their doorstep, silent for a moment.

'Is he asleep? Upstairs?' I finally asked. 'Shall I go and jump on his bed and surprise him?'

'He's not here,' said Joel. 'Tony went to Kiev.'

That completely startled me. Kiev? I couldn't even begin to imagine why Ant would go there. 'But . . . but . . . I've come all this way,' I began to protest. 'He didn't tell anyone he was going to Russia.'

Ellery began to laugh. Joel gave an exasperated sigh. 'It's a nightclub,' he snapped. 'I'm going back to bed.'

Joel disappeared back into the house. 'I'll drive you to Kiev,' Ellery offered. 'I'll just put some pants on. Come in and wait.'

In the car, on the way there, I explained to Ellery how I'd had a misunderstanding with Ant and he'd left the country without saying goodbye. Ellery was very impressed that I had followed Ant. 'You've come all that way?' he repeated several times, his voice filled with awe.

He dropped me on a corner and indicated the nightclub. I thanked him and was about to get out of the car when something occurred to me. Something Ellery had said to Joel. *'You've heard Tony talk of Stephen.'* Suddenly that simple sentence seemed horribly ominous as I imagined all the things that could have been said. 'Is he going to be pleased to see me?' I asked.

Ellery hesitated for a moment before replying. That hesitation was telling. 'A good-looking boy like yourself. I can't imagine why he wouldn't be thrilled,' Ellery said gallantly.

I wasn't convinced. I thanked him again for the lift and said good night. I was beginning to feel uncertain. A nightclub wasn't the place for our reunion. It would be impossible to talk. As I joined the queue to go in, I realised I wasn't even dressed for going out. I was just wearing a pair of jean shorts and a T-shirt. When I paid the admission I was told to check my clothes down to my underwear at the coat check. I was completely bewildered. I was aware I looked a bit casual, but it wasn't that bad. 'Excuse me?'

There were people queuing behind me and the guy was impatient. 'Check your clothes down to your underwear,' he repeated. 'You are wearing underwear?'

I nodded and the guy directed me over to the coat check. The black guy who'd been ahead of me in the queue was slipping out of his jeans. Evidently it was the thing to do, but I was confused. What sort of places was Ant frequenting? 'This *is* a nightclub, isn't it? For dancing?' I asked the black guy and he nodded.

I stripped down to my underwear and stuffed my wallet into one of my socks. I wasn't sure what I was going to find when I walked through into the club: an orgy or a dance floor. In fact, it was something in between the two. Kiev was having a foam party.

The guys on the dance floor were up to their eyes in foam. It pumped out of a machine onto the dance floor, which had been encircled by a tarpaulin wall to contain the foam. Even so, it oozed out through the gaps where people made their way on and off the dance floor. As I walked forward to get a better look, a swirl of foam oozed across the floor to greet me.

I stood to the side and watched. It did look like fun. The boy standing next to me began to talk. 'I lost one of my contact lenses in there,' he complained. 'I know, expensive. But I couldn't have worn my glasses here. No way. But now I can only see out of one eye. Can you tell me, is that Cuban boy over there flirting with me? I can't see well enough to tell.'

The Cuban boy was in fact looking me over with obvious approval, his fingers resting lightly against his immense crotch. I assured my half-blind friend that the Cuban boy was indeed looking our way and hurried off. I could not afford any distractions. I had waited far too long for this moment. A muscular black man strode past me towards the dance floor, his eyes running over me as he walked by. For a moment, I felt very tempted to follow and dance next to him. His eyes had offered such a clear invitation. But I took a deep breath and made myself walk up the stairs instead. I needed to find Ant quickly and the best view would be from the upper level. It also seemed like a good idea to get some distance between myself and all that bare flesh and sexual heat.

The dance floor was a striking spectacle from above. All those writhing muscular bodies, wrapped hard up against one another or dancing joyously with their hands in the air. But when the music plunged into a slower song, the mood changed.

The lighting grew dark and mysterious. The dry-ice machine whirled vapours of shrouding mist across the dance floor. The song had no lyric at all, just an eerie hypnotic electronic beat. Below me, the scene began to assume a malevolent aspect.

It was as if I was poised at the edge of a pit, a pit filled with men, some of the most beautiful men I had ever seen. But these men were in distress. They raised their hands in terror, clamouring for help. While around them, a relentless sea of froth rose higher and higher, threatening to overwhelm them. I shuddered and shut my eyes. I did not want to see Ant's face amongst that multitude of men. I didn't open my eyes until that unsettling music ended and slid into a familiar up-tempo dance song.

By then, everything was changed. The mists had dissipated. The lights were flashing golden and bright upon the dancers again. It had been the ominous light, the mist, perhaps my own exhaustion that had warped my perception. I was reminded as I gazed down on those dancing that this was a night of celebration. The smiles on those handsome faces below me were ecstatic. They laughed. They kissed. They embraced. They must have all seen the same news reports that I had.

I could not see Ant anywhere on the dance floor. Finally, just as I was beginning to panic that I'd never find him, I spotted him waiting at the bar to be served. Curiously there was a dollop of foam poised on his head to which he was seemingly oblivious. It was like a sign. I turned away from the dance floor and hurried across to the stairs. I scurried down them, a feverish excitement coursing through me.

I was moving towards him, my eyes taking in the tan he had acquired on the beach, the way his broad back glistened with sweat or maybe residue from the foam, the fancy Ralph Lauren underwear he wore (probably bought especially for tonight), when I had a sudden intense attack of nerves. I stopped in my tracks, rendered immobile by a crippling uncertainty. I felt so acutely unsure of my reception that it was impossible for me to just stroll up and tap Ant on the shoulder.

What if his face fell when he saw me? It would be too devastating.

I decided to put some distance between us. To position myself in his line of vision so that his gaze could fall on me naturally and I could analyse the look on his face at that moment. That look was vital. I felt sure I would be able to judge from his face how he felt about me.

The bar was accessible from all four sides. I squeezed through the throng of people until I was positioned directly opposite Ant, the bar between us. I stood staring at him, waiting for him to notice me, to sense that he was being watched. But Ant's eyes were doggedly fixed on the barman as he competed for his attention. As he waited, he nodded his head to the rhythm of the music. The barman served the person next to Ant and Ant looked away exasperated.

It was then that his eyes met mine. His face froze. Poised perfectly still, only his eyes seemed alive. He stared at me so intently, I felt as if all my secrets had been revealed. Slowly, a smile began to grow on Ant's face until it was wide and radiant.

I knew such a sense of joy at that moment. A shiver of pleasure prickled across my neck and up over my cheeks. My mouth gaped open in a dopey grin. Then, abruptly, we were interrupted. A barman planted himself between the two of us and Ant was lost to view. 'What do you want?' the barman asked me.

I knew the answer to that.

'Him,' I said, pointing. 'Behind you. I want him.'

The barman swivelled to look.

'With the foam on his head?'

I nodded.

Ant was looking puzzled. The barman grinned at me and moved over to Ant to deliver the message. Meanwhile, I began to push my way through the guys clustered round the bar to get to the other side. But as I moved, I kept my eyes fixed on Ant. I watched the barman lean across the bar and whisper in his ear. I saw the secret smile dawn on his face. Then his eyes looked for me, found me gone and a brief flicker of panic crossed his face. His disappointment was stamped so forlornly over his face, I felt unbearably touched. I called out his name but my voice was lost in the din of the music and the voices. Ant's eyes darted about in all directions and I lifted my hand and waved. He saw me then and he waved and began to push back through the people around him.

Suddenly a new song struck up and a spotlight, dazzling in its brightness, illuminated the bar next to where Ant had been standing. A muscular guy clad in tight leather briefs sprang up into the circle of light. He stood, face impassive, swaying to the music, his hands loosely fondling his crotch. The guys standing around the bar roared their approval and surged forward. I found myself looking twice at the dancer. There was something very familiar about him. Then I realised he was on the cover of a porn magazine I had at home under my bed.

In a matter of seconds there were twice as many people separating me from Ant. They were grudging or downright unhelpful about allowing me to squeeze any closer. I squirmed and pushed and apologised and offered the fact that I was from Australia by way of explanation.

Then I saw it. Just beyond the massive shoulders of the guy planted so resolutely in front of me. A dollop of foam crowning a close-cropped head. I craned forward. Then I recognised his hand, grasping the guy's shoulder in front of me for balance. Ant's blunt solid fingers. The scar on the index finger. The silver handcuff bracelet on his wrist, which Carson had given him for his birthday one year. I wrapped my own hand over the top of his and squeezed, and his face appeared, peering hopefully over the bodybuilder's shoulder. I had to lean against that big slab of beefcake as I craned forward on the tips of my toes to raise my mouth to Ant's.

We kissed. His mouth tasted of cinnamon chewing gum. Then I felt his arms go around me and run all over my body. It was only when they delved down the back of my underwear that I opened my eyes in surprise. That seemed a little fresh.

They weren't Ant's hands. They belonged to the body-builder who was wedged between us. 'Great butt,' he informed me, raising his eyebrows and winking.

'I know,' said Ant loudly, pushing himself past the guy and appearing alongside me. 'And I've had my eye on it for a lot longer than you have.'

I yelled in his ear. 'Can we get out of here? Go for a walk along the beach instead?'

Ant nodded. He led me over to the coat check and we grinned at each other as we dressed. Neither of us tried to talk over the music.

Outside, I cuffed the foam off his head and we both laughed. 'How'd you get foam on your head?' I teased him, and though Ant grinned, he looked a little guilt-stricken.

Ant took me by the shoulders and changed the subject. 'What are you doing here?' he asked. 'I thought I was delirious and had started seeing things. One second you were there across the other side of the bar, and the next you vanished. I thought you were an apparition.'

'Let's walk,' I said, tugging him by the hand.

'Okay,' he agreed and led me down the street, past a string of slightly dilapidated hotels, their facings highlighted in an array of pastel colours.

Neither of us spoke for a moment or two. I didn't even dare look at him. I lowered my eyes and looked at the pavement, which to my surprise was pink. Then Ant squeezed my hand and glanced across at me. 'I still can't believe you're here. It's been a day for surprises. Wonderful surprises,' he added with a grin.

I hesitated before I spoke. 'I do know that the news from Vancouver . . . is especially significant for you.'

Ant glanced sharply at me, caution in his eyes.

'Kip came looking for you one night,' I continued. 'Instead he found me and somehow, as we talked, your secret . . . spilt out.'

Still Ant was silent. When we reached the Amoco gas station

on the corner, he turned, tugged my hand and we crossed the street to walk down Fourteenth. I could smell the scent of the sea in the air.

'I owe being here to Kip, actually. He lent me the money to come. He wants you to come home . . . but not half as much as I do, Ant.'

My voice quavered as I said his name. At that same moment, a guy walked past and barked 'Faggots!' at us.

Automatically we released each other's hands and walked faster. Ocean Drive loomed in front of us. An explosion of bright lights, Latin music and sports cars.

'We'll walk on the beach. Get away from all this,' said Ant.

He crossed the street and I followed. We stopped where the sand began and slipped our shoes off. Then we began to walk, past the toilet block that was gaudily painted pink and green, down towards the water. The beach was completely deserted. We were quite alone. There was no-one to shout 'Faggot!' at us but I was acutely aware that Ant had not reached for my hand again. I did not feel confident enough to stretch my fingers out to find his.

'But why did you come all this way?' he asked, his voice puzzled. 'You could have written a letter.'

That was my cue. I knew what had to be said, what I'd always been afraid to say because I was so fearful of rejection.

'I couldn't say it in a letter. It had to be said face to face,' I began and then I hesitated. I stopped walking, planted myself firmly in the sand and seized his hand, forcing him to stop too. As he turned to me questioningly, I continued. 'You see, I've had a secret too, Ant. Something our circumstances or just my own insecurity wouldn't allow me to confess to you.'

I felt so horribly apprehensive and exposed, I hesitated. 'What?' said Ant, his voice filled with concern. 'Something awful?'

'Oh no, something quite wonderful,' I said lightly. 'A secret love.'

I could feel Ant's breath on my cheek as he craned closer to me. Smell a trace of his cologne on the warm sea breeze that whipped around us.

'Haven't you guessed? It's you, Ant. I love you and I have loved you ever since I met you.'

I had never said those words aloud to anyone and truly meant them before.

But that in itself was a problem. My words sounded as light at that moment as they had when I'd uttered them so insincerely in the past. My declaration hung between us, its lame inadequacy becoming more pronounced with every moment of silence that passed between us. Such proclamations had been robbed of their power, right there in America, by their constant repetition in films and television shows. The setting was spectacular – the lapping of the waves, the palm trees and the lit-up line-up of pastel deco hotels – but it was impossible to bring anything fresh to such a tired sentence, even though I'd waited more than three years to say it.

Ant said nothing. It was too dark to read his expression. Back towards the city, perched on top of a tall building, a clock displayed the time and temperature. Seventy-nine degrees. One-thirty in the morning. It reminded me that I hadn't slept properly for close to twenty-four hours and I began to wonder if it was a mistake to attempt such a crucial conversation when I was at such a low physical ebb.

Ant turned and ambled the few metres down to the water's edge. I watched him with dismay. He hadn't fallen into my arms and kissed me. Instead he had put a distance between us.

As he stared out at the water he remarked, 'Today has been an extraordinary day.'

This was not the reply I had hoped for.

Ant had changed the subject.

I managed to mumble my agreement, but I was choked up with disappointment. I knew he was referring to the AIDS conference news. Why hadn't he said, 'I love you *too*'?

'I can't describe how it felt, seeing that newspaper headline this morning,' Ant continued. 'I mean, I'm not sinking all my hopes into these new drugs. I know that it's early days and this initial promise may not be fulfilled.'

His voice sounded so forlorn and childlike, it tore at me. Even as he began to turn back towards me, I was running to him. I seized him and pulled him hard against myself.

'Ever since this morning, all day, I've been hugging this news to myself, this gift, too scared to unwrap it in case I should find there's actually nothing inside the glitzy wrapping paper – no gift, no miracle after all. But I do want to hope, Stephen. I'd like to believe that I've just had my life given back to me.'

He paused for a moment and pulled back from me. I could see his tears glistening in the dark. 'And if it's not a miracle, if it just gives me more time, I'll be grateful for that. A few more years of good health. But the one thing I'm absolutely certain of is that I won't waste my time. I'm going to choose very carefully.'

I was beginning to sense where this conversation was headed: that I was not going to be included in his choice for his future. If he was going to choose carefully, then naturally all my mistakes and indiscretions would be reconsidered. If common sense and caution were to prevail, my hopes were ludicrous.

But I couldn't bear to hear that rejection spoken aloud. Better for him to say nothing and allow myself to go on wondering and hoping that maybe one day . . .

I put my hand over his mouth and hushed him. 'Don't speak,' I whispered in his ear. 'Just hold me for a little, instead, if you don't mind. Just for a moment.'

His arms wrapped around me so swiftly. He drew me against himself and I rested my head against his chest. I let a few silent tears fall and hoped he might feel the wetness through his T-shirt and be made to feel repentant for being so cruel.

It was only very gradually that I became aware that this was not a hug of consolation. At first it was just his heartbeat in my ear, so strident and accelerated. Then I noticed his hands, how they seemed to linger as they ran over me. He wasn't patting me on the back. They felt more like caresses.

But it was something else that told me that this trip hadn't been in vain. Told me unmistakably. Ant didn't need to speak. Something that had been numbed, deadened by fear and anxiety and grief, stirred and swelled and spoke for him.

I looked up at Ant curiously, pressing myself against him a little to be sure. His smile was luminous white in the dark, like the cresting waves behind him. His hands clutched me and he clasped me hard against himself.

'Actually, I have a real present for you,' I whispered in his ear. 'Something I've been saving to give to you for many long years.'

'I can't wait to unwrap it,' Ant whispered back.

And he couldn't. He started right there and then on the beach.